HOME AND THE WORLD IN SLOVAK WRITING

Home and the World in Slovak Writing

A Small Nation's Literature in Context

EDITED BY KATARINA GEPHARDT,
CHARLES SABATOS, AND IVANA TARANENKOVÁ

McGill-Queen's University Press
Montreal & Kingston • London • Chicago

ISBN 978-0-2280-2405-7 (paper)
ISBN 978-0-2280-2406-4 (ePDF)
ISBN 978-0-2280-2407-1 (ePUB)

Legal deposit first quarter 2025
Bibliothèque nationale du Québec

Printed in Canada on acid-free paper that is 100% ancient forest free (100% post-consumer recycled), processed chlorine free

u. slovak arts council

Supported with public funds provided by the Slovak Arts Council. This publication reflects solely the views of its authors, and the Council cannot be held responsible for the information contained therein.

McGill-Queen's University Press in Montreal is on land which long served as a site of meeting and exchange amongst Indigenous Peoples, including the Haudenosaunee and Anishinabeg nations. In Kingston it is situated on the territory of the Haudenosaunee and Anishinaabek. We acknowledge and thank the diverse Indigenous Peoples whose footsteps have marked these territories on which peoples of the world now gather.

Library and Archives Canada Cataloguing in Publication

Title: Home and the world in Slovak writing : a small nation's literature in context / edited by Katarina Gephardt, Charles Sabatos, and Ivana Taranenková.
Names: Gephardt, Katarina, editor | Sabatos, Charles, editor | Taranenková, Ivana, 1976– editor
Description: Includes bibliographical references and index.
Identifiers: Canadiana (print) 20240473493 | Canadiana (ebook) 20240473523 | ISBN 9780228024057 (paper) | ISBN 9780228024071 (ePUB) | ISBN 9780228024064 (ePDF)
Subjects: LCSH: Slovak literature—20th century—History and criticism.
Classification: LCC PG5407.H66 2025 | DDC 891.8/709—dc23

This book was typeset by Sayre Street Books in 10.75/13.75 Minion Pro.
Copyediting by Kathryn Simpson.

Contents

Figures

FOREWORD

Slovak Literature and Central Europe

Daniel W. Pratt

Slovak literature appears to be in the midst of a golden age, judging by the articles in this collection and the wealth of contemporary translations. Slovak writers, now freed from the ideological necessities of nation building, socialism, and "catching up," have built upon the legacy of the interwar era and post-war generation to expand the scope, themes, and structures of Slovak literature. The result has been an explosion of excellent literature that includes topics beyond the previous ideological themes, while also including authors from the peripheries and minority groups within Slovakia. This makes Slovak literature a particularly vibrant tradition, able to build on past works while also developing in unexpected ways. With the current degree of literary experimentation and exploration, Slovak literature has transformed from a hidden gem to a rich and stable tradition in the centre of Europe.

Perhaps most remarkably, Slovak literature is hitting a high mark domestically at the same time as a group of talented and dedicated translators are exposing the rest of the world to it. Slovak literature is being translated primarily into the languages of their neighbours, i.e., German, Czech, Hungarian, and Polish, but the new English-language versions show a burgeoning wider reach. The English-speaking world can access some of the latest Slovak literature almost simultaneously with its new developments, a true rarity for Central European cultures. The Hungarian *Nyugat* writers, for example, rarely reached a broader audience, with a few notable exceptions; Polish literature of the interwar era only became more widely known after the Second World War with the development of Slavic departments and émigré translators. Some of the best interwar Czech literature, such as the novels of Vladislav Vančura, remains untranslated or in small, out-of-date editions. Perhaps only the Czech literature of the Prague Spring and normalization could compete with the contemporary case of Slovak literature on the world stage, when editions of Václav Havel, Bohumil Hrabal, and Milan Kundera emerged in English shortly after their publications in Czech. This situation of contemporary Slovak literature, with its domestic strength and quality of translation, bodes well, both nationally and internationally.

The combination of the new translations and the new directions of Slovak literature make the current collection even more necessary. It adds much needed cultural context to contemporary Slovak literature, allowing new (and old) readers to gain insights into the more recent literary developments and currents in Slovakia. Compared to the countries it borders, very little Slovak literature had been translated until recently, making Slovakia something of a special case in the Central European region. Czech and Polish literature has been widely translated into English, and Hungarian has received more translation recently as well, with the rise of László Krasznahorkai in particular, although less than either Czech or Polish unfortunately. Austrian literature benefits from German being a widely spoken language, making access to the Austrian tradition much easier than any of the Slavic or Hungarian ones. Ukrainian literature has received more attention of late, sadly due in part to interest following the Russian invasion, but Slovak literature has remained largely a terra incognita, despite its quality. This makes Slovak literature a curious case; as Robert Pynsent has claimed, "Slovak literature has not grown in isolation but a certain isolation has been imposed on Slovak literature."[1] Slovak culture has been influenced by Central European and world literature, but it has largely remained unexamined from the outside, at least for now.

As a scholar of Central Europe, I would like to point to some of the convergences and divergences of those currents in the broader region. Slovak literature has existed largely in the shadows of its neighbors, suffering from Magyarization under the Austro-Hungarian Empire and marginalization during the Czechoslovak period. However, the world's ignorance of Slovak literature has provided it with a particular advantage because it has been able to develop largely without the pressures of the world market. As it now moves to a more global audience, Slovak literature can rely on a rich local heritage and extra room to expand. Some

Slovak literature has developed in line with other Central European literatures, as will be shown below, but this leaves room for avenues of development that are distinctly Slovak. By placing the Slovak tradition in the context of Central Europe, I want to point to exactly what makes Slovakia a unique tradition, and a particularly vibrant one, today.

TRAUMA AND HISTORY

One of the most prominent themes in Central European literature since the Second World War has been the historical narrative. Three distinct eras can be discerned: in the immediate aftermath of the war, many authors turned to semi-autobiographical texts about the war itself. This kind of "testimonial art" investigated the traumas experienced by Central Europeans, giving voice to the horrors of the war. Later, because the Socialist governments in East Central Europe kept a strict control over the historical narrative, fiction, especially unofficial fiction, played a strong role in developing alternatives to the official, ideologically constructed narratives of the past. During this period, authors traced the traumas of the last century, while not overlooking the atrocities committed by members of their own communities. This more critical approach begins after the Thaw and continues well into the post-socialist period. Finally, more recently, authors have turned towards an entirely new set of paradigms, focusing on the haziness of memory, the inability to trace history as it happens, an analysis of new eras of history, and the murkiness of individual responsibility.

From the earliest Thaw works, Slovak and Central European literature has turned towards the historical record. In chapter 1 of this volume, Rajendra Chitnis cites Alfonz Bednár's cycle *Hodiny a minúty* (Hours and minutes, 1956) as a turning point in post-war Slovak literature, and this text revisits the historical record of the war, the Slovak Uprising, and the more recent past. In undermining the heroic story of the Uprising, Bednár challenged the reigning narrative of history put forward by the Communist Czechoslovak authorities. The title itself reminds the reader that even if time goes by, there are still similarities and overlap between the Nazi and Communist eras, deeply undercutting the progressive narrative of Marxist ideology. One theme of this early turn towards the historical narrative was the testimonial novel, a form that lay between autobiography and novel. Chitnis also focuses on Ladislav Mňačko's

Death Is Called Engelchen (*Smrť sa volá Engelchen*, 1959, trans. 1963), which distinctly lay between journalism and the novel. Mňačko blurs the line between fiction and non-fiction, creating what we can call testimonial art, i.e., fictionalized accounts of actual events experienced by the author.

In the rest of Central Europe, testimonial art focused largely on two experiences: the occupation and subsequent chaos, or the persecution and deportation of Jewish citizens. Josef Škvorecký's first novel *The Cowards* (*Zbabělci*, 1958, trans. 1979), written in 1948–49 but published a decade later, addresses his experiences of the end of the war in a novelized version of himself. His main character Danny has been a forced labourer for the German war machine, and he ends up fighting alongside the Red Army against the Nazis. However, in what will become a major theme in Central European literature, Danny does not fight out of any ideological commitment, but rather to impress his beloved Irena. In Bohumil Hrabal's *Closely Watched Trains* (*Ostře sledované vlaky*, 1965, trans. 1968), the main character Miloš Hrma also commits an act of heroism not because of any real commitment to the Czech anti-fascist cause, but rather because he overcame his fears about sexual inadequacy. In line with these Czech novels, the Polish author Tadeusz Konwicki's first novel *Rojsty* (Swamps) was written in the immediate post-war years, but only published in 1956. Like Danny and Hrma, Konwicki's hero Stanisław enters the partisan movement more out of love than from a sense of duty. However, Konwicki's text is far more critical of the entire partisan project and the tradition of Polish uprisings.

In the Polish tradition, there arose a distinct line of texts drawing attention to the suffering of others as witnessed by the authors and narrators. Czesław Miłosz's poetry of this era contains numerous references to his experiences of the war, notably his collection *Ocalenie* (Rescue, 1945) that included his famous poems "A Poor Christian Looks at the Ghetto" and "Campo dei Fiori." The first describes the Nazi destruction of the Warsaw Ghetto during the Ghetto Uprising of 1943. The lyric ego acknowledges his own responsibility for and impotence towards the death around him.[2] The latter poem questions human's ability to ignore the death and destruction around them, questioning the very humanity of humans. The lesson that comes at the end of the poem is that bearing witness to such events is the moral imperative for those who survived. This moral can be ascribed to Zofia Nałkowska and her collection

Medallions (*Medaliony*, 1946, trans. 1999), a series of short stories that came out of her investigations as a member of the Central Committee for the Investigation of German Crimes in Poland. Nałkowska's text offers stories without commentary, slyly exposing many of the antisemitic attitudes in Poland, but without addressing them directly.

Jewish authors also contributed to the testimonial literature of the immediate post-war era. In the Czech lands, both Jiří Weil and Arnošt Lustig drew on their own experience of the Second World War in their works. Weil's *Life with a Star* (*Život s hvězdou*, 1949, trans. 1989) was unfortunately published just after the communist coup, and it received a harsh critical reception as a result. Lustig's first collection of stories, *Night and Hope* (*Noc a naděje*, 1957, trans. 1962), fictionalized his own experiences during the war and in a concentration camp. In Poland, Tadeusz Borowski remains one of the foremost documenters of the concentration camps, with his *This Way for the Gas, Ladies and Gentlemen* (*Pożegnanie z Marią*, 1948, trans. 1967), even though he was not Jewish. His time in Auschwitz, described in a satirical tone, has become one of the most widely read accounts of the camps, alongside Primo Levi and Elie Wiesel.

Most probably due to Hungary's role as Nazi ally in the Second World War and then the economic hardships in the country due to paying reparations, Hungarian literature did not turn to the same subject matter. Most novels of the post-war era looked to the present day and the changes in contemporary Hungary or described eras further back in time. It would take several years before Hungarian novelists turned to the horrors and traumas of the war. After the 1956 revolution, novelists began to explore the interwar era, searching for answers for why the country had been led into fascism. Géza Öttlik, for example, explored the problems of the interwar society in his novel *The School at the Frontier* (*Iskola a határon*, 1959, trans. 1966), showing how his generation was taught and focusing on the social divisions of the country. The novel portrays the harsh schooling of young men, examining the disciplinary processes by which fascism could take hold.

In the 1960s, with the greater relaxation of censorship in the entire region, Hungarian authors finally looked back at the wartime period, just as other Central European authors would turn to questioning the entire historical narrative. Tibor Cseres's novel *Cold Days* (*Hideg napok*, 1964, trans. 2003) points to the absurdity of history and the ordinary people behind the most gruesome actions. The novel takes place during the Hungarian massacre of Jews and Serbs in Novi Sad, marking an important move towards literature that takes a more critical stance toward the country, the historical narrative, and the understanding of the past. Additionally, it was one of the first texts to address the ethnic strife in Hungary and its former borderlands. Central European literature as a whole continues to struggle with the legacy of imperial diversity (and the loss of much of it after the Holocaust) to the present day.

More critical approaches to the historical legacy of the war and history generally would emerge over the entire Central European area from the late 1960s onward. Novels moved beyond the scope of witness testimonies, relying less on semi-fictionalized accounts and adding more critical voices to the discussion. This turn was represented in Slovakia by the pioneering novels of Pavel Vilikovský and Ján Johanides, both of whom took on diverse subject matter. Vilikovský calls into question the very structures of historical speech in *Ever Green Is ...* (*Večne je zelený ...*, 1989, trans. 2002). Peter Darovec points to the graphic design of the novel in chapter 2, showing how it is meant to evoke ideologically motivated history textbooks. Moreover, using the character of a senile spy begs the question of who crafts the historical narrative. Even if Vilikovský uses an outlandish character, the novel nonetheless sheds doubt on how history was marshalled for ideological causes.

The rest of Central Europe followed suit, shining a light on the troubling past while critiquing the native populace for some of its roles over the past century. In his chapter, Chitnis compares Johanides to Bohumil Hrabal's later work *Příliš hlučná samota* (*Too Loud a Solitude*, completed 1976, published 1989, trans. 1990), showing the connection between their outlooks on history. Hrabal also effectively portrays the violence and destruction of historical forces in Central Europe in his novel *I Served the King of England* (*Obsluhoval jsem anglického krále*, completed 1971, published 1984, trans. 1988). Its main character Jan Dítě (whose last name means "child") moves from petty entrepreneur to waiter to Nazi supporter to owner of a large hotel, a purchase funded by stolen Jewish stamps, to enlightened labourer in the Šumava forests. The novel is told from Dítě's perspective, allowing him to craft a positive narrative of his experiences, deconstructing the myths of heroism, resistance, and collaboration. This kind of deconstruction was common throughout the region, especially in the Hungarian works of Péter Esterházy, Magda

Szabó, and György Konrád, the Polish works of Tadeusz Konwicki, and the Franco-Czech novels of Milan Kundera.

Although some authors would reject historical narratives of heroism, Dítě's example would also fuel the motif of the petty hero. Darovec addresses the "little" person as a typically Central European theme, in which a petty hero fails to do much in terms of "big" history, but nonetheless achieves the audience's admiration through their little attempt to change the course of history itself.[3] Hrabal's Hrma plays a distinctively petty heroic role in *Closely Watched Trains*, but this theme would become considerably more popular in the post-socialist era with the work of Petr Šabach, such as his collection *Hovno Hoří* (Shit burns, 1994), the basis for the film *Pelíšky* (Cosy dens, 1999). Although Dítě already somewhat deconstructs this formula, it would become a popular motif throughout the region. The fact that the Slovak writer Pišťanek deconstructs this formula as well coincides with the work of Hrabal and others who sought to complicate the nostalgic version of the trope.

Building on the legacy of the generation born between 1900 and 1940, the post-socialist novelists turned again to history, but in quite different ways. Zora Prušková tackles the new streams in historical narratives in chapter 4 in this volume, focusing on the plurality of memory and the lack of a single historical narrative. Peter Krištúfek, for example, plays with the earlier testimonial form in his *The House of the Deaf Man* (*Dom hluchého*, 2012, trans. 2015) by beginning with a personal archive. The so-called kaleidoscopic form of history, one that shifts form with each successive historical era, demonstrates a move towards acknowledging the shifting nature of history and the lack of objectivity in understanding it. Instead of merely providing alternative understandings of history, this generation of authors rejected the very objective claims of historical analysis itself.

The rejection of historical objectivity dovetails with several other authors in the Central European region. As early as the 1990s, Jáchym Topol challenged historical accounting in his postmodern novel *City, Sister, Silver* (*Sestra*, 1994, trans. 2000). The novel portrays the years around the Velvet Revolution, and the main character travels throughout the former Czechoslovak lands, even to Subcarpathian Ukraine. The novel questions the role of the Czechs in their history and ends without a clear definition of that role. Perhaps a more direct comparison to this new line in Slovak literature comes from the Hungarian writer Péter Nádas, whose *Parallel Stories* (*Párhuzamos történetek*, 2005, trans. 2011) follows two families, one Hungarian and one German, through the twentieth century. The scope of the text belies any clear historical storyline and showing the multiple available interpretations of historical events. Olga Tokarczuk's *House of Day, House of Night* (*Dom dzienny, dom nocny*, 1998, trans. 2002) focuses on one region of Poland, but through that focus tells the story of several figures over 800 years. Instead of telling a single narrative, however, the text revolves around individual vignettes that mark her initial foray into the so-called "constellation novel."

More recently, there has also been a move beyond the historical novel of Central Europe to ones that encompass a far larger area, and far bigger concerns than national or regional ones. Tokarczuk's *The Books of Jacob* (*Księgi Jakubowe*, 2014, trans. 2021) follows the self-proclaimed messiah Jakub Frank throughout Central Europe but also into Ottoman Turkey and the Holy Roman Empire, all while discussing European Enlightenment more generally. László Krasznahorkai began with more allegorical work centred in his native Hungary, but since then has built a more global perspective, writing on Europe and New York in *War and War* (*Háború és háború*, 1999, trans. 2006) and the entire world and its history in *Seiobo down Below* (*Seiobo járt odalent*, 2008, trans. 2013). Although such a scope does not seem to be evident yet in Slovak literature, there does seem to be a move beyond the borders of Slovakia itself.

In chapter 8 of this volume, Tamara Janecová looks at expatriate and cosmopolitan writings, and this seems to be a truly unique form of writing in Central Europe. Instead of taking on the scopes that Tokarczuk and Krasznahorkai do, there is a line of Slovak literature that focuses on the migrant experience. The Czech writer Iva Pekárková covered some of the same ground in her early novels from the 1990s, but the Slovak novelists Ivana Dobrakovová and Zuska Kepplová mark new territory in their stories that are more grounded in their authors' migratory experience of contemporary Europe. The depiction of the migratory Slovak in these stories reaches far beyond the early twentieth-century Pennsylvania steelworkers of Thomas Bell's 1941 *Out of This Furnace*, showing Slovakia's new place in Europe. I expect that there will be a more widespread trend of migratory literature across Europe and the world, placing Slovakia amongst the avant-garde of this new literary movement.

NEW COMMUNITIES, NEW WRITERS

Slovakia's new place in Europe coincides with the building of new communities, and these new communities need new voices to tell their stories. Well into the twentieth century, the typical writer from Central Europe was male and interested in questions about the nation. Three chapters in this collection show how both the authors and their topics have shifted away from this older construction: Ivana Taranenková shows how the self has become a more legitimate topic for literature, particularly a self that is divorced from national concerns; Radoslav Passia addresses the wealth of new regional literature, one that by nature challenges ideas of a homogeneous nation; and Rafał Majerek discusses the thriving new line of women's writers in Slovakia. Released from the discussions of the nation and its history, writers across Central Europe have diversified, as have their themes.

As Passia discusses in chapter 7, Central Europe more generally has turned again towards more regionalism, partially as a showcase for the diversity of each country. The Second World War left the region devoid of much of the diversity it had; most of the Jews were murdered and many who stayed left during antisemitic movements under socialism, the post-war population transfers made states more ethnically homogeneous, and immigration to Central Europe has only recently been on the rise. In lieu of a Western-style diversity based on years of migration and their colonial legacies, Central European culture has returned to examine the diversity it does have, both ethnically and regionally.

In Poland, the Silesian identity has gained considerable strength in the past few years, partially thanks to a number of novels and reportage works set in the region. Tokarczuk's *House of Day, House of Night* looks at Lower Silesia, and Szczepan Twardoch has become one of the great voices of Upper Silesia. Twardoch's *Drach* (Dragon, 2014) is set in the area between Gliwice and Rybnik, where the German-Polish border once lay, taking place over the last century. The story focuses on the linguistic and cultural mixing of the area, incorporating untranslated passages in German, Polish, and Silesian. Twardoch himself has become an avid supporter of Silesian rights, arguing for greater autonomy and a strong Silesian identity. Zbigniew Rokita tells the story of Silesia, its diversity, and his family's story in his award-winning reportage work *Kajś* (Somewhere, 2020). On the other side of the country, Paweł Huelle has been focusing on the distinctive culture and history of Gdańsk and its environs. In the Czech lands, the focus on regional identity is perhaps best seen in Květa Legátová's novel *Jozova Hanule* (Joza's Hanule, 2002) that looked at the Moravian Wallachia's experience of the Second World War through the eyes of a Prague woman hiding in the region.

With these new avenues for writing, a new set of writers has emerged in Central Europe. Women now make up a large number of contemporary writers across Central Europe, from the immensely popular Tokarczuk to the punkish Dorota Masłowska, whose debut novel *Snow White and Russian Red* (*Wojna polsko-ruska pod flagą biało-czerwoną*, 2002, trans. 2005) received as much shock as it did praise. In the Czech Republic, Petra Soukupová has written intimately honest texts in which history takes a back seat. Her novel *K moři* (To the seaside, 2007) tells the story of a family going on vacation, but with Socialist repression in the background. Without an intimate knowledge of the history of Czechoslovakia, the reader would not even realize that politics had played a role, defying the typical emphasis on the historical narrative.

Hungarian literature had focused on the borderlands and non-metropoles much earlier than Slovak literature did, but only more recently has literature become more diverse in ethnic terms. Lakatos Menyhért played an enormous role in developing Romani literature in Hungarian, particularly with his *The Color of Smoke* (*Füstös képek*, 1975, trans. 2015). Magda Szécsi has continued in this line, and her *Cigánymandala* (*Gypsy Mandala*, 2007) emerged to both critical and popular acclaim. Both the Czech lands and Poland have lagged in terms of developing a more robust literature from their ethnic minorities, but they have contributed more in terms of queer literature. In Poland, the legacy of Witold Gombrowicz looms large over queer literature, and there is a clear line from him to more modern works such as Michał Witkowski's novel *Lovetown* (*Lubiewo*, 2005, trans. 2009), which became a surprise hit. Despite increased homophobic activities and laws, Poland's culture continues to include more discussions of LGBTQ+ subjects, both in the contemporary age and in the historical context. In the Czech lands, Zuzana Brabcová's novel *Rok perel* (Year of the pearls, 2000) was one of the first to deal with lesbian love and has become a part of the Czech LGBTQ+ canon. Slovak literature and criticism have recently turned towards LGBTQ+ topics as well, particularly after the murder of two gay men by a far-right extremist in October of 2022. Ivana Hostová, the author of chapter 6, has contributed elsewhere to this emerging field.[4]

NEW CRITICAL PARADIGMS

Because of the changes in scope, motifs, and authors, there is a need for new critical paradigms across the Central European space. In the case of Slovakia, the previous attempts to create an English-language study of Slovak literature tried to show first and foremost that Slovak literature was worthy of reading. Peter Petro makes this the centre point of *A History of Slovak Literature*, calling Slovak literature the "perennial Cinderella of central European literature."[5] When competing against other nations for attention, Slovakia was at a disadvantage for its size, "newness," and the lack of Western knowledge of its cultural history. This focus on the "existence" of Slovak literature in its own right, not as a subsection of Hungarian or Czech literature, is reflected in Vladimír Mináč's assertion that "For many decades, we have been convincing ourselves and others that we exist."[6] Now that Slovakia exists as its own country, there is less of a need to write simply to prove the value of its culture, the existence of its culture, or the very existence of the nation itself.

Because Slovak literature can now turn away from questions of national existence, literary criticism can also turn from advocating for it as well. The current volume does exactly that, and it belongs to a new turn in scholarship about "national" traditions. I use quotation marks here, because the current volume as well as others about the region defy the traditional national narratives of literary development. The aim of the current volume is not to be total and comprehensive, but rather like the historical novels of the present age, this book contains a pluralistic vision of Slovak literary history. No single voice is dominant, but rather the diversity of interpretations and methodologies takes centre stage. This book also features a diverse set of scholars, both from Slovakia and elsewhere, both women and men, and incorporating a diverse set of texts, methodologies, and stances. Such breadth is exactly what is needed to address a thriving literary field, instead of the more traditional, monologic narrative of historical development.

The current volume also mirrors some of the other recent books published about Central European literature. Tamara Trojanowska, Joanna Niżyńska, and Przemysław Czapliński's *Being Poland: A New History of Polish Literature and Culture since 1918* (2018) and Katarzyna Fazan, Michał Kobialka, and Bryce Lease's *A History of Polish Theatre* (2022) both take a similar approach. *Being Poland* states this goal at the outset, claiming, "This book embraces a different model of authorship: it offers a polyphonic model of cultural analysis ... [capitalizing on] multiple intellectual, cultural, generational, and institutional perspectives, as well as a variety of theoretical tools and approaches."[7] Their book lives up to this promise, including scholars from all over the world, addressing literature and culture in all varieties of the concept of "Poland." This makes the present volume a timely addition to the new scholarship on Central Europe, but one that finally brings a real spotlight to Slovak literature.

Slovak literature today remains an exceptional literary tradition in Central Europe, not because it has been overlooked for so long, but because it is so vibrant, with a rich scholarly community and dedicated translators. I have always appreciated Central European literature in all its constitutive elements, but at the moment there is truly something exciting about Slovak literature. The rest of the literary world seems to feel the same way, as Slovak writers are winning more awards than ever before, being translated more than ever before, and being analyzed more than ever before. This collection helps celebrate a new golden age of Slovak literature, one that we are privileged to have some access to in the English-speaking world.

NOTES

1 Pynsent, *Modern Slovak Prose*, 37.

2 Jerzy Andrzejewski makes a similar move in his *Holy Week* (*Wielki Tydzień*, 1945, trans. 2007).

3 For more on the trope of the petty hero, see Pehe, *Velvet Retro* (particularly ch. 4, "Petty Heroism: Nostalgia for Resistance"), 84–100.

4 See for example Hostová, "Queer Perspectives in Translation Studies."

5 Petro, *A History of Slovak Literature*, 156.

6 Mináč, *Dúchanie do pahrieb*, 59.

7 Trojanowska, Niżyńska, and Czapliński, *Being Poland*, xv–xvi.

BIBLIOGRAPHY

Hostová, Ivana. "Queer Perspectives in Translation Studies: Notes on Two Recent Publications." *World Literature Studies* 14, no. 1 (2022): 61–78.

Mináč, Vladimír. *Dúchanie do pahrieb*. Bratislava: Slovenský spisovateľ, 1989.

Pehe, Veronika. *Velvet Retro: Postsocialist Nostalgia and the Politics of Heroism in Czech Popular Culture*. New York: Berghahn, 2020.
Petro, Peter. *A History of Slovak Literature*. Montreal: McGill-Queen's University Press, 1995.
Pynsent, Robert, ed. *Modern Slovak Prose: Fiction since 1954*. Hampshire and New York: Palgrave Macmillan, 1990.
Trojanowska, Tamara, Joanna Niżyńska, and Przemysław Czapliński, eds. *Being Poland: A New History of Polish Literature and Culture since 1918*. Toronto: University of Toronto Press, 2018.

Acknowledgments

In November 2019, only a few months before the COVID-19 pandemic isolated us in our respective homes and countries, the co-editors of this book first met at an event that brought together critics and publishers of Slovak literature. Co-organized by the University College London School of Slavonic and East European Studies and the Institute of Slovak Literature of the Slovak Academy of Sciences, the meeting was a part of a series of events called "Raising the Velvet Curtain: Slovak Literature since 1989," which commemorated the thirtieth anniversary of the Velvet Revolution by promoting Slovak literature in the United Kingdom. Julia Sherwood, a prolific translator of Slovak literature to English who planned the series, invited Katarina Gephardt to discuss her ideas for collaboration on a book on Slovak literature. The need for a text such as *Home and the World in Slovak Writing: A Small Nation's Literature in Context* had first become apparent to Katarina when she struggled to find English-language sources on Slovak literature for her course syllabus on Central European literature in translation a decade earlier. She had the opportunity to discuss her ideas for the book with the conference participants and met Ivana Taranenková and Charles Sabatos, who joined her as co-editors of this book and whose expertise in Slovak literature and comparative literature was essential to the success of the project. We owe an immense debt of gratitude to Julia for connecting us and providing a forum in which scholars from different countries and continents could discuss how to promote Slovak writing in a wider global context. We also appreciate her suggestions for this project and the opportunity to interview her about her work as a translator.

In its structure and coverage, this book functions as a collectively written monograph rather than a collection of essays. The chapters were authored by native speakers of English as well as non-native speakers who wrote their essays in English or Slovak. The manuscript could not have been completed without the contributors' willingness to write original chapters that followed a similar structure and covered key historical contexts, themes, and texts. We thank all of the contributors for agreeing to share their expertise and being open to feedback, which made our collaboration both effective and rewarding. The chapters that Katarina Gephardt and Charles Sabatos translated from Slovak required a level of involvement on the part of the authors that is not typical of edited collections. All quotations from Slovak sources in English that do not include references to published translations were translated by the co-editors or chapter authors.

Our editor at McGill-Queen's University Press, Richard Ratzlaff, provided insightful and generous feedback that challenged us to broaden the contexts and the potential audiences for this book. We are deeply thankful for his interest in Slovak literature, encouragement, and confidence in the viability of this project. We thank Kathleen Fraser, the managing editor at McGill-Queen's University Press, for her patient answers to our questions and for helping us complete the publication process. We appreciate the diligent editorial assistance of Kathryn Simpson, our copyeditor, and Elise Noelle Good, our graduate student assistant at Kennesaw State University, who clarified and polished the language and standardized the format of the manuscript. We are grateful to John Havard, the English Department chair at Kennesaw State University, for his support of Katarina's work on the project and Anne R. Richards and Radoslav Passia for their helpful advice and feedback. We also thank Marielena Zajac for compiling the index.

Our work on this project and the publication of this book would not have been possible without the generous support of several institutions. The Institute of Slovak Literature of the Slovak Academy of Sciences (Ústav slovenskej literatúry SAV) provided substantial funding for the publication costs. The Slovak Arts Council (Fond na podporu umenia) supported most of the translation work. The Norman J. Radow College of Humanities and Social Sciences and the English Department at Kennesaw State University provided funding for research, book production costs, and the support of our graduate student research assistant.

HOME AND THE WORLD IN SLOVAK WRITING

Introduction

Katarina Gephardt, Charles Sabatos, and Ivana Taranenková

Slovakia's share of the global literary market can be fairly described as minuscule, which is determined by the country's population of five million and its recent history. Prior to the end of the Cold War, limited cultural contact with the Anglophone world restricted the volume of translations of Slovak literature into English. The state also tended to support translations into the languages of other socialist countries. Between 1832 and 1989, only about sixty books containing English translations of Slovak literature were published, while since 1989, over a hundred such translations have appeared, most of them in the new millennium.[1] The most recently published English translations have attracted the attention of reviewers, but literary criticism on Slovak literature has been limited in the Anglo-American context. This book strives to fill that gap by mapping the transformations of Slovak literature with a special focus on contemporary texts, while also providing contexts to support a wider, global circulation of Slovak writing.

The increasing speed of translation into English makes it possible for Slovak literature to reach audiences beyond its regional or European contexts, entering "world literature" in the sense Rebecca Walkowitz conceptualizes it in *Born Translated: The Contemporary Novel in an Age of World Literature*, as the condition in which "many contemporary works will seem to occupy more than one place, to be produced in more than one language, or to address multiple audiences at the same time."[2] The translation of Slovak literature is not driven by global demand, and Slovakia has not produced a writer with an international reputation as the Czechs have in Milan Kundera. What sustains the process of translation are relationships among authors, translators, and small publishing houses. A remarkable example is a series of Slovak fiction edited by Julia Sherwood, an influential, prolific translator of Slovak literature into English and published by Seagull Books, a press with a focus on literature in translation that was founded in India and established a branch in the United Kingdom as an alternative to major publishers. The press website describes the mission of the Slovak series as introducing "works by writers from Slovakia, a country whose literature has so far remained in the shadow of its neighbours in Central Europe and not available to a wider readership."[3] Most of the books included the series were first published within the past decade, which indicates that the lag between the publication of the Slovak originals and translations is shrinking. Nevertheless, at this point in time, most Slovak literature is not "born translated," or "*written for translation* in the hope of being translated," or "*written as translations*, pretending to take place in a language other than the one in which [it has], in fact, been composed."[4] However, there are exceptions. For example, Pavol Rankov's *It Happened on the First of September (or Some Other Time)* (*Stalo sa prvého septembera (alebo inokedy)*, 2011, English trans. 2020), which features a multiethnic setting in Southern Slovakia before the Second World War, is keenly aware of translation as a theme, and the novel has been translated into twelve languages.[5] The millennial generation of writers who have had the opportunity to travel and become fluent in other languages shows a growing awareness of global audiences, most notably in fiction depicting expatriate life or in multimodal poetry that is written in English or incorporates foreign words and cultural references.

The small size of Slovakia determines its literary production as well as the reception of Slovak writing abroad. In this respect, its literary landscape is similar to that of other small nations, and Slovak literature belongs to the category of "small literatures," which developed in conjunction with nineteenth-century national movements and justified their existence with arguments for political and cultural emancipation inspired by Johann Gottfried Herder's concepts. Pascale Casanova describes this trend as "the Herderian revolution," which led to significant dependence of the literary landscapes created through this process on non-literary national or political criteria.[6] From the perspective of Casanova's argument in her influential *The World Republic of Letters*, Slovak literature belongs to a lesser developed literary space, which alternately strives for "assimilation" and "differentiation" in relation to "a dominant literary space."[7] On the one hand, Slovak literature legitimized itself through imitation and appropriation of the structures and forms of dominant literary spaces, which is evident, for instance, in the repeated calls for the development of the social problem novel. On the other hand, Slovak literature underscored its unique features as the foundation for its sense of self-worth. The perceived developmental delay of Slovak literature in relation to literatures of dominant cultures also led to ambivalent responses. The literary establishment felt the need to "catch up" with the trends of dominant literatures, while also celebrating belatedness as a youthful promise of future development.[8]

The historical factors that determined "smallness" continue to impact the circulation of small literatures in translation. In their edited volume *Translating the Literatures of Small European Nations*, Rajendra Chitnis and Jakob Stougaard-Nielsen define "small" as relating "less to the size of the nation or historical subservience to empire than to the hegemonies of transnational publishing" that limit the diversity of works available in translation to readers of English.[9] They qualify Casanova's conception of the relationship between small and dominant literatures and point out that it tends to "replicate and perpetuate stereotypes from popular cultural geography and geopolitical imagination."[10] Challenging literary critics who perceive the predicament of small literatures as "irredeemably sad and unfortunate," Chitnis and Stougaard-Nielsen point out that "smallness is not only lamented, but also celebrated (even fetishized), accepted, denied, ignored, or dependent on perspective," positions influenced by how writers situate themselves in relation to "big" literatures.[11] The case of Slovakia confirms that smallness has its drawbacks but also advantages. While the circulation of Slovak literature in translation may still be limited for the reasons cited by Chitnis and Stougaard-Nielsen, writers benefit from state-sponsored grant awards, which contribute to generic and stylistic diversity of published texts and open doors to debut writers. The small size of the country makes it possible for marketing to happen organically through literary events and the word of mouth, and so the literary scene is not subjected to the level of commercializing pressure that drives publishing in the United Kingdom or the United States.

A less favourable consequence of smallness is the struggle for visibility in relation to dominant languages and cultures, a determining factor in Slovak literary history, which has always been shaped by the influences of larger nations, including the Hungarians, the Czechs, and the Russians. Robert Pynsent's collection *Modern Slovak Prose* (1990), one of the few existing book-length studies of the subject in Anglo-American criticism, notes that "Slovak literature has not grown in isolation but a certain isolation has been imposed on Slovak literature."[12] The aim of this book is to help bring it out of such isolation by complementing the efforts of translators who promote and disseminate Slovak literature abroad. The essays included in this volume tell the story of how a small nation's literature can survive and thrive despite – and perhaps, on occasion, thanks to – a smaller domestic audience and relatively limited circulation in English translation. The selection of texts, marketing, and reception of translations raise issues of access, value, influence, and audience. Slovak literature has faced challenges similar to those of other small nations, yet the fact that prior to 1918, Slovaks did not live in a state defined by national affiliation has made the cultural role of literature particularly significant and has hampered its wider circulation. The evolution of the stories that the Slovak tell about themselves in literature and public discourse have been shaped by several key factors: the myths of the past, geographical location, association with Central Europe, and the struggle for independent statehood.

Pynsent opens his subsequent essay "What about the Slovaks [?]" with a tongue-in-cheek but pithy statement that captures the predicament of nineteenth-century Slovaks: "If Jane Austen had known about the Slovaks, and if she had lived for a couple of decades longer, she might have written, 'It is a truth universally acknowledged that a nation in possession of language must be in want of a state.'"[13] Although a distinct Slovak nationality has existed in some form for centuries, Slovakia's relatively brief history of free cultural development as a modern nation dates back only to the founding of Czechoslovakia in 1918, and its independent statehood only began (apart from the wartime Slovak state) with the breakup of the joint republic in 1993. Slovakia's destiny has thus been shaped by its predicament as a small nation, "one whose very existence may be put into question at any moment; a small nation can disappear and it knows it."[14] There is an element of risk or contingency in the very existence of the Slovak nation that shapes its literature and culture.[15] Compounded by Slovakia's small size, its history presents a unique set of circumstances that shape Slovak national identity and literary production. Slovak literature of the nineteenth and twentieth centuries responded to these circumstances by developing two complementary strategies. On the one hand, it searched for its place in a broader literary space, and, especially during periods of relative autonomy from ideological pressures, borrowed impulses for its development from world literature, which were often absorbed through feverish translation of key literary texts. On the other hand, Slovak literature tended to accentuate and even invent its uniqueness, by turns erecting and dismantling its self-identifying mythologies.

What Pynsent raises in his essay is the "Slovak Question," which encompasses "national and constitutional problems in addition to economic, social, cultural [as well as] the problem of relationships between the Slovaks and their neighbors."[16] Pynsent goes on to scrutinize mythical versions of the Slovak past that were forged in the nineteenth century by national revivalists, who invented traditions and codified the Slovak language in order to validate the concept of a distinct Slovak national identity. In order to justify Slovak claims to autonomy within Hungary, they traced a thousand years of national existence back to the Slavic Greater Moravian Empire in the ninth and early tenth centuries. Although the initial objective of the Romantic historiographers was to boost national confidence and support the struggle for national rights, other myths produced before the advent of professional historiography also contributed to a sense of inferiority, conjuring the image of a small nation of plebeians without its own history, perpetually oppressed by its overlords, the Hungarians, and later, the Czechs. Such distortions of Slovak history were perpetuated during the era of interwar Czechoslovakia, the Slovak state during the Second World War, and especially during the four decades of socialist establishment, when they were further inflected by the mandates of Marxist-Leninist historiography.[17] Despite Slovak historians' recovery work and revisions of such distortions following 1989, mythical versions of Slovak national history persist in political discourse, journalism, and popular culture.

Slovakia's geographical location, which impacts its national security and foreign policy, has also shaped its myths of national identity. In national mythology, "the geographical centre of Europe is situated in Slovakia" – a problematic assumption because both the geographical location of Europe's centre and its cultural perception are debatable.[18] Nevertheless, as Alexander Avenarius points out, "its conceptual essence is clear" because it describes the syncretism of the Central European space, which is positioned at the crossroads of the East and the West and continually negotiates their influences.[19] Avenarius traces the historical roots of such adaptation of Eastern and Western influences to the ninth-century mission of the Byzantine monks Constantine and Methodius, who brought Christianity to the Slovak territory and symbiotically combined elements of Eastern (Byzantine) and Latin Church elements in their liturgy, which had broader cultural influence. Another important milestone in the development of a shared Central European identity was the Turkish threat associated with the Ottoman invasion that persisted from the sixteenth to the early eighteenth centuries.[20] Since the Turks occupied a significant part of Hungary, important institutions of the kingdom moved to the Slovak territory, which played a key role in "the collision of the two worlds."[21]

Central Europe is a contested term with a complex history that can nevertheless be useful in determining which aspects of Slovak literature are unique and which are regional. The Czech historian Miroslav Hroch points out that the concept is both a geographical reality and a construct and traces it to the Reformation, which, unlike in Western Europe, ended with a compromise and a push for religious toleration. The other aspect that is unique to Central Europe is "the remarkable discontinuity of its evolution," which means that unlike Western European nation states, none of the modern states of the region "evolved in continuity out of the Middle Ages and into a modern nation state" but were taken over by larger units.[22] The region fell under the German influence, which became especially pronounced following the unification of Germany, although in the case of western Ukraine, eastern Poland, and Lithuania, the degrees of German and Russian influence shifted over time, which contributes to the instability and complexity of the macroregion as a concept. Hroch points out that "efforts toward national emancipation in other parts of Europe, whether Catalan, Welsh, Flemish or Ukrainian, have emerged out of a distinct and culturally definable concept of the nation and national interests, and this preceded the emergence of the concept of a nation based on a political definition."[23] But in Central Europe, national movements seeking emancipation usually subscribed to the same cultural and linguistic conception of the nation as that of the dominating German movement."[24] The strong cultural participation of the Jewish population was another key factor that contributed to "the complicated overlapping of identities in Central Europe,"[25] which Milan Kundera describes as "maximum diversity in minimum space."[26]

Slovakia's situation was both characteristic of the region, along with lines described by Hroch, and unique in that there was no history of statehood corresponding with Slovak ethnicity to draw on in the Middle Ages and further complicated by the dual impact of Hungarian and German domination prior to 1918. The Central European dimension of Slovak identity played an important role following the dissolution of the Habsburg Empire and in the founding of Czechoslovakia in 1918 and was suppressed during the Cold War, when Czechoslovakia was a part of the Warsaw Pact and economically tied with the East, only to resurface after 1989, leading to strategic groupings of Central European states such as the Visegrád Four. The Cold War, which divided Europe into the West and the East, contributed to the decline of the concept of Central Europe, which was revived by intellectuals and dissidents such as Czesław Miłosz and Milan Kundera as a counterpoint to Soviet political domination and enforced Russian cultural influence. In "The Tragedy of Central Europe," Kundera strategically defines the concept in relation to "to the word 'Europe' ... not [as] ... a phenomenon of geography, but a spiritual notion synonymous with the word 'West.'"[27] In the context of the European Union, the concept of Central Europe continues to carry such a strategic function.

The instability of the concept of Central Europe raises the question of whether the literature of the region shares certain common Central European traits and to what extent such a legacy influences Slovak literature. As Kundera and others suggest, the quintessential characteristics of Central European literature emerge from the legacy of the declining Austro-Hungarian Empire and manifest in Franz Kafka's writing or in interwar texts such as Jaroslav Hašek's *The Good Soldier Švejk* (*Osudy dobrého vojáka Švejka za světové války*, 1921–23) or Joseph Roth's *The Radetzky March* (1932). These texts share "an unheroic and perhaps subconscious focusing on absurdities" and "an atmosphere of decline, of an irresistible downward slide," and a "resigned acceptance."[28] Contemporary Central European writers continue to draw on this legacy in their representation of the impact of European integration and the forces of globalization on their countries as well as a counterpoint to nationalism. Reflecting on the question "Is There a Central European Identity in Literature?," Ewald Osers ends with further questions: "In conclusion one is bound to ask whether a politically restructured and nationally fragmented Central Europe will sustain a mid-European identity in literature. Might there not be a deliberate change of climate from inward-looking, gently self-pitying fatalism to a European-Community-oriented optimism? A deliberate effort to shake off whatever heritage is left of the old monarchy and to become 'Westerners?'"[29] Contemporary Slovak literature seems to suggest that the cultural legacy of Central European literature is very much alive, but the "self-pitying fatalism" is balanced with oblique, ironic perspectives on the dominant economic and political forces of our time through the perspective of twenty-first-century everymen and everywomen. In this respect, Slovak literature can serve as a case study of how the culture of a small nation historically conditioned by the struggle for national self-determination draws on its broader regional affiliation to sustain itself under the pressures of globalization, while also drawing new inspirations from a wider world.

The struggle for statehood is perhaps the most uniquely determining factor that has shaped Slovak national identity, yet there is nothing self-evident or teleological about Slovakia's evolution toward independent statehood, even though hindsight may suggest such an inevitable developmental path. The relationship between the nation and the states that the Slovaks inhabited was subjected to several "historical reversals," which, as Rudolf Chmel points out, "speak more of a disintegration of national identity and adaptability than a continuity of political thought and its construction."[30] It is paradoxical that although "the altogether natural interest in Slovak self-identification and self-determination was often interpreted as extremism," none of the twentieth-century state forms that the Slovaks entered into "were accompanied by a plebiscite or by some other unambiguous expression of the will of the people."[31] Along their journey through the turbulent twentieth century, the Slovaks found themselves on several forking paths at which they could well have been swallowed by another state. At each juncture, tensions arose between the nation's orientation inward, focused on exploration of roots and sites that could help define its identity, and outward, looking toward Western Europe, Russia, or more recently, the United States as its global anchor for economic and cultural influence and national security. These clashing orientations also inform the development of Slovak literature, which oscillates between domestic traditions and a wide range of foreign influences in response to regime changes and ideological shifts.[32] If it appears that this volume presents a predominantly positive picture of the development of Slovak literature after 1989, it is because the period from the Velvet Revolution to the present is the first longer, uninterrupted era in which Slovak writing could enjoy creative freedom and develop in contact with global trends.

The paradoxical, Janus-faced Slovak identity, which looks both inward and outward in its self-definition, buoyed by grandiose myths of origin and plagued by a sense of inferiority that stems from its historical statelessness prior to 1918, co-evolves with the country's literary production throughout Slovakia's complex and turbulent twentieth-century history. Therefore, we begin this introduction by first mapping essential historical and cultural contexts for twentieth and twenty-first-century Slovak literature, which is the focus of this book. The concluding part of the introduction situates our book in relation to the limited existing Anglo-American criticism on Slovak literary production.

MILESTONES, CONTINUITIES, AND RUPTURES: SLOVAK HISTORY AND LITERATURE FROM 1918 TO THE PRESENT

In the years leading up to the First World War, Slovakia was still known as "Upper Hungary," but the nineteenth-century national revival movement had laid the foundations for Slovak national identity and aspiration to autonomy within the Austro-Hungarian Empire. In the course of the nineteenth century, the Slovak national revival led to the codification of standard Slovak. The revival movement, led by Ľudovít Štúr, also contributed to the education of Slovak intellectual elites, accelerated the cultural development of the Slovaks, and built the foundations for the future development of Slovak literature.[33] The poet Janko Kráľ introduced a new poetics that combined inspirations from Slovak folk genres and Western Romanticism.[34] By the turn of the twentieth century, the fruits of this nineteenth-century revival movement were being crushed by Magyarization, or the imposition of Hungarian (Magyar) identity and the suppression of minority groups throughout the Hungarian Kingdom. For example, the Apponyi school legislation of 1907 aimed at the Magyarization of elementary schools in Upper Hungary, which affected the education of future Slovak intellectuals. One of these was Pavol Országh Hviezdoslav, who began writing in Hungarian before he became a major Slovak poet who responded to the First World War with his famous *Bloody Sonnets* (*Krvavé sonety*, 1914, trans. 2018). In this climate, the function of Slovak literature was defensive and organized around the promotion of the national cause: the protagonists, whether authors or literary characters, were the champions of the nation, and those who were not loyal to the cause, even when they did not actively oppose it, were seen as antagonists. Other causes, such as the rights of women, were subordinated to the national cause, even though the national movement also invested women writers with a degree of cultural authority.

Toward the end of the First World War, the fate of the Slovaks was far from obvious since they had never shared a common state with the Czechs and were in many respects culturally different from them. The idea of a common state was rooted in the two nations' respective nineteenth-century national revival movements, both of which posited the ideal of Slavic brotherhood. During the war, Slovak politicians, who had pursued the program of national self-determination and autonomy within Hungary, were paralyzed by the "anti-Slavic hysteria" of Austro-Hungarian authorities, who were wary of popular sympathies for Russia and Serbia.[35] The impetus for the idea of Czechoslovakia came from abroad, from exiled politicians seeking a solution to the predicament of Czechs and Slovaks after the anticipated disintegration of the Austro-Hungarian Empire. In Paris, Tomáš Garrigue Masaryk, Eduard Beneš, and Milan Rastislav Štefánik were lobbying for the idea. The powers of the Entente were initially reluctant to support the small nations' struggle for self-determination because they hoped for a separate peace agreement with Austria-Hungary, which they saw as an instrument of Germany. When these hopes failed, the politicians in exile established the Czechoslovak National Council in Paris with branches in the United States and Russia, which was later transformed into a provisional Czechoslovak government. Drawing on Štefánik's French government contacts, they also established Czechoslovak legions, which fought on the Western front as well as in Russia, bolstering the credibility of future Czechoslovakia as an ally of France and other Western powers. In the United States, the large Slovak emigrant community pushed for Slovak autonomy through the Cleveland Memorandum issued by the Slovak League in 1915, which called attention to the predicament of the Slovaks within Hungary, and the Pittsburgh Agreement, signed in May 1918 at the occasion of Masaryk's visit in the United States, in which the Slovak and Czech expatriate communities expressed support for the founding of independent Czechoslovakia.

The Czechoslovak idea did not take root easily in the Slovak political climate. Despite the impact of Magyarization on Slovak-Hungarian relations, the most apparently feasible option was achieving autonomy within the post-imperial Hungarian state. After all, Slovaks and Hungarians shared a thousand years of Slovak history and culture, and many members of the not yet numerous Slovak intelligentsia of the time had been Magyarized in order to be able to pursue professions in the Austro-Hungarian Empire. Slovak infrastructure or political and institutional life were not prepared for the establishment of Czechoslovakia. Slovak politicians were divided into Protestants with a pro-Czech orientation such as Vavro Šrobár or Ivan Dérer and Catholic nationalists who tended to push for Slovak autonomy within Hungary. Nevertheless, even the nationalist leader Andrej Hlinka, a Catholic priest who was not fond of the Czechs because of their "anti-Catholic radicalism and was impressed by their political vitality," eventually conceded that "the thousand-year marriage with the Hungarians has failed; we have to separate."[36] In the wake of that realization, the association with the Czechs appeared not only the most pragmatic option, but also the only viable option to Slovak politicians of all stripes.

Two days after the founding of Czechoslovakia in Prague in October 1918, an assembly of representatives of Slovak political parties adopted the Declaration of the Slovak Nation, also called the Martin Declaration. The assembly declared itself the National Council of the Slovak "branch" of the united Czechoslovak nation. This was undoubtedly an important document and the first expression of Slovak aspiration to statehood independent of Hungary. However, in its focus on separation from Hungary, it also contained many ambiguities, which became a point of contention in interwar Czechoslovakia, particularly the term "branch," which could be interpreted as a bid for autonomy and self-government within Czechoslovakia by Slovak nationalists but was also used in arguments for a unitary Czechoslovak nation by the Prague government.[37] The integration of Slovakia into Czechoslovakia was more complicated than the path to political consensus among Slovak politicians. The state administration was run by Hungarians or by Magyarized Slovaks, and the southern border between Hungary and Slovakia was not determined. In the end, this meant that making the territory of Czechoslovakia as conceptualized on paper a reality required a military takeover by Czechoslovak troops and the importation of Czech bureaucrats to replace officials loyal to Hungary. These interventions took place in a social climate affected by high rates of unemployment, poor supplies, hunger, and social unrest, which culminated in the establishment of a short-lived Soviet-style Slovak Republic in Eastern Slovakia, an attempt to restore greater Hungary with the help of the Soviet Union from Budapest. These rocky beginnings, the asymmetry in the levels of cultural and economic development between the Czechs and the Slovaks, and the centralism of the Prague government contributed to tensions between the Czechs and the Slovaks in interwar Czechoslovakia and to the disintegration of the country in the face of Nazi aggression in 1939.

In the cultural sphere, the end of the First World War and the establishment of Czechoslovakia brought radical changes that reoriented Slovak literature toward the wider world, especially Western Europe, and allowed it to absorb foreign influences more freely. This was reflected in more systematic and wide-ranging translation activity aimed at a public now educated in Slovak not only at the elementary but also at the secondary and university levels. Most immediately, Slovak culture was shaped by the influx of Czech intellectuals, university professors, teachers, and artists.

The dominant critical polemics of the interwar period responded to the increased foreign influences and tensions between the older generation's concerns about the maintenance of national traditions and the younger generation's absorption of influences from the neighbouring Czechs and, more broadly, from European Modernism or proletarian internationalism.[38] The ideological and aesthetic diversification of the younger generation of Slovak intellectuals and writers in response to Western ideas induced moral panic in the older generation. Some critics, as for example Pavol Bujnák in 1925, warned that due to foreign influences Slovak literature "is ceasing to be Slovak, in many of its expressions is Slovak only in its language, but is miles away from us in [the] spirit" of creating a unified, amalgamated national life.[39] At the meeting of the Association of Slovak Writers in Bratislava in the same year, the influential Štefan Krčméry recognized the foreign influence in the "cultural conflagration" that was taking place in Slovak culture as inevitable and even essential, but argued that "we should infuse it with our own color," "maintain our own content," and "create our own forms."[40] The generation of writers and critics who had become established before 1918 were concerned with the continuity of national development, whereas the younger generation, influenced by diverse currents of thought from abroad, were seen as potentially threatening this continuity with foreign fads and a feverish push for innovation. However, it was impossible to channel the diverse influences into one current, and interwar Slovak literature became more diverse with respect to ideology, aesthetics, and poetics.[41] Slovak writers were catching up with late-nineteenth-century Western European literary trends such as aestheticism, decadence, and naturalism, even while the concepts of broader modernist movements such as symbolism, futurism, Dadaism, surrealism, and expressionism began to reach the Slovak literary scene.

Released from the obligatory defence of the national cause, Slovak interwar poets absorbed a wide range of foreign influences and fell into several loose groupings that drew inspiration from various intellectual and ideological currents of European modernity. Proletarian poetry by leftist intellectuals were grouped around the magazine DAV, which featured, among others, the multi-faceted poetry of Laco Novomeský. The echoes of symbolism and decadence culminated with the influential work of Ján Smrek and Emil Boleslav Lukáč. The Catholic "moderna" movement of poet-priests included key figures such as Rudolf Dilong and Janko Silan. The surrealists, who first shocked the Slovak literary scene with Rudolf Fabry's iconoclastic collection *Uťaté ruky* (Severed hands, 1935), also included Vladimír Reisel and Štefan Žáry. These diverse poetic currents were inspired by the poets' own activity as translators. Continuing the modernization of Slovak poetry as represented by the symbolist poetry of Ivan Krasko prior to 1918 and its departure from stylized language and traditional form characteristic of the pre-First World War generation, the interwar poets drew on spoken Slovak vernacular and tended to adopt free verse. The role of the poet also shifted, becoming "neither a bard nor a preacher, neither a prophet nor a scourge" but "above all a citizen" of the new Czechoslovak state.[42] Writers were also citizens of Europe, if not the world, who registered the iconoclastic and hedonistic trends of the 1920s and later the ominous political developments of the 1930s.

During the interwar period, Slovak prose fiction absorbed Western European influences, which had already shaped poetry earlier in the twentieth century. Like in the parallel case of poetry, the openness to foreign influences, the diversification of Slovak political life, the increased opportunities for publishing in Slovak-language periodicals, and the wider range of professional paths open to the new generation of writers produced several different distinct "schools" of fiction as well as highly original individual figures. It is therefore difficult to generalize about the broader trends, but the key features that interwar Slovak fiction shared with the currents of European modernism are the exploration of archetypal layers of collective memory, the focus on individual psychology, the shift to urban settings, the search for universal truths in the aftermath of the First World War and in response to the political turmoil of the 1930s, as well as a conscious effort at stylistic innovation to reflect the ever-shifting new realities of this period. Some writers of the prewar literary scene continued writing after 1918 and retrospectively reassessed nineteenth-century traditions. Janko Jesenský's novel *Demokrati* (*The Democrats*, 1934, 1938, English trans. 1961) satirizes Slovak social and political life. Timrava, a major woman writer of this era, concluded her career with an autobiographical re-evaluation of women's participation in the national movement in *Všetko za národ* (All for the nation, 1926). Ladislav Nádaší-Jégé, who was a medical doctor by profession and was fluent in several languages, drew inspiration from his familiarity with European literature in prose influenced by Zola's naturalism, for example in his autobiographical novel *Cesta životom* (Life journey, 1930), which explores the human factors underpinning the decline and corruption of the Austro-Hungarian Empire.

Interwar fiction writers also returned to the central themes of nineteenth-century realism represented by figures such as Martin Kukučín, Jozef Gregor Tajovský, and Timrava, which put emphasis on village life as the core of Slovak identity.[43] The relationship between rural and urban life, the village and the city, remained central in the works of the Slovak Moderna (the Modern School). Urban settings, virtually absent in nineteenth-century Slovak writing, became more common in interwar Slovak fiction, reflecting the development of urban life and of Bratislava as a new metropolitan centre of Slovakia. The increased international influences manifested in the younger interwar generation in a variety of ways that stemmed from different experiences of the wider world. Some writers, such as Ján Hrušovský and Tido J. Gašpar, responded directly to their personal experience of fighting in the First World War. Gejza Vámoš, a Slovak writer of Hungarian-Jewish descent, drew on his experiences in Prague as a medical student and doctor in *Atómy Boha* (God's atoms, 1928), a novel that scandalized Slovak public opinion with its deterministic and pessimistic view of humanity and its violation of social taboos.[44] When Vámoš's dark view of humanity was validated by the antisemitism of the late 1930s, he emigrated first to China, then to Brazil, and spent the rest of his life in exile. Another writer who cultivated a cosmopolitan identity as a European, Ivan Horváth, studied in Paris during the 1920s and travelled widely to European cultural capitals. He explores the motif of the journey in *Vízum do Európy* (Visa to Europe, 1930), a collection of short fiction that takes the reader to various European cities and features characters of different nationalities. Looking toward the East yielded radically different results in the writing of the most prominent interwar representative of proletarian prose, the Czech-born Peter Jilemnický. His early novel *Víťazný pád* (Victorious fall, 1929) draws inspiration from his personal experience as a teacher in the provincial region of Kysuce and participates in the lyrical revaluation of Slovak village characteristic of the interwar period. Following his stay in the Soviet Union, documented in *Dva roky v kraji Sovietov* (Two years in the land of the Soviets, 1929), he aligns his fiction with the tenets of socialist realism in novels that focus on the living conditions and political struggles of the Slovak agricultural workers, foreshadowing a trend that would dominate Slovak literature after the Second World War.

On the other hand, the new generation also re-envisioned domestic settings and demythologized the nineteenth-century realist conception of the Slovak village. One of the most remarkable literary phenomena of this period was Milo Urban's *Živý bič* (The living whip, 1927) which offers a defamiliarizing, unsentimental view of Slovak village life irrevocably altered after the First World War, which disrupted its self-contained isolation. Jozef Cíger Hronský's *Jozef Mak* (1933, trans. 1985) also challenges the picture of village life as presented in the realist "classics" by exploring the psychological experience of poverty and suffering of a Slovak Everyman, "a common human being, a mere statistic, whom no one longed for at his birth and no one will miss at his death! ... a cipher, worth mentioning just as a part of humanity but never in his own right."[45] In the so-called "naturist" fiction of the 1930s and the 1940s, which is characterized by lyricized prose and reliance on folktale narrative elements, village life is reconsidered as an archetype of human experience through its proximity to nature rather than as a source of national identity.

The status of Slovakia within Czechoslovakia shifted in the course of the interwar years, which became evident at the outbreak of the Second World War. Throughout the interwar period, the concept of "Czechoslovakism," which envisioned one amalgamated nation of Czechs and Slovaks, presented a challenge for mutual relations. The nationalist Slovenská ľudová strana (Slovak People's Party), led by Andrej Hlinka, became increasingly radicalized in response to the Prague government's centralist policies. One of the key figures whose political positions evolved during this period and who briefly represented Slovakia in the Prague government was Jozef Tiso, a Catholic priest and the future president of the wartime Slovak state.[46] Slovak politicians gained confidence when during the years leading up to the war it appeared that Slovakia, located farther east, could serve a defensive function in the event the Czech lands were occupied by Germany. Instead, Slovakia once again became the object of Hungary's expansionist ambitions. The two parts of the republic increasingly grew apart under the different threats they faced (Hungarian and German).

In the late 1930s, Slovak literature became more topical in response to these troubling political developments. The Congress of Slovak Writers in 1936 directly challenged the political forces of the time, which was evident in Laco Novomeský's speech: "We want the Slovak cultural efforts to be truly cultured and play an honourable and a significant role in building a new culture of humanity saturated with genuine human aspirations and defending it against the attacks of barbarism, whether it calls itself 'ardent nationalism,' 'racial superiority,' 'clerical and religious salvation' or directly 'fascism!'"[47] The congress proclaimed its allegiance to humanist ideals, which united writers regardless of whether their politics leaned toward the left or the right, and declared that Slovak writers maintained friendly relations with Czech writers on terms of equality, a significant position in the context of the tense mutual political relations between the two nations in the late 1930s. Emil Boleslav Lukáč published a collection of poems under the title of *Moloch* (1938), which evokes a civilization threatened by the forces of barbarism. In the poem "Europa," he draws on Greek mythology as a shared foundation of European civilization to lament the impending fate of the continent: "A lover seized by a bull/ not divinely transformed ... Where, oh, where / Is that blood-red, brutal animal carrying you off?"[48]

In September 1938, Germany, Italy, Great Britain, and France signed the Munich Agreement, which dictated that Czechoslovakia must surrender its border regions (the so-called Sudetenland) to Nazi Germany. Czechoslovak President Edvard Beneš, Masaryk's successor, resigned and went into exile. In the following month, as German troops occupied the Sudetenland, Hlinka's Slovak People's Party proclaimed Slovak autonomy, which the Prague government was forced to accept. Jozef Tiso's negotiations about territory with the Hungarians failed, and the decision was relegated to Germany and Italy. As a result, Hungary took over a large part of the Slovak territory, including the second largest town of Košice and 40 per cent of agricultural land and the southern part of Carpathian Ukraine following the Vienna Arbitration mediated by Nazi Germany and Italy. Hitler invited Jozef Tiso to Berlin and presented him with "an unambiguous choice: an immediate declaration of independence, or the prospect of the division of Slovakia between Germany, Poland, and Hungary."[49] As a result of this personal intervention by Adolf Hitler, the Slovak parliament proclaimed an independent Slovak state on 14 March 1939. The Western part of Czechoslovakia, or what was left of the Czech Lands, became a Protectorate of Nazi Germany. Ultimately, Hitler used the unresolved national tensions within Czechoslovakia as "a detonator, justifying aggression and occupation as a result of 'internal disintegration.'"[50]

The wartime Slovak Republic was used by Nazi Germany as a model state that showcased its role as a liberating rather than an occupying force. The state was dependent on Nazi Germany in its foreign policy, "halfway between an occupied country or protectorate ... and a sovereign state under German influence."[51] As an ally, Slovakia participated in the 1939 campaign against Poland and in the war against the Soviet Union starting in 1941, and declared war against the US and Great Britain along with Nazi Germany. Also, the role of the Slovak state mandated by agreements signed with Nazi Germany was to support the war effort with supplies of armaments and raw materials. The authoritarian rule of Hlinka's Slovak People's Party exercised increasing levels of control on public life, but the party leaders disagreed on the model of dictatorship that they considered best suited for the country. Tiso's faction advocated for a "people's Slovakia" governed by conservative, paternalist values and hierarchies, relying on the support of the Catholic Church. Vojtech Tuka's faction, bolstered by the fascist Hlinka Guard led by Alexander Mach, embraced the model of "Slovak national socialism."[52] The darkest aspect of the dictatorship was its antisemitism, which first led to propaganda that fuelled popular sentiment against the Jewish citizens of Slovakia, then to legislation that severely curtailed their civil rights, and, eventually, starting in 1942, to the state-sponsored deportation and killing of the Jewish population in Slovakia and the "Aryanization" (confiscation and redistribution to non-Jews) of their property. The Romany community also suffered from discrimination and restricted civil rights, and in the last year of the war, German SS units committed mass killings of Romany in central Slovakia.[53] The legacy of the Second World War Slovak state, especially its systematic liquidation of the Slovak Jewish community that permanently altered Slovak society and the problematic role of the Catholic Church in the events, continues to haunt Slovak politics and culture, including literature. For example, the film *The Shop on Main Street* (dir. Ján Kadár, 1965), an adaptation of a novella by Ladislav Grossman that won an Oscar for Best Foreign Language Film, depicts the cowardice and greed that led provincial Slovaks to participate in Aryanization and the Holocaust. More recently, Viliam Klimáček's play *Holokaust* (2012) revisits the tragic events of this period and examines ordinary Slovaks' motives for complicity with the fascist regime.[54]

The impact of the wartime authoritarian state on the literary scene was complex and shifted in the course of the war. During the early years of the Second World War, Slovak culture retained relative autonomy under the Slovak state, which meant that some of the modernist trends that emerged in the interwar period could continue to evolve. This allowed, for example, the publication of the best-known and most accomplished products of "naturist" fiction, Margita Figuli's *Three Chestnut Horses* (*Tri gaštanové kone*, 1940, trans. 2014) and Dobroslav Chrobák's *Drak sa vracia* (Dragon returns, 1942). František Švantner's *Nevesta hôľ* (The bride of the glades, 1946), written during the war, was published shortly after. On the other hand, the Slovak state relied on the national mythology of the millennium of Slovak struggle for freedom, and its nationalism was used to justify harsh antisemitic policies. The position of Slovak writers in relation to the regime was far from unitary and evolved over time from the early acceptance of its existence as perhaps inevitable in the context of Central European historical developments to the eventual rejection of the regime during the final years of the Second World War.[55]

The wartime Slovak resistance was divided in its aims and strategies. The communists, who had links with Moscow, envisioned a future in which Slovakia would be a part of a wider Soviet federation or even the

Soviet Union itself. The liberal intelligentsia, tied to Beneš's government in exile (first in Paris and later in London), especially the Protestants who were marginalized by the Catholic state, wanted a restoration of Czechoslovakia in a more equitably federal form. By the end of the war, the Soviet Union, in line with the anti-Hitler coalition, also strategically supported the renewal of Czechoslovakia, which led the Slovak communists to subscribe to this objective. In late 1943, when Germany's eventual defeat became more obvious, the communist and civil groups signed the so-called Christmas Agreement and established the Slovak National Council as a joint resistance authority. Their main objective was to help the Allied front and open the path for the Soviet Army advancing toward the Carpathians, which led to the events of the Slovak National Uprising. Without time for adequate coordination and strategic planning with the Soviets, the partisans of various nationalities, who had begun to attack collaborators and Germans in the mountains of Central Slovakia, spontaneously occupied whole villages and valleys. In response, the Germans began to occupy Slovakia with the agreement of the Slovak government, which had lost control of the situation, and after a two-month struggle, the Uprising was defeated in August 1944.

The Slovak National Uprising failed in some of its key objectives, but it was significant as the culmination of Slovak anti-fascist resistance, and, since the Allies recognized the army of the Uprising as an Allied force, provided credibility to the Slovak aspiration to participate as equals in the re-established postwar Czechoslovakia. The government of the Slovak state compromised itself by collaborating with Nazi Germany in the brutal suppression of the Uprising, which involved the burning of many villages and summary executions. The traumatic experiences of the Uprising were a frequent theme in socialist-era literature, most notably in Ladislav Mňačko's *Death Is Called Engelchen* (*Smrť sa volá Engelchen*, 1959, trans. 1961), which explores the human dimensions and the psychological impact of the partisan struggle.

In the period immediately following the end of the Second World War (1945–49), cultural life briefly returned to a limited form of pluralism, which became increasingly constricted while Czechoslovakia moved toward another form of totalitarianism. The sphere of culture, just like the rest of Slovak society, cleansed itself of fascist elements, and nationally oriented literature – which had been so dominant – became suspect in this atmosphere. Influential writers who had served as cultural representatives of the old regime such as Jozef Cíger Hronský and Rudolf Dilong emigrated, opening a divide between domestic and exile literature that was to continue for decades. The writers who remained shared the platform of antifascism and dedication to the rebuilding of the country, but beyond those fundamental values, their views on the function of literature diverged greatly. The rural-oriented naturists and urban-oriented surrealists continued to publish their work, some of which had been produced during the war. A shared feature of the literature of this transitional period is its existential anxiety in the aftermath of the war and in response to enforced collectivism, whether fascist or Marxist. In this respect, Slovak literature was still following a broader European movement toward existentialism. After 1949, this existential trend could freely develop only among exiled writers.

Leftist ideologues, whose power grew in the aftermath of the war, exerted increasing influence in debates on the function of literature. Following the communist takeover of power in February 1948, the ideological pressure was compounded by systematic liquidation of alternative visions of literary life. During the early 1950s, the Czechoslovak communist leaders followed Stalin's USSR in imposing strict control over all spheres of culture, including literary life. Enforced unity was considered essential in combatting external (Western) and internal enemies (even within the party's own ranks). The state systematically liquidated all institutions associated with democratic literary life and reorganized both the publishing industry and literary associations in new institutions that were subjected to state control. Despite earlier attempts to formulate a humanist conception of socialist literature, the tenets of socialist realism, which put literature in the service of ideology and mandated its appropriate content, became the only viable model for literary production. Institutions that did not subscribe to or promote the agenda of socialist realism were abolished; writers whose work did not correspond with its tenets were pushed out of public life.

Embraced by some writers and reluctantly adopted by others, socialist realism openly promoted and engaged with the ideals of communism, focusing on approved themes such as the fight against fascism, gratitude for the liberating role of the USSR, industrialization, and collectivization. The purpose of this literature was to bolster the leading role of the communist party in history and support the development of class consciousness among the population. The poetry that fit these criteria offered a celebratory, rose-coloured view of reality and elevated diction that looked forward to brighter tomorrows. Fiction featured schematic plots and stereotypical battles between heroes and villains that resembled fairy-tale archetypes. Writers who fell out of favour resorted to "writing for the drawer" for decades, and their texts were published much later, in the 1960s or even the 1990s.

The system rewarded authors who wrote "engaged" literature that aligned with the tenets of socialist realism and supported the regime with various benefits, including prizes, special editions, large print runs, financial bonuses, and even free vacations. The less pliable writers were subjected to repression, forbidden to publish, barred from other employment that corresponded with their level of education, or imprisoned. The privileging of writers of working-class origins over established intelligentsia and professionals was another form of control. Literary criticism was also used as an instrument of intimidation and enforcement of the norms of socialist realism, which contributed to the atmosphere of terror. The benefit of the mass popularization of ideologically "engaged" literature, along with the relative democratization of education (with the exclusion of "class enemies"), was dramatically increased interest in reading literature, and literary discussions were conducted in various public spaces, including workplaces.

The early sign of the post-Stalin Thaw in Czechoslovakia was the push to rehabilitate communists who had been executed or imprisoned after staged trials in the 1950s or persecuted and banned from public life. A few writers dared to openly critique the human failings that had compromised the socialist regime, most notably Alfonz Bednár in *Sklenený vrch* (The glass mountain, 1954) and *Hodiny a minúty* (Hours and minutes, 1956), Ladislav Mňačko in *Oneskorené reportáže* (Belated reports, 1963), Dominik Tatarka in "The Demon of Conformism" (*Démon súhlasu*, 1963, abridged trans. 1987), and Milan Rúfus in the collection *Až dozrieme* (When we are ripe, 1956).[56] Such exceptional texts were published in the midst of a broader debate on the need for literature to present a comprehensive picture of human experience, one not only focused on social movements and issues, but also on the individual consciousness.

In the more relaxed political climate, historians and politicians reopened the question of Slovak autonomy and the debate about a potential federative reorganization of the state that would give equal representation to the Slovaks. This debate was also driven by economic concerns. The sweeping rehabilitation of political prisoners in the early 1960s included Slovak intellectuals who had been condemned as proponents of "bourgeois nationalism" such as Gustáv Husák, who was to play a major role in Czechoslovak politics of the coming decades.

By the early 1960s, the country was in an economic crisis because its centrally planned economy could not keep up with the scientific and technological revolution in the West. Slovakia was at an added disadvantage because it tended to supply raw materials and semi-finished products to the Czech lands, which produced more profitable finished goods. It turned out to be impossible to implement economic reform without political reform that would modify the centralizing role of the communist party. By early 1968, the period that became known as the Prague Spring, the party leadership led by the Slovak politician Alexander Dubček allowed a significant degree of democratization in public life, which was especially evident in the freedom of the press. In Slovakia, the magazine *Kultúrny život* served as a venue for public debates about urgent social, political, and cultural issues, including the question of the federation and the relationship between the East and the West. The young generation was influenced by Western popular music that permeated Czechoslovakia, especially rock and roll, which introduced them to alternative values that emphasized individual freedom.

During the periods of the Thaw and the Prague Spring, the schematic aspects of socialist realism came under scrutiny. Some writers recognized that the overly optimistic picture of the postwar reality did not capture the negative side of the period: the staged trials, the scrutiny of the class backgrounds that impacted employment, forced resettlement, the persecution of priests and believers, and general abuses of power. The principal issue or problem that was characteristic of Slovak literature between 1956 and 1970 was the recovery of individual experience beyond "the typological heroism" and "the ideal of social engagement" and the return to the representation of imperfect, authentic humanity in literary works.[57] How this was to be accomplished, however, was a matter of debate, and different generations and groups varied in their approaches. The middle generation, whose ideological views were formed by the Second World War and the Uprising, defended its established status and argued for reforming socialist realism. They continued to subscribe to communist ideals and tended to focus on the human flaws that hampered their implementation. In contrast, the younger generation of writers born in the 1930s and 1940s, such as Ján Johanides, Pavel Hrúz, Rudolf Sloboda, Vincent Šikula, and Pavel Vilikovský, drew inspiration from Western literature and the interwar domestic tradition in their neo-modernist formal experimentation and their focus on existential questions and individual experience. Their writing inaugurated key trends that influenced later generations of Slovak writers.

In poetry, the temporary "thaw" opened possibilities for imagining poetics that diverged from official, ideologically inflected poetry. New loosely connected groups of poets promoted the integrity of content and form in poetic expression. The "concretists" or the Trnava group, which was initiated by the prominent poet Miroslav Válek, highlighted sensory specificity as a challenge to ideologically mandated content. A more radical group known as the "Osamelí bežci" (Lone Runners), which was motivated by a quest for ethical autonomy and briefly organized around the journal *Mladá tvorba*, examined the lyrical subject as a construct, challenging the assumptions of ideologically engaged poetry as well as the aestheticizing, utopian tendencies of the concretists. Ivan Štrpka later reformulated the program of the "lone runners" with a focus on "open poetry" that recorded the state of human consciousness in its pure or raw state, unprocessed by language or poetic processes.[58]

The increasing plurality of public and political life was perceived as a threat by the Soviet leaders, and in August 1968, the troops of the Warsaw Pact invaded Czechoslovakia.[59] A faction of communist politicians, the so-called "realists," which included Gustáv Husák, who eventually replaced Alexander Dubček as the first secretary of the Communist Party of Czechoslovakia, considered the invasion an inevitability and an opportunity for career advancement. Under the conditions of limited state sovereignty and under the directives of the Soviet leadership, these politicians began a process of "normalization," or consolidation of neo-Stalinist state power. As a result of the reforms, the Constitutional Act on the Czecho-Slovak federation was eventually passed in the fall of 1968, but since the objective of normalization was a restoration of the central role of the communist party, the extent of the federal competencies of Slovak institutions was limited, especially in the economic sphere.[60] A lost or broken generation of writers was once again interrupted in its relatively free creative pursuits and subjected to ideologically driven critique, censorship, and profiling after 1968. Nevertheless, this generation laid the foundations for the development of postmodernism in the 1990s.

The process of "normalization" had far-reaching consequences in the cultural sphere that shaped the development of Slovak literature in the decades that followed. Literary institutions were subjected to purges, and censorship reasserted its grip on literary production. Texts and writers that did not subscribe to the tenets of socialist realism were once again repressed, but this repression was often less direct than in the 1950s; only a few writers were imprisoned, and state power preferred to use manipulation, corruption, and training of writers and critics to make them comply with its agenda. The state attempted to raise a new generation of writers and critics to support the production of acceptable socially engaged literature. There was some divergence among the proponents of socialist realism, with some advocating a less dogmatic and more aesthetically nuanced approach that, to some degree, allowed for the focus on the individual in broader social or historical contexts and made it possible for some formerly sanctioned writers to publish again in the late 1970s. Nevertheless, the press regularly attacked writers for escapism, whether to the past or to the private sphere, which led to a loss of confidence for some writers and paralysis or writer's block for others.

Writers responded to this situation in several different ways. One group emigrated to the West, such as Jaroslava Blažková (who moved to Canada), to avoid repercussions for their social activism and writing that they had produced during the more liberal period of the 1960s. Another group was subjected to personal restrictions and interventions, especially those who were expelled from the Slovak Writer's Union and banned from publication, such as Dominik Tatarka, who became involved with the dissident movement produced texts that were later published as *Písačky* (Jottings) and *Navrávačky* (Recordings, both 1988) during his period of "internal exile."[61] Their disappearance from the literary scene cleared the stage for less talented and more conformist writers who produced the type of writing required by the regime. Those who refused to comply with the state-mandated standards for literary production once again resorted to "writing for the drawer," like Pavel Vilikovský, whose books *Eskalácia citu* (An escalation of feeling), *Kôň na poschodí, slepec vo Vrábľoch* (*A Horse Upstairs, A Blind Man in Vráble*), and *Ever Green Is …* (*Večne je zelený …*) were all published in 1989, a number of years after they had been written (the latter two appeared in English translation in 2002).

During the 1970s, normalization also increased the ideological pressure on poetry, which was evident in a special section devoted to poetry in the political weekly *Nové slovo* edited by a poet of the older generation, Vojtech Mihálik. Some poets escaped the political pressure by focusing on private themes associated with childhood, the landscape, and cultural memory. During the 1980s, a younger generation of poets introduced greater spontaneity and authenticity that stemmed from personal experience. By the mid-1980s, this generation of poets, which included Štefan Moravčík, Daniel Hevier, Viliam Klimáček, Ivan Kolenič, and Tatiana Lehenová, challenged the taste and ideological expectations of official critics and editors.

The writers who retreated into the past tended to reconceptualize the nation in response to the establishment of the compromised Czechoslovak federation of 1968, which nevertheless represented some progress toward Slovak national emancipation. Their shared objectives were to represent the past through the prism of individual or regional experience and to restore a sense of continuity and national identity in reaction to disruptive historical developments. The damaging effects of the forced internal exile and restrictive censorship limited the range of human experiences that could be represented in literature (for example, Christian or spiritual themes were suspect) and disrupted the free development of Slovak literature in response to postmodern and other global trends, which only became possible in the late 1980s and 1990s.[62] There was also a less visible, "hidden history of humiliation and sleepless nights," which shaped a whole generation of writers.[63] Nevertheless, unofficial spaces in which intellectual debate and cultural development could preserve some continuity remained, including informal debate clubs, meeting places such as cafes, or alternative theatre groups, which paved the way for cultural development in an open society after 1989. The underground circulation of literary magazines that began in the 1980s provided the foundation for the later pluralistic differentiation of periodicals in an open society. During the last two decades of its existence, the communist regime and its official representatives in literary institutions shifted toward an increased emphasis on aesthetic criteria and a greater openness to innovative approaches, which allowed some writers to return from either enforced or voluntary internal exile. Partly due to the relatively less restrictive conditions for cultural life in Slovakia, dissident literary circles were smaller than in the Czech Republic and centred on Prague and the Charter 77 movement.

The "Velvet Revolution," which led to the fall of the communist regime in November 1989, resulted from a complex combination of domestic political, social, and economic problems as well as a favourable international situation.[64] As a result of normalization, the attitude of the population toward the communist party was mostly that of opportunism among its remaining supporters or resignation and indifference among the majority. By the 1980s, the standard of living in Slovakia increased as the state subsidized essential food items and encouraged consumption as an antidote to political unrest. However, the centrally planned economy failed to compete with Western market economies and supply the demand for consumer goods. Shortages caused dissatisfaction and increased the impact of corruption and the black market. The growing dissident movement, although more diffuse than in the Czech regions, was increasingly visible and vocal in its protests against violations of human rights, restricted religious rights, and environmental pollution. Mikhail Gorbachev's rise to power and the reform movement of perestroika in the USSR further undermined the regime, which had been legitimized by the Soviet invasion in 1968 and bolstered by occupying Soviet troops. Poland's Solidarity Movement and the mass emigration of people from the socialist German Democratic Republic brought the situation in the Soviet Bloc to a tipping point. In Czechoslovakia, the opposition to the regime culminated in student demonstrations in Bratislava and Prague in November 1989. After the student protest in Prague was violently suppressed by the police, a series of demonstrations, a general strike, and the absence of any support from the Soviet side led to the establishment of a new government that included representatives of the dissident movement. Václav Havel was named the president of Czechoslovakia and Alexander Dubček returned to politics as the chairman of the federal parliament. Občianske fórum (Civic Forum) and Verejnosť proti násiliu (Public against Violence) emerged as the leading political forces and the precursors of new political parties.

The transition to a democratic government (free elections took place in 1990 and again in 1992) and the market economy exposed and aggravated the economic and constitutional asymmetries between Slovakia and the Czech lands. Slovak economy relied on heavy industry with a focus on armaments, which were not in high demand after the end of the Cold War. As early as 1990, the pressure of Czech centralism became evident in the dispute over the name of the country, in which the Slovak side preferred the hyphenated name Czecho-Slovak Republic. The hyphen became a point of contention and an occasion for displays of nationalism in both parts of the federation. When the dissatisfaction with high inflation and unemployment, especially in the provinces, led to the election victory of the populist Movement for Democratic Slovakia led by Vladimír Mečiar, the negotiations over the division of powers between the federal and national government bodies became increasingly fraught. In the Czech Lands, the winner of the election was the right-wing Civic Democratic Party led by Václav Klaus, who pushed for faster economic transformation. Slovakia, with its armaments factories and eastward oriented heavy industry, was perceived as a burden in such a vision of future development. Despite popular demand for a referendum, the two leaders eventually signed agreements that led to the peaceful dissolution of Czechoslovakia in December 1992.[65]

The independent Slovak Republic was quickly recognized by neighbouring states and world powers and gradually joined major international organizations. However, the corruption of the Mečiar government, the signs of its potential pro-Russian orientation, and the controversial policies toward the Hungarian minority spurred by the Slovak National Party (SNS), which was a part of the government coalition, led to the gradual exclusion of the Slovak Republic from the first group of Central European candidates for accession to NATO and the European Union. The country changed course only after the 1998 election, when the results did not allow Mečiar to form a government and a coalition of other parties formed a pro-Western government led by Mikuláš Dzurinda. This new government eventually made it possible for Slovakia to sign the Schengen Agreement in 2003 (implemented in 2007), to join the European Union and NATO in 2004, and to adopt the Euro before its Central European neighbors in 2009. Nevertheless, the historically determined uneven development between the capital and the provinces as well as the deeply rooted tensions between pro-Western and pro-Russian political orientation continue to impact Slovak culture and politics.

The Slovak literary scene also connected with Western trends through institutions; for example, the Slovak branch of the PEN Club was re-established in 1989, and the feminist association and publisher ASPEKT was founded in 1992. The centrally run state publishers and journals were replaced with a wide range of private publishing houses and literary periodicals. In 1996, the National Centre for Literature (later the Centre for Information on Literature and currently the Slovak Literary Centre) was founded for the promotion of Slovak literature abroad. The dismantling of the state-sponsored literary establishment also had some negative effects. The quality of publications, especially in the selection and marketing of translations that was driven by profitability, declined, and books became more expensive for average Slovaks, which put pressure on publishers and limited print runs.

Following the division of Czechoslovakia and the founding of the independent Slovak Republic in 1993, tensions increased between intellectuals and writers who embraced secular liberalism and those who turned to nationalism (a group that paradoxically included both conservative Christians and former communists), which was reflected in the division of writers' organizations. During the 1990s, the Mečiar regime impacted the liberalization of cultural life, but the pressure was not strong enough to reverse the trajectory of increasing pluralism. The opening of the literary scene to different types of writers and styles and the unhampered experimentation with postmodern trends paved the way for the development of contemporary Slovak literature in the new millennium.

In the 1990s, Slovak literature became "decentralized, liberalized, democratized, differentiated."[66] Features of alternative literature such as anti-literariness, irony, grotesque, improvisation, and democratization of language that had emerged during the socialist era manifested more openly as belated postmodernism in the prose of this decade. For example, Stanislav Rakús, who had published shorter works in the 1970s, published his first novel *Temporálne poznámky* (Temporal notes, 1993) based on his autobiographical experiences as a lecturer.[67] The poets of the 1990s engaged in formal experimentation, deconstructed "the central position of the traditionally conceived lyrical subject" and problematized the capacity of language or poetry to "mediate experience, knowledge, or any universal values."[68] One of the most significant poets of this decade was Mila Haugová, who scrutinized the feminine as a visceral, mythological, and philosophical being-in-the-world.

Democratization also allowed writers to openly re-assess the past. In his novella *But Crime Does Punish* (*Trestajúci zločin*, 1995, trans. 2022), Ján Johanides conjures a scene in which, in the aftermath of 1989, officials reopen a mass grave from the Second World War to bury socialist-era secret service files on top of the unidentified dead: "And then the files started to rain on the skeletons ... In a matter of minutes, the skeletons were covered in a layer of files. Next, it was the turn of the quicklime ... A layer of documents, then a layer of lime. And again, like layers in a cake."[69] The powerful symbolism of the scene encapsulates the dilemma of the postsocialist reckoning with the past in Slovak society of the 1990s, in which both forgetting and remembering had troubling implications. Since 2000, the pluralization and individualization of literary life has continued, which is evident in the proliferation of literary institutions, publishers, and periodicals as well as the numbers of literary publications. Although commercialization presents a challenge that affects the quality of literary production, the grant support system of the Ministry of Culture also increases the diversity of writers and publications.[70] A new generation of writers have moved beyond postmodern paradigms, which, on the one hand, manifests as "the 'return' of the subject," with attempts to "mediate a plausible 'living world'" as filtered through individual experience.[71] On the other hand, in contrast to the backlash against enforced socialist collectivism of the previous decade, the millennial generation also embraced new forms of social engagement in their literary expression. Experimental poetry has increased its focus on communication with the reader, often in dialogue with visual arts and technology, through its use of multimedia and computer-generated language. The younger generation of poets also shows a renewed interest in the subject and social issues. Contemporary prose has turned to re-exploring various aspects of social reality distorted by the past. In addition to the autobiographical turn that re-examines individual and generational experience, writers also re-evaluate historical events, foreground gender issues, reconsider the relationship between home and the world in response to expat experience, and highlight the significance of minorities and regions in relation to national identity.

SLOVAK LITERATURE IN ENGLISH-LANGUAGE CRITICISM AND TRANSLATION AFTER 1989

The period since 1989 has been formative and significant for the development of literary criticism within Slovakia, with the emergence of scholars (including several contributors to this volume) whose work is not influenced by the ideological restrictions of the previous regime. However, most of their research has not previously been translated into or published in English.[72] The handful of reference works translated into

English and published in Slovakia itself before 1989 were mostly broad overviews whose critical analysis was limited to the then-acceptable Marxist standpoint.

The situation in English-language criticism improved in the decade after 1989, largely due to Robert Pynsent of the School of Slavonic and East European Studies (SSEES) at University College London. As the organizer of a conference on Slovak literature at SSEES in 1987, Pynsent brought together leading British, Slovak, and other international scholars, including his own mentor at Cambridge, Karel Brušák, who "initiated the serious study of Slovak in the United Kingdom," as well as the long-term SSEES lecturer David Short, the American scholar and translator Norma Rudinsky, and the Slovak-Canadian Peter Petro, among others.[73] Their contributions were published in Pynsent's edited volume *Modern Slovak Prose: Fiction since 1954*, which appeared three years later, after the fall of the communist regime. As Susie Lunt has noted, this volume (which includes Pynsent's essay on Ján Johanides and chapters on such writers as Dominik Tatarka, Ladislav Ballek, and Dušan Dušek) "is the first such book to be published in the West on this significant period in Slovak literary history and one of the first to present truly engaging, non-establishment interpretations of contemporary Slovak works."[74]

Peter Petro translated Martin M. Šimečka's *The Year of the Frog* (1993), the first full-length work of Slovak prose published in English after the revolution, followed by the concise but comprehensive *History of Slovak Literature* (1995).[75] In the final chapter, which covers most of the twentieth century, Petro provides short overviews of the 1960s and the normalization period (1970s–80s), with profiles of Dominik Tatarka representing the former, and Ladislav Ballek and Milan Rúfus the latter, briefly mentioning the "young and unorthodox voices" such as Dušan Mitana, Rudolf Sloboda, and Pavel Vilikovský.[76]

Rajendra Chitnis's 2004 monograph *Literature in Post-communist Russia and Eastern Europe* remains the most recent comprehensive overview of late twentieth-century Slovak literature. Comparing work by Pavel Vilikovský, Peter Pišťanek, Dušan Mitana, Ivan Kolenič, and Balla to that of their Czech and Russian contemporaries, Chitnis suggests that "the writers of the [1988–98] Changes frequently appear far more confident about their understanding of the nature not only of art, but also of human existence, than much 'liberal' literature of the preceding period."[77] In the same year, the first volume of a wide-ranging reference source on literature of the region, Marcel Cornis-Pope and John Neubauer's four-volume *History of the Literary Cultures of East-Central Europe* (2004–10) was also published. It includes substantial discussions of Slovak literature, especially in Dagmar Kročanová's discussions of literary journals, censorship, and several periods of Slovak drama in the third volume. While all of these provide helpful background, perhaps the most intriguing is the "meta-critical" analysis of Slovak literary historiography itself, in which Kročanová examines the "pitfalls" of writing literary histories in a small nation whose culture and literature are "saturated with politics and ideology."[78]

While the scholarship of Pynsent, Petro, Chitnis, and Kročanová brought attention to postsocialist Slovak writing, particularly fiction, the writers themselves remained largely inaccessible in translation, except for individual stories by Mitana, Sloboda, Vilikovský, and Johanides in *Description of a Struggle* (1994), the most comprehensive English-language anthology of East European fiction in the decade after 1989.[79] However, Slovak works from 1989 and after slowly began to appear in English, beginning with Vilikovský's *Ever Green Is ...*, which was published in 2002 as part of the "Writers from an Unbound Europe" series from Northwestern University Press.[80] Established to capitalize on the wave of interest in the former Eastern Bloc following the fall of communism, Northwestern's series was not as influential as the series Philip Roth had edited for Penguin Books, "Writers from the Other Europe," but unlike Roth's, it included a significant number of women writers (including the future Nobel laureate Olga Tokarczuk) and had a broader geographical coverage, with authors from nearly every country in the region. While the translation did not make Vilikovský a well-known name among English-speaking readers, its long-term impact may be seen more indirectly, as shown in two articles on Central European literature by Julian Evans, which appeared less than two years apart in the *Guardian*. In July 2002, Evans notes perceptively that "Western support for dissident Czech writers before 1989 was just that – Slovakian writers were not included. It may be time for British publishers to realise that on the other side of the Moravian forests there are overdue discoveries to be made."[81] He then gives the example of Vilikovský's *Ever Green Is ...* (which was not yet available in English, although the translation came out a few months later). In May 2004, Evans again calls Slovak "one of the least known Slavic literatures," but adds, "At least we have ... a novel by Pavel Vilikovský, *Ever Green Is ...*, the fictional autobiography of a senile bisexual spy that is rife with mischief."[82]

In both of his articles, Evans also mentions Pišťanek's *Rivers of Babylon*, which appeared in English a few years later (vol. 1 in 2007, vols 2–3 in 2008) from Garnett Press, an imprint of Queen Mary University of London. It received an enthusiastic review in the *Times Literary Supplement* by Tim Beasley-Murray, who called it "a worthy heir to Rabelais, Balzac, and Gogol" and concluded with the "hope that Peter Petro's sober, judicious and accurate translation, expertly edited and introduced by Donald Rayfield, has some success in the English-speaking world and helps it on the path to world domination."[83] As with the case of Vilikovský, Pišťanek's "success" was rather relative since Garnett's distribution was even more limited than Northwestern's, but two decades after the Velvet Revolution, the two most influential writers of the post-socialist transition had finally been made available in English.

In 2011, Garnett Press published another translation, Daniela Kapitáňová's *Cemetery Book* (originally published in 2000 under the pseudonym Samko Tale, which is also the name of the narrator and protagonist). Magdalena Mullek's review in *Asymptote*, which compares the novel to both Faulkner's *The Sound and the Fury* and Dostoevsky's *Notes from Underground*, suggests: "Just as Samko's unexpected turns of phrase jolt us out of everyday language, Kapitáňová's novel jolts us out of our everyday literary expectations."[84] This book is perhaps most notable, however, as the first full-length Slovak novel translated by the London-based Julia Sherwood, also a former student of Robert Pynsent at SSEES. Sherwood's productivity as a translator in the following decade rivalled Pynsent's critical output in the decade after 1989; in addition to publishing translations (sometimes more than one per year) by such writers as Balla, Jana Juráňová, and the more recently established novelists Uršuľa Kovalyk and Ivana Dobrakovová, she helped to establish new series of Slovak literature in English with both Seagull Books, based in Kolkata, and Karolinum Press, based in Prague. Together with Magdalena Mullek, she co-edited *Into the Spotlight* (2017), an anthology of contemporary Slovak writing, and the two have also developed an informative website in English (both translators discuss their activities later in this volume).[85]

While the number of Slovak translations into English has thus increased greatly over the past decade, thanks primarily to Sherwood,

Mullek, Janet Livingstone, and several other translators, the number of literary studies in English devoted to Slovak literature has not grown apace – in fact, it seems to have decreased. The historian Alexander Maxwell, whose *Choosing Slovakia* (2009) examines nineteenth-century national identity, often contradicts received opinion in Slovak scholarship in a manner similar to Pynsent, but his arguments are generally convincing, as in his criticism of contemporary Slovak historians who, "expecting Štúr to proclaim the Slovaks a 'nation' speaking a 'language,' have been extraordinarily unwilling to confront the fact that Štúr described the Slovaks as 'a tribe [*kmen*]' speaking 'a dialect [*nárečja*].'"[86] The cultural-linguistic anthropologist Jonathan Larson's *Critical Thinking in Slovakia after Socialism* (2013) is another example of research in an adjacent field with useful insights for literary scholars, particularly in his reports of field work observing how high school students learned to analyze literary texts:

> Pedagogues I interviewed specified that in Eastern Europe literature provides an important method for helping people understand better the historical realities in which they have lived ... To what extent and in what ways, in reality, has the consumption of literature in time and space yielded more enlightened, critical societies? ... Literature's civic magic, I argue, lies in layered sociocultural assumptions about criticism that have just as much to do with reading literature to cultivate taste and distinction as with doing so to cultivate dispositions for self-reflexive, independently minded, contextually grounded political analysis.[87]

As Larson concludes, "Literature represented an artifact of cultural and cultivated distinction as well as a civic imperative" in the post-socialist Slovak educational system, but the "objectification" of critical discourse "might serve to draw attention to certain domains of social activity as criticizable (such as the hypocrisy and vices of the powerful), while avoiding others (such as attitudes toward Roma or other ethnic minorities)."[88]

The present volume is intended to fill a crucial gap in comparative Slavic literary scholarship by bringing together the work of leading scholars in the field to examine the development of contemporary Slovak literature. In its focus on contemporary literature, this volume follows

Robert Pynsent's collection *Modern Slovak Prose*, which evaluated the socialist-era Slovak literary scene, but also complements Peter Petro's *History of Slovak Literature*, whose broader coverage essentially ends at the Velvet Revolution.

OVERVIEW OF THE VOLUME

The aim of our collection is to map the key milestones and themes in the development of Slovak literature. Most Slovak literature translated into English was originally published within the past century, so the primary historical focus of our book is the period from the 1989 to the present, even though some of the chapters also examine the nineteenth and early twentieth-century roots of the more recent literary developments. Since it is not possible to contain a comprehensive survey of Slovak literature in the scope of this volume, the chapters cover pivotal historical moments and literary themes. Each chapter combines foundational historical cultural contexts with closer analysis of representative texts. Whenever possible, the chapter authors highlight texts that have been translated into English, and our appendix includes a selective list of translated works that can serve as a starting point for a reading list of Slovak literature in English translation. The rationale for our focus on Slovak texts available in English translation, in particular, is that it is through those translations that Slovak literature enters global circulation, which is a relatively recent phenomenon. The other reason stems from the inevitable limitations of the expertise and background of the co-editors and contributors. Another book could be written, for example, on Slovak literature in German translation or in translations into Slavic languages.

We have also strategically limited the genres that we cover to focus on ones that are more widely accessible in English translation, particularly prose fiction and poetry, which means that genres such as drama and, with a few exceptions, non-fictional prose are missing from our picture of the Slovak literary scene. We believe that such a selective approach makes the book more relevant to scholars of other "small" literatures looking for ways to introduce those literatures to a broader audience. In other words, the book is structured as a selective rather than comprehensive introduction to contemporary Slovak literature, while also serving as a case study of how a "small" literature interacts with global trends. We hope that the individual chapters make Slovak literature in English translation accessible to readers who do not read Slovak and serve as a bridge between Anglo-American and Slovak criticism on Slovak literature.

We begin with two chapters that are historical in focus, covering two key twentieth-century milestones that continue to shape contemporary literature, the post-Stalin liberalization and the decade of transition that followed the Velvet Revolution of 1989. The rest of the chapters cover key themes and issues that are central to contemporary literature, while also tracing their genealogies in the past: the tension between subjectivity and history in fiction, poets' choice between social engagement and formal experimentation, the contrasting orientations on domestic settings in regional writing and foreign settings in emigrant and expat literature, and, last but not least, on the increasingly prominent role of Slovak women's writing. The concluding section of the book shines a light on the practice of translation in a case study of a specific translation and an interview with a translator.

Chapter 1, "Slovak Literature and the Post-Stalin Liberalization" by Rajendra Chitnis, covers the period from 1956 to 1970, offering useful background on the handful of Slovak works from that era that have appeared in English translation (mainly by Ladislav Mňačko and Dominik Tatarka) as well as on writers like Jaroslava Blažková and Ján Johanides who first emerged at that time and had an important influence on post-1989 writing, but have not been adequately translated to date. Chitnis's chapter also offers the important reminder that the Slovaks were often stylistically and thematically ahead of their better-known Czech counterparts and were never as deeply divided by censorship: "By 1970, so many major Czech names from the 1960s had been excluded from sanctioned publication that dissident critics could legitimately ask whether sanctioned or unsanctioned literature represented the 'real' Czech literature of the period. This question could never seriously be asked of Slovak literature."

Peter Darovec's "Literature of the Transition" (chapter 2) examines two lines of transition from state socialism into the post-socialist period: that of "continuous" transition represented by the reappearance of Pavel Vilikovský, one of the most original voices of the liberalizing 1960s, and that of "ruptured" transition represented by Peter Pišťanek. Despite their considerable differences, both authors, Darovec suggests, "address similar issues in a similar way, among which are the problem of national identity and especially the need to change the traditional myth-building approach to it." Written in the 1970s, Vilikovský's *Ever Green Is ...* was published only months before the revolution in 1989, while Pišťanek's *Rivers of Babylon* brought an entirely new vision into Slovak literature that foreshadowed the unrestrained corruption of the 1990s.

Ivana Taranenková's "Writing the Self from Autobiography to Autofiction" (chapter 3) focuses on the intersections of life writing and fiction in contemporary Slovak "autofiction." The chapter maps the historical transformations of Slovak autobiographical writing in the context of the imperative to privilege the collective over the individual. Taranenková draws attention to the shift that has taken place in Slovak literature in the new millennium: the "return" of the subject, the renewed focus on authenticity, and the foregrounding of problems associated with individual identity in conjunction with global cultural trends that involve post-postmodern developments. She points out the transformative potential of the concept of autofiction in the Slovak literature of the late twentieth and early twenty-first centuries. Drawing on historical context, Taranenková further traces the transition from autobiography to autofiction in the works of influential writers, including Dominik Tatarka, Ján Rozner, Martin M. Šimečka, Rudolf Sloboda, Veronika Šikulová, Balla, and others. The chapter shows how "after decades of the marginalization of the self and the privileging of objectivity, contemporary Slovak literature finds itself in a situation of hegemonic subjectivity, which filters the world through a strictly delimited self."

In chapter 4, "History and Memory: Rewriting the Past," Zora Prušková examines Slovak historical fiction since 2000 that focuses mainly on events and traumas of the twentieth century. She calls attention to memory as a construct and explores alternatives to official histories that had been suppressed in Slovak literature as well as alternative ways of translating memory into narrative. Prušková points out that Slovak historical fiction in the new millennium "does not aim at an explanation but rather at an understanding, approximation, and preservation of the historical event in a state of balanced entropy." In recent examples of the genre, the essence of the historical era or event is not depicted in broad epic chronotopes but in the intimate spaces of individual and communal lives as exemplified by three types of postmillennial historical narratives in her chapter. She outlines these three types of postmillennial historical narratives that share the common interest in archival materials and filter the past through individual or family memory – *The House of the Deaf Man* by Peter Krištúfek, the novella *Konvália* by Denisa Fulmeková, and the memoir by Alta Vášová *Ostrovy nepamäti* (The islands of unforgetting). These authors avoid the ideological constraints of earlier historical novels, choosing rather to "self-consciously explore history as a continually shifting process, the tenuous nature of memory, and the complicated connections and discrepancies between words and images."

The two chapters focused on poetry examine two progressive trends in contemporary Slovak poetry. These complementary trends represent the different responses of new generations of Slovak poets to the liberalization of the cultural sphere after 1989: increased social engagement and more radical experimentation. The first response, which Viliam Nádaskay maps in chapter 5, "Poetry and Social Engagement," reconceptualizes the relationship between poetry and social engagement in a post-socialist society. In contrast with the apparent social engagement that was mandated by the state as a reflection of party allegiance during the socialist era, contemporary poets tend to focus on themes and causes at the intersection of individual and collective identities, "demonstrating that poetry can serve a social function without resorting to being one-dimensional, unnecessarily straightforward, or mediocre." Nádaskay traces the evolution of the concept of social engagement and its perception from socialist through post-socialist to the current situation. During the 1990s, poetry lost its traditional role as the moral authority for Slovak society. Nádaskay points out that the situation has changed in contemporary poetry of the new millennium, and poetry of engagement has become a rising phenomenon in Slovakia, diverging into various forms and modes. Through his analysis of such poets as Michal Habaj, Katarína Kucbelová, and Mária Ferenčuhová, Nádaskay suggests that they can reclaim the social function of the genre through an assertion of their individual and artistic identity. He stresses that even though "writers of today refuse to perform the role of officially designated consciousness, to be *committed*, they seem to no longer mind to *engage*, to include moral and ethical messages that are necessary for poetry to be actually *engaging* as well."

Ivana Hostová's "Subversion and Experimentation in Contemporary Slovak Poetry" (chapter 6) reflects on the most innovative trends in the development of Slovak poetry after 1989. Her chapter focuses on another type of poets' reaction to the state-mandated literature of the past, an experimental line of writing that characterised Slovak poetry in the late 1990s and the opening decades of the twenty-first century. Hostová suggests that poets emerging in the 1990s, including Peter Macsovszky, Peter Šulej, and others "embraced a poetically subversive gesture leaning towards various forms of non-traditional and innovative writing procedures where shock and radical break with conventional literariness was a key element." Whereas during the decade following the revolution experimental and formally innovative poetry was initially perceived as subversive departure from state-sponsored literature and was subsequently coopted by the Mečiar regime, experimental approaches became more mainstream with Slovakia's return to Western-oriented political development in the new millennium. The new generation of poets adopts a wide range of "experimental approaches that often verge on poetic research and frequently transgress the boundaries of media, arts, and literary and academic writing." In the context of Slovakia's membership in the European Union and NATO and the corresponding outward orientation of Slovak culture, a new generation of poets including Nóra Ružičková, Marianna Mlynárčiková, and Zuzana Husárová have followed globalizing trends toward an increasingly conceptual poetic approach.

In chapter 7, "Regional Writing and Domestic Inspirations," Radoslav Passia examines an aspect of Slovakia that was historically repressed and remains somewhat overlooked even today: its inner diversity, both regional and ethnic. These aspects are visible in the so-called regional prose, which focuses mainly on social contexts, regional details, and linguistic and cultural specifics of a narrowly limited geographical space while also foregrounding space as a category. Through his exploration of the linguistically and culturally distinct areas of southern and eastern Slovakia, Passia sheds light on the contributions of Hungarian and Rusyn writers and the still-emerging literary tradition of the Roma. He points out that "each of these minorities enters the majority cultural space with a different cultural and historical background and distinct representations in contemporary Slovak literature, which feature their specific thematic and narrative elements."

Chapter 8, "Expatriate and Cosmopolitan Writing" by Tamara Janecová, analyzes another subset of Slovak writers whose work has partially eluded full integration into Slovak literary history: those who have moved abroad and, in some cases, even into foreign languages. She contrasts émigré writers who left after 1968, such as Jaroslava Blažková and Irena Brežná, with the younger generation of voluntary expatriates like Ivana Dobrakovová and Zuska Kepplová. Although the motivations for leaving home differ, moments of confrontation between home and abroad that question their identity come to the fore in the prose of both generations. The writing of these authors thematizes personal experiences of living abroad and presents intimate accounts of women disconnected from their domestic ties and relationships. They are thus linked by "the themes of identity and loneliness, gendered perspectives, and the personal focus of the narration."

Rafal Majerek's analysis in the chapter titled "Women's Writing and Social Change" (chapter 9) examines the concepts of gender and feminism as they relate to the contemporary Slovak context. Majerek shows how women's writing gradually overcomes silencing and marginalization of the past, gaining recognition for its quality and assuming its central place in contemporary Slovak literature. After a detailed overview of critical writing on women's issues, Majerek offers a comparison of two of the most distinct voices in current Slovak fiction, Jana Juráňová and Uršula Kovalyk, suggesting that their "perspectives increase the visibility of historical and contemporary aspects of women's experience, while also reflecting the heterogeneity of the contemporary forms of women's writing." As a significant part of the authorial gesture of these women writers, he highlights their social engagement.

The section entitled "Coda: Translators and Translations" opens with "Translating Politics and the Politics of Translation," in which Magdalena Mullek takes a personal approach, using her own choices as the translator of Pavol Rankov's novel *It Happened on the First of September (or Some Other Time)*, a popular novel that traces the story of Czechoslovakia through thirty years of political turmoil. Through a case study of her work on translating the novel, Mullek considers the contemporary politics of translation and its effect on publishing this and other Slovak works in English. She also analyzes the process of translation and the choices she made to communicate Slovak politics and history to readers outside the original cultural context.

The coda section also includes an interview with the translator Julia Sherwood in which she reflects on the rewards and challenges associated with publishing and promoting English translations of Slovak literature, as well as bibliographies of Slovak prose and poetry written since 1989 that have been translated into English.

We hope that this collection, bringing together leading researchers and exceptional emerging scholars, can take English-language criticism on Slovak literature a significant step forward and form a foundation and inspiration for future scholarship, much as *Modern Slovak Prose* did over thirty years ago. Although only one chapter is directly devoted to gender studies, the volume reflects the much larger place of Slovak women writers, both at home and in translation, compared to their role in 1990. Since far more of the authors discussed below are available in English than was the case with Pynsent's collection (and in recent years, they have begun to appear much sooner after their original Slovak publication than was previously the case), we also see this increased availability of translations as an invitation for specialists of world literature to integrate some of these writers into their teaching, as another step toward bringing Slovak literature out of its longstanding and undeserved isolation.

NOTES

1 For a concise overview of the history of English translations of Slovak literature and its most prominent translators, see Ľudmila Pánisová's introduction to a special journal issue on the topic, "The Shadow Heroes of Translation: On Translators of Slovak Literature into English," 1–18.

2 Walkowitz, *Born Translated*, 6.

3 See https://www.seagullbooks.org/books-by-series/the-slovak-list/.

4 Walkowitz, *Born Translated*, 4.

5 Magdalena Mullek, who translated the novel into English, discusses the process of translating *It Happened on the First of September* in this volume (see "Coda: Translators and Translations").

6 Casanova, *The World Republic of Letters*, 75, 105.

7 Ibid., 179.

8 For a study of the use of these complementary strategies on the part of the representatives of "small literaratures" in relation to nationalism, see Macura, *The Mystifications of a Nation*.

9 Chitnis, Stougaard-Nielsen, Atkin, and Milutinović, eds, *Translating the Literatures of Small European Nations*, 3.

10 Ibid.

11 Ibid.

12 Pynsent, *Modern Slovak Prose*, 37.

13 Pynsent, "What about the Slovaks[?]," 9.

14 Kundera, "The Tragedy of Central Europe," 35.

15 Milan Kundera describes this predicament as "a wager, a risk; [the small nations] are on the defensive against history, that force that is bigger than they, that does not take them into consideration, that does not even notice them" ("Die Weltliteratur," 284). The influential Slovak critic Peter Zajac also considers the sense of contingency and risk as one of the determining factors that shaped Slovak culture and literature from its beginnings in "Slovak Literature as Adventure."

16 Ibid., 59.

17 For an account of the complexity and the ideological work of the myths of Slovak history and their literary uses, see Škvarna, "Koncepty slovenských dejín a deformácie historickej pamäti," 191–216, and Rudinsky, *The Context of the Marxist-Leninist View of Slovak Literature 1945–1969*.

18 Avenarius, "Epilogue," 322.

19 Ibid.

20 For an account of the impact of the Turkish threat on the representation of the Turks on Slovak collective identity and literature, see Sabatos, *Frontier Orientalism and the Turkish Image in Central European Literature*.

21 Avenarius, 313.

22 Hroch, "Central Europe," 26.

23 Ibid., 28.

24 Ibid., 26.

25 Ibid., 29.

26 Kundera, "Die Weltliteratur," 284.

27 Kundera, "The Tragedy of Central Europe," 33.

28 Osers, "Is There a Central European Identity in Literature?," 48, 51.

29 Ibid., 53.

30 Chmel, "The Slovak Question in the 20th Century," 63.

31 Ibid., 63–4.

32 Our brief historical survey of the historical evolution of Slovak literature is indebted to the comprehensive volumes by Šmatlák et al., *Dejiny slovenskej literatúry* II and Marčok et al., *Dejiny slovenskej literatúry* III. Our objective is to provide a framework through which readers less familiar with Slovak literature can situate the historical moments covered in the individual chapters.

33 For an overview of Slovak Romanticism, see Petro, *A History of Slovak Literature*, 64–92.

34 For a more detailed account of Slovak Romanticism, see Zajac, Schmarcová et al., *Konfigurácie slovenského realizmu.*
35 Lipták, *Slovensko v dvadsiatom storočí*, 58.
36 Kosatík, *Slovenské století*, 38. On Hlinka, see Felak, *At the Price of the Republic.*
37 For a discussion of this problematic term, see Kosatík, *Slovenské století*, 37.
38 For a brief account of modern Slovak literature, see Petro, *A History of Slovak Literature*, 130–53.
39 Qtd in Šmatlák, *Dejiny*, 279. See Šmatlák, 275–83, for a discussion of the tensions between different conceptions of literary development,
40 Qtd in Šmatlák, *Dejiny*, 279.
41 For further information on the literature of Czechoslovakia in the interwar period, see Šámal, Pavlíček, Barborík, and Janáček, eds, *Literární kronika první republiky.*
42 Šmatlák, *Dejiny*, 294–5.
43 For an overview of Slovak realism, see Petro, *A History of Slovak Literature*, 93–129.
44 Charles Sabatos is currently preparing his English translation of *Atómy boha* (God's atoms) for publication.
45 Hronský, *Jozef Mak*, 9. (The protagonist's last name, "Mak," means "poppy-seed" in Slovak.)
46 On Tiso, see Ward, *Priest, Politician, Collaborator.*
47 Qtd Šmatlák, *Dejiny*, 434.
48 Lukáč, "Europa," 24.
49 Lipták, "Slovakia in the Twentieth Century," 259.
50 Ibid., 258.
51 Ibid., 260.
52 Ibid., 262.
53 For an account of the treatment of the Jewish and Romany citizens in the Slovak state, see Lipták, "Slovakia in the Twentieth Century," 264–6.
54 For criticism on Slovak literature and the Holocaust, see, for example Hučková, "Forgotten Prosaic Works," 153–66, and also Prušková, "I Didn't Want to Be a Jew," 221–4.
55 See Šmatlák, *Dejiny*, 441.
56 Rajendra Chitnis examines these texts more closely in chapter 1 of this volume.
57 Marčok, *Dejiny*, 38.

58 The innovative tendencies of this group influenced the further development of Slovak poetry after the Velvet Revolution of 1989. For a detailed account of the alternative movements in Slovak poetry of the 1960s, see Marčok, *Dejiny*, 98–117.

59 A useful overview of this period is Williams, *The Prague Spring and Its Aftermath.*

60 For an account of reform socialism and the push for the Czecho-Slovak federation in the 1960s, see Sikora, "Slovakia and the Attempt to Reform Socialism in Czechoslovakia, 1963–1969" and Žatkuliak, "Slovakia's Position within the Czecho-Slovak Federation, 1968–1970."

61 For more on Dominik Tatarka's dissident writing, see Sabatos, "Can the Dissident Speak?," 74–88. In chapter 3 of this volume, Ivana Taranenková discusses the publication history of Tatarka's texts.

62 See chapter 2 by Peter Darovec in the present volume.

63 Marčok, *Dejiny*, 43.

64 Western scholarship on the Velvet Revolution (known as the "Gentle Revolution" in Slovak) has focused predominantly on the Czech experience; for a Slovak-focused account see Krapfl's *Revolution with a Human Face.*

65 For more detailed accounts of the fall of the communist regime and the decade of the transition, see Lipták. "Slovakia in the Twentieth Century," 293–305 and Štefanský, "The Fall of Communist and the Establishment of an Independent Slovakia," 351–69.

66 Passia and Taranenková, *Hľadanie súčasnosti.* See also their contributions in chapters 3 and 7 of this volume.

67 In chapter 2, Peter Darovec analyzes the key fiction writers of this transitional period.

68 Passia and Taranenková, *Hľadanie súčasnosti*, 113. For a more detailed discussion of how the poetry of the 1990s paves the way for contemporary poetry, see Nádaskay's and Hostová's discussion of these complementary trends in chapter 5 and chapter 6.

69 Johanides, *But Crime Does Punish*, 60. In his afterword to the English translation, Robert Pynsent suggests that the scene was inspired by a specific mass murder of Carpathian Germans on Švédské šance, a hill in Moravia, but Johanides heightens the symbolic potential of the scene by locating it in Central Slovakia, the region associated with the Slovak National Uprising, and leaving the victims unspecified.

70 For an account of Slovak literary life in the new millennium, see Passia and Taranenková, *Hľadanie súčasnosti*, 21–35.
71 Ibid., 17.
72 For examples of Slovak literary scholarship in English, including an article on Slovak literary scholarship and Slovak literary historiography, see the special issue of *Slovenská literatúra* 61, no. 6 (2014), https://www.sav.sk/?lang=sk&doc=journal-list&part=list_articles&journal_issue_no=11113393.
73 Pynsent, *Modern Slovak Prose*, ix–xi.
74 Lunt and Milenkovic, *Slovakia*, 116.
75 Petro, *A History of Slovak Literature*, and Šimečka, *The Year of the Frog*.
76 Ibid., 156.
77 Chitnis, *Literature in Post-Communist Russia and Eastern Europe*, 15.
78 Roberts, "Overcoming Czech and Hungarian Perspectives in Writing Slovak Literary Histories," 377.
79 March, *Description of a Struggle*.
80 *Ever Green Is ... Selected Prose* also includes the short story "Everything I Know about Central Europeanism" (1996) as well as another novella published in 1989, *A Horse Upstairs, A Blind Man in Vráble*.
81 Evans, "Rebels against Reality."
82 Evans, "Continental Shelf."
83 Beasley-Murray, "Stoker Supreme," 22.
84 Mullek, "*Samko Tale's Cemetery Book* (review)."
85 "Slovak Literature in English Translation."
86 Maxwell, *Choosing Slovakia*, 122.
87 Larson, *Critical Thinking in Slovakia after Socialism*, 159.
88 Ibid., 177–8.

BIBLIOGRAPHY

Avenarius, Alexander. "Epilogue: The Basic Problems of Slovak History and Historiography." In *A Concise History of Slovakia*, edited by Elena Mannová, 307–14. Bratislava: SAV, 2000.

Beasley-Murray, Tim. "Contemporary Slovak Literature, the Devilish Pact with Theory, and the Genitalists." In *Slovakia after Communism and Mečiarism*, edited by Kieran Williams, 79–88. London: School of Slavonic and East European Studies, 2000.

– "Stoker Supreme." *Times Literary Supplement*, 29 February 2008, 22.

Casanova, Pascale. *The World Republic of Letters*. Translated by M.B. DeBevoise. Cambridge, MA: Harvard University Press, 2004.

Chitnis, Rajendra, Jakob Stougaard-Nielsen, Rhian Atkin, and Zoran Milutinović, eds. *Translating the Literatures of Small European Nations*. Liverpool: Liverpool University Press, 2020.

Chitnis, Rajendra. *Literature in Post-Communist Russia and Eastern Europe: The Russian, Czech and Slovak Fiction of the Changes 1988–98*. London: Routledge-Curzon, 2004.

Chmel, Rudolf. "The Slovak Question in the 20th Century." In *Scepticism and Hope: Sixteen Contemporary Slovak Essays*, edited by Miro Kollár, 59–96. Bratislava: Kalligram, 1999.

Cornis-Pope, Marcel. "East-Central European Literature after 1989." In *History of the Literary Cultures of East-Central Europe, Vol. 4, Types and Stereotypes*, edited by Marcel Cornis-Pope and John Neubauer, 561–630. Amsterdam: Benjamins, 2010.

Economist. "And the Winner Is," 16 August 1997, 42.

Evans, Julian. "Continental Shelf." *Guardian*, 1 May 2004. https://www.theguardian.com/books/2004/may/01/featuresreviews.guardianreview34.

– "Rebels against Reality." *Guardian*, 27 July 2002. https://www.theguardian.com/books/2002/jul/27/featuresreviews.guardianreview2.

Hroch, Miroslav. "Central Europe – The Rise and Fall of a Historical Region." In *Central Europe: Core or Periphery?*, edited by Christopher Lord, 21–34. Copenhagen: Copenhagen Business School Press, 2000.

Hron, Madelaine. "*Ever Green Is …* (review)." *Slavic and East European Journal* 47, no. 1 (2003): 132–3.

Hronský, Jozef Cíger. *Jozef Mak*. Translated by Andrew Cincura. Bloomington: Slavica Publishers, 1985.

Hučková, Dana. "Forgotten Prosaic Works: Forming a Literary Image of the Holocaust in Slovak Literature of the 1940s and 1950s." *Poznańskie studia slawistyczne*, no. 12 (2017): 153–66. https://doi.org/10.14746/pss.2017.12.10.

Johanides, Ján. *But Crime Does Punish*. Translated by Julia Sherwood and Peter Sherwood. Prague: Karolinum Press, 2022.

Kapitáňová, Daniela. *Samko Tale's Cemetery Book*. Translated by Julia Sherwood and Peter Sherwood. London: Garnett Press, 2011.

Kollár, Miro, ed. *Scepticism and Hope: Sixteen Contemporary Slovak Essays*. Bratislava: Kalligram, 1999.

Kosatík, Pavel. *Slovenské století*. Prague: Torst, 2021.

Kundera, Milan. "Die Weltliteratur." In *World Literature: A Reader*, edited by Theo D'Haen, César Domínguez, and Mads Rosendahl Thomsen, 283–94. London and New York: Routledge, 2012.

– "The Tragedy of Central Europe. *New York Review of Books* 31, no. 7 (1984): 33–8.

Krapfl, James. *Revolution with a Human Face: Politics, Culture, and Community in Czechoslovakia, 1989–1992*. Ithaca: Cornell University Press, 2013.

Larson, Jonathan. *Critical Thinking in Slovakia after Socialism*. Rochester: University of Rochester Press, 2013.

Lipták, Ľubomír. *Slovensko v dvadsiatom storočí*. Bratislava, Kalligram, 2011.

– "Slovakia in the 20th Century." In *A Concise History of Slovakia*, edited by Elena Mannová, 241–306. Bratislava: SAV, 2000.

Lukáč, Emil Boleslav. "Europa." In *Moloch*, 25–6. Bratislava: L. Mazáč, 1938.

Lunt, Susie, and Zora Milenkovic. *Slovakia*. Oxford: Clio, 2000.

Mackie, John. "The Pop Star Prof: UBC Retiree Was the Ringo Starr of Czechoslovakia." *Vancouver Sun*, 10 January 2019. Accessed 15 July 2022. https://vancouversun.com/news/local-news/the-pop-star-prof-ubc-retiree-was-the-ringo-starr-of-czechoslovakia.

Macura, Vladimír. *The Mystification of a Nation: "The Potato Bug" and Other Essays on Czech Culture*. Translated by Hana Píchová and Craig Cravens. Madison: University of Wisconsin Press, 2010.

Marčok, Viliam et al. *Dejiny slovenskej literatúry III: Cesty slovenskej literatúry druhou polovicou XX. storočia*. Bratislava: Literárne informačné centrum, 2006.

Maxwell, Alexander. *Choosing Slovakia: Slavic Hungary, the Czechoslovak Language and Accidental Nationalism*. London: I.B. Tauris, 2009.

Mňačko, Ladislav. *Death Is Called Engelchen*. Translated by George Theiner. Prague: Artia Pocket Books, 1961.

Mullek, Magdalena. "*Samko Tale's Cemetery Book* (review)." *Asymptote*, April 2012. https://www.asymptotejournal.com/criticism/daniela-kapitanovas-samko-tales-cemetery-book/.

Pánisová, Ľudmila. "Introduction: The Shadow Heroes of Translation: On Translators of Slovak Literature into English." *Bridge* 2, no. 1 (2021): 1–18.

Partridge, James. "Slovak: Literary Translation into English." In *Encyclopedia of Literary Translation into English*, vol. 2, edited by Olive Classe, 1292–5. Chicago: Fitzroy Dearborn Publishers, 2000.

Passia, Radoslav and Taranenková Ivana, eds. *Hľadanie súčasnosti: Slovenská literatúrazačiatku 21. storočia*. Bratislava: Literárne informačné centrum, 2014.

Petro, Peter. *A History of Slovak Literature*. Montreal: McGill-Queen's University Press, 1995.

Pišťanek, Peter. *Rivers of Babylon*. Translated by Peter Petro. London: Garnett Press, 2007.

Prušková, Zora. "I Didn't Want to Be a Jew (Nechcel som byť žid)." In *Handbook of Polish, Czech, and Slovak Holocaust Fiction: Work and Contexts*, edited by Elisa-Maria Hiemer, Jiří Holý, Agata Firlej, and Hana Nichtburgerová, 221–4. Oldenburg: De Gruyter, 2021.

Pynsent, Robert. "Appendix: The Uncensored Text of Robert Pynsent's Introduction to *Scepticism and Hope*." In *Slovakia after Communism and Mečiarism*, edited by Kieran Williams, 115–25. London: School of Slavonic and East European Studies, 2000.

– *Modern Slovak Prose: Fiction since 1954*. Basingstoke: Palgrave MacMillan, 1990.

– *Questions of Identity: Czech and Slovak Ideas of Nationality*. Budapest: Central European University Press, 1994.

– ed. *Reader's Encyclopedia of East European Literature*. New York: Harper Collins, 1993.

– "Video-Nasties: The Last Decade of the Slovak Twentieth Century through the Eyes of Peter Pišťanek." In *Slovakia after Communism and Mečiarism*, edited by Kieran Williams, 89–109. London: School of Slavonic and East European Studies, 2000.

– "What about the Slovaks [?]" In *Scepticism and Hope: Sixteen Contemporary Slovak Essays*, edited by Miro Kollár, 9–26. Bratislava: Kalligram, 1999.

Roberts, Dagmar. "Overcoming Czech and Hungarian Perspectives in Writing Slovak Literary Histories." In *History of the Literary Cultures of East-Central Europe*, vol. 3, *The Making and Remaking of Literary Institutions*, edited by Marcel Cornis-Pope and John Neubauer, 377–84. Amsterdam: Benjamins, 2007.

Rudinsky, Norma. *The Context of the Marxist-Leninist View of Slovak Literature 1945–1969*. Pittsburgh: Carl Beck Papers in Russian and East European Studies, 1986.

Sabatos, Charles D. *Frontier Orientalism and the Turkish Image in Central European Literature*. Lanham, MD: Lexington Books, 2020.

Sikora, Stanislav. "Slovakia and the Attempt to Reform Socialism in Czechoslovakia, 1963–1969." In *Slovakia in History*, edited by Mikuláš Teich, Dušan Kováč, and Martin D. Brown, 299–314. Cambridge: Cambridge University Press, 2011.

"Slovak Literature in English Translation," http://slovakliterature.com/index.html.

Slovenská literatúra (special journal issue in English) 61, no. 6 (2014). https://www.sav.sk/?lang=sk&doc=journal-list&part=list_articles&journal_issue_no=11113393/.

Šámal, Petr, Tomáš Pavlíček, Vladimír Barborík, and Vladimír Janáček, eds. *Literární kronika první republiky: události, díla, souvislosti*. Prague: Academia, Památník národního písemnictví, Ústav pro českou literaturu AV ČR, 2018.

Šimečka, Martin. *The Year of the Frog*. Translated by Peter Petro. Baton Rouge: Louisiana State University Press, 1993.

Škvarna, Dušan. "Koncepty slovenských dejín a deformácie historickej pamäti." In *Kontakty literatúry: modely, identity, reprezentácie*, edited by Magdalena Bystrzak, Radoslav Passia, and Ivana Taranenková, 191–216. Bratislava: Veda, 2020.

Šmatlák, Stanislav. *Dejiny slovenskej literatúry II (19. storočie a prvá polovica 20. storočia)*. Bratislava: Literárne informačné centrum, 2007.

Štefanský, Michal. "The Fall of Communist and the Establishment of an Independent Slovakia," In *Slovakia in History*, edited by Mikuláš Teich, Dušan Kováč, and Martin D. Brown, 351–69. Cambridge: Cambridge University Press, 2011.

Timrava [Božena Slančíková]. *That Alluring Land: Slovak Stories*. Translated by Norma Rudinsky. Pittsburgh: University of Pittsburgh Press, 1992.

Vilikovský, Pavel. *Ever Green Is …* Translated by Charles Sabatos. Evanston: Northwestern University Press, 2002.

Walkowitz, Rebecca L. *Born Translated: The Contemporary Novel in an Age of World Literature*. New York: Columbia University Press, 2015.

Ward, James Mace. *Priest, Politician, Collaborator: Jozef Tiso and the Making of Fascist Slovakia*. Ithaca: Cornell University Press, 2013.

Williams, Kieran, ed. *Slovakia after Communism and Mečiarism*. London: School of Slavonic and East European Studies, 2000.

Zajac, Peter, Ľubica Schmarcová. *Konfigurácie slovenského romantizmu: synopticko-pulzačný model kultúrneho javu*. Brno: Host, 2016.

– "Slovak Literature as an Adventure." In *One Hundred Years of Slovak Literature: An Anthology*, edited by Stanislava Chrobáková. 14–23. Bratislava: LIC, 2000.

Žatkuliak, Jozef. "Slovakia's Position within the Czecho-Slovak Federation, 1968–1970." In *Slovakia in History*, edited by Mikuláš Teich, Dušan Kováč, and Martin D. Brown, 315–29. Cambridge: Cambridge University Press, 2011.

CHAPTER ONE

Slovak Literature and the Post-Stalin Liberalization, 1956–70

Rajendra A. Chitnis

Between Stalin's death in 1953 and the retrenchment that followed the Moscow-led military intervention in Czechoslovakia in August 1968, the cultures and societies of Communist Central and Eastern Europe experienced a period of liberalization known in the Soviet case as the Thaw. A comparative study would show, however, that the timing, length, and extent of this liberalization varied not only between but also within different countries, as the Slovaks and Czechs exemplify. Some Soviet cultural historians even argue that signs of liberalization in the Soviet Union pre-date Stalin's death, while the degree to which culture and society "refroze" afterwards also varies between and within countries. Despite interruptions, instances of censorship, and an enduringly antagonistic atmosphere, Slovak literature enjoyed one of the longest and most sustained periods of liberalization in the bloc, from at least 1956 to 1970, more comparable to Polish and Hungarian than Czech. We might attribute this longevity to a new national self-confidence deriving from Slovak resistance at the end of the Second World War, unmatched in the Czech context, a sense that the Communist takeover had been substantially enacted and imposed on Slovaks from Prague, where support for the ideology was stronger, and, at least in urban cultural centres like Bratislava, a greater, earlier openness to liberalizing currents emanating from the USSR, Poland, and Hungary. As a result, several generations of writers were able to emerge and develop, transforming the idea of Slovak literature and sowing the seeds that would flourish after the fall of Communism in 1989. To date, however, none of these writers, from what

Peter Darovec and Vladimír Barborík call "one of the strongest generations ever to emerge in Slovakia," has achieved an international reputation comparable to their Czech counterparts.[1] This chapter examines the reasons why and highlights some examples of what international readers have been missing.

For liberal commentators at least, the post-Stalin liberalization and the post-communist period discussed in later chapters are linked culturally as times when the inward-looking, didactic, collectivizing, mythopoetic nationalist tradition embraced by the independent Slovak fascist puppet state during the Second World War, easily adapted to the Stalinist model after 1948 and reasserted by the post-independence populist-nationalist government in 1993, was vigorously countered by a more open, varied, anti-schematic, experimental approach that synchronized Slovak literature with contemporaneous Western thought and aesthetics.[2] Darovec and Barborík, in their 1996 homage to the periodical *Mladá tvorba*, the hub of new writing and literary debate in the period, wrote: "From 1956 to 1970, *Mladá tvorba* organically created the space for a form of culture, many dimensions of which were only able to manifest themselves fully twenty years after its demise."[3] In Slovak literature, as elsewhere, the post-Stalin liberalization began with calls for the abandonment of the Soviet cultural model of socialist realism, imposed in Czechoslovakia in 1949, the release of literature and writers from uncritical service to the communist party and its ideology, and for a much broader understanding of what constituted socialist literature, with an emphasis on individual artistry rather than political conformism. The eventual effect, however, was a powerful renewal of creative practice, marked by a westward turn. Writers reconnected with earlier modernist trends in Slovak literature, notably Symbolism and Surrealism, and with fashionable American influences like Hemingway and the Beat Generation or European existentialism, Theatre of the Absurd, new-wave cinema, the *nouveau roman*, or nascent post-structuralism.

More Czech writers from the post-Stalin liberalization became Western intellectual household names than at any other time in Czech literary history, including Václav Havel (1936–2011), Bohumil Hrabal (1914–1997), Milan Kundera (1929–2003), or Josef Škvorecký (1924–2012). By contrast, to date only one Slovak novel from the period has been commercially published in English translation, *The Taste of Power* (*Ako chutí moc*, trans. 1967, Slovak 1968) by Ladislav Mňačko (1919–1994).[4] Two

English-language anthologies of Czech and Slovak literature published commercially in the late 1960s, at the height of international interest in Czechoslovakia, reflect this imbalance. Oxford University Press's *Czech and Slovak Stories* (1967), edited and translated by Jeanne Němcová (dates unknown), comprises works by sixteen Czech writers and two contemporary Slovaks, Jaroslava Blažková (1933–2017) and Anton Hykisch (b. 1932), while Penguin's *New Writing from Czechoslovakia* (1969), edited and translated by George (Jiří) Theiner (1926–88), includes just three Slovaks – Blažková, Ján Johanides (1934–2008), and Miroslav Válek (1927–1991) – alongside twenty-three Czechs. A truer reflection of the quality and importance of the Slovak writing of this period is not found until the publication in 2015 of *The Dedalus Book of Slovak Literature*, an anthology of thirteen texts dating from 1888 to the early 2010s, with no fewer than five drawn from the 1960s.

We can most easily attribute the previous neglect of Slovak literature to its lack of a distinct international reputation. In the popular imagination, "Czechoslovak" literature was satisfactorily represented by Czech literature and Slovak had limited ability to promote itself at this time without relying on Prague and Czech-speaking gatekeepers, to whom it was also relatively unknown. Some deeper reasons are explored in the following pages. First, Slovak literature liberalized earlier and more radically than its Czech counterpart, in the mid-1950s, but unfortunately when world attention was focused on events in the USSR, Poland, and Hungary, not an unfamiliar part of still hard-line Czechoslovakia. Secondly, Western gatekeepers, while paying lip service to a work's literary qualities, prioritized literature that criticized life in communist society.[5] By the mid-1960s, when interest turned towards Czechoslovakia, this approach favoured certain Czech writers, who had found their political voice as proponents of reform-communism, over Slovak (and indeed other Czech) writers who sought to engage more with the preoccupations of world literature. Thirdly, between 1970 and 1989, far more Czech than Slovak writers, many of them already internationally established names, found themselves excluded from sanctioned publication and, again for Cold War political reasons, they formed the focus of publishers' efforts. Finally, the themes of Slovak Thaw literature, particularly the focus on the Slovak experience in the Second World War, perhaps did not appeal as much as the Czech focus on the post-war experience of Stalinism.

Theiner justifies the imbalance between Czech and Slovak in his anthology by claiming: "had this anthology been compiled in something like 1960 instead of 1967, the Slovaks would undoubtedly have outnumbered the Czechs. Since the early sixties, however, it is the Czechs who have come into prominence, with the Slovaks quite noticeably lagging behind."[6] In reality, though, it was the Czechs who were catching up. Inspired by developments in Hungary and Poland, the post-Stalin liberalization began earlier in Slovakia and, despite frequent pressure from hostile Party ideologues, including what Pynsent terms a "brief re-Freeze" between 1959 and 1963,[7] it was more sustained than in Czech literature. For Slovak literary historians, the decisive year is 1956, which saw the publication of works including *Až dozrieme* (When we are ripe), a self-consciously sombre and introverted cycle by the Slovak poet Milan Rúfus (1928–2009), *Hodiny a minúty* (Hours and minutes) by Alfonz Bednár (1914–1989), a cycle of short novels juxtaposing the end of the Second World War and the early communist period, and the overt political satire, "The Demon of Conformism" (or perhaps "consent") (*Démon súhlasu*, abridged trans. 1987) by Dominik Tatarka (1913–1989), both discussed below. *Mladá tvorba* was launched in September of that year. It featured poets like Rúfus, Válek, Lýdia Vadkerti-Gavorníková (1932–1999), Ján Ondruš (1931–2000), and others associated with the so-called Concretists or Trnava Group, and prose writers including (in order of appearance) Blažková, Johanides, Rudolf Sloboda (1938–1995), Vincent Šikula (1936–2001), Pavel Vilikovský (1941–2020), Pavel Hrúz (1941–2008), Dušan Mitana (1946–2019), Dušan Dušek (b. 1946), and Alta Vášová (b. 1939). By contrast, its notional Czech equivalent, *Květen*, an outlet for new poetry first published in September 1955, was closed in 1959 after ideological criticism.[8] In 1958, Škvorecký's *The Cowards* (*Zbabělci*, 1958, trans. 1970), a novel describing the final days of the German occupation in a provincial Czech town from the scornful perspective of an adolescent boy, was withdrawn and not republished until 1964.[9] It was not until 1963 that Czechs saw the first performance of Havel's *The Garden Party* (*Zahradní slavnost*, trans. 1969) and the publication of works including Hrabal's *Perlička na dně* (The little pearl on the sea-bed, stories from which first appeared in English translation in *The Death of Mr Baltisberger* [1975]), the first volume of Kundera's *Laughable Loves* (*Směšné lásky*, trans. 1974), and *Mr Theodore Mundstock* (*Pan Theodor Mundstock*, trans. 1968) by Ladislav Fuks (1923–1994).

When international interest did turn to Czechoslovakia, in the early 1960s, it centred on Prague. In a pioneering BBC radio programme made in 1962 about the pressures facing writers in contemporary Czechoslovakia, the English poet A. (Alfred) Alvarez (1929–2019) contrasts his experience there with Poland, noting: "Czechoslovakia is one of the most rigidly orthodox of all the Eastern European countries. The ruling elite may decry the cult of personality, but it remains as near Stalinist as makes no difference. Prague is thick with red stars, red flags, Russian propaganda. And many of the writers I met there were orthodox communists."[10] He remarks of the cautious Czech approach to liberalizing the arts: "For every two steps forward there must be at least one official step back."[11] Conversely, in the printed version of the broadcast, published in 1965, he acknowledges how much Czechoslovakia has changed in the intervening time. All these assessments, however, reflect that Alvarez only speaks to Prague-based Czech intellectuals to form an understanding of situation in the whole country, whereas had he gone to Bratislava in 1962, he might have found at least pockets more comparable to Poland and Hungary.

Western intellectuals and publishers enlisted translated literature from the communist bloc in the Cold War against communism. Recalling visits to Prague in 1964 and 1965 by the leading English theatre critic, Kenneth Tynan (1927–1980), and a director of the Royal Shakespeare Company, John Roberts, Michelle Woods notes: "Western interest in Czechoslovak literature and film of the 1960s was predicated on the narrative of resistance to neo-Stalinism, to the prospect of a cultural thaw motoring a political thaw behind the Iron Curtain, and ultimately, to the validation of Western democracy. In this schema, John Roberts, sitting in the Divadlo na zábradli [The Theatre on the Balustrade, where Havel's 1960s plays were performed], needs no Czech to understand the relevance of the laughter around him; it signals to him that it will be relevant to a Western audience because it signals dissent."[12] By the late 1960s, Czech writers like Havel, Klíma, Kundera, Škvorecký, Pavel Kohout (b. 1928), and Ludvík Vaculík (1926–2015), all of whom were translated with varying success into English and other major Western languages in the late 1960s and 1970s, fitted this schema far better than their Slovak counterparts, with the exceptions of Mňačko and Tatarka. The narrative of "writers against rulers"[13] masked for Western readers the fact that, apart from Havel, all these writers were Party members who had supported the communist takeover in February 1948, several had held in some cases very senior positions in the party during the Stalinist period and, especially in the cases of Kohout, Kundera, Mňačko, and Tatarka, had conducted a very public literary journey from Stalinist fervour to critical opposition. Western commentators focused instead on the stand these writers took against censorship and Soviet authoritarianism, the role they played in foreshadowing and shaping "Socialism with a human face," the reform-communist programme launched in the "Prague spring" of 1968, and the price that they later paid for it, following the Soviet-led military intervention in Czechoslovakia in August 1968 and the replacement of the reform-communist leadership in April 1969. Western publishers and critics were able to present and interpret their texts in the narrow context of communist repression, an approach that, though often reductive, was also exploited by writers like Havel, Klíma, Kundera, and Škvorecký to increase the appeal of their work.[14]

This picture excludes the most significant Slovak interventions in cultural politics, which came much earlier and often behind the scenes of state-wide gatherings, and were not always incorporated into official records.[15] René Bílik detects glimmers of liberalization in Slovak literature as early as 1953, in a debate in successive issues of the Writers' Union weekly, *Kultúrny život*, about the Socialist Realist novel *Pokolenie v útoku* (A generation on the attack, 1952) by Peter Karvaš (1920–1999). For Bílik, by openly weighing the ideological merits of the novel against its aesthetic shortcomings, the exchanges "indicated signs of a shift in values inside the awakening literary organism."[16] In 1955, alongside articles "focusing on intellectual life in Poland, Hungary, and Yugoslavia i.e. in the Soviet bloc countries in which people enjoyed a larger degree of freedom of speech,"[17] *Kultúrny život* published an outspoken attack by Tatarka on the sacred cow of Slovak socialist realism, *Drevená dedina* (The wooden village, 1951) by František Hečko (1905–1960).[18]

By common assessment, at this time Slovak liberalizers differed from their Czech counterparts not so much in their aspirations as in their apparent resilience in the face of the hostility of the Party establishment. The most significant challenge yet mounted by Czech and Slovak writers to the Stalinist status quo came at the Second Congress of the Writers' Union in April 1956, where, as Marci Shore describes, Mňačko and Tatarka were among those to perform "rituals" of self-criticism for their earlier support for Stalinism.[19] Juraj Marušiak concludes, however, of the aftermath: "Whereas in the Bohemian lands the Czechoslovak Party leadership successfully managed to compel or persuade writers to capitulate, i.e., to distance themselves from the Second Congress, in Slovakia they did not enjoy the same success. Although the Slovak writers were not more radical in their requirements than their Czech colleagues, they resisted more efficaciously."[20] Alfred French makes a similar distinction regarding the party's preparations for the Third Congress in 1963, of which he remarks: "the crackdown after 1956 was thought to have taught the Czech writers an adequate lesson, and the wild men among the Slovaks were not expected to export their rebellious attitudes to Prague."[21] He associates the relative assertiveness of Slovak writers with the revival of Slovak nationalism, arguing that the Slovak wing of the communist party, which was seeking a "better deal for Slovakia" and themselves, allied itself with reformers and treated the rehabilitation of Husák and Novomeský as a rehabilitation of the nationalism for which they had previously been convicted.[22]

Theiner's explanation for the bias towards Czech in his anthology reflects that after 1963, it was mostly Prague-based Czech writers who became more visibly politically engaged. The situation by this time in Slovak literature is encapsulated for Bílik in a remark at the 1963 congress by the writer and Party functionary, Vladimír Mináč (1922–1996): "There is not and cannot be unity of method in socialist literature either. This goes against the nature of art, which in every case is the fruit of individuality. That is why the only wise policy in this area ... is a policy of tolerance."[23] Bílik points out that Mináč is simply acknowledging the prevailing reality, which bears comparison with the more consensual strategy being adopted by the Hungarian Communist Party under János Kádár, in the wake of the Soviet invasion there in 1956. We might therefore ascribe the subsequent quieter development of Slovak literature compared to Czech in the 1960s either to an exchange of creative freedom for a tacit agreement to stay out of politics, or to what, from a Western perspective, would be regarded as a more normal literary situation, a healthy separation of art and politics, in which writers see their work as a fundamentally personal matter, not part of a campaign, though it may ultimately constitute a more complex processing of the experience of the period.[24]

Remnants of this context perhaps explain why Slovak literature experienced more continuity in literature in the 1970s and 1980s period than its Czech counterpart. Liberalization in both literatures gradually ended in the wake of the Soviet-led military intervention in Czechoslovakia in August 1968 and the replacement of the party's reform-communist leader, the Slovak Alexander Dubček, in April 1969 by Husák, who instituted the policy of normalization that gave its name to the last two decades of communist rule in Czechoslovakia. The Czech émigré literary historian Antonín Měšťan claims, however: "it is well known that the pressure of the so-called normalization after 1968 was significantly weaker in Slovakia ... and reprisals against writers and the whole intelligentsia did not attain the same intensity as in Bohemia and Moravia."[25] By 1970, so many major Czech names from the 1960s had been excluded from sanctioned publication that dissident critics could legitimately ask whether sanctioned or unsanctioned literature represented the "real" Czech literature of the period. This question could never seriously be asked of Slovak literature. Figures like Johanides and Šikula could not publish in the early 1970s, but they returned later in the decade with their masterpieces; meanwhile others, like Dušek, Mitana, Rúfus, and Vášová, preserved some memory of the aesthetics of the preceding period.[26] As a result, unlike in Czech literature, where post-1989 critics typically marginalized works sanctioned for publication during the normalization as artistically and morally compromised, Slovak writers from the 1960s liberalization remained central to literary life after 1989, some, like Johanides and Vilikovský, through new works, others, like Blažková and Sloboda, more as influences cited by new writers.

In the 1970s and 1980s, Western publishers were almost exclusively attracted to those Czech writers who had figured prominently in 1967–68 as advocates of reform-communism, were now only able to publish in samizdat or abroad, and typically either emigrated or joined the Czechoslovak dissident movement, in which Tatarka was one of the few Slovak participants. Theiner, as an émigré in England after 1968, became a major gatekeeper to literature from Czechoslovakia in the English-speaking world, especially as editor of *Index on Censorship*, a position that demanded a focus on persecuted writers. Měšťan notes, moreover, that Czechs were much more successful than Slovaks in establishing publishing operations abroad devoted to unsanctioned writing from Czechoslovakia, which became a key source of texts with potential for translation in the West, and these featured Slovak writers only minimally.[27] For example, of 227 publications listed on the website of '68 Publishers, founded in Toronto by Škvorecký and Zdena Salivarová

(b. 1933), only five are by Slovaks, including two by Tatarka.[28] Index, in Cologne, alongside Tatarka also published Mňačko, Ivan Kadlečík (1938–2014), Milan Šimečka (1930–1990), and his son, Martin Šimečka (b. 1957). The émigré writer Dušan Šimko (b. 1945) was the only Slovak to publish a work with Rozmluvy in London.

A perhaps final factor influencing the relative invisibility of Slovak literature in this period may be the crucial difference in its historical focus. During the post-Stalin liberalization, writers throughout the bloc, typically supporters of communism approaching middle-age, took the opportunity to confront their youthful ideals with the reality of the years since the Party takeover, in works often characterized as "literature of disillusion." In the mid-1950s, the focal point for Slovak writers remained the war, specifically the Slovak National Uprising of August 1944 and its aftermath, understood as a decisive episode in the shaping of Slovak national identity and the cradle of Slovak post-war idealism. In his classic study of Slovak history between 1900 and 1968, Ľubomír Lipták writes: "for the fate of our nation and country [the Uprising] is of primary significance, standing on the threshold of a new era ... the heroism of soldiers and partisans ... made it possible for a 'rebel regime,' a progressive Slovak government, to develop and take shape freely on the liberated territory and to a certain extent fix itself in the consciousness of the people."[29] The significance of the Uprising would, however, be lost on international readers, since "even broad-brush volumes covering hundreds of pages by English, German, French or American military historians mention the Slovak National Uprising at best in a few superficially and erroneously formulated lines; there are textbooks and syntheses about the war in which there is no mention of it."[30] By contrast, Czech writers, writing in the 1960s, when international attention had turned to Czechoslovakia, focused on Stalinism, often using stereotypical Cold War images like show-trials, purges, prison camps, censorship, secret police informers, collectivization, overweening bureaucracy, and the oppressive incursion of ideology into everyday life that appealed to Western publishers.

The first book-length work of Thaw literature from Czechoslovakia published in English was in fact a Slovak novel about the Uprising, Mňačko's *Death Is Called Engelchen* (*Smrť sa volá Engelchen*, 1959, trans. 1961), translated by Theiner, who was working at the time at its publisher, Artia, a state-run exporter of Czechoslovak culture with limited ability to reach wide audiences. The text, also translated into other European languages at the time, was undoubtedly chosen because of its domestic success, which led quickly to television and cinema adaptations, its fit with the Western canon of war fiction, the debt it owed to *A Farewell to Arms* – Western reviewers characterized Mňačko as a "Red Hemingway"[31] – and the high profile of its author, a prominent communist journalist who had repudiated his own Stalinist past and embraced destalinization in 1956.[32] Its publication and translation coincided with the brief Re-Freeze identified by Pynsent, which placed Bednár's *Hodiny a minúty* out of favour, and one can only speculate about how a translation of Bednár's far more distinctive and better written cycle, which powerfully portrays many of the aspects of Czechoslovak Stalinism listed above, might have affected international perceptions of Slovak literature.

Mňačko, the only Slovak writer with book-length translations in English in this period, himself readily acknowledged that his work was driven by campaigning tendentiousness that owed more to journalism than literary ambition. With *Death Is Called Engelchen*, he sought to bring to public awareness the German destruction and massacre of the village of Ploština, near his birthplace in eastern Moravia, on the Slovak border, in April 1945, which he witnessed as a partisan. He recalls telling a Czech editor that it was "not a novel in the true sense of the word, in the book I tried to capture events that I had experienced personally, it is therefore more a novel-chronicle of one partisan village in the Vizovice hills."[33] He wrote comparably of *The Taste of Power*, which came out in English and German translation in 1967, before it had appeared in full in Slovak: "I wanted to write a political pamphlet wrapped into novel form, because as literature of fact it would not have had a hope of publication ... I am not one of those writers who lays claim to eternity. My strength – if I may say so of myself – was the burning relevance of my chosen subject, above all from a social and moral perspective."[34]

In *Death Is Called Engelchen*, the events leading up to the destruction of Ploština are narrated by Volodia, Mňačko's fictionalized younger self, to a nurse while recovering in hospital. The novel still bears comparison with socialist realism, especially Czech accounts of the violent expulsion of Bohemian Germans from Czechoslovakia in the summer of 1945 like *Nástup* (Advance, 1951) by Václav Řezáč (1901–1956), the "Inferno" part of a planned trilogy, in which the work of anti-fascists is dark, dangerous, and remorseless, German brutality and cunning is limitless, and glory and triumph are virtually absent. *Death Is Called Engelchen* is, however, more decisively a story of failure, of errors made by Volodia's partisan band that led to Ploština's destruction but make Volodia the man he is. In *The Taste of Power*, set in the 1960s, the Uprising explicitly symbolizes ideals betrayed in the subsequent decades. These ideals centre on a model of masculinity epitomized by Volodia, active, courageous, unflinching, ascetic, comradely, honourable, passionate but chivalrous towards women, which has been lost in peacetime by the Party man in *The Taste of Power*, who has instead become soft, embourgeoisé, vain, paranoid, manipulative, and crass.

The privileging of political relevance over artistry also applies to the text from 1956 most vaunted by Slovak critics, Tatarka's *Démon Súhlasu* ("The Demon of Conformism"), described by Peter Petro as "one of the most outspoken literary works published in Eastern Europe at the time," but only available in English in Petro's heavily abridged journal translation.[35] As Marcela Antošová and Veronika Cillingerová discuss, commentators typically consider "The Demon of Conformism" a satirical pamphlet, at the "interface" between literature and journalism.[36] The grotesque parable again features an authorial alter-ego narrator, who, in a private conversation with a senior figure in the Writers' Union, declares that the system has corrupted writers, rendering them mere puppets. The senior figure agrees, but then in public he mocks this view and humiliates the narrator, who thus discovers the difference between agreement in private and in public, an early literary articulation of the notion of the "split personality" in authoritarian society popularized by dissidents during the normalization. In a reiteration of Hans Christian Andersen's "The Emperor's New Clothes," the narrator belatedly realizes that he and his contemporaries have been possessed by the "demon of consent," the security of unanimous agreement, which he now regards as "resignation," "the honest citizen's expression of helplessness or the clever man's hypocrisy,"[37] and, in keeping with Soviet writers at the same time, he calls for renewed "sincerity in literature."[38]

Texts like "The Demon of Conformism" and *The Taste of Power*, despite their acknowledgment of personal error, lack humility and repentance and retain the hierarchical, didactic understanding of the writer that the outstanding Slovak literature of the Thaw rejects in favour of ambiguity, uncertainty, complexity of theme and structure, and a collaborative relationship between writer and reader. Tatarka suggests that during the Stalinist period, when writers were most lauded as leaders, oracles, and teachers of their nation, they had in practice ceased to be so, but by recovering their ability to speak in their own voices, they can authentically resume this role. Mňačko's alter-ego in *The Taste of Power* is a disillusioned photographer who has witnessed his friend's rise from partisan to party boss, has seen both sides of power, but only reported on one side until now. He is no more than an observer, a recorder, with limited responsibility for what has happened. Tatarka suggests that all writers like him fell under a spell from which they have awoken. The "demon of consent" and the "taste of power" serve as substitutes for any penetrating insight into how idealism becomes corrupted.

This narrative of a corrupted idealism that might be purified again is replaced in Bednár's *Hodiny a minúty* (Hours and minutes), the outstanding work of fiction about the Uprising and arguably of the Slovak Thaw, by a rejection of utopian ideology, which is typically placed in the mouths of German officers and refers to Nazism, but for the implied reader manifestly applies to Stalinism too.[39] The cycle is one of the earliest sanctioned works in the bloc to assert their ideological and practical equivalence. Instead of a mythicized history marked by ruptures, revolutions, and new beginnings, Bednár shows the troublesome continuity of history experienced by individual human beings, who bring their imperfection and the past with them. He portrays the aftermath of the Uprising as a time of chaos and terrible brutality, in which people's actions are typically motivated by fear and self-preservation rather than principle, and military and moral leaders, whether commanders of partisans, German officers or priests, repeatedly express their impotence and uncertainty about the right course to take. While continuing more radically the deconstruction of the communist-nationalist myth of the Uprising found tentatively in his first novel, *Sklený vrch* (The glass peak, 1954), he also lays the foundation for the more universal examination of the contemporary human condition undertaken by writers like Johanides, Šikula, and Vilikovský. The narration, moving backwards and forwards in time as it reveals the details of different characters' lives, their interconnectedness, and their inner worlds, asserts that everything is complicated. Few characters are unambiguously heroic: broadly positive characters, including Slovak peasants and partisans, have flaws, notably antisemitism, while typically negative characters, including some Germans and the priest, are portrayed with relative authorial sympathy.

Bednár's desire to re-examine the memory of recent years is captured at the beginning of the title story, when a character on a plane in 1952 looks down at the land below and sees "the recent past, into which people no longer like to look and which they no longer understand well either."[40] In each story, he juxtaposes the aftermath of the Uprising with the early communist period, not to contrast wartime Nazism and post-war Stalinism, but to reveal the overlaps between them. Unlike the preaching of Mňačko and Tatarka, Bednár trusts the reader to make the right inferences, for example, when a German officer, condemning Nazism, promises himself to "never, ever again believe in an idea, because when a human being believes in an idea, even murdering turns into a monotonous chore that constantly has to be made more interesting," or when a Slovak peasant, looking forward to the liberation, claims: "No one will track what people are saying and thinking any more."[41] The implied reader cannot but read the way one character describes fascism, at the very centre of the cycle, as simultaneously a description of Stalinism:

> Terrified hearts, bowed heads, bent spines, false words or words that are blasphemously stupid and empty, a world smashed to pieces, surrounded by borders, indifference to human dignity and worth, people in prison, in camps, stripped of respect, humiliated, many already tortured to death and very many beaten up. Informers surround everyone. All this is Fascism and unfreedom. People today lie with words, they lie in the press, judges have ceased to be judges, they confiscate property from whomever they like, the newspapers are censored, telephones are bugged, they drive people to work like cattle, they torture and tyrannize people.[42]

To emphasize the connection, the hearer responds with words that she will later repeat identically when describing her attitude to communism: "nowadays everyone lives just according to their instincts. They avoid danger ... These days the only way to live is to turn others in or let oneself be turned in."[43]

The communist takeover is shown to have allowed disreputable people to take power and property for themselves and hide acts of criminality and collaboration that they or family members committed during the war. In the first story, "Susedia" ("Neighbours"), the son of a man hanged by the Germans for allegedly assisting the partisans and harbouring a Jewish family becomes a local official and persecutes the daughter of his father's neighbour as a "class enemy" to perpetuate the falsehood that her father betrayed the partisans and the family, when in fact it was his own father who did so. Interceding on her behalf, the parish priest says pointedly to a former partisan, turned communist official: "After all, you are, I hope, more just than the Germans."[44] In the most controversial final story, "Rozostavaný dom" ("A half-built house"), which was fiercely attacked by critics on publication, a poor peasant, who deserted the partisans, became a bandit and then informed on the partisans to the Germans, joins the local party militia after the war, has a farmer evicted during the collectivization, seizes his land to build himself a grotesque villa and, in a gesture reflective of his and the party's hubris, uproots the cross that the farmer had placed there.

The "half-built house," a reference both to the villa and a utopian communal housing block under construction in the nearby town, a death-trap where a character dies after falling, throwing herself or being pushed down an unfinished lift shaft, serves as a metaphor for Slovak communist society, the construction of which may yet be completed successfully, or may not. A camp survivor compares the new housing estates to concentration camps.[45] Throughout the cycle, Bednár associates the Uprising and communist takeover with the modernization and urbanization of Slovak life. While the settings of the Uprising narratives are pre-industrial rural communities, terrorized by alien modern weaponry and warfare, the communist-period settings are urban, signalled by technology like planes and wirelesses, and by unhappy, alienated human beings living alone, in dysfunctional nuclear families or fractious, ideologized workplace collectives. Foreshadowing a central theme of Šikula's writing, what the "half-built house" is missing or has lost is represented by the cross, described as a "symbol of love and respect for the human being,"[46] by the eponymous cradle in the second story, which has been passed around the village for generations to be used by each new baby, by various older peasants who reject their sons' espousal of communism, especially collectivization, and notions like the collective guilt of Germans, by certain nurturing female characters like the persecuted daughter in "Neighbours," who intuitively recognize and selflessly perform their duty to help others, and by the quiet, self-renewing beauty of nature, especially woodland, fleetingly glimpsed and often destroyed amid the violence.

In the title story, Bednár introduces the figure of the alienated, disillusioned urban male intellectual who would become so prominent in Slovak and Czech Thaw literature in the 1960s, supplanting the Socialist Realist/Hemingway hybrid epitomized by Volodia in *Death Is Called Engelchen*. Mitúch is from a farming family but consistently referred to by his academic title, "engineer," which differentiates him from his calm, clear-thinking farmer-brother and indicates his psychological detachment from his roots, an implicit cause of his alienation and uncertainty. Crucially, unlike Tatarka's and Mňačko's anti-heroes, he is not a disillusioned idealist, but, reflecting the influence of French Existentialism, is unconvinced of any ideals, caught between the two sides and dismissive of both. Bednár highlights how easily the heroic status of partisan is unjustly obtained or conferred, noting "they only considered him a partisan at home, where no one differentiated too much between the men who were in the uprising against the Germans."[47] During the Uprising, the commander of Mitúch's regiment defected to the Germans, and Mitúch deserted, disguised as a peasant.

Lost and lonely, Mitúch is drawn to his former classmate, Gizela Gáborová, who appears to be caught in a similar situation. In *Death Is Called Engelchen*, Mňačko sentimentalizes a superficially comparable affair between Volodia and a Jewish woman as an oasis of tragic love amid the inhumanity. Gizela, however, is a conventional femme fatale, who encouraged her collaborator-husband to seize property from wealthy Jews and inform the Germans of their whereabouts, then, as a widow, prostituted herself to German officers. She exploits Mitúch like the Germans, seducing him because she hopes he will intercede for her with the partisans. In the early 1950s, when the two meet again, she has become a communist secret police agent. At this point, Mitúch recognizes the difference between them, and is not prepared to surrender to the despair, misanthropy, and self-hatred that enable Gizela to justify her selfishness and indifference to suffering. His arduous race up a mountain in the last hours and minutes of the German occupation, bleeding from a gunshot wound, through a field of unburied corpses, in an attempt to stop the partisans killing a good German soldier that the reader knows is futile, becomes a metaphor for the Sisyphean task Mitúch takes on to live at peace with himself and others. This Existentialism-influenced diminishing of the goal in favour of the path taken resonates especially in the context of post-Stalinist societies retreating from utopianism and pervades the work of the next generation of Slovak writers.

A comparable figure to Mitúch appears in Johanides's early short story, "Nerozhodný" ("Indecisive"), also set in the aftermath of the Uprising, which opens his first collection, *Súkromie* (Privacy, 1963) and was translated into English by Denis Dobrovoda for *The Dedalus Book of Slovak Literature*. Where Mitúch is an engineer, the unnamed central character is a surgeon, an ironic profession given that, as the title suggests, he is an indecisive man. Whereas Mitúch eventually gains the reader's sympathy, Johanides's surgeon, appropriately for a story about indecisiveness, is a more ambiguous character. He struggles to act because of his propensity to think and his tendency to rationalize his own and others' behaviour based on theories and models he devises could represent either a lack or excess of empathy. The key incidents in his life have ostensibly taught him that whenever he does reach a decision, it causes harm: a girl commits suicide after he refuses to marry her, while after he identifies the source of a typhoid epidemic, a mob beat the disabled man responsible to death.[48] The reader may sympathize with his revulsion at the inherent harmfulness of human existence, which culminates in Czech literature in the Taoist Haňťa in Hrabal's *Too Loud A Solitude* (*Příliš hlučná samota*, completed 1976 but published in 1989, trans. 1990), who in the face of the horrors of the mid-twentieth century has retreated to a cellar to read and pulp books. Equally, however, where Haňťa is accused of laziness, the reader may suspect the surgeon of cowardice and consider him an example of the over-sensitive modern intellectual, who has lost grip of any guiding principles and is crippled by despair.

Johanides achieves this ambiguity by avoiding a structure that provides an order to or interpretation of events, reflecting the influence of the *nouveau roman*. Few of his works are presented as conventionally narrated plots, but instead require the reader to immerse themselves fully in the text and participate in the construction of story and meaning. In "Indecisive," the reader is further disorientated by the unusual second-person narration, which, according to Pynsent, was borrowed from *Second Thoughts* (*La Modification*, 1957, trans. 1958) by Michel Butor (1926–2016) and epitomizes what conformist critics at the time considered superfluous, pretentious formalism.[49] For Pynsent, the narrating voice speaks to the surgeon "as a typical intelligentsia representative of this father's generation."[50] It might also, however, be the voice of his conscience, reflecting on his wasted life, or the thoughts flashing through his head as his life ends. It is critical, mocking and accusatory, and though centred on the surgeon and his actions, has the effect of implicating the reader and author in the same habit of over-thinking.

The unsympathetic reader may conclude that this habit causes the disastrous ending to the story. The surgeon has reluctantly agreed to the request of an acquaintance, a partisan whom he has been surreptitiously supplying with medicine, to leave his elderly father and go to the mountains to treat wounded partisans. In the taxi there, however, they are stopped by German soldiers, who, in contrast to their normal portrayal, seemingly want to avoid violence. Distracted by thoughts he cannot remember, the surgeon fails to pay attention to his friend's instructions about how to act in this situation and leaves the car absent-mindedly holding his revolver, possibly causing the Germans to open fire. It is, however, unclear whether he is pointing his gun at a German officer or handing it to him. The officer disarms and then shoots him, before himself surrendering his gun and allowing the partisan to execute him. In a possible gesture to prevailing ideological correctness, the decisive revolutionary alone survives the encounter. The reader, however, is left more memorably with the image of a small dead bird which had flown into the surgeon's window and which he is still clutching in his hand. Throughout his fiction, Johanides acknowledges the contemporary human being's experience of life as senseless and fragile, which the bird symbolizes, but, like Vilikovský, over the advocacy of tradition and community in Bednár and Šikula he privileges the role of creativity and imagination in the effort to overcome it.

A different French influence is found in the work of Jaroslava Blažková, by far the most prominent female representative of the so-called 1956 Generation, whose hugely popular first novel, *Nylonový mesiac* (A nylon moon, 1961), to date untranslated into English, was quickly compared by reviewers to the French *succès de scandale*, *Bonjour Tristesse* (1954, trans. 1955) by Françoise Sagan (1935–2004). In this period of so-called cultural liberalization in Czech and especially Slovak literature, the dominance of male writers is striking, and seems to reflect a reassertion under communism of the limited range of subjects, styles, and genres considered appropriate for women writers, and also the dominance of men in senior positions in publishing and the Writers' Union and among literary critics. In this chapter, as in Slovak surveys and histories of the period, the studies by French and Pynsent or anthologies in translation, women writers barely figure, and we can undoubtedly attribute the rise of Slovak literary feminism since the 1980s to the striking absence of female subjectivity – and its appropriation by male writers – in the preceding period. At an event in Oxford in November 2019, Blažková was the first person mentioned by the leading contemporary writer Uršuľa Kovalyk (b. 1969) when she was asked to name the three authors most important to her. In *Nylonový mesiac*, the male central character is bored of his girlfriend, a nurse who is desperate to get married, and breaks up with her after a brief affair with a more exciting, uninhibited colleague, who in turn ends their relationship because she finds him too conventional. The tension in the novel between social norms and individual freedom is reflected in Blažková's writing, which often balances between prevailing political and social expectations of literature and their subversion; for this reason, her work was censored in the early 1960s and publicly attacked for its eroticism and perceived immorality. Her work further echoes the democratic, emancipated spirit of the late fifties and sixties in the West in its lively, idiosyncratic use of colloquial language, comparable to Škvorecký, with whom she worked in Canada at '68 Publishers after emigrating in 1968.[51]

The contrasting Slovak and Czech experiences of the post-Stalin liberalization are captured in the titles of two celebrated works, Rúfus's verse cycle *Až dozrieme* (When we are ripe, 1956) and Josef Topol's play *Konec masopustu* (The end of Mardi Gras, 1962). While Czech literature experienced the 1960s as a time of carnival before order is restored, for modern Slovak literature, the post-Stalin liberalization represented a coming-of-age. It is the Slovak writers who came to prominence during this period whom we have to thank for the rich variety of literature that has emerged since 1989 and is documented in the rest of this book.

NOTES

1 Darovec and Barborík, *Mladá tvorba*. In fact, this "generation" included writers born between the 1910s and 1940s.

2 Scholars variously formulate this division among Slovak intellectuals. For the nineteenth century, Robert Pynsent distinguishes between the

easternizing Romantic nationalism of Ľudovít Štúr (1815–1856) and the Westernizing realism of Štefan Launer (1821–1851) (see Pynsent, "What about the Slovaks?," 10–13). For the post-1989 period, Timothy Beasley-Murray writes of the polarization between "Urbanists" and "Ruralists": "The Urbanists … are largely middle-class professionals, living in the cities of Bratislava and, to some extent, Košice … Their notion of Slovakia is of a pluralist society which belongs to a broad European family of nations … The Ruralists … are largely based rurally or in the recently urbanized working class, or in some cases are former members of the Communist nomenklatura. In essence, their understanding of Slovakia is an exclusive, nationalist one, and their notion of Slovak culture is traditionalist." See Beasley-Murray, "Contemporary Slovak Literature," 80–1.

3 Darovec and Barborík, *Mladá tvorba*, 1.

4 Given the target audience of this volume, my discussion focuses on English-language translations. Unlike Ľudmila Pánisová, I distinguish between state-sponsored translations published in Czechoslovakia, which fall into a broad understanding of cultural diplomacy, and those commissioned by British or North American commercial publishers based on anticipated reader interest (cf. Pánisová, *Slovenská literatúra v anglickom preklade*, 38–9). My account of what was translated from Slovak literature in this period relies, like Pánisová, on Kovtun, *Czech and Slovak Literature in English.*

5 In his foreword to *The Taste of Power*, Max Hayward remarks revealingly: "It is usual in discussing works of this kind to emphasize that though they are mainly of documentary interest, they also have some literary worth." Hayward, "Foreword," 8–9.

6 Theiner, "Introduction," 19.

7 Pynsent, "Introduction," 9. As discussed in the introduction to the present collection, Pynsent's volume constitutes the most detailed study in English to date of Slovak literature between 1954 and 1989.

8 Darovec and Barborík, *Mladá tvorba*, 7. Both *Mladá tvorba* and *Květen* faced ideological criticism from adherents of Stalinist socialist realism, but – in a pattern repeated in this period – Slovak writers seemed better able to withstand Party pressure than their Czech counterparts. In its thinking and language, *Květen* in hindsight remained beholden to a relatively narrow understanding of Socialist literature. By contrast, the first editor of *Mladá tvorba*, Jozef Kot (b. 1936), highlights the youthful independence that drove its emergence "not from above, by decree, but as a spontaneous

manifestation of the movements of young writers," who were students at the Arts Faculty of Comenius University in Bratislava.

9 A less celebrated Slovak counterpart to *Zbabělci* was Hykisch's first novel, *Krok do neznáma* (*A Step into the Unknown*), printed in 1959 but immediately pulped and not republished until 1963.

10 Alvarez, *Under Pressure*, 50–1.

11 Ibid., 68.

12 Woods, *Censoring Translation*, 2. As Theiner notes, alongside politics, cinema paved the way for Western interest in literature from Czechoslovakia (see Theiner, "Introduction," 13). Following Western arthouse festival successes, the Oscar for Best Foreign-Language Film was awarded in 1966 to a Slovak-language film, *The Shop on Main Street* (*Obchod na korze*, 1965), directed by Ján Kadár (1918–1979) and Elmar Klos (1910–1993), and in 1968 to the Czech-language *Closely Observed Trains* (*Ostře sledované vlaky*, 1967), directed by Jiří Menzel (1938–2020) and based on a 1965 Hrabal short novel.

13 *Writers Against Rulers* is the English title of *Spisovatelé a moc* (1969, trans. 1971) by the journalist Dušan Hamšík (1930–1985), about the 1967 Fourth Congress of the Czechoslovak Writers' Union, where many of these writers spoke out against party cultural policy, and its aftermath.

14 Woods pointedly asks: "Has the West misread Havel's plays by deeming them and producing them as political for its own ideological and economic ends?" (Woods, *Censoring Translation*, xiii.) In 1990, in the afterword to the first post-Communist Czech edition of his first novel, *The Joke* (Žert, 1967, trans. 1969), Kundera decried the narrow political reading of the work abroad.

15 For example, in April 1948, a group of Slovak socialist writers and critics, including Tatarka, drafted a "Manifesto of Socialist Humanism," just before the Congress of National Culture that would establish cultural policy in newly communist Czechoslovakia, which may be read as a compromised and contradictory attempt to preserve some creative freedom in the face of Party censorship and the imposition of Soviet cultural bureaucracy and socialist realism. Mária Bátorová notes that, despite references to the manifesto in discussion, its text does not appear in the congress minutes (see Bátorová, *Dominik Tatarka*, 14).

16 Bílik, *Duch v reťazi*, 51.

17 Marušiak, "Unspectacular Destalinization," 837.

18 See Marušiak, "Unspectacular Destalinization," 835–6 for more details. In 1994, Peter Pišťanek (1960–2015) parodied the novel in the second volume of

his *Rivers of Babylon* trilogy, where the "wooden village" refers to the cluster of kiosks selling black market goods opposite the Hotel Ambassador.

19 See Shore, "Engineering in the Age of Innocence," 413–14, 417–18. In 1950–52, Mňačko, Tatarka, and other Slovak writers had written approvingly about the Stalinist purges of literature, which culminated in the execution of Vladimír Clementis (1902–1952), the Slovak Communist politician and former leading figure behind the major Slovak interwar avant-garde periodical, DAV, and the imprisonment of others associated with DAV, including the poet Laco Novomeský (1904–1976) and Gustáv Husák (1913–1991), who would in 1969 become Party general secretary and in 1975 the last Communist president of Czechoslovakia. Bátorová suggests that Tatarka's support was motivated by "his confidence in the correctness of Communist ideas and the reliability of the forced confessions of those tried, together with fear at the time for his own existence and psychological intimidation in a period of brutal political purges that reduced intellectuals to lapses of this kind. Tatarka would alternatively have had to fade from public view and his exhibitionist character would not permit this." See Bátorová, *Dominik Tatarka*, 23.

20 Marušiak, "Unspectacular Destalinization," 849.

21 French, *Czech Writers and Politics*, 173.

22 French's study remains the standard English-language account of Czech literature and politics in this period, but this section constitutes the only significant discussion of a distinctively Slovak context, and Mňačko and Tatarka are the only Slovak writers mentioned in the book. See French, *Czech Writers and Politics*, 168–76.

23 Qtd in Bílik, *Duch na reťazi*, 59.

24 Indeed, of major Czech writers of the 1960s who adopted a comparable approach, Hrabal's success came later, while prose writers like Fuks, Věra Linhartová (b. 1938), and Vladimír Páral (b. 1932), the playwright Josef Topol (1935–2015), or the playwright and prose-writer Alena Vostrá (1938–1992) were either unsuccessful when translated or, like their Slovak counterparts, not translated at all.

25 Měšťan, "Česká a slovenská exilová literature," 35. The scope for Slovak literature to develop separately, even amid the straitened circumstances of the 1970s, increased following the federalization of Czechoslovakia in October 1968, which led to the establishment of a separate Union of Slovak Writers and Ministry of Culture. Perhaps most importantly, the leading Czech literary ideologues and functionaries in the Writers' Union and other

cultural bodies before and after 1969 were almost entirely loathed, mediocre placemen who commanded little respect from their peers as artists, which could not quite be said of their Slovak counterparts, including Válek, Slovak minister for culture from 1970–88, Kot, and Mináč. As secretary of the Writers' Union after 1980, the respected novelist, Ladislav Ballek (1941–2014), oversaw an earlier and much more far-reaching response to Soviet *glasnost'* than took place in Czech literature.

26 In 1976, Šikula published *Majstri* (The master carpenters), the first volume of a saga set in Western Slovakia around the time of the 1944 Slovak National Uprising. Johanides returned to publication in 1978. Thanks to his historical novel, *Marek koniar a papež uhorský* (Marek the groom and the Hungarian pope, 1983), Donald Rayfield judged Johanides as probably "the only living Slovak novelist whose claim to European stature, and on posterity, is convincing." See Rayfield, "The Use and Abuse of History," 118.

27 See Měšťan, "Česká a slovenská exilová literatura," 38–9. Měšťan attributes the limited Slovak presence to a Slovak unwillingness to collaborate with Czechs, motivated by nationalism.

28 See "Soupis vydaných knih," accessed 22 July 2022, https://www.skvorecky.cz/?p=3804.

29 Lipták, *Slovensko v dvadsiatom storočí*, 214–15. The uprising, planned in the spring of 1944 by a unified resistance of democrats and communists, the Slovak National Council, was triggered by the German decision in August 1944 to occupy Slovakia and stop partisan disruption of its supply lines to the eastern front. Rebels liberated and for two months held territory in central and eastern Slovakia. The resulting de facto German occupation of Slovakia was marked by brutal reprisals, while partisans hid in the mountains and worked to hasten the progress of the Soviet liberation. For a detailed account, see Prečan, "The Slovak National Uprising."

30 Lipták, *Slovensko v dvadsiatom storočí*, 217.

31 Harkins, "Ladislav Mňačko, *The Taste of Power*," 502.

32 French records: "His wide circle of powerful friends, his Party status, and his reckless and violent personal manner made him a formidable opponent," 192.

33 Mňačko, "O Ploštine," 5.

34 Mňačko, "Pár slov po dlhých rokoch," 183.

35 Petro, *A History of Slovak Literature*, 145. See Tatarka, "The Demon of Conformism," 285–97.

36 Antošová and Cillingerová, "Timeless Message of Dominik Tatarka," 50.

37 Tatarka, *Démon súhlasu*, 59.

38 The title of an essay by the critic Vladimir Pomerantsev (1907–1971) in the Soviet literary journal *Novyi mir* in December 1953.

39 The English translation of Bednár's cycle by David Short is forthcoming in the Karolinum Press's Modern Slovak Classics series.

40 Bednár, *Hodiny a minúty*, 174.

41 Ibid., 181, 209.

42 Ibid., 220.

43 Ibid., 221, repeated 255.

44 Ibid., 98.

45 Bednár's portrayal of mothers precariously ferrying prams and small children across the building site strongly foreshadows the portrayal of a suburban high-rise estate under construction in the satirical Czech film, *Prefab Story* (*Panelstory*, 1979), by Věra Chytilová (1929–2014).

46 Ibid., 264.

47 Ibid., 200.

48 Disability, typically presented as a metaphor of vulnerability that highlights both the capacity of human beings for cruelty and offers a kinder concept of humanity, is a recurring theme in Slovak Thaw literature, notably in Šikula's "With Rozarka" and Vilikovský's "Escalation of Feeling I," both translated in the same anthology.

49 See Pynsent, "Ján Johanides," 82.

50 Ibid.

51 Blažková's most prominent counterpart in poetry was Vadkerti-Gavorníková, who, like Blažková in her short fiction, blurs the female perspective with the child's, two identities at once central and peripheral in traditional, conservative society, and whose spare, unsentimental verse directly contradicted conventional expectations of women's poetry.

BIBLIOGRAPHY

Alvarez, A. [Alfred]. *Under Pressure: The Writer in Society: Eastern Europe and the U.S.A.* Harmondsworth: Penguin, 1965.

Antošová, Marcela, and Veronika Cillingerová. "Timeless Message of Dominik Tatarka in His Work 'The Demon of Conformism.'" *European Journal of Science and Theology* 13, no. 3 (2017): 47–58.

Bátorová, Mária. *Dominik Tatarka: The Slovak Don Quixote.* Frankfurt am Main: Peter Lang, 2015.

Beasley-Murray, Timothy. "Contemporary Slovak Literature, the Devilish Pact with Theory, and the Genitalists." In *Slovakia after Communism and Mečiarism*, edited by Kieran Williams, 79–88. London: SSEES, 2000.
Bednár, Alfonz. *Hodiny a minúty*. Bratislava: Slovenský spisovateľ, 1956.
Bílik, René. *Duch v reťazi*. Bratislava: Kalligram, 2008.
Darovec, Peter, and Vladimír Barborík. *Mladá tvorba 1956–1970–1996*. Levice: L.C.A., 1996.
French, Alfred. *Czech Writers and Politics, 1945–1969*. Boulder: East European Monographs, 1982.
Hamšík, Dušan. *Writers against Rulers*. London: Hutchinson, 1971.
Harkins, William E. "Ladislav Mňačko, The Taste of Power." *Slavic Review* 27, no. 3 (1968): 501–2.
Hayward, Max. "Foreword." In Ladislav Mňačko, *The Taste of Power*. Translated by Paul Stevenson, 5–10. New York: Praeger, 1967.
Karpinský, Peter, ed. *The Dedalus Book of Slovak Literature*. London: Dedalus, 2015.
Kovtun, George. *Czech and Slovak Literature in English* (1988). Accessed 22 July 2022, https://www.loc.gov/rr/european/bibs/csle.html.
Lipták, Ľubomír. *Slovensko v dvadsiatom storočí*. Bratislava: Kalligram, 2011 [1968, 1998].
Marušiak, Juraj. "Unspectacular Destalinization: The Case of Slovak Writers after 1956." *Hungarian Historical Review* 5, no. 4 (2016): 834–53.
Měšťan, Antonín. "Česká a slovenská exilová literatura: shody a rozdíly." In *Česko-slovenská vzájemnost a nevzájemnost*, edited by Ivo Pospíšil and Miroslav Zelenka, 34–40. Brno: Masarykova univerzita, 2000.
Mňačko, Ladislav. "O Ploštine." In *Smrť sa volá Engelchen*, 5–9. Bratislava: Europa, 2016.
– "Pár slov po dlhých rokoch." In *Ako chutí moc*, 179–83. Bratislava: Europa, 2016.
Pánisová, Ľudmila. *Slovenská literatúra v anglickom preklade*. Nitra: Univerzita Konštantína Filozofa, 2014.
Petro, Peter. *A History of Slovak Literature*. Montreal: McGill-Queen's University Press, 1995.
Prečan, Vilém. "The Slovak National Uprising: The Most Dramatic Moment in the Nation's History." In *Slovakia in History*, edited by Mikuláš Teich, Dušan Kováč, and Martin D. Brown, 206–28. Cambridge: Cambridge University Press, 2011.
Pynsent, Robert B. "Introduction." In *Modern Slovak Prose: Fiction since 1954*, edited by Robert B. Pynsent, 1–39. Basingstoke, London: Macmillan, 1990.

– "Ján Johanides: The Consistency of Blood." In *Modern Slovak Prose: Fiction since 1954*, edited by Robert B. Pynsent, 79–107. Basingstoke, London: Macmillan, 1990.
– "What about the Slovaks?" In *Scepticism and Hope: Sixteen Contemporary Slovak Essays*, edited by Miro Kollar, 9–25. Bratislava: Kalligram, 1999.
Rayfield, Donald. "The Use and Abuse of History in Recent Slovak and Georgian Fiction." In *Modern Slovak Prose: Fiction since 1954*, edited by Robert B. Pynsent, 114–24. Basingstoke, London: Macmillan, 1990.
Shore, Marci. "Engineering in the Age of Innocence: A Genealogy of Discourse inside the Czechoslovak Writers' Union, 1949–1967." *East European Politics and Societies* 12, no. 3 (1998): 397–441.
"Soupis vydaných knih." Accessed 22 July 2022. https://www.skvorecky.cz/?p=3804.
Tatarka, Dominik. *Démon súhlasu*. Bratislava: Slovenský spisovateľ, 1969.
– "The Demon of Conformism." Translated by Peter Petro. *Cross Currents* 6 (1987): 285–97. Accessed 22 July 2022. https://quod.lib.umich.edu/c/crossc/ANW0935.1987.001/297:34?rgn=author;view=image;q1=Caraion%2C+Ion.
Theiner, George, "Introduction." In *New Writing from Czechoslovakia*, edited by George Theiner, 13–23. Harmondsworth: Penguin, 1969.
Woods, Michelle. *Censoring Translation: Censorship, Theatre, and the Politics of Translation.* London, New York: Bloomsbury, 2012.

CHAPTER TWO

Literature of the Transition: Between Neo-modernism and Postmodernism

Peter Darovec

The fall of the communist regime in 1989 brought almost immediate and fundamental changes in virtually all areas of social life. Of course, this also applied to the field of literature, which until then had been under the strong ideological pressure and governmental control of the repressive political regime. This mainly manifested itself externally, in the changing system of prohibitions and restrictions on the publishing possibilities of many authors, as well as in the texts themselves, by enforcing the unified ideological-aesthetic poetics called socialist realism. This was an officially compulsory creative method, actually rather a doctrine, a set of elements that were required throughout the era of communist party rule – although not every period was compelled to adhere to it in the same way. In the Stalinist 1950s, socialist realism was a canon directed by decree, in the more relaxed 1960s, it was a partially ignored canon, the 1970s brought a canonical "recidivism" within the scope of the so-called political "normalization," and in the "perestroika" of the late 1980s, the socialist realist canon was ironized and parodied.

After 1989, with the overall liberalization and democratization of society, the literary system also changed rapidly. Literary production opened up to a broader range of values, situated itself pluralistically, and became markedly differentiated. It also adapted to the introduction of market mechanisms and coped with the dramatic change in the position of writers and literature in society.[1] However, the fundamental changes that were directly linked to the revolutionary fall of the communist regime were only in the area of literary "activity" or life, i.e., the non-textual circumstances of literature. Thus, the socio-political transition undoubtedly had a fundamental effect on the literary transition, but the two areas of activity were not simply parallel. Describing the transitional transformations of literary poetics, in the context of the overall social transformation, is considerably more complicated. On the one hand, in exceptional cases, these changes can be traced long before the political change. On the other hand, the process of literary transition was not completed until several years after the drastic political transition. This diverse and variable process of literary transition can also be described with the help of the part-contradictory, part-complementary poetics of neo-modernism and postmodernism. Although the transition phenomena are associated mainly with the Velvet Revolution of 1989, we can only understand them if we return to their genesis in the two short phases when the restrictive regime was eased: the 1960s and late 1980s, respectively.

Postmodernism is generally considered as the condition of late capitalist culture and society.[2] This has been true for Western Europe since the late 1950s, especially in the 1970s and 1980s, when several basic texts defining both the postmodern and postmodernism were written. In the late 1980s, the postmodern was a widely discussed phenomenon in the West that could be grasped from many different aspects, and it was even difficult to define its boundaries. Andreas Huyssen, for example, has said that "the amorphous and politically volatile nature of postmodernism makes the phenomenon itself remarkably elusive, and the definition of its boundaries exceedingly difficult, if not per se impossible."[3] In the Western world, the postmodern is defined in several ways: both cultural: "non-realistic and non-traditional literature and art of the post-Second World War period," which "takes certain modernist characteristics to an extreme stage," and social: "aspects of a more general human condition in 'late capitalism.'"[4] None of these characteristics is applicable to the Central European and thus Slovak situation before 1989.[5] In the Soviet bloc, of course, the state of late capitalism was not a relevant term. In this politically and culturally isolated world (with the possible exception of Yugoslavia, which was then more open to Western culture) there was no general sense of postmodern life or society, as presented by Jean-Francois Lyotard in his influential book *The Postmodern Condition: A Report on Knowledge*. Nevertheless, in retrospectively examining the transition of Slovak literature from the officially required socialist realism to the living form of literature as an adequate voice in post-revolutionary social discourse, we can identify decisive elements associated with the postmodern gesture, partly beginning in the pre-revolutionary period. In other words, the authors of the transition applied postmodernist methods, especially in their early work, without being familiar with the formal concept of postmodernism, but their work can be fully read in line with postmodernist poetics.

The postmodernist replacement of the totalitarianism of grand narratives by a plurality of *petits récits*, or small narratives, took place in Slovak reality under a totalitarian government with an official, constitutionally enshrined grand narrative.[6] Reflecting on the Slovak literature of transition is thus primarily an attempt to specify, for the purposes of historical poetics, significant and productive ways of overcoming socialist realism and the normalization period's lethargy in literature. At the same time, it involves the naming of the liberating process, the emancipation of literary thinking from the long-lasting stereotypes of the National Revival period, which from Romanticism to socialist realism sought to shape Slovak national consciousness on the basis of ideologically utilitarian myths. Thus, the literature of transition can also be understood as a "myth-busting" literature, examining and questioning various socio-political myths, but especially those of a national-social nature.

THE TWO LINES OF LITERARY TRANSITION

From today's perspective, it is possible to identify two basic lines of literary transition – continuous and ruptured. The first comes from the period before normalization, the relatively liberal, relaxed 1960s. Especially in the work of the young authors of the time, this line postulated the humanist-oriented neo-modernist literature of the subject, an empathic interest in human intimacy, the inner and particularly emotional experience of the surrounding world and the subject in it. This is documented by the keywords used in the titles of emblematic prose works from this period: *Súkromie* (Privacy, 1963) by Ján Johanides, *Narcis* (Narcissus, 1965) by Rudolf Sloboda, and *Citová výchova v marci* (Sentimental education in March, 1965) by Pavel Vilikovský. This neo-modernist line thematizes the need to find the last remnants of reality and authenticity in the modern world of simulacra. It is a line of continuity because it emerged from the modernist and avant-garde traditions of the interwar period, maintained at least a limited impact on Slovak literature even later during "normalization," and remains inspiring to this day. This neo-modernist line never lost the basic modernist need to search for a deeper meaning, but since the 1960s, this search for meaning has sometimes been carried out with the help of postmodernist techniques of textual creation such as elements of intertextuality, textual self-referentiality, the game of mystification with the reader, and so on. Their work is a postmodernism *avant la lettre*, i.e., the presence of elements and tendencies of postmodernism in literary works themselves before Slovak authors used postmodernism as a signpost.[7] This line of literary transition will be represented in this chapter by Pavel Vilikovsky's short prose work *Večne je zelený* (*Ever Green Is ...* 1989, trans. 2002).

The second line of transition has its source in the liberalizing perestroika atmosphere of the late 1980s, at the time of the normalization regime's death throes, as it gradually transformed into a self-parody. Fittingly, a parodic-comic way of depicting reality before and after the revolution is typical of the work of authors whose literary work was shaped in the unofficial scene of the late 1980s, who made their debut in magazines just before the Velvet Revolution, and who published their first books only at a relatively mature age after the revolution. Peter Pišťanek, Dušan Taragel, and Igor Otčenáš represent a diametrically different alternative to the above-mentioned neo-modernist line of transition. Instead of the non-modernist empathic approach, their writing prefers positions of ironic distance and concretization. It is, thus, a line of rupture, a sharp, often parodic demarcation not only of the official doctrine of socialist realism, but also of intellectual neo-modernist subjectivism. The gesture of these authors also took the form of a radically ironic intertextual reassessment of virtually all contemporary icons and ideologically motivated socio-political myths. It was a literature of "subverting the canon" by using persiflage transcription and pastiche.[8] In the world of total semantic emptiness presented by these authors, there is no need to ask questions about the deep meaning of the world and life. Instead, they initiate various games with contexts, languages, and literary genres, blurring the boundaries between discursive art and pop culture. Most of the important publications of these authors date back to the post-revolutionary 1990s, when they became foundational for the short-lived dominant trend of postmodernism in Slovak literature. Readers perceived their texts in the context of a new postmodern social situation, to which they were ideologically and aesthetically suited.

However, their postmodernist poetics, paradoxically, were also partially formed in the pre-revolutionary period, when one could not speak of a postmodern era in Slovakia and a broader awareness of postmodernism as a literary trend was not yet present in the country. This line of transition will be demonstrated in Peter Pišťanek's novel *Rivers of Babylon* (1991, original title in English, trans. 2007).

In both of the lines outlined in this chapter, this manifestation of postmodern trends in Slovak literature independently of the Western literary movement seems to serve as indirect evidence of the primacy of artistic production over the influence of external stimuli in the publication of literature. Both works discussed below illustrate what Fredric Jameson has called the "proper use" of postmodernism, which is not only "the description of a particular style," but also "a periodizing concept whose function is to correlate the emergence of new formal features in culture with the emergence of a new type of social life and a new economic order – what is often euphemistically called modernization, post-industrial or consumer society, the society of the media or the spectacle, or multinational capitalism."[9] Yet neither Vilikovský's nor Pišťanek's postmodernism emerged in a postmodern political situation. At that time, there was no post-industrial consumer society in Slovakia, much less a society of media or international capitalism, but rather the seemingly frozen time of communist normalization (when Vilikovský created his text) or the attempts at small shifts under perestroika (when Vilikovsky's prose was published and Pišťanek's poetics began to emerge). The postmodern situation did not reach Slovakia until the 1990s, when the writing of both of these authors found new readers and became widely accepted because it addressed the pressing issues of postrevolutionary Slovak society. After the revolution, the two of them became the most prominent representatives of contemporary Slovak literature.[10]

PRELUDE TO TRANSITION: A CASE OF SATIRE UNDER "NORMALIZATION"

The ironization of national myths during the period of social transition was not limited to the relatively closed space of highbrow literature. Even in the pre-revolutionary years, it was a frequent topic of wider discourse. This is shown, for example, by the extremely popular parodic dramatization of the life of the Slovak national hero, the bandit Juraj

Jánošík. However, the real object of parodic ridicule is not the real life of a relatively insignificant thief and robber, but the long-term creation of ideological myths around him. The comic drama *Jááánošííík* by Stanislav Štepka was performed for decades by the "Radošinské Naïve Theater" (Radošinské naivné divadlo), and it can be quoted by generations of spectators to this day. This also applies to the comedy duo Milan Lasica and Július Satinský. Their comedy was based on an ironic shift of the most banal life situations into the space of nonsense, which unmasked both the banality of the era and the regime. However, their work was not a direct political satire and did not have such an ambition. It playfully yet thoroughly exposed the ideological language of power. The absurd position of their lyrics was not a comical escape from serious reality; on the contrary, it was a sophisticated way of revealing the comfortable conventionality of thinking. Their texts on clichés about the Slovak national mentality, which addressed it with skeptical, humour, and without romantic pathos, were typical in this context. Their work also included songs in which they also ironically dealt with national, cultural, and political myths. One example can be seen in Lasica's lyrics for the title track of the album *My* (We), released by Lasica and Satinský together with the musician Jaro Filip in 1987, two years before the revolution:

We are a dovelike nation
no one will give us anything
everyone just yells at us
it's known about us
Where none of us just cut the skin
feathers are flying out of us in a moment
sometimes it makes us terribly angry
for we are not as stupid
as we look.
We didn't explode the atom
that's true and so what?
Try to count, lovely people
the noggins we broke
We haven't offered the world
the Pythagoras theorem
And yet we're here
and you'll just have to deal with it

Even though we're still a little young
we don't want anyone's advice
but nonetheless we like
to sigh from time to time
We are a dovelike nation
no one will give us anything
everyone just yells at us
in a word we know about us.[11]

Despite the various restrictions on their public appearances during "normalization," Lasica and Satinský's work became the well-known and quoted "public property" of people from various social groups. Their bizarre humour seemed simple and therefore very accessible to a wide range of audiences. In fact, it was a significant intellectual gesture in which absurdity was both a source of comedy and thematized as the era's most characteristic phenomenon.

THE LINE OF CONTINUOUS TRANSITION: PAVEL VILIKOVSKÝ'S *EVER GREEN IS …*

The prose work of Pavel Vilikovský (1941–2020) represents a unique connection between the two indicated lines of transition. Its ideological and aesthetic frameworks, continuously constructed over half a century, have their basis in the neo-modernist poetics of the 1960s, when the author made his debut. But his two most influential books, published a few months before the 1989 revolution, use the textual techniques typical of literary postmodernism. Neither were written in the relatively tolerant 1960s, when they could have been published in book form. Both came from the time of the author's partially voluntary, partially enforced publication ban under "normalization." *Ever Green Is …* was actually written in the first half of the 1970s, while the novella *A Horse Upstairs, a Blind Man in Vráble* was created between 1983 and 1985, so it had a shorter wait until its publication. At first, this work, with its sophisticated composition, looks like "only" a refined and self-referential postmodern textual game. But its main theme reveals a suggestive personal statement that presents the most important things in human life. In this case, finding oneself through a deep relationship with one's mother is a feeling of authentic love, which results, however, in a controversial act: euthanasia. In this essential point, the search for real emotion, Vilikovský remains quite firmly modernist or neo-modernist in this novella, despite the markedly postmodern stylization of the text. The modernist need to search for meaning, at least the last traces of it even in a seemingly meaningless world, is repeated in several of his later works.

However, *Ever Green Is ...*, a burlesque novel of radical irony that is still appreciated by both critics and readers, is an interesting exception to this neo-modernist framework. It was after this book appeared that Pavel Vilikovský's exceptional position in the Slovak literary context was established.[12] He became an "ambassador of his own brand," the laureate of many Slovak and foreign literary awards, and certainly the most widely translated Slovak writer.[13] This comic yet frightening prose quite consciously works with a non-existent morpheme of meaning and accepts the existence of a meaningless world. It is a book of purely postmodernist laughter at this absence of meaning, which has been described by Tibor Žilka as "persiflage, parody or pastiche of meaningless public speeches and scientific reports, but also of literature itself."[14] At first glance, this remarkable novella is a short and frivolous literary grotesque. Even its plot is not particularly highbrow: it is actually a spy story that ironically refers to the genre of easy-reading adventure fiction, as well as conspiracy theories (which still remain so popular today). It is narrated by an old, retired, and mostly senile secret agent, who is constantly convincing the reader that it was his secret actions that shaped (at the very least) the twentieth-century history of Central Europe: "Really, the single reward is the awareness that you have helped to turn the wheel of history; to the left or the right, that's all the same, the main thing is whether it moves."[15]

On his missions, the fictitious agent also encounters real – if sometimes obscure – historical figures, from the famous spy Mata Hari to Hitler during his imprisonment after a failed coup. Of course, despite the use of numerous real historical facts, the novella's history of Central Europe is quite different from the one we know from history books, the genre referred to by its graphic design (which prints "keywords" in the margin, taken at random from the text). The agent's version of a textbook is an absurd alternative to the equally unreliable ideologically motivated history textbooks then used by the educational system of the authoritarian regime. The alternative historicism of this prose is thus not ironically directed towards history itself, but towards its utilitarian interpretations.[16] This persiflage style of "historiographic metafiction" is a playful subversion of ideological myths of various provenance about the modern history of Central Europe.[17]

Ever Green Is ... combines playfulness as a creative principle with radical irony. This is "above all, discrimination against all cardinal paradigms that have only one global significance; at the same time, it opens up space for multi-meaning play, for polylogos, allegory, reflection."[18] All of this relativizing radical irony pits the work against the Slovak literary tradition, which often had a clear tendency leading to the construction and confirmation of statements that could be used as "truths" even in non-literary socio-political contexts.[19] Thus, the Slovak tradition mostly leaned towards the Eastern type of understanding of the word in literature, as Jurij Lotman states in connection with Russian culture: "The problem of the relativity of the word is essentially inherent in West European culture. It differs from the relationship that Russian culture has with the word, in which it reciprocates not as conventionally bound to the truth, but as closely connected with it."[20] The radical irony in Vilikovsky's novella not only relativizes the word and unbinds it from its close relationship with the truth, but even relativizes the very category of truth. Nothing can be seriously claimed here, so the truth gives up a non-binding narration: "In fact irony may be the only way we can be serious today. There is no innocence in our world."[21]

Vilikovsky's "game of irony" involves history, literature, and linguistics, but ultimately the reader, the addressee of the story.[22] At the end, he himself becomes a character, who is tied up by the secret agent: the narrator. The reader is bound here literally by rope, but also metaphorically by the spy's narration, which shows the power ambitions of the ideological narrative towards its audience. In this case, it is both literal and frightening that "a game with language" also means "a game with the reader."[23] The totalitarian language thus reaches the centre of the work's meaning. It is a comical yet at the same time serious variation on the period's semantically emptied language of power. We should keep in mind that the text was written during the deepest repression of the 1970s "normalization," and, as the author later recalled, he actually wrote it for his own amusement during boring and mandatory ideological lectures, without expecting that it might later be published.[24] Language as a tool of power is a key problem of the work, even when not explicitly stated. The character of the manipulative spy directly merges with narration, and he himself is only "a dummy assembled from a language that indicates nothing, and yet is a real force."[25] Vilikovský draws attention to the power potential of language and at the same time shows its inability (including the language of historiography) to name reality in a relevant way. This is Vilikovsky's special contribution to alternative historicism, which is not "truer" than official historicism, but is equally fictional. Neither should be trusted, but both can be entertaining. An appropriate distance must be kept from both, and this "distance has been signalled by irony."[26] Any historical narrative is described here as suspicious simply because it is constructed by language, as suggested by Valér Mikula: "If language is secretly used to deceive, then openly and profusely deceiving means showing that the purpose of language is deception."[27] Within the range of Vilikovský's story, language is both violated and violating, but in any case, it is no longer naming reality.

Eco has pointed out that "books are made only from other books and around other books."[28] *Ever Green Is ...* is a book of contexts, and its basic constructive principle is to refer to other books. This intertextuality has a meaningful form: "Vilikovský uses intertextual linking primarily to create lexical, syntactic and stylistic prototypes, which he presents to the recipient. Thus, he does not presuppose his awareness of the content, but rather of the form, and activates this awareness."[29] Quotations, paraphrases, and allusions are more a presentation of a certain type of language in this case rather than a direct reference to specific texts.[30] In fact, there are several quotes from fictional texts that were invented only for this occasion, producing an intertextual game for the other person. It emphasizes the specific language used to convey information rather than the information itself. *Ever Green Is ...* is a book about languages, a book of many languages, which are implied in the narration. In the sphere of the ironic effect of quotations and allusions, it primarily faces the language of ideology and power. The empty objectifying scientific language or, in contrast, long-winded poetic language, also has a comical effect. The polyphony of the text is based on the constant alternation of different stylistic segments: the agent's narration combines the speech of various historical figures together with encyclopedic information from various fields, including geography, demography, political science, and sexology, as well as the theory of interrogation. The informative value of these linguistic fragments is nullified by the context – especially by the total unreliability of the narrator, who appropriates them.

Ever Green Is ... also expresses skepticism toward the possibilities of reason. If reality can no longer be named by language, then it can no longer be understood with reason. The novella is the story of the agent's journey through Europe, ultimately reaching Slovakia. It is thus an allusion to the Enlightenment travel literature, to gaining experience, to the educational novel. However, education does not take place here, because "if the educational novel lives on from the fact that experiences lead to an inner transformation of the character, in Vilikovsky's case, on the contrary, they lead to its constant self-affirmation."[31] Other passages that are reminiscent of the educational novel are those with a direct didactic effect, which the agent often includes in his story. His lessons for his "young friend" (the reader, who at the climax of the book is also surprisingly revealed to be the agent's unrecognized son) actually do take place in the Enlightenment-rationalist style. But the modern reader of Vilikovsky's "Enlightenment prose" finds only that reason as a tool for knowing the world can no longer be trusted. The narration thus parodies itself: "Parody has perhaps come to be a privileged mode of postmodern formal self-reflexivity because its paradoxical incorporation of the past into its very structures often points to these ideological contexts somewhat more obviously, more didactically, than other forms."[32] Vilikovsky's text is not a satire that ridicules irrationality with Enlightenment reason. It is a pastiche, because "unlike persiflage, in which there is always a moment of parody (mockery), pastiche is the neutral practice of this mimicry ... without a satirical impulse, without laughter and without the belief that outside the temporarily accepted distorted speech there is something like healthy linguistic normality."[33] The realization of this pastiche is then the exuberant grotesque of the meaningless world.

Ever Green Is ... is a comical and skeptical subversion of various national and social myths that have conformed to tradition and the authoritarian regime. It is also an indirect dispute with the then-influential concept of the communist and nationalist writer Vladimír Mináč, who in his essay collection "Dúchanie do pahrieb" (Blowing on the embers, 1970) not only reflected on the meaning of Slovak national existence at the beginning of normalization, but also shaped it, using his position of authority to ideologically seize Slovak national history.[34] With his high pathetic language, Mináč built a myth of the Slovaks as a pure, innocent, hardworking nation that had created values inconspicuously but over centuries. "Even if we do not have our own history in the conventional sense of the word, if we do not have our feudal history, we still have our past, our ancestors, our continuity."[35] That continuity is precisely the peaceful work whose the results have been taken away from the Slovaks by various violent foreigners.[36] The Slovaks just have to endure their invasions: "For many decades, we have been convincing ourselves and others that we exist ... Thank God, we're still alive. The rock cracks, the oak tree breaks, but we stand firm, we're standing and we'll keep on standing, we are and we will be, we exist and we will exist."[37] In Vilikovsky's ironic subversion, it is just that type of violent foreigner, the spy, who describes the Slovaks in nearly the same way: "All nations want to plow a deep furrow in the history of humanity, they want to surpass themselves, but so far, they haven't been able to reach knee-high; only Slovaks, the children of God, see the meaning and fulfillment of their existence in the simple fact that they exist. Who else knows how to have such childlike pleasure: 'Two hundred years have gone by already, and we're still here! There must be something behind it! We're still here, and that can't just be an accident!' And then, full of enthusiasm, they determine a clear goal: 'Let's keep right on existing!'"[38] Actually, it is the narrator's non-Slovak origin that generates the grotesque comedy resulting from his culture shock in his encounter with Slovak reality. The sophisticated foreigner from the West is confronted with the disarming naturalness and simplicity of Slovakia and the Slovaks. He also comments with ironic distance on the conventionality and insignificance of Slovak culture and literature: "Without the Slovak countryside there would be no Slovaks and without Slovak writers there would be no Slovak countryside ... at least certainly not today. These days if a Slovak wants to recover in the lap of virginal nature, he or she simply opens some prominent work of Slovak literature. Don't worry, in Slovak literature all works are prominent, and so catch on with everyone. Do you speak Slovak? You are as many people as the languages you speak, you anthropoid."[39]

The agent arrives in central Slovakia shortly after the First World War to carry out his secret mission disguised as a Czech tourist – which is an emblematic comic character in Slovak jokes about their neighbouring nation, which has mostly played the dominant role in their mutual relations.[40] Disguised in this way, the spy rapes a Slovak cowherdess immediately upon arrival. Referring to himself as "the first Robinson Crusoe in the forests of Turiec," he discovers that his "girl Friday" suffers from vaginismus, while he suffers from priapism:

> I wouldn't have minded her so much if she had only been Friday, but since she was also Monday, Tuesday, Wednesday, Thursday, Saturday, and Sunday, it literally drove me to despair. I feverishly attempted the most various methods to end this involuntary symbiosis once and for all; I alternated a rough physical pressure – in the given case, it would be better to call it anti-pressure – with persuasion, in deep hopelessness I finally grasped – they don't say it for nothing, that a drowning man would even grasp at straws – at the pseudo-scientific theories of the Viennese Jew Freud, at the "so-called," as he said himself, *sogennante Psychoanalyse* ... The dear cowherdess, marked with long centuries of social and national oppression, immediately and entirely ungroundedly, but in view of the prevailing tone of our conversations quite understandably, began to think that she had a soul. At that moment I realized that the symbiosis with the cowherdess's lovely though not particularly clean body was barely bearable, but it could be borne; a symbiosis with her so-called soul, however ... Nothing else was left for me to do but to pitilessly destroy this pitiful monster and replace it with a psychological prosthesis, which I myself had to make.[41]

In this absurd and physically grotesque scene, the two remain "connected" for nine months until the birth of their son: the later fictitious addressee of the spy's story. During that period of waiting, the spy didactically lectures to the shepherdess, who later becomes the first female associate professor (*docentka*) in Slovak history.

As Valér Mikula has noted, "Awareness of one's own illusiveness is the greatest force of art in the postmodern era, perhaps even a hidden grain of optimism."[42] However, this does not apply to the unrecognized illusiveness of grand narratives, especially those that affect national consciousness and national history.

THE LINE OF RUPTURED TRANSITION: PETER PIŠŤANEK'S *RIVERS OF BABYLON*

In contrast to the highbrow, intellectual, even elitist gesture of neomodernist psychological-analytical prose, Peter Pišťanek (1960–2015) selected provocatively low themes and environments. With his debut novel *Rivers of Babylon* (1991), published a year and a half after the revolution, and his subsequent collections of shorter prose, *Mladý Dônč* (Young Dônč, 1993) and *Sekerou a nožom* (With an axe and a knife, 1999), Peter Pišťanek showed a dramatically different alternative. The range of characters from the social underworld (mobsters, prostitutes, etc.) or lower social classes (workers, villagers) also corresponded to this. His exuberant writing about these people with their simple and superficial thinking was a consciously ironic confrontation with the modernist exploration of complex mental life. At the same time, it was a declaration of interest in the real world, not in academic and intellectual constructs. In media interviews Pišťanek liked to ironize the then-predominant form of highbrow literature, which he saw as ridiculously unbelievable, invented, and distant from reality: "Usually it was about some kind of intellectual world, where for example, the husband is an astrophysicist who's dying and doesn't want to tell his wife, a professor of ballet."[43] In contrast, Pišťanek's simple characters do not think much about themselves. It is enough for them to satisfy their basic, often only primary bodily needs. Their life goals are limited to an undisguised desire for power and material gain. The radical irony, in whose framework the author grants his characters only the lowest life motivations, allows for no exceptions. All of the characters in his literary world act with the same self-centred selfishness, including those whose social status would presuppose a higher intellect, outlook on life, and perhaps even morality. But even the minor characters of intellectuals, artists, or politicians have the same banal focus on their own interests as do the author's typical social outsiders. Tomáš Kubíček talks about the vegetative hedonism of Pišťanek's characters: "The heroes of these worlds do not perceive their existence in them as wrong. They do not find their non-participation in great history unfortunate. They don't resist fate and they don't fumble desperately at the wheel of history. They simply are (in different forms, in these different worlds)."[44]

The theme of the "little" person who does not and cannot influence the course of history is a typically Central European theme. Even in this respect, however, Pišťanek was not a humble follower of the tradition, but rather an ironic violator of it. His "little" people do not act in the spirit of tradition as pitiable victims of "big" history. On the contrary, they live quite contentedly in history and the social regimes that history brings with it, because they have no moral or ethical problem in adapting to degrading conditions. From such characters and their natural environments, the author was able to create his bizarre literary world. Despite the comic hyperbole, he was able to report with cruel accuracy on the actual Slovak social reality under socialism and later also the early post-revolutionary capitalism. Pišťanek wrote about the types of people he knew in detail. He understood their behaviour and was able to perfectly imitate their mannerisms and significant speech expressions. He inserted peripheral, sub-standard language registers into his prose to an unprecedented extent. The numerous vulgarisms have the functional and simultaneously comical effect of linguistically and psychologically portraying his characters and their environment. His explicit depiction of sexuality, which had previously been taboo in Slovak literature, has a similar impact.[45] With all this, Pišťanek transcended the boundaries of what was until then perceived in the Slovak cultural context as the space of highbrow literature. He quite consciously flirted with this highbrow literature as well as the genres of popular or commercial literature, and this specific display of postmodernist intertextuality significantly expanded his possibilities of expression. His radical irony is aimed at both high culture and degenerate forms of mass culture: the title *Rivers of Babylon* itself ironically alludes to the Biblical tradition (albeit in connection with prostitution) and at the same time to its lowbrow pop music adaptation by Boney M. According to Linda Hutcheon, "Postmodernism's relationship with contemporary mass culture is not, then, just one of implication, it also one of critique."[46] The result of this conglomeration of meanings is an extremely comical and absurd bizarreness, which paradoxically enough, can realistically portray actual life. Despite his strongly postmodernist stylization, Pišťanek is also a realistic writer, and taking into account the harshness of his themes and motifs, we can also speak of hyperrealism. In Pišťanek's early writings, he and his friend Dušan Taragel called their common style "brutalist realism."[47]

All this also applies to his cult novel *Rivers of Babylon*. On the one hand, "it belongs to the texts of Slovak literature in which the peak stage of postmodernism became manifest, where any residual traces of modernism are already absent."[48,49] On the other hand, it is a social novel that, with cruel black humour, precisely shows the state of society at a moment of great social change. It is a revolutionary novel in its poetics, and at the same time a novel that was created at the time of the revolution, whose theme is the revolutionary period. It even anticipates, to an almost visionary extent, the fundamental changes in Slovak society during the turbulent 1990s, which at the time the novel was written had not yet become apparent.[50] Thus, it not only captures the period of its origin, but also rather prophetically anticipates the state of society in the years after its release.

Rivers of Babylon is the story of a young man from a village, Rácz, who goes to work in the city. The settlement of towns by villagers is the basic defining story of twentieth-century Slovak history. Perhaps it is because of this universality that the novel is not set in an explicit time and space. Yet according to the conditions it portrays, we can reliably identify the setting as the Slovak capital Bratislava at the end of the 1980s and beginning of the 1990s, i.e., just before, during, and after the revolution. In the novel, we follow Rácz's brutally direct and rapid journey from the boiler room of the hotel where he finds his first job upon his arrival, to the economic and power control of the entire city. His "revolutionary" change of status from a social outsider to a hegemon is represented spatially in the novel. The hot underground space of the boiler room can also be interpreted as an ironic version of hell with Rácz as the devil who "ascends to heaven" and becomes a perverted god. From the periphery of the village and then the basement of the boiler room, he quickly moves to an apartment upstairs in the hotel and finally to a luxury villa, whose location high above the city evokes a fairy-tale castle with Rácz as the ruler of the town.

The entire plot of the novel is an ironic persiflage of the typical Slovak fairy-tale narrative about a young villager who goes out into the world and surprisingly achieves success, marrying a princess and gaining the kingdom. His success is the result of his archetypal innocence and simplicity; in one version of this tale ("Foolish Johnny") even outright stupidity. In Pišťanek's adaptation, the protagonist's traditionally valued simplicity becomes Rácz's primitive animality, which no one in the city can resist, neither the women he picks for sex nor the men who serve him because they are afraid of him. Unlike the fairy-tale action of good deeds, in this rewriting the protagonist's uncontrolled brutality leads to his success. He always acts like a ruthless aggressor, and those surrounding him reward him with respect and reverence. The rise to power of this straightforward rural primitive speaks to the specific transitional state of society that made it possible. It is contingent on the state of society at a sensitive historical moment, as Rudolf Sloboda perceived in a contemporary review: "Pišťanek's sociological scope is accurate: such a predator can – and must, I suppose! – exist now and today. He feels it himself, at the end he pacifies the predator a little, legalizes him. His role is finished."[51] Rácz's primitive mafia methods fit right (and only) into the transition phase. He enters the story as a social outsider and in the standard state of society would have remained there. But he succeeds, although he does not develop at all, remaining equally rude and limited throughout the novel. This is "a travesty of the Bildungsroman, a novel of development based on the story of integration into society, the acceptance of world conditions."[52] Rácz does not have to adapt to the conditions of this specific world. He himself is their direct consequence, the personification of this social situation. In his review of the translation for the *Times Literary Supplement*, Tim Beasley-Murray described Rácz as "less a character than the embodiment of a Nietzschean will to power."[53,54] In the revolutionary situation of social transition, power lies on the street, and it is the brutally simple and simply brutal Rácz who has the force to pick up that power. Pišťanek's novel dynamically accumulates a number of bizarre elements; it is a comic hyperbole, it is full of absurd black humour, but at the same time it is an exact reflection of Slovak life in revolutionary times, as well as post-revolutionary times to come. Although paradoxically it was written at the very beginning of the "wild" 1990s, it is often described as a key Slovak novel of those times, as a part of them as well as a representation of them.[55]

While *Rivers of Babylon* graphically evokes a specific historical period, it is not an explicitly political novel. In fact, it shows almost none of the revolutionary events that dramatically changed the state of the country in late 1989 and early 1990. The demonstrations of hundreds of thousands of people in the centre of Bratislava, where Rácz's fictional hotel is located, do not appear in the novel at all. These socio-political processes lie outside the viewpoint of the characters surrounding Rácz. They appear on their mental horizon only when they can bring these characters some personal benefit. In this, too, Pišťanek's novel is ironically factual and sociologically accurate. Disillusionment is a basic characteristic of Pišťanek's fictional world. He perceives the motivation of his characters and their social environment without illusions, but all grand narratives, especially ideologically motivated ones, turn out to be equally disillusioning.

The author's rationalizing outlook unmasks their pathos as false and outdated, far removed from lived reality. The ironization of traditional narratives and conservative myths takes many forms in Pišťanek. It disturbs, for example, the typical Slovak (and literary) narrative about the Slovak village as a space of moral purity in comparison with the amoral city.[56] Pišťanek's disillusioning version of the village is connected with the city by the identical absence of any values. In both spaces, there is an equally primitive desire for property and obtaining physical pleasure. However, in the uneducated countryside, no one even tries to disguise this behaviour. Pišťanek also intensively subverts the widespread national self-myth of the Slovaks as an extremely generous nation, which is poles apart from the brutal selfishness of his characters. However, this selfishness is not limited to Slovaks; foreigners who appear in this environment for whatever reason are exactly the same.

Disillusionment is also often associated with the motif of work, which the national-communist intellectual Mináč (previously mentioned in connection with Vilikovský) had moved to the level of national myth: "But if the history of civilization is the history of labor, a construction that is interrupted by history but always victorious again and again, then so is our history."[57] Pišťanek is thus another author who enters into a polemic with Mináč's pathetic cult of manual labour as the privileged foundation on which he builds the proletarian myth of Slovak history. In contrast to this ideological illusion, in *Rivers of Babylon* Pišťanek shows types of people he has observed in real life, who are definitely not defined by their relationship to work. On the contrary, these modern-day "proletarians" are eager to avoid their boring work, to get rid of it, to transfer it someone else by deceit. Significantly, this is the point of the opening scene of the novel, in which the old stoker in the hotel's boiler room transfers his work duties to the naive Rácz, whose social success begins at the moment when he himself violently forces others to carry out this same manual labour. Pišťanek's factual rewriting of illusory narratives turned out to be closer to reality than the empty stereotypes promoted by socialist ideologues.

The ironic rationalization of myths and self-myths is most easily achieved from a position of distance. In *Rivers of Babylon*, one such disinterested observer of specifically Slovak national qualities is the Swedish "bisexual tourist" Hurensson. As a foreigner without any emotional connection to the country and its inhabitants, Hurensson's ironic "Western" rationality stands in contrast to the thematized Slovak national pathos. He pays particular attention to the hypertrophied national and personal self-confidence of the Slovaks, in which nothing is hidden:

> This is a nation of the underestimated, it occurs to Hurensson. They could have given the world some of the most brilliant artists, ballet dancers, and scientists – at least that's what they claim. But why didn't they – that's the question? Hurensson found out about the existence of this nation only because of its ridiculously cheap prostitutes, willing to put up with anything that doesn't leave visible traces. Only then did he find out from the residents of this nation about the apparently famous artists, astronomers, and inventors whom he'd never heard of before. But so far Hurensson has only been able to meet cheap whores, black market hustlers, arrogant waiters and taxi drivers, lazy room-maids and venal policemen. However, Hurensson does not condemn anyone outright. He believes the milieu in which he circulates as a bisexual tourist has shaped his opinion. He has no doubt that this nation is composed not merely of parasites and fools, but also of honest and educated working people. The point is that Hurensson has never yet met such people, nor even found a trace of their existence. He needn't give a toss.[58]

Hurensson's non-illusory observation of the Slovaks is not only the discovery of their national self-myths, but also an exact description of the current strategies for survival of certain human types in a society in transition. These people need to re-orient themselves in a changed world. At the same time, however, these types of people like to blame their life failures on the adverse circumstances of great history. Waiting for a coffee in the hotel café, Hurensson reflects further:

> This small nation with its artificially hypertrophied and incomprehensible national pride is a nation of geniuses misunderstood and unrecognized by the rest of the world, he feels. They all believe that they're better than they seem at first sight. The young hustler and unlicensed taxi driver thinks he is an artist. The blond whore never fails to stress that she was originally a ballet dancer. The stooped porter with spidery bony fingers who takes your bags turns out to have been at one time a lecturer at the evening university, now closed, of Marxism-Leninism. He was a philosopher, or so he says. Whatever they do now is only temporary, done out of necessity.[59]

We can see that Pišťanek's cynical foreigner Hurensson has much in common with the equally cynical foreign spy in Vilikovsky's *Ever Green Is ...*

Hurensson and the spy, both of whom are suspicious individuals, report an unflattering message about the Slovaks. This is all the more ironic because it comes from people who are the only ones with the slightest reason to deal with this small unknown nation somewhere in Central Europe, and even their reason was only the possibility of cheaply satisfying specific physical needs. Their sexual exploitation of Slovak men and women is a parodic update of the basic Slovak myths, which "dramatize our suffering self-stereotypes: the myth of the millennium of slavery, the myth of the sacrifice of history, and partly the myth of plebeianism."[60]

CONCLUSION

Ever Green Is ... and *Rivers of Babylon*, both essential works of Slovak prose, were published only two years apart, one just before and the other just after the 1989 revolution. Their authors belonged to different generations; they had different life experiences, and their poetics came from different sources. Nevertheless, in their groundbreaking fiction, they address similar issues in a similar way, among which are the problem of national identity and especially the need to change the traditional myth-building approach to it. Both work with postmodernist skepticism, scrutiny, de-tabooing, and a disillusioned, grotesque humour.

Of course, similar manifestations of postmodernism prior to the postmodern social situation can be found in the work of other authors besides Vilikovsky and Pišťanek. We can find similarly productive national "myth-busting" in different variants of persiflage-style alternative historicism. The neo-modernist line of transition can be found in Rudolf Sloboda's 1968 collection *Uhorský rok* (Hungarian year), while the second, newer line of transition is seen in Igor Otčenáš's *Keby* (If, 1998), another ironic version of a history textbook, which in this case describes Slovak history after the victory of Nazi Germany in the Second World War. Otčenáš's work ironically assumes that Slovaks would have adapted to permanent Nazi totalitarianism in virtually the same way as they actually did adapt to postwar communist totalitarianism.

Both lines of transition of Slovak literature outlined above proved to be productive and at the same time influential for creating the basic forms of post-revolutionary Slovak literature. Along with the rather surprisingly continuous creativity of authors who were established as early as the mid-1960s, the newer postmodernist line of writing was at least as prominent on the post-revolutionary literary scene. "A phenomenon that could be described as a spatialization of time has arisen, in which works that were created half a century ago, those from twenty years ago, those from the last decade, and those that are being created now, are appearing together for the first time."[61] In the 1990s, the postmodern gesture was more visible in various forms, from intellectual academic postmodernism to Pišťanek's harsh prose of ironic reality. During that decade, as Ivana Taranenková explains, "the postmodern line of writing emphasized the playfulness and sophistication of literary texts, as well as mystification, irony, and experimentation, associated with questioning the category of subject, authenticity, and basic experience."[62] After the relatively rapid exhaustion of the potential of postmodernist poetics, the neo-modernist literature of the subject and authenticity was re-evaluated in the new millennium.

Both of these lines have also significantly contributed to the strengthening of a modern and authentic national self-confidence, which can now afford the self-ironic gestures of rejecting the creation of affirmative illusory myths. This is an important contribution of literature to the maturation of Slovak social discourse. The "myth-busting" of the literature of transition in the years before and after the revolution can therefore be seen as a direct movement to the present. Ultimately, the years of transition are the starting point for most literary overviews of contemporary Slovak literature.

NOTES

1 The status of the writer as well as literature has been socially marginalized in the post-revolutionary years, but at the same time it has become authentic and, above all, more independent of state power and ideology.

2 Jean-Francois Lyotard connects the manifestations of postmodernism with the postmodern era, the beginning of which is defined by the end of the postwar reconstruction of (Western) Europe: "This transition has been under way since at least the 1950s, which for Europe marks the completion of reconstruction." *Postmodern Condition*, 3.

3 Huyssen, *After the Great Divide*, 58–9.

4 On the distinction between "postmodernity" and "postmodernism," see for example Ruth Mayer: "Postmodern is the term for the cultural-historical era after modernity, including the aesthetic-philosophical concepts and cultural

configurations of this period … By contrast, the term postmodernism refers to literary styles and cultural phenomena for this era." "Postmoderne/Postmodernismus," 618.

5 Hawthorn, *Concise Glossary of Contemporary Literary Theory*, 110.

6 Lyotard, *Postmodern Condition*, 31.

7 Darovec, *On, Pišťanek*, 152.

8 Rédey, *Subverzia kánonu slovenskej prózy v novele Petra Pišťanka Mladý Dônč*, 5.

9 Jameson, *Cultural Turn*, 3.

10 Evidence of this assertion can be found in the prestigious survey of the literary journal *Platform for Literature and Research*, where dozens of relevant writers, editors, and critics selected the most important works of contemporary literature. In a survey on the topic "Three Decades of Slovak Literature (1989–2019)," the prose of Pavel Vilikovský and Peter Pišťanek dominated by a large margin (Barborík, "Anketa").

11 Lasica, Satinský, and Filip, *My*.

12 At the time of its publication, *Ever Green Is …* was already considered a "groundbreaking book" (Resutík, "Pavel Vilikovský," 124) and the status of a "literary event" (Čúzy, Darovec, Hochel, Kákošová, *Panoráma slovenskej literatúry*, 68).

13 Barborík, "Byť vyslancom vlastnej značky," 4.

14 Žilka, "Slovak Postmodernism," 415.

15 Vilikovský, *Ever Green Is …*, 18.

16 Alternative historicism is one of the postmodernist realizations of the literature of transition. Its search for counterfactuality is disrupted by the concept of historical grand narratives. Just as in modern historiography, it serves to examine other possible scenarios of historical events for a better understanding and interpretation of the historical scenario that actually took place (Ferguson, *Virtual History*), so in literature it is a game of meanings that refers to the plurality of truth.

17 Hutcheon, *Poetics of Postmodernism*, 105.

18 Žilka, *Téma a štýl v postmodernizme*, 21.

19 As early as the Slovak national revivalist tradition of the nineteenth century, we find many texts that deviate significantly from the actual course of historical events. This was not about questioning or verifying history, but an attempt to reconstruct it. It was one of the tools for promoting the Slovak political agenda that was used due to the lack of other options, especially by means of literature. Since the Second World War, voluntary or forced

affirmation of totalitarian ideologies and regime doctrines has been added to the construction of national consciousness.

20 Lotman, "Myslenie kritiky," 9.
21 Hutcheon, *Poetics of Postmodernism*, 39.
22 Eco, "Postscript," *Name of the Rose*, 68.
23 Hutcheon, *Poetics of Postmodernism*, 21.
24 Vilikovský, "Moji Rumuni mi rozumejú," 9–18.
25 Mikula, "Krajnosťou k miernosti," 45.
26 Hutcheon, *Poetics of Postmodernism*, 39.
27 Mikula, "Krajnosťou k miernosti," 51.
28 Eco, *Name of the Rose*, 44.
29 Dvořák, "K některým problémům intertextuality," 37.
30 Rajendra Chitnis has compared the "patchwork of quotations" in *Ever Green Is ...* with the Czech novelist Bohumil Hrabal's *Dancing Lessons for the Advanced in Age* (Taneční hodiny pro starší a pokročilé, 1964), "where the stream of language pouring from the narrator's mind represents life and resistance to the positivist use of language which seeks to restrict that life" (*Literature in Post-Communist Russia and Eastern Europe*, 32).
31 Zajac, "Inkognito, ergo sum (*Večne je zelený ...*)," 4.
32 Hutcheon, *Poetics of Postmodernism*, 35.
33 Zajac, "Inkognito, ergo sum," 4.
34 Mináč thus continues the Slovak tradition of creating national identity through "active atavism," as defined by Robert Pynsent: "By active atavism I mean a seeking out and even inventing of ancestors and ancestral characteristics." *Questions of Identity*, 59.
35 Mináč, *Dúchanie do pahrieb*, 66.
36 Mináč combines the older national myth of the thousand-year oppression of the Slovak nation with the current communist ideology: "The myth of the thousand-year national servitude is the product of specific historical conditions and distinct national relations of the nineteenth century. ... The interpretation of historical servitude has been enriched with a new dimension in the intentions of historical materialism: class oppression" (Krekovič, Mannová, Krekovičová, *Mýty naše slovenské*, 72–5).
37 Mináč, *Dúchanie do pahrieb*, 59.
38 Vilikovský, *Ever Green Is ...*, 79.
39 Ibid., 83.
40 Sabatos, "Czechs, Sex, Spies, and Torture," 184–6.
41 Vilikovský, *Ever Green Is ...*, 103–4.

42 Mikula, "Krajnosťou k miernosti," 47.
43 Taragel, "Spisovateľ Peter Pišťanek."
44 Kubíček, "O hranicích nímandslendu a pasti nadinterpretace," 405.
45 Pynsent, "Video Nasties," 89.
46 Hutcheon, *Poetics of Postmodernism*, 41.
47 Pišťanek and Taragel, "Autorské poznámky," 269.
48 Taranenková, "*Rivers of Babylon*,"186.
49 In Pišťanek's case, however, it is not a question of fulfilling a universal postmodernist canon, but rather of his own use of some postmodern forms of textual creation to create a special poetics and a special prosaic worldview. In addition, it should be recalled that Pišťanek began writing this novel at a time when he had no access to information on the theoretical aspects of postmodernism.
50 Pišťanek actually had the first version of the novel ready before the revolution; in 1988 he read from it aloud to his friends. In the revolutionary months during which Pišťanek worked as a parking guard in the centre of Bratislava, where mass demonstrations were taking place, the novel was partially rewritten and completed very quickly.
51 Sloboda, "Niekoľko poznámok k Riekam Babylonu," 40.
52 Taranenková, "Rivers of Babylon," 193.
53 Beasley-Murray, "Stoker Supreme," 22.
54 Rajendra Chitnis has written on Pišťanek's work as a form of Bildungsroman; see Chitnis, "Žiť plným životom," 28–30, and *Literature in Post-Communist Russia and Eastern Europe*, 51–8.
55 Malíček, "Pamäť deväťdesiatok," 23.
56 In the Slovak cultural tradition, the village has always been understood as a domestic space, which is understandable and therefore accepted. On the other hand, Slovaks did not inhabit cities for the most part and considered them to be foreign, unknown, with different standards of behaviour, and therefore unacceptable.
57 Mináč, *Dúchanie do pahrieb*, 71.
58 Pišťanek, *Rivers of Babylon*, 88.
59 Ibid., 87–8.
60 Krekovič, Mannová, and Krekovičová, *Mýty naše slovenské*, 16.
61 Zajac, "Slovenská literatúra deväťdesiatych rokov v obrysoch," 79.
62 Taranenková, "Koncepty súčasnosti," 142.

BIBLIOGRAPHY

Barborík, Vladimír. "Anketa Tri desaťročia slovenskej literatúry (1989–2019)." Platforma pre literatúru a výskum, 2019. https://plav.sk/node/171.

– "Byť vyslancom vlastnej značky. Rozhovor s Pavlom Vilikovským." *Dotyky* 6, no. 7 (1993): 4–7.

Beasley-Murray, Tim. "Stoker Supreme." *Times Literary Supplement*, 29 February 2008, 22.

Chitnis, Rajendra. "Žiť plným životom: moc v kolektíve v próze Petra Pišťanka." *Romboid* 34, no. 8 (1999): 26–30.

– *Literature in Post-Communist Russia and Eastern Europe: The Russian, Czech and Slovak Fiction of the Changes 1988–98*. London: Routledge-Curzon, 2004.

Čúzy, Ladislav, Peter Darovec, Igor Hochel, and Zuzana Kákošová. *Panoráma slovenskej literatúry*. Bratislava: Slovenské pedagogické nakladateľstvo, Mladé letá, 2006.

Darovec, Peter. *On, Pišťanek*. Bratislava: Literárne informačné centrum, 2020.

– *Pavel Vilikovský alebo Prepísať sa k citu, prečítať sa k zmyslu*. Bratislava: Kalligram, 2007.

Dvořák, Antonín. "K některým problémům intertextuality v próze Pavla Vilikovského *Večne je zelený*." *Slovenské pohľady* 106, no. 8 (1990): 37–9.

Eco, Umberto. *The Name of the Rose*. Translated by William Weaver. San Diego: Harcourt Brace Jovanovich, 1984.

Ferguson, Neil. *Virtual History: Alternatives and Counterfactuals*. New York: Basic Books, 2000.

Hawthorn, Jeremy. *A Concise Glossary of Contemporary Literary Theory*. London: Edward Arnold, 1992.

Hutcheon, Linda. *A Poetics of Postmodernism: History, Theory, Fiction*. London, New York: Routledge, 1988.

Hutchinson, Peter. *Games Authors Play*. London, New York: Methuen, 1983.

Huyssen, Andreas. *After the Great Divide: Modernism, Mass Culture and Postmodernism*. London: Macmillan, 1988.

Jameson, Fredric. *The Cultural Turn*. London: Verso, 1998.

Krekovič, Eduard, Elena Mannová, and Eva Krekovičová. *Mýty naše slovenské*. Bratislava: Premedia Group, 2013.

Kubíček, Tomáš. "O hranicích nímandslendu a pasti nadinterpretace. Průhledy do světa Ľudevíta Dônče a spisovatele Petra Pišťanka." *Slovenská literatúra* 49, no. 5 (2002): 404–9.

Lasica, Milan, Július Satinský, and Jaroslav Filip. *My*. Bratislava: Opus, 1987.
Lotman, Jurij. "Myslenie kritiky." *Literárny týždenník* 1, no. 9 (1988): 9.
Lyotard, Jean-Francois. *The Postmodern Condition: A Report on Knowledge*. Translated by Geoffrey Bennington and Brian Massumi. Manchester: Manchester University Press, 1984.
Malíček, Juraj. "Pamäť deväťdesiatok, na čítanie i do zbierky." *Knižná revue* 29, no. 4 (2019): 23.
Mayer, Ruth. "Postmoderne/Postmodernismus." In *Metzler Lexikon Literatur und Kulturtheorie*, edited by Ansgar Nunning, 5th ed. Stuttgart: J.B. Metzler, 2013.
Mikula, Valér. "Krajnosťou k miernosti, obscénnosťou za lepšiu budúcnosť." *Slovenské pohľady* 105, no. 8 (1989): 45–6
Mináč, Vladimír. *Dúchanie do pahrieb*. Bratislava: Slovenský spisovateľ, 1989.
Otčenáš, Igor. *Keby. Rýchle dejiny budúcnosti Slovenska*. Bratislava: L.C.A. and Filmservice Slovakia, 1998.
Passia, Radoslav, and Ivana Taranenková, eds. *Hľadanie súčasnosti. Slovenská literatúra začiatku 21. storočia*. Bratislava: Literárne informačné centrum, 2014.
Petro, Peter. "Rivers of Babylon: Peter Pišťanek's Novelistic Trilogy," *Trans*. Accessed January 2022. https://www.inst.at/trans/14Nr/petro14.htm.
Pišťanek, Peter. *Rivers of Babylon*. Translated by Peter Petro. London: Garnett Press, 2007.
Pynsent, Robert. *Questions of Identity: Czech and Slovak Ideas of Nationality and Personality*. Budapest: Central European Press, 1994.
– "Video Nasties: The Last Decade of the Slovak Twentieth Century through the Eyes of Peter Pišťanek." In *Slovakia after Communism and Mečiarism*, edited by Kieran Williams, 89–109. London: School of Slavonic and East European Studies, 2000.
Rédey, Zoltán. *Subverzia kánonu slovenskej prózy v novele Petra Pišťanka Mladý Dônč*. Nitra: Univerzita Konštantína Filozofa v Nitre, 2007.
Resutík, Milan. "Pavel Vilikovský: Večne je zelený!" *Slovenské pohľady* 105, no. 7 (1989): 123–4.
Sabatos, Charles. "Czechs, Sex, Spies, and Torture: Slovak Identity as Translation in Pavel Vilikovský's *Ever Green Is …*" *Comparative Literature Studies* 40, no. 2 (2003): 173–92.
Sloboda, Rudolf. "Niekoľko poznámok k Riekam Babylonu." *Dotyky* 4, no. 2 (1992): 40.
– *Uhorský rok*. Bratislava: Smena, 1968.

Šútovec, Milan. "Začiatok sedemdesiatych rokov ako literárnohistorický problém." *Slovenské pohľady* 105, no. 1 (1989): 29–43.

Taragel, Dušan, "Spisovateľ Peter Pišťanek: Písať sa mi už nechce, ale iné robiť neviem." SME, 14 January 2010. https://kultura.sme.sk/c/5188469/spisovatel-peter-pistanek-pisat-sa-mi-uz-nechce-ale-ine-robit-neviem.html.

Pišťanek, Peter, and Dušan Taragel. "Autorské poznámky." *Sekerou a nožom.* Levice: L.C.A., 1999.

Taranenková, Ivana. "Premeny poetík? (Niekoľko poznámok k reflexii slovenskej literatúry po roku 1989)." *Slovenská literatúra* 56, no. 6 (2009): 72–9.

– "Koncepty súčasnosti po konci postmoderny." *Litikon* 3, no. 2 (2018): 137–52.

– "*Rivers of Babylon* – postmoderný Bildungsroman, román konca dejín." *Slovenská literatúra* 65, no. 3 (2018): 183–97.

Vilikovský, Pavel. *Ever Green Is …* Translated by Charles Sabatos. Illinois: Northwestern University Press Evanston, 2002.

– "Moji Rumuni mi rozumejú (rozhovor s Pavlom Vilikovským)." *RAK* 4, no. 6 (1999): 9–18.

Zajac, Peter. "Inkognito, ergo sum (*Večne je zelený …*)." *Literárny týždenník* 2, no. 26 (1989): 4.

– "Prelomové či svoje? Skica o slovenskej literatúre deväťdesiatych rokov." *OS-Fórum občianskej spoločnosti* 3, no. 2 (1999): 74–7.

– "Slovenská literatúra deväťdesiatych rokov v obrysoch." *Host* 17, no. 5 (2001): 79–86.

Žilka, Tibor. *Téma a štýl v postmodernizme (Postmodernistické aspekty prozaických textov).* Nitra: Pedagogická fakulta Ústav literárnej a umeleckej komunikácie, 1991.

– "Slovak Postmodernism." In *International Postmodernism.* Edited by Hans Bertens and Douwe Fokkema, 413–18. Amsterdam: J. Benjamin, 1997.

CHAPTER THREE

Writing the Self from Autobiography to Autofiction

Ivana Taranenková

In 1850, the Slovak Romantic poet Mikuláš Dohnány wrote in his journal: "The awareness that I am writing about myself has arrested my pen, for I always want to introduce others, to showcase the virtues of others. I was looking for a character for my novella, but in vain, and I did neither want to invent lies nor write untruths. So what else can one then give the nation, if not oneself?"[1] Dohnány's reflection foreshadows a characteristic preoccupation in Slovak literature of the next century, which questions the viability of representations of the self in a literature that had been bound with a collective identity from its beginnings.

During the process of national revival, individualism and subjectivity were suspect because writers and critics prioritized the collective definition and defence of the nation. The demand to transcend the boundaries of subjectivity and individualism remained urgent in the course of the twentieth century, when Slovak literature, just like other literatures of the so-called Eastern Bloc, was subjected to ideological pressure. The emphasis on subjective points of view and authentic representations of the self in literature became more pronounced during the periods of relative loosening of ideological pressures. Following November 1989, literary representations of the self that highlighted subjectivity and authenticity were pushed to the background in the literary production of the new generation, which responded to the dominant postmodern trends that proclaimed the death of the subject. The "return" of the subject, or the renewed focus on authenticity and foregrounding of problems associated with individual identity in Slovak literature, takes place during the first decade of the new millennium in conjunction with global cultural trends that involve post-postmodern developments.

In the rest of this chapter, I map the transformations and the limitations that shaped the literary representations of the self in Slovak literature during specific periods of artistic and cultural development. I pay special attention to the changes in autobiographical literature, which has long been considered a privileged space for representing the self with the indisputable status of referentiality,[2] while not considering this type of literature as a strictly limited genre.[3] Instead, I also focus on the transformative potential of the concept of autofiction in the Slovak literature of the late twentieth and early twenty-first centuries, which has made it possible to plausibly articulate the experience of the subject in relation to the world and the self in the wake of the postmodern questioning of subjectivity.

HARNESSED BY HISTORY: THE EVOLUTION OF THE LITERARY SELF

Normative discursive practices that prescribed models for literary and cultural representations of the self in Slovak literature originated in the nineteenth century. Their form was primarily determined by the ideologically conditioned affiliation with a collective identity, which stemmed from social and historical developments. The construction of the self ("I") was tied with the march of history that was assumed to result in – depending on the dominant ideology – national or class emancipation. Since the beginning of the national movement in the 1830s, individualism was thus considered to be a manifestation of different, Western cultures. Both Czech and Slovak literature decisively rejected the Romantic conception of individualism: "The rejection of Romantic aesthetics as a whole along with all its ideological consequences (while some of its elements were selectively adopted) in conceptualizing 'Slavic poetry' was an attempt to formulate essential differences between Slavdom and the Western world, which was stereotyped as a world of crass materialism (represented primarily by England with its industrial and commercial activity) and of revolt against the established order (represented by France, still marked by the memory of the Revolution)."[4] For the Slovak national revivalists, Byronism, in particular, embodied an extreme form of individualism, and the figure of Lord Byron continued to challenge the major ideologues of the Slovak national movement, particularly Ľudovít Štúr and Svetozár Hurban Vajanský, throughout the nineteenth century. They viewed the separation of the individual from the collective as a threat to the still emerging and fragile national and cultural identity, which is based on the principles of objectivity, harmony, and moderation. Similar objections were later raised against modernist movements, which were perceived as excessively individualistic.

Literary representations of the individual "I" were also conditioned by the role of the writer as a representative of the national movement during this period. Jozef Miloslav Hurban, a prominent writer associated with the Slovak National Awakening, formulated his ideal of the writer ("poet," since poetry was the highest form of art according to the aesthetic criteria of the period) as a figure elevated above everyday existence but also closely associated with the national collective: "We don't want the poet to walk before us and lament, but expect him to stand high above us and draw us toward him in grief and joy with his resounding song and thus reach us and our hearts."[5] The ideal poet of the national movement was a bard rather than a Byronic hero.

Nineteenth-century autobiographical literature also weighed the legitimacy of representing the self. Literary criticism of this period highlighted the documentary function of autobiographical literature and the social and historical dimensions of the relationship between the subject and its environment. Critics privileged texts that captured important historical events such as the witness accounts of the participants of the 1848–49 Revolution or the memoirs of the leading figures of the National Awakening.[6]

The privileging of social and historical perspectives over problems of individual identity was driven by the unique political imperative of Slovak national emancipation, yet the question of the self in autobiographical writing also intersected with similar debates on the legitimacy of literary representations of the self in the broader context of European literature. Laura Marcus examines autobiographical discourses that set out to establish the norms for an "ideal" autobiographical text and determine practices for appropriate literary representation of the self during the nineteenth century. Model autobiographical texts were ones that represented exemplary and singular lives. The texts that did not fit this model were accused of vanity and egotism. Individual texts representing the authorial self had to continually legitimize themselves and reconcile the tension between the subject and the other, the public and the private, revelation and secrecy, while they strove to maintain "respectability."[7] Similar legitimizing discourses also appear in Slovak literature of this period.

In nineteenth-century Slovak literature, the legitimacy of autobiographical writing is measured, above all, by national affiliation. Slovak autobiographical texts do not present any lives, but "Slovak" lives, which is reflected in the titles of memoirs from this period such as Gustáv K. Zechenter-Laskomerský's *50 rokov slovenského života* (50 years of Slovak life, journal 1911–15, book 1956)[8] and Elena Maróthy Šoltésová's *Sedemdesiat rokov slovenského života* (Seventy years of Slovak life, 1925).[9] The strong association between the individual "I" and the national collective meant that Slovak autobiographical prose was not yet confronted with questions associated with egoism, frivolity, or vanity, which were debated in British literature of the Victorian period.

The emphasis on public lives in autobiographical texts also conditioned the reception of nineteenth-century Slovak women's autobiographies.[10] Women's autobiographical writing, with its focus on intimate spaces and everyday experiences, did not necessarily promote the national cause. This trend is evident in Šoltésová's account "Umierajúce dieťa" ("The dying child," 1885), which later became the basis for her novel *Moje Deti* (My children, 1923–24).[11] Both texts capture the brief lives and deaths of the author's two children, a son and a daughter. Although the novel, published later, was exceptionally successful and belongs to the most translated texts of Slovak literature, the shorter prose narrative "Umierajúce dieťa" was met with reactions that criticized its excessive subjectivity and sentimentality, impulsiveness, and a lack of objectivity. Šoltésová's autobiographical writing is in line with the poetics of women's autobiography as described by feminist scholars in the 1970s. Such texts, situated in the domestic sphere, appeared to be set outside of the grand events of public history that dominated men's autobiographies.

The emphasis on individual identity in Slovak literature has historically been associated with periods when the ideological pressure to privilege collective identity was lifted. In the twentieth century, the exploration of the self was also the focus of the representatives of the Slovak literary "moderna" (the modern school) and interwar writers, who were catching up with the modernizing processes that had already taken place in European literatures in previous decades. The reception of their writing was no longer hampered by ideological obstacles, and, in the pluralist atmosphere described as "opening of the windows" to Europe (a metaphorical term used for the unobstructed absorption of contemporary European artistic, aesthetic, modernist, and later avantgarde trends), writers enjoyed a greater degree of artistic autonomy. Nevertheless, even in interwar literature, the role of the writer as a cultural representative was not questioned but coexisted with the modernist focus on the self. On the one hand, this preoccupation with the self stemmed from the crisis of modern humanity and the relativization of traditional values, and on the other hand, it allowed for the autonomy of the creative subject, capable of transforming reality through art.

In the course of the 1920s and 1930s, a new type of literature emerged, one that privileged the representation of social phenomena over aesthetic qualities. This early form of socially engaged literature eventually evolved into socialist realism after 1948, and the literary representations of the self were once again subjected to ideological pressure, this time of the dogmatically modified Marxism (of Soviet provenance), and individualized identity was suppressed by collective identity determined by class affiliation in schematic literary works that systematically served political imperatives. The self was once again bound with the public sphere and the inexorable march of history. In this context, the apparently timid and measured call for individuality by the twentieth-century literary critic Alexander Matuška at the Writers' Conference of 1952 was in fact quite bold, yet it is impossible to miss the echoes of the previous century's imperative for literature to transcend the self: "We have to solve a difficult dilemma: To be personal and at the same time above personality; to be subjective but move beyond subjectivity; to attach to something outside of the self but remain ourselves ... Subjectivity and individuality mean nothing more, but neither anything less than to personally speak of that, which concerns us all. But in order to speak, I first have to be somebody. And that means that I have to reach the level of this age, both mentally and emotionally, I must know and must feel."[12]

The specific individual, their experience of the world, the private dimension of human life, their authenticity and right to grieve became the slogans of the post-Stalin Thaw, the decade starting in the late 1950s, when literature once again opened to diverse, individualized voices. The very titles of key prose texts of the 1960s such as the collections of short stories by Ján Johanides's *Súkromie* (Privacy, 1963) and Pavel Vilikovský's *Citová výchova v marci* (Sentimental education in March, 1965) or

Rudolf Sloboda's novel *Narcis* (Narcissus, 1965) signal the change. Following 1968, literary representation of the self was once again complicated because normalization and the associated political repression put increased ideological pressures on artists, in some cases sanctioning them and banishing them from public life.

In the second half of the twentieth century, most Slovak autobiographical texts stay connected with pivotal historical events, memories of the Second World War and later the Slovak Uprising. This group of texts included the memoirs by the interwar generation, who were compromised by their political engagement during the period of the wartime Slovak state but rehabilitated during the 1960s. One of the notable exceptions to this trend was Rudolf Sloboda's novel *Narcis*. The novel was the starting point of the writer's autobiographical project that spanned decades and balanced at the boundary of fact and fiction. The inspiration for the novel was Sloboda's own experiences, including dropping out of the university, working as a coal miner in the Ostrava region, and returning home. Whereas Sloboda's early texts conceal their autobiographical origins, his later prose openly abandons the literary pretence of a fictional narrative in favour of open self-revelation. Autobiographical narrative approaches also shape the form of his texts.[13]

In the broader global context, the literary representation of the autonomous subject, or the authentic self, in Slovak literature was complicated by the rise of postmodernism, which questioned the correspondence between language and reality (and therefore also between fact and fiction) and declared that the subject was a linguistic construct. In Slovak literature, these postmodern trends were fully actualized after 1989 and shaped the literature of the 1990s, which represented another phase of unobstructed reflection and reception of contemporary trends among artists liberated from the ideological pressures of the socialist period. Authors who first appeared on the literary scene during this decade avoided references to life experience and enclosed themselves in the text, or in their own problematized subjectivity, which was the result of the "decentering of identity into multiple subject positions."[14]

In the Slovak literature of the 1990s, the postmodern self avoided interactions with the outside world, and any attempt at authentic self-expression was a priori suspect as an untrustworthy repetition of outdated artistic forms. The postmodern self was preoccupied with its own problematized solipsistic subjectivity. The protagonists of Balla's prose published in the early 1990s can serve as examples of this phenomenon. The central theme of Balla's debut collection of stories, *Leptokaria* (1996), is the threatening impact of the everyday, intimately familiar world that leads not only to the disintegration of reality, but also, ultimately, to the physical dissolution of the self.

The narrator of the first story of the book entitled "Infekcia" ("Infection") is unsettled by the furniture in the house that he inherits from his parents. The reason for his anxiety, fears, or terrors is the fact "that it is I, that part of myself, which has through its extended existence in this apartment incarnated into the old, kind, and otherwise certainly innocent furniture."[15] The protagonist sees the destruction of the furniture as the only solution to this crisis. Therefore, the narrator and his friend, who shares his fears and experiences similar delusions, gradually destroy wall paint and haul away carpets, floorboards, and linoleum. The renovation of these furnishings does not provide an escape since the new items are infected with the narrator's existence at an ever-increasing pace. It is the insistence of this existence that ultimately makes it impossible for the protagonist to make any connections with the outside world because he permeates and contaminates the things that surround him, and they turn back on and threaten their originator. The self becomes a source of monstrosity and perpetual anxiety. In his debut, Balla introduces the concept of "dual-selfness" ("die Zweisamkeit"), an extreme form of loneliness, in which the self becomes a monad: "By the way, an attribute of duals-selfness: unitariness. Dual-selfness is also unitariness; unitariness is an attribute of dual-selfness. By the way, another attribute of dual-selfness is, naturally, loneliness."[16]

Despite the "linguistic turn" in the cultural paradigm of postmodernism and its skepsis, which inspired Balla's early writing and the Slovak fiction of the 1990s, anthropological and existential dimensions of autobiographical writing could not be simply pushed to the background. In the postmodern situation and even in its aftermath in the new millennium, autobiographical writing accepted the interplay of and tension between the factual and the fictitious, the authentic and the constructed through the medium of language and linguistic schemes. The concept of autofiction, which was first introduced by the French writer Serge Doubrovsky, challenges established definitions of genre: "An autofictional text purports to be both fictional and autobiographical, and thus represents a paradox in the traditional understanding of genre ... In the age of postmodernity and the media, it is considered one option of self-presentation, one that is mostly adopted by French authors due to its origins in this literary scene marked by specific traditions."[17]

Autofiction gradually became a significant phenomenon in contemporary globalized literature and culture, and Slovak literature followed this trend after 2000. In autofiction, the self represents a "situated subjectivity ... situated in time, in space and corporeal being."[18] This anchoring of the subject in a specific social, historical, and physical time and space is connected with the ambition to "to represent the truth, however subjective it could be,"[19] while also restoring "affect."[20] The post-postmodern subject does not give up in its attempts to formulate its authentic life experience in the world. In the new millennium, such "situated subjectivity" is not merely confined to the limits of individual lives, but also becomes a starting point for reflections on history and for social engagement with urgent contemporary issues. The subject makes such attempts at authentic self-expression despite the awareness that any kind of subjective and individual experience, or, in fact, reality, is filtered through language as a literary medium and can draw on fictional narrative strategies.

THE RETREAT FROM HISTORY

Even before the 1990s, when Slovak literature could freely engage with postmodern trends and their skepticism about the authentic self, preoccupation with subjectivity had been strongly represented in the texts of authors who had produced samizdat or exile literature. This type of autobiographical literature was considered a witness testimony of the resistance against the ideology of the former regime, in which the individual human experience, or existential situation, was confronted with the officially mandated narratives of history. Such moments are present in the autobiographical texts of Dominik Tatarka, Janko Silan, Juraj Špitzer, Albert Marenčin, Ivan Kadlečík, or Martin M. Šimečka.

Some of these texts, however, deviate from the framework of traditional autobiography and bear features of autofiction. In this respect, they overlap with texts written in other circles or in later years. The parallel trend toward autofiction is also evident in the autobiographical writing of Rudolf Sloboda, which was continually published as part of official literature during several decades, from his literary debut

(1965) until his suicide (1995), as well as the prose of Ján Rozner, which could only be published during his lifetime and appeared only in the new millennium.

The affinity of these texts, published in different contexts and under different conditions, is determined not only by common themes and autobiographical writing characteristic of autofiction (fragmentary narratives, generic heterogeneity, repetition of motifs), but also by their shared setting in Bratislava during the second half of the twentieth century. Texts by various authors produced in different circumstances suggestively evoke the same neighbourhoods of Bratislava and its surroundings. They feature some of the same prominent figures of contemporary cultural life, whether the representatives of the official culture that supported the regime such as the literary critic Alexander Matuška and the writer Vladimír Mináč or the members of intellectual circles that fell out of favour with the regime, including Ján Kalina, Agneša Kalinová, Juraj Špitzer, Albert Marenčin, and others.

Existence on the margins of society after a forced retreat from history and under the persecution of the regime, which destroyed the public lives of intellectuals who fell out of favour, intervened in their private lives, and watched their every step, are also the dominant themes of the autobiographical writing of the prominent Slovak writer Dominik Tatarka, who entered the literary scene with existential short stories in the 1940s and became an established writer with his avant-garde novella *Panna Zázračnica* (The miraculous virgin, 1944). Following the Second World War, he subscribed to the ideology of the new regime and wrote several novels that were in line with the mandates of socialist realism. In the late 1950s, he turned into an advocate of political reform, and his literary production returned to existential themes. After 1968, he fell victim to political repression due to his opposition to the Warsaw Pact occupation of Czechoslovakia, could not publish his work, and lived under the surveillance of the secret police. He was one of the few Slovak intellectuals who signed Charter 77 and was connected with the Prague dissident circles.

The autobiographical texts Tatarka wrote while he was side-lined from public and cultural life, ones with particularly complicated paths toward publication, preserved some of the key themes of his earlier work, but radically changed in form and style.[21] These texts were published abroad as a trilogy entitled *Sám proti noci* (Alone against the night, 1984), *Písačky* (Jottings, 1984), and *Listy do večnosti* (Letters into eternity, 1988). The author himself described these texts as "jottings," which highlighted their fragmentary character and generic heterogeneity.[22] As Fedor Matejov points out, the texts consist of "diary entries, memories, notes, amateurish interpretation of dreams, reactions in the form of pamphlets addressed to former writer colleagues and commenting on the social conditions of normalization, mailed and not mailed, and fictitious letters addressed mostly to women."[23] Women, and Tatarka's erotic interactions with them, are at the core of his "jottings." Sexuality, in its sacramental and authentic dimensions, thematized quite openly in the context of the otherwise prudish Slovak literary scene, takes centre stage in Tatarka's life following his banishment from public life. Even this private sphere does not provide a refuge for the writer as an individual because the secret police used female agents to compromise Tatarka. In addition to the themes related to sexuality and politics, Tatarka's "jottings" also explore the memories of his earlier life, particularly of his loved ones, especially his mother, and his childhood and youth in his native region. During the final phase of his life, Tatarka's writing serves as a mode of self-preservation and becomes the only validation of his identity, which the regime had taken away from him, as well as a reminder of the fullness of his life experience in the hostile environment of normalization.

The autobiographical books by Ján Rozner, the novel *Seven Days to the Funeral* (*Sedem dní do pohrebu*, 2009, trans. 2024), the collection of stories "Noc po fronte" ("The night after the front," 2010), and the short narrative *Výlet na Devín* (Trip to Devín, 2011) were written in Munich during the 1970s, after Rozner moved there as an exile in 1977. Even though these texts originated outside of the geographical and temporal sphere of official Slovak literature, Rozner managed to forge a link between the past and the present.[24] On the one hand, his prose depicts the typical fate of a Central European intellectual, whose life unfolds amidst the turmoil of history only to be cast out, forgotten, onto its periphery. In this respect, his texts are related to those of his contemporaries such as Tatarka. On the other hand, they also anticipate the dominant trends of Slovak prose in the new millennium in their use of autofictional elements. Whereas *Seven Days to the Funeral* centres on a private event – the death of a spouse – which was compounded by social circumstances that contributed to its heightened public visibility, "Noc po fronte" and *Výlet na Devín*, which are set between 1935–45, foreground the predicament of the subject amidst of the turbulent historical events of the twentieth century.

Seven Days to the Funeral depicts the seven days of preparation for the funeral of Zora Jesenská, the author's wife, who died of leukemia on 21 December 1972. Both Jesenská and Rozner were publicly known figures. Jesenská was a prolific translator who came from a culturally prominent family; she was a niece of the classic Slovak writer, Janko Jesenský. She gained public attention with her translation of Boris Pasternak's *Doctor Zhivago*, which could be published in Czechoslovakia in 1969 only thanks to the inertia that briefly sustained the process of cultural liberation inaugurated by the Prague Spring. Rozner was the son of a Jewish father and a German mother born in Bratislava. He came from a poor family and due to his origin was threatened with internment during the period of the Slovak state. In the postwar period, he became a leading publicist and literary critic who supported the communist regime, even though he was not a party member. However, partly in response to the suppression of the political reform process, he gradually re-evaluated his position. His marriage to Jesenská, who was thirteen years older, was perceived as a union that bridged a divide, not only because of the age difference between the spouses, but also because of their different social status.

During the 1960s, the couple supported the democratizing and reform processes, and so they were deeply affected by and opposed to the Warsaw Pact invasion. Jesenská participated in a demonstration against the regime, where she fell victim to police brutality. For both spouses, the normalization brought existential problems: They could not work, their names could not be mentioned publicly, and their books and translations were taken out of circulation. These are the reasons why the communist regime used Jesenská's funeral to demonstrate the reach of its power. However, *Seven Days to the Funeral* is not only a witness testimony about the period of normalization and the repressive practices of the communist regime, but also consists of multiple additional layers that reflect the author's personal life and Slovak culture.

The text constitutes a compact whole, with a plot contained in the period of seven days and methodically divided into chapters that count down the time from one event to another, from the wife's passing to her funeral. These seven days also function as a transfer station between two phases of the writer's life and dramatize the process of mourning.

Despite the marked emotional distance and reserve, accentuated by third-person narration, as well as the narrator's obsessive effort to methodically capture every detail, the intimate dimensions of the death of the partner are inextricably tied with the public and social aspects of the event. Rozner's narration is motivated by his effort to reconstruct his own world and life following the departure of the person who gave it meaning: "Many people realised after a long time that they had failed in their own eyes, that they hadn't done what they had set out to do, that was the way of the world, the world was one big nuisance, particularly this narrow world he lived in, he was fed up with it, he had no desire to be some kind of luminary in this world. So he deliberately decided to withdraw into himself, until he shrank into a luminary that was invisible, she was the only one who could still see what he was and that had given his life a purpose, but now those seeing eyes were gone, he was invisible."[25] The story protagonist's desire for marginalization, which is more implied than openly expressed, alternately becomes a refuge and a source of frustration and self-deprecation. In the wake of the political events of 1968, such marginalization becomes a part of both spouses' daily existence and represents a parallel but constantly present theme of Rozner's narrative. After their participation in the lively cultural activity of the past decades, normalization casts the couple out on the periphery, into banal everyday existence, to which they both have to adapt.

Nevertheless, Jesenská's death had implications that reached beyond the private sphere and turned into a public and consequently also a political event. It exposed the stupidity and the brutality of the regime, which persecuted and obstructed individual lives even in extreme life circumstances. In Jesenská's native town, Martin, where the funeral was to take place, her acquaintances were ordered not to attend, and the secret police scrutinized every aspect of the ceremony, including the music that was to be played. The prominent Slovak translator Jozef Felix (who had translated Dante, among others) had to leave his post as a university professor for giving a speech at Jesenská's funeral.

Jesenská's family origin not only affected her relationship with Rozner and put a distance between the couple, but also impacts the preparations for her funeral and turns her death and private mourning into a public event. It violates the intimate aspects of the funeral, makes it impersonal, enforces formal rules, and compels the protagonist to perform tasks that he cannot identify with and comply with "what is proper." When addressing these aspects of the event, the narrator deploys marked irony, which exposes the snobbery, hypocrisy, and provincialism of his environment and confirms the protagonist's peripheral position. The embodiment of this inauthenticity is the death mask, which Jesenská's relatives insist on having produced because to them it represents an expression of social respect toward the memory of the departed. However, given Jesenská's actual social ostracization before her passing, the mask is only a tragicomic payback of what the community is convinced is owed to her. The protagonist realizes all this yet complies with the requests.

The tasks associated with the funeral – the selection of the epitaph, the writing of the obituary, the filling of envelopes, the writing of lists, the bureaucratic obligations (the surrender of the identification document, the arrangement of the death certificate) – function as motifs that trigger a thread of memories. By the same token, they substitute for the funeral rituals of the past and fragment the process of mourning into a series of banal mechanical acts. Ultimately, Rozner analyzes the funeral itself from the perspective of a dramaturg (the author worked as a theatre dramaturg at one point).

The emotional distance, the laconic reflection on one's own psychological state, along with the methodical precision of the account and the accumulation of details, present the only possible forms of remembering for Rozner. He eliminates emotions, rationally evaluates them, and brackets them in order to maintain his focus. That is when he feels relief, just like when he does in the sterile hotel room in Martin, where he spends the night before the funeral. The reliability of this method is only illusory, though. Even though Rozner does not explicitly discuss the process of remembering as a distinct theme, he subtly relativizes it in order to be able to admit, in the conclusion of the novel, the possibility of manipulating memories and being manipulated by them: "His memory was like a sieve, making things up or changing details of things he was trying to recollect ... there was something inside him that was manipulating his own recollections."[26] Passages such as these foreground the autofictional character of Rozner's text, which connects it with several literary texts of the first decades of the new millennium.

A decade later, in the 1980s, Martin M. Šimečka also delivers a testimony on life on the periphery and out of favour with the regime during the period of normalization in *Vojenská knižka* (The military record,

1981), *Výpoveď* (The notice, 1982), *Žabí rok* (*The Year of the Frog*, 1983, trans. 1993), *Džin* (The genie, 1987), and *Záujem* (Interest, 1997). The first four books were initially published by a foreign exile publisher. *Záujem*, which was published by Torst, a Czech publishing house, portrays the reality of life after November 1989 and confirms that the protagonist of the book is not interested in living at the centre of historical events. As the son of the dissident Milan Šimečka, who experienced a fate similar to those of Tatarka and Rozner, the author acutely feels the everyday reality of socialism, which gradually strips him of his youthful ideals. He cannot get an education adequate to his capabilities and makes a living with occasional jobs (stoker, nursing assistant, hardware store salesperson). His prose texts complement his father's reflections on politics and the public sphere. In contrast to his father's focus, Šimečka privileges the private sphere and everyday experience, which are aspects of life that his father ostentatiously neglects in his focus on history. Nevertheless, the public sphere occasionally threatens the younger Šimečka's retreat into privacy, for example, when he is arrested along with his father and also interrogated by the secret police. In moments such as these, the autobiographical protagonist of *The Year of the Frog* realizes that his life does not belong to him, that much of it was predetermined: "The first of the two months that I stole from the State by refusing to work went by, and I saw that the time was not mine at all. It did not belong to me, as I had hoped. I distributed it among others in a way that did not suit me."[27]

His reaction to the deranged and often grotesque times is markedly physical; he finds temporary relief in ascetically pushing his body to the limit of exhaustion by jogging. His disgust with the everyday impositions of the regime is also manifested physically in the form of nausea. The concluding scene of the book symptomatically captures the state of physical disgust by depicting the protagonist venting his frustration caused by a difficult life situation (mind-numbing work, imprisoned father, mother suffering from self-destructive tendencies, partner's ectopic pregnancy, death of his friends' newborn child) during a run, when he discovers that he is trampling on mating frogs:

> A spasm of revulsion yanked me out of my rhythm and threw me high into the air. It forced out of me a desperate yelp that lit the fuse of my remaining energy and drove me sprinting through what became a horrible stretch of the road. For the old foliage turned to

> frogs. As I approached them, the horror concentrated my vision, and I saw big toads, green-brown with immovable eyes, as they lazily hopped along the warm asphalt. This time they were double-headed monsters with goggle eyes, because they had made on that fateful day the decision to mate. Each female toad carried on her back the male, who held on to her like a child ... Then I saw the car. It approached mercilessly. I had no time to close my eyes or stop by ears: there was the slapping sound of popping under the tires and out flew pink entrails as the glued bodies exploded, slippery flesh quivered, and the little tails of intestines stuck to the road.[28]

The last book of the autobiographical series, *Záujem*, is the author's reckoning with "life in history" as well as the euphoria that followed the Velvet Revolution of 1989. Ultimately, Šimečka's autobiographical protagonist is skeptical of his father's utopian ideas about the purpose of history and his son's mission; he views it an assignment that he does not subscribe to: "I am expected to approach life as one great homework. And ... that homework is assigned by him."[29] His distaste for history lingers even after the fall of communism, which opens new opportunities: "I am no hero. I never was one and won't be because I don't have courage to do anything, in my whole life up to this point I have refused to act or speak in any way, and my heroism stems only from my voluntary inaction being mistaken for resistance."[30] The book captures the moment of transition from the fall of communism to "Mečiarism," and the protagonist's existential skepticism does not leave him even when he considers the post-communist reality: "I transferred into another regime and gained new classmates, all intellectuals. We met often, perhaps in the fear that we could dissolve in what we had brought about, freedom, which looked as helpless as clusters of drunks on street corners."[31]

Rudolf Sloboda's early autobiographical prose reflects a similar desire to remain on the periphery and a skeptical perspective on pivotal historical events. The social transformation following 1989 is the focus of his later fiction, particularly the novel *Krv* (Blood, 1991). As Zora Prušková points out, although Sloboda's oeuvre does not explicitly foreground its autobiographical character, it can be read as one "great text" focused on the examination of the author's existence: "The reader thus comes into contact with a specific kind of half-acknowledged autobiography, in which he can decode the didactically motivated pictures of life simultaneously as mystification, ironic self-reflection, but also as an urgent, almost therapeutic erasure of the frustrated experience of existence."[32] It is such blurring of the boundaries between fact and fiction, reality and imagination, as well as the precisely defined anchoring of the writing subject in a concrete time and location and the understanding of writing as an existential activity that once again bring us to the characteristics of autofiction. The author makes the autobiographical foundations of his writing fully visible during the last years of his life, when he repeatedly returns to the concept of memory in various texts. His texts are generically heterogeneous, mediate philosophical reflections in accessible ways, comment on the social situation, banal scenes from family life and his native village, and lyricized memories of his parents and childhood. Sloboda's autobiographical protagonist finds himself in a situation different from the predicament of the writers of the above-mentioned texts; he considers himself a member of the official culture. Nevertheless, he maintains a position of an outsider, a folk sage, who approaches intellectual activity and life itself as a dilettante. His exile is voluntary; he observes events from a frog's-eye view, emphasizes the pettiness of human motives, and grounds high-minded reflections with references to mundane everyday reality. (For example, in his memoir [1996], he immediately follows his reflection on Hegel's philosophy with a reference to the construction of an outhouse.) His confrontation with history, which also impacted the texts of his predecessors and contemporaries, is not as sharply delineated. It resembles Šimečka's pose in his refusal to serve as an agent of history and his emphasis on the abnormality of the environment in which he finds himself. Sloboda's position on the post-1989 social changes is similarly skeptical to Šimečka's: "When the 'elders' exited the scene, the citizens did not know whom they really defeated and what to rejoice over. That is why various individuals tried to muddy the waters, obscure social truths and spread unrest more or less without a cause, if we assume that humans are decent creatures. If we know that humans are animals, it is clear to us that even a case such as the following one is possible: a communist, a chief editor of a prominent journal, joins the journal of the opposition, and is immediately appointed as its associate editor. All hidden human perversions take on public form in these times."[33] Despite an altered social reality, he lives in stagnant times; he remains "a killed man," as he put it in his important novel *Rozum* (Reason, 1982). It is not historical time, the time of great events, but time that in the context of Central European culture the Czech writer and historian Josef Kroutvor describes as provincial time: "Provincial time disintegrates, it is no longer controlled by consciousness. Individual timelines do not correspond with one another; everyone lives their everyday reality. History loses its foundation; life orients itself according to biological rhythm. The arrested time accumulates problems; stores the time not lived in the subconscious. The clash between ahistoricity and everyday reality produces sudden explosions of the imagination, temporal escapes into imaginary events."[34] Such tension among banality, arrested time, and great events stimulates the imagination and provides one of the essential sources of Sloboda's autobiographical writing.

THE RECOVERY OF THE SELF IN CONTEMPORARY LITERATURE

One of the most prominent features of contemporary Slovak literature is the recovery of the subject – the self, which significantly shapes the fictional worlds of individual literary texts. The problems associated with personal identity – its continual definition and affirmation – become a central theme in Slovak prose of the new millennium. The attention given to individual identity also manifests in the genre forms that harken back to classical literature, especially in the prose of the youngest generation. Their writing draws on the elements of the Bildungsroman, and occasionally takes on the form of the novel of disillusionment (novel of "lost illusions"). It is precisely this egocentric aspect of contemporary Slovak literature, which has enabled Slovak authors to formulate concepts of reality, reconstruct the outlines of their perceived life experiences. They return to the theme of history through narratives in which the march of history fatally impacts personal lives, while abandoning any principles of objectivity.

The principal stage for the appearance of the recovered self is autofiction, which takes on heterogeneous forms, ranging from fragmentary notes or simulated journal entries to structured narratives, in which we can identify features of various subgenres including the historical novel, the social novel, or the family saga. These autofictions focus on intimate aspects of life, aim at the reconstruction of life experiences, recover worlds that have been irretrievably lost in the past. These are the characteristic features of, for example, Etela Farkašová's novel *Stalo sa* (It happened, 2005), an autobiographical record of the writer's mother's death, Jaroslava Blažková's *Happyendy* (Happyends, 2005), or the memoir-style fiction in Pavel Vilikovský's prose collection *Čarovný papagáj a iné gýče* (The magical parrot and other kitsch, 2005). Vilikovský imports the questions about the possibility of authenticity, genuine emotion, and spontaneity from the postmodern phase of his work into the new millennium, but his newer work becomes significantly less skeptical. In the short stories included in the above-mentioned collection entitled "Gašpar, Melichar, Baltazárová" (Gaspar, Melchior, and Ms Balthasar) and "Pán spomienok" (The master of memories), in which he writes about his father, foreground the central motif of autofiction, the unreliability of memory. The narrator accepts its unreliability, and the memories, even though they may be invented, of dead family members or places that have vanished provide an escape from the troubling and hostile present and offer a degree of satisfaction.

The narrative features of autofiction are also evident in the recent prose of Alta Vášová. Her book *Ostrovy nepamäti* (Islands of unforgetting, 2008) uses fragmentary texts to reconstruct a family history and empathetically parallels the author's own life situations with the destiny of the Czech writer Božena Němcová. The fragments of memories and events in the text are patched together without regard for chronology; they become layered, shifting, and mutually illuminating, even while the outside world is dramatically changing all around. In Vášová's book, memory originates like landmasses by sedimentation of memory layers, but it never stagnates and is ever shifting and subject to entropic change, which leads the author to skeptically describe the process as "unforgetting." The book focuses on self-examination, allows the writer to retreat into peaceful solitude and explore the world and especially herself from that vantage point. Solitude, Vášová's privileged theme, becomes a space of freedom and true independence. It allows the narrator to leave things unsaid and remain invisible.

The autobiographical book by the poet Mila Haugová, *Zrkadlo dovnútra* (Inward mirror, 2009), also stems from focused introspection motivated by the effort to "take possession of one's life:" "I will attempt to create a text out of the interconnected fragments of my life, a text that would aim its unique beam to illuminate it, along with, in the background or in the foreground, my contemporaries and the world that I've been a part of."[35] The title itself, "Inward mirror," forecasts the author's premise in the first chapter of her book, which carefully outlines her methodology: "These are going to be subjective memoirs. Subjective writing, stories, photographs, documents, and subjective interpretation."[36] Haugová's autobiography does not lose sight of history or external reality, but they interest her only as far as they impact her own life, especially through the arrest of her father for political reasons in the 1950s. By the same token, the author declares her goal to reconstruct a whole and recreate it "from individual fragments."[37]

Haugová does not question the possibility of accessing or reconstructing one's own identity or affirming one's self, nor does she foreground the self as a construct.[38] Right at the beginning she rigorously asserts: "Writing, my writing, has always been a self-preserving activity for me."[39] By writing about herself, Haugová achieves separation, objectification, and ultimately alienation of her identity: "And now suddenly one more building, an autobiography ... What is it that I am really building now? A house. One more house? But I won't live in it, I build it so that I can separate yet another house from myself. To the extent that it becomes a new reality. A different life."[40] Autobiography thus lays bare the labour involved in the reconstruction of one's identity and its significant elements of performativity. Haugová's remarkable, at times almost non-literary methodical approach highlights the aspect of autobiography that has characterized the genre since the era of Romanticism, which is "curiosity about one's own self."[41]

A strong autobiographical subject is also at the centre of the generically heterogeneous books of Veronika Šikulová. Her autobiographical writing continually probes intimate family relationships with her father (an influential writer of the second half of the twentieth century Vincent Šikula), her mother, partner, and children. Starting with brief and fragmentary forms such as lyrical sketches and short stories, she moves toward larger, more focused narratives such as her novel *Miesta v sieti* (Dwellings in a web, 2011) or *Medzerový plod* (Foulbrood, 2014). In the first book, the destinies of three women in one family of Slovak-Hungarian origin (a grandmother, mother, and daughter) intersect with the historical events of the twentieth century. The second book focuses on the illness and death of the protagonist's mother.

The epicentre of Šikulová's prose is the specifically delimited space of home, not only in the topographical but also in the intimate sense of word, as an object of everlasting nostalgic longing, even in texts set in the larger world, whether it is France or the United States. In Šikulová's writing, the source of values stems from the past, the world of her childhood, which is idyllic and quite perfect. The tension between the present, in which Šikulová's protagonist, passing from book to book, is an adult woman, a mother, and a wife, and the past, in which she was a carefree child surrounded with loving parents, grandparents, and extended family, functions as the central theme of her prose. The protagonist laments the passage of time, in which the familiar world gradually shrinks and vanishes, leaving only the frustrating and disillusioned present, the prosaic world of obligations.

This motif is also quite pronounced in the book *Medzerový plod*, which depicts the terminal illness of the narrator's mother. The title, "foulbrood," is a term that describes a symptom of an infection of a bee colony that leads to its demise. The mother's terminal illness confirms the final extinction of the narrator's intimately familiar world caused by the departure of her loved ones: "Her house, hive, was struck by a plague ... The garden has deteriorated; only birds fly over it like petals. Clinical finding: She is a foreigner in the world."[42] The stream of free associations continually oscillates between two forms of the protagonist's world. There is the hostile world of the present, the space in which she is overcome by anxiety, in which she does not understand her husband and his strange hobbies (accumulation of boxes, detachment from his family), the world, that is "strange," full of "trouble," a world devoid of fragrance and colour, without childhood magic: "The household of our heroine is somehow strange. The scents have faded ... Also, her husband is strange. Recently he has been bringing boxes home. He has always collected boxes, but now his obsession with paper boxes borders on passion."[43] In this world, the heroine is a stranger, she cannot relate to her grown-up role of a woman, wife, mother. In contrast with the hostile present, there is the colourful world of the past, the time of her childhood, when she was a daughter, a companion in childhood games, a rebellious girl. The narration almost manically recalls all characteristics of that "lost time," when an ordinary day was filled with magical details and adventures, and even family harmony:

> Since she was a child, she had always somewhat idealized the world that surrounded her, the sun, the night sky, the moon, which grows and shrinks like a bubble from a bubble ring, the stars shining in the

> sky, fragrant flowers in the garden with beautiful names and colors, trees growing upward and deep into the earth, their crowns similar to temples full of heavenly birds, the earth inhabited with millions of organisms covered with fur or feathers, good and kind, taking care of their sweet and playful young, beautiful smooth stones, which, when split, sometimes glittered like the precious stones in mother's rings and the fairytales that their parents read to her and her sister … a world in which mom and dad loved each other, joked together in the kitchen, in which dad sat at the piano and sang loudly, in which mother sat by her sewing machine, with in which she could instantly conjure a piece that looked like it had come from Paris.[44]

Šikulová's narrator does not depict her past as tied with great historical events, with social movements, despite her assertion that "the last century, with its war and the socialist era, is very familiar to her. She feels that she has arisen from it, and it is only ending now, which somewhat extends her age."[45] The narration is dominated by exclusively subjective, even intimate aspects of the past, and the era before 1989 is represented as an idyllic time of her childhood and coming of age, without any disruptive impact of the regime. She takes a similar position toward the present; the hostility of adult life is associated with the hostility of her surroundings, whether at home ("She returned home. She did not like the evenings in the kitchen, the dim, weak, and unfriendly light from the economical bulb, potato peels on the counter, potatoes in the pot, unfinished on the plate, she is boiling the water from them in the pot")[46] or in public ("Today's stage sets disgust her. Everywhere, even in galleries and churches, she senses hypocrisy and pretense").[47] Šikulová's autobiographical protagonist seeks refuge from the reality of adulthood in the private sphere: in domestic work, cooking, gardening, and care for loved ones. For her, these are not banal and routine acts; they function as rituals, which she uses to preserve the continuity of family memory and prove her worth to her ancestors: "She was afraid that mother would die and leave her in the world alone, that her world would shrink, sadden, that she won't have anyone to obey, to whom to show that she is good, that she can and does take care of her children well, that she can dress nicely, that she writes books and can entertain and please those around her. Someone else may consider her obedience and desire to remain a daughter a lack of freedom, but she felt good, and took this for a joyful sign of the immortality of our essence."[48] Šikulová's writing itself – extroverted, insistent, associative, at times too loud, too full of lyrical reflection and hedonistic celebration of the private sphere – functions as a form of defence against shrinking, dissolution, mortality – the "plague" that inevitably reaches every human life.

THE TRANSFORMATIONS OF THE IRONIC SELF AFTER POSTMODERNISM

The transformation of the representations of the self is also evident among authors who do not explicitly claim to write autobiographically, even though autobiographical elements appear in their writing. In texts by the key representatives of Slovak postmodernism such as Pavel Vilkovský, Peter Pišťanek, Balla, and Peter Macsovszky, who characteristically filter reality, tradition, and language through the lens of irony, the shift toward modification of perennial themes and increased subjectivity is evident. Peter Macsovszky's novel *Making Skeletons Dance* (*Mykať kostlivcami*, 2010, trans. 2024) is an interesting example of this trend. During the 1990s, the writer's poetry inaugurated the poetics of "sterility," which explored the potential of language and poetry (a type of meta-poetry). In contrast, his novel is a quasi-modernist return to existential themes and belongs to the genre of the "book of the father" (also present in Hungarian literature).

With ostentatious misanthropic gestures, Macsovszky exposes absurdity and mortality as the only certainty in the absence of any other integrating purpose. Any attempts to evade or deny this reality is presented as a lie, illusion, or simply folly. He not only returns to the modernist and avant-garde moments of the first half of the twentieth century, but also points to the central theme of contemporary prose, the so-called myth of the novel. The starting point for Macsovszky's obsessive, insistent exploration is an archetype of the father, primarily a literal father in the biological sense and symbolically a father as a figure that represents "the way of the world" and, therefore, a propagator of deceit and lies, against whom the sons rebel and whom they denounce.

Emotional connection and engagement are currently the central themes of even writers such as Balla, who in the 1990s introduced a combination of the grotesque absurdity and ironic distance in his fiction. In Balla's novel *Veľká láska* (*Big Love*, 2015, trans. 2019), the protagonist fails to establish a relationship with his partner and weighs their capacity to connect with others. The result is a consciousness of loss and melancholy. Like his postmodern precursors, Balla's protagonist Andrič remains isolated and fails to connect with the outside world, and like, other men, is "not really aware of most things or events, but simply make[s] them up, relying on misinterpreted allusions and superficial observations, but has no way to understand the way of the world and the rules that govern it."[49] However, in contrast with Balla's postmodern protagonist, he acknowledges his longing for authenticity, fulfillment, and closure, for participating in "a human story with twists and turns and a cathartic ending."[50]

In the novel *In the Name of the Father* (*V mene otca*, 2011, trans. 2017), Balla transcends the limits of tortured subjectivity and focuses on an analysis of family relations. Family ties are marked by permanent feelings of guilt, failure, and inadequacy. Sons hate their fathers and disappoint their mothers; fathers are indifferent to their sons; husbands cheat on their wives. The reasons for starting a family are rooted in human stupidity, habit, or hypocrisy. The constant features of Balla's fictional world include egotism, extreme loneliness, alienation, disgust with life, or crushing banality of everyday existence inflected by the atmosphere of a specific district town in southern Slovakia. This location is one of the autobiographical signals of the novel because it depicts the author's native town of Nové Zámky, including specific street names. The motto of the book is an excerpt from the permit for the construction of a specific family home from 1967. The protagonist's son, just like the author, is an office worker and a writer.

The title can be interpreted on several levels. One of them consists of the memories of the protagonist, the first-person narrator, the father and the husband, which are presented as fragments of past events, fantasies, or even old dreams and given equal weight in the narrative. Balla's protagonist is convinced of his own superiority and authority. He is a predator, an alpha male, and the only person in his community not capable of pretending that he cares about anyone else but himself. He considers emotional expression a weakness. The power of this provincial predator over others is based on the consciousness that he is a part of a larger plan and associated with a higher power that is embedded in the concrete foundations of his detached family house.

The narrator wants to deploy the special power of his house as an instrument of domination that keeps the inhabitants of the town apathetic and resigned. Under the concrete of his cellar grows the sacred tree of the ancient Germans *yggrasil* and springs the well *hwegelmir*. A living current flows through the walls. Like Balla's earlier story, "Infection," the house does not become a family nest, a symbol of shared intimacy, but a monstrous space representing the futility of life, alienation, threat, and even destruction. As the narrative progresses, it becomes evident that the protagonist's life is also ultimately banal and a waste of time, and thus will become a part of the great forgetting and vanishing that is the inevitable fate of all, and "everything that once was has now vanished, evaporated, gone."[51] This recognition culminates in the last part of the book, when the protagonist discovers that the effect of the house had been eliminated by the mysterious builder. Therefore, the narration of the father, initially intended to demonstrate power over others, gradually disintegrates and all that is left is an "everyman," a retired salesclerk, who is trying to cover up his failures and losses.

This ultimately raises the question of the narrator's identity. It could be the protagonist's younger son, who is a writer and who, as the title indicates, addresses the reader "in the name of the father." The father is mirrored in his son, just like the son is mirrored in his father: "I wasn't aware of being observed. But my younger son had been observing me. And that is one of the reasons he began to hate me. Mind you, he would have ended up hating anyone if he had observed them for long enough."[52] It is symptomatic that in the emotionally intense passage that depicts the scene of the mother's death in the novel, the voices of the characters, the father and the son, merge because they articulate a common failure, which was the abandonment of the mother and the wife. However, the son who creates the father's portrait also becomes his judge. At the level of the book that refers to the Christian prayer, the novel's critique is aimed not only at a specific father, but also at the father as a symbolic figure representing divine authority, a representative of the patriarchal order. At the end of the book, all that is left is a tired, worn out, and resigned old man, whose life has been reduced to "fragments, cliffs looming up from the grey sea of oblivion."[53] Balla's narration manifests a continual desire for a higher meaning in life and close connections with loved ones: "After all, I tried for a long time to reach a state of finality. Now even the imperfections have become perfect and final."[54] This aspiration is evident in the scene, in which the protagonist's younger son sits on the bedside of his dying mother: "As he sat by her bedside with his head in his hands he suddenly saw his mother's face crumbling into another that seemed more truthful and convincing, eventually turning into the maternal face that he'd sought in vain in his mother's visage ever since he was a small child, this face now rose to the surface, engulfing the previous face and displaying a surprising presence of mind, in the circumstances unexpected, even suspicious."[55] The melancholy of Balla's protagonists, their desire for what seems unreachable, their feelings of loss, themes that also appear in the writing of other former postmodern proponents of irony, are reminiscent of an older form of irony, which surprisingly returns in the post-postmodern situation. This is Romantic irony, as Hegel described it in *Aesthetics*. Just like the subjects of Romantic irony, the protagonists of these texts rely on their excessive individualism, the focused egocentrism that requires the casting off of all ties. On the one hand, their "craving for the solid and the substantial ... does want to penetrate into truth and long for objectivity, but, on the other hand, cannot renounce [their] isolation."[56]

CONCLUSION

The literary representations of the self and the manifestations of individualism and subjectivity in Slovak literature had been determined by ideological pressure and became more pronounced only during brief periods when social and political restrictions were temporarily lifted. The writers of the National Awakening emphasized collective national identity, and the developments following 1945 shifted Slovak writers' focus to class identity. Therefore, in the Slovak context, the literary self was harnessed by the march of history, which filtered individual and private elements of literature through collective imperatives. Autobiographical women's writing was the exception, since the lives of women were defined by the private domestic sphere and by family relations.

Existence on the periphery, whether voluntary or enforced by political power, occasionally made it possible for writers to focus on the subject, on authentic and individual human experience, which was situated in opposition to faceless power structures. Following 1989, the death of the subject proclaimed by postmodernist theorists once again marginalized any preoccupation with individual identity and its literary representation. Since the start of the new millennium, the self and the subjective perspective have once again shaped the fictional worlds of contemporary Slovak literature in conjunction with global literary trends.

Issues associated with identity – its continual redefinition and affirmation – become a central and dominant theme in Slovak prose after 2000. Subjective perspectives filtered through the optics of gender, social class, or regional identity are characteristic of literary representations of the present and privileged over other narrative approaches. In the most recent book by Ivana Dobrakovová, the novel *Pod slnkom Turína* (Under the sun of Turin, 2021), the narrator concludes: "It was a centripetal movement: I was gradually moving further inside, enclosing myself … I was preoccupied by my internal monologue, which was occasionally interspersed with voices."[57] This quotation captures the characteristic approach to narration in most contemporary Slovak prose: the surrounding world permeates the text only to the extent to which the dominant subject, who does not even attempt objectivity, allows. Vladimír Barborík observes that "the self as the center of the fictional world" simultaneously becomes its "unbreachable boundary."[58] Barborík points out the marked absence of the authorial narrator from "the artistically more ambitious" contemporary Slovak prose, which ultimately also leads to the disappearance of "the tools for the construction, naming, and analysis of a broader, socially defined reality, the reality of relationships that extend beyond the limited perspective of the individual."[59] It therefore appears that after decades of the marginalization of the self and the privileging of objectivity, contemporary Slovak literature finds itself in a situation of hegemonic subjectivity, which filters the world through a strictly delimited self. The question that remains is whether such pervasive subjectivity will eventually create a demand for literature about people and the world beyond the self.

NOTES

1 Dohnány, *Listy a denníky*, 135.

2 "For a long time, up until the 1960s, autobiographies had been considered as a sort of historiographical writing, as texts that are 'true' or at least 'truthful' reports of a person's life. Since these life reports are written by the very person who has lived this life him or herself, autobiographies were often read as 'authentic' descriptions of what had really happened. This understanding of autobiography goes along with biographical readings of literary texts in general that are still being practiced, especially by nonprofessional readers, today." See Wagner-Egelhaaf, "Introduction: Autobiography/Autofiction across Disciplines," 1.

3 "Autobiography is more than just a literary genre – if it is a genre at all. Its manifold aspects, which have been discussed by literary scholars from the nineteenth century up to the present day, are closely connected with the core features of literature itself." Ibid.

4 Macura, *Znamení zrodu*, 206.

5 Hurban, "Básne Karla Sabinu," 102.

6 For example, the memoirs by the leading figures of the National Awakening: Ján Kollár and Ján Francisci.

7 Marcus, *Auto/biographical discourses*, 11–55.

8 The text was originally serialized in the journal *Slovenské pohľady* under the title "Môj vlastný život" (My own life) in 1911–15.

9 As Marcus shows, the parallel privileged subjects in the British context were professional men, who replaced the function of the model lives of the saints. Ibid., 26.

10 "Women are more often linked to unassuming and artless form of personal writing, neither needing or being capable of the self-vindication of public man." Ibid., 47. Barbara Johnson's "My Monster/My Self" also addressed the problem of legitimacy in nineteenth-century women's autobiographical writing: "The problem for the female autobiographer is, on the one hand, to resist the pressure of masculine autobiography as the only literary genre available for her enterprise, and, on the other, to describe a difficulty in conforming to a female ideal which is largely a fantasy of the masculine, not the feminine, imagination" (Johnson, "My Monster/My Self," 10).

11 The subtitle of E.M. Šoltésová's "Umierajúce dieťa" ("The dying child") introduces "Úryvky z denníka matky" ("Fragments from a mother's journal"), which clearly shows that the author bases her authority for publishing her autobiographical and intimate text from her identity as a mother, or identity that is not self-centred, but determined by her relationship with another, her child. The same strategy is evident in the writing of her friend, Terézia Vansová, who did not directly depict her life, but inscribed her autobiographical text into the biographies of her loved ones, her mother (*Terézia Medvedecká*, 1900) and husband (*Ján Vansa*, 1926–27, in journal form under the title *Môj muž*/My husband).

12 Matuška, *Za a proti*, 451.

13 See Prušková, *Rudolf Sloboda*, 15.

14 Leitch, *Literary Criticism*, 22.

15 Balla, *Leptokaria*, 6.

16 Ibid., 23.

17 Gronemann, "Autofiction," 241
18 Gibbons, "Contemporary Autofiction," 130.
19 Ibid., 118.
20 Ibid., 130.
21 Tatarka texts were prepared for publication in exile by the historian Ján Mlynárik. The trilogy that he edited, *Sám proti noci* (1984) a *Písačky* (1984), *Listy do večnosti* (1988), is accepted in current publishing practice as an authoritative presentation of Tatarka's "jottings," even though with some critical commentary. Tatarka's final book *Navrávačky* (Recordings, published in samizdat in 1987, in exile in 1988), originated from a transcription of recorded interviews with the author. For more on this text, see Sabatos, "Can the Dissident Speak?"
22 Michaela Jurovská points out the parallels between Tatarka's writing and the concept of autofiction (Jurovská, "Písačky Dominika Tatarku alebo O slobode," 238).
23 Matejov, *Lektúry*, 217.
24 Only a few of Rozner's texts were published during his lifetime, as for example a chapter from the novel *Seven Days to the Funeral* in 1989 in the exile journal *Listy* published in Rome.
25 Rozner, *Seven Days to the Funeral*, 53–4.
26 Ibid., 416.
27 Šimečka, *The Year of the Frog*, 85.
28 Ibid., 159.
29 Šimečka, *Záujem*, 58.
30 Ibid., 88.
31 Ibid., 113.
32 Prušková, *Rudolf Sloboda*, 11, 13.
33 Sloboda, *Krv*, 71–2.
34 Kroutvor, *Potíže s dějinami*, 72.
35 Haugová, *Zrkadlo dovnútra*, 10.
36 Ibid., 9.
37 Ibid.
38 "Autobiography as my finger pointing at myself." Ibid., 11.
39 Haugová, *Zrkadlo dovnútra*, 9.
40 Ibid., 54.
41 Müller-Funk, "Rod jako narativní konstrukce identity," 59.
42 Šikulová, *Medzerový plod*, 199.
43 Ibid., 15.

44 Ibid., 44.
45 Ibid., 45.
46 Ibid., 43.
47 Ibid., 47.
48 Ibid., 49.
49 Balla, *Big Love*, 26.
50 Ibid., 26.
51 Balla, *In the Name of the Father*, 24.
52 Ibid., 18.
53 Ibid., 88.
54 Ibid., 83.
55 Ibid., 82.
56 "The next form of this negativity of irony is, on the one hand, the vanity of everything factual, moral, and of intrinsic worth, the nullity of everything objective and absolutely valid. If the ego remains at this standpoint, everything appears to it as null and vain, except its own subjectivity, which therefore becomes hollow and empty and itself mere vanity. But, on the other hand, the ego may, contrariwise, fail to find satisfaction in this self-enjoyment and instead become inadequate to itself, so that it now feels a craving for the solid and the substantial, for specific and essential interests. Out of this comes misfortune, and the contradiction that, on the one hand, the subject does want to penetrate into truth and long for objectivity, but, on the other hand, cannot renounce his isolation and withdrawal into himself or tear himself free from this unsatisfied abstract inwardness." Hegel, *Aesthetics*, 66.
57 Dobrakovová, *Pod slnkom Turína*, 55.
58 Barborík, "Ja: jedna (jediná?) podoba súčasnej prózy," 50.
59 Ibid., 55.

BIBLIOGRAPHY

Balla. *Leptokaria*. Levice: L.C.A, 2000.

– *Big Love*. Translated by Julia Sherwood and Peter Sherwood. London: Jantar Publishing, 2019.

– *In the Name of the Father*. Translated by Julia Sherwood and Peter Sherwood. London: Jantar Publishing, 2017.

Barborík, Vladimír. "Ja: jedna (jediná?) podoba súčasnej prózy: (Kepplová – Kopcsay – Modrovich – Piussi – Rosová)." *Romboid: literatúra / umelecká komunikácia* 47, no. 7 (2012): 50–5.

Dobrakovová, Ivana. *Pod slnkom Turína*. Bratislava: PT Marenčin, 2021.
Dohnány, Mikuláš. *Listy a denníky Mikuláša Dohnányho*. Edited by Rudolf Chmel. Martin: Matica slovenská, 1971.
Gibbons, Alison. "Contemporary Autofiction and Metamodern Affect." In *Metamodernism: Historicity, Affect and Depth after Postmodernism*, edited by Robin Van Den Akker, Alison Gibbons, and Timotheus Vermeulen, 117–30. London, New York: Rowman Littlefield, 2017.
Gronemann, Claudia. "Autofiction." In *Handbook of Autobiography/Autofiction*. Edited by Martina Wagner-Egelhaaf, 241–6. Boston, Berlin: De Gruyter, 2018.
Haugová, Mila. *Zrkadlo dovnútra*. Bratislava: Koloman Kertész Bagala, 2009.
Hegel, Georg Wilhelm Friedrich. *Aesthetics: Lectures on Fine Art*. Vol 1. Translated by T.M. Knox. New York: Oxford University Press, 1975.
Hurban, Jozef Miloslav. "Básne Karla Sabinu." *Tatranka* 2, no. 1 (1841): 102.
Kroutvor, Josef. *Potíže s dějinami*. Praha: Prostor, 1990.
Johnson, Barbara. "My Monster/My Self." *Diacritics* 12 (Summer 1992): 2–10.
Jurovská, Michaela. "Písačky Dominika Tatarku alebo O slobode." In Dominik Tatarka, *Písačky pre milovanú Lutéciu*, 233–51. Bratislava: LIC, 2013.
Leitch, Vincent B. *Literary Criticism in the 21st Century*. London, New York: Bloomsbury Academic, 2014.
Macsovszky, Peter. *Mykať kostlivcami*. Bratislava: Drewo a srd, 2010.
Macura, Vladimír. *Znamení zrodu*. Praha: H&H, 1995.
Marcus, Laura. *Auto/biographical Discourses: Theory. Criticism. Practice*. Manchester and New York: Manchester University Press, 1994.
Matejov, Fedor. *Lektúry*. Bratislava: Slovak Academic Press, 2005.
Matuška, Alexander. *Za a proti*. Bratislava: 1975.
Müller-Funk, Wolfgang. "Rod jako narativní konstrukce identity." *Aluze* 14, no. 2 (2010): 59–69.
Prušková, Zora. *Rudolf Sloboda*. Bratislava: Kalligram, 2001.
Rozner, Ján. *Seven Days to the Funeral*. Translated by Julia Sherwood and Peter Sherwood. Prague: Karolinum Press, 2024.
Sabatos, Charles. "Can the Dissident Speak? The Czech Woman Writer in the Work of Roth and Tatarka." *World Literature Studies* 9, no. 4 (2017): 74–88.
Šidák, Pavel. "Pojem 'modus' a genologická taxonomie." In Matěj Antoš, Petr Hrtánek: *Přízraky a masky. Gotický modus v české postmoderní próze*, 16–44. Ostrava: Ostravská univerzita, 2017.

Šikulová, Veronika. *Medzerový plod*. Bratislava: Slovart, 2014.

Šimečka, Martin M. *Záujem*. Praha: Torst, 1997.

– *The Year of the Frog*. Translated by Peter Petro. New York: Simon & Schuster, 1996.

Vajanský, Svetozár Hurban. "Verše Janka Jesenského." *Národnie noviny* 36, no. 66, 67 (1905): 3–4.

Wagner-Egelhaaf, Martina. "Introduction: Autobiography/Autofiction across Disciplines." In *Handbook of Autobiography/Autofiction*, edited by Martina Wagner-Egelhaaf, 1–18. Boston, Berlin: De Gruyter, 2018.

CHAPTER FOUR

History and Memory: Rewriting the Past

Zora Prušková

In the new millennium, the increasing distance from Slovakia's turbulent twentieth-century history has led to reflection on its significance in various spheres of cultural life, including literature. Writers of the generation that grew up during the Cold War era but reached adulthood in a more democratic and open society move away from the ideologically driven and apparently objective historical fiction of the socialist era to the exploration of subjective experience in Slovakia's history, often with a particular focus on the controversial era of the Second World War Slovak state. Their historical fiction raises questions about the role of human psychology, empathy, social cohesion, and value systems in historical processes.

The revolutionary change that followed 1989 opened the space for writing about history through the lens of personal memory and autobiography. Reflective memory did not play a prominent role in the historical fiction of the 1990s, perhaps because the generation of writers that were entering the literary scene during this decade did not yet have sufficient distance from, or time to reflect on, the events of the twentieth century.[1] The new millennium registered a shift toward experimentation with genres and points of view in historical fiction. Free of the mandate to adhere to a particular version of history, post-millennial Slovak historical fiction calls attention to memory as a construct. The novels explore narratives that challenge official histories and had been suppressed in Slovak literature as well as alternative ways of translating memory into narrative. The French philosopher and anthropologist Maurice Merleau-Ponty emphasizes that memory involves a relationship between preservation and forgetting:

> The problem of memory is at dead end as long as we hesitate between memory as preservation and memory as construction. We will always be able to show that consciousness finds in its "representations" only what it has put into them, that memory is thus construction – and that, however, behind the construction there must be another memory which evaluates the products of the first, a past given gratuitously and in inverse ratio to our voluntary memory ... Then there would not be this alternative between preservation and construction. Memory would not be the opposite of forgetting, for we would see that true memory is found at the intersection of the two ... We would see that explicit recollection and forgetting are two modes of our oblique relation with a past that is present to us only through the determinate emptiness that it leaves in us.[2]

Transcribed in literary form, the past is a construction in the sense suggested by Merleau-Ponty, one in which the story of individual characters reflects the collective consciousness of a shared experience. Such a construction is not always verifiable with reference to historical facts. Historical fiction does not aim at an explanation but rather at an understanding, approximation, and preservation of the historical event in a state of balanced entropy. In the process of transcribing memory, the past is as unfamiliar as the future. Given this dual ontological nature of historical fiction, the clearest indicator of its true nature is the choice of genre, which reflects the authors' values as well as the degree of their aesthetical inventiveness or unproductive mannerism.

The tendency to rewrite history through the perspective of individual subjects, whose interpretations of events may expose the unreliability and instability of official histories, stems from the re-evaluation that took place in Slovak historiography following 1989, which foregrounded the importance of generational memory. For example, one of the leading historians involved in this process, Ľubomír Lipták (1930–2003), who had been excluded from public life because his interpretation of Slovak history did not correspond with the philosophical principles of Marxism-Leninism, prefaced the second edition of his magisterial *Slovakia in the Twentieth Century* (1968, 1998) with a reflection on the historical position of his own generation:

> I would be gratified if this book did not only provide readers with an account of Slovakia in the twentieth century, but also serve as a witness statement of one generation, or at least a part of it. It was the second generation that was educated in their mother tongue after 1918 and entered a more modern and urban society. It was born in a parliamentary democracy but spent most of its life under dictatorships. It survived seven major political, state, and ideological takeovers and regime changes, and it was liberated several times ... Defeats and victories are so intertwined in its experience that it is sometimes hard to differentiate one from the other. In this respect it is a genuine, typical part of Slovakia's twentieth-century history.[3]

Lipták's reflection on his generation's role in the events of the twentieth century, which acknowledges that history is always written from a particular vantage point, is an important rhetorical move informed by poststructuralism, one that anticipates the development of contemporary Slovak historical fiction and its treatment of generational memory. The historian's foregrounding of the subjective perspective on historical processes also opens opportunities for rewriting events from the perspective of the succeeding generation. Departing from the ideologically rigid Marxist interpretation of history as a reflection of class struggle, Lipták's book presents Slovak history in a dynamic way, as an interplay of simultaneous forces, and highlights regional differences in the experience of events, particularly the Second World War.

Contemporary Slovak historical fiction reflects this shift in historiography in its experimentation with narrative structure and perspective. Lipták's interest in the local or regional experience of history pioneered a renewed focus on the paradox of the history of small nations among the intellectuals of the succeeding generation. For example, the Slovak philosopher František Novosád's article "Smaller Nations" (2019) traces the importance of culture for small nations that had to struggle for statehood and traces their efforts to legitimize their existence through culture rooted in folk traditions to the work of the German thinkers Herder and Hegel.[4] The rewriting of history, which even in an open society involves a degree of selection, with some events foregrounded and others omitted or suppressed, is inflected by the smallness of Slovakia, which, as I show in the following analysis, puts particular pressure on balancing individual experience and collective history.

The interest in the role of subjective experience in the rewriting of history has opened possibilities for Slovak literature to play an increasingly important role in this process since 1989. There were some signs of the focus on subjective history in the 1970 and 1980s, a period that provided opportunities for using the historical narrative as an instrument for increasing public consciousness of important historical events. This mandate meant that writers were granted a degree of creative freedom, as long as they adhered to the ideologically prescribed format of historical writing. The main condition was that personal testimony was not to be foregrounded, and, therefore, any elements associated with personal history had to align with the ideologically privileged connection with broader social and historical forces. Personal histories were in the background of these novels and provided a source of inspiration but were never conveyed in the form of subjective accounts. The opportunities to filter memory through emotional experiences, including trauma, were not acceptable because they did not follow the official mandate to approach history selectively or fit the expectation of straightforward accounts. Despite these restrictions, Slovak historical fiction included some significant deviations from the rules, which signalled the great aesthetic potential of memoir writing.

Some examples of this approach produced successful historical fiction during the 1970s and 1980s. Family sagas like Peter Jaroš's *Tisícročná včela* (Millennial bee, 1979, film adaptation 1983) and Vincent Šikula's trilogy *Majstri* (Masters, 1976), *Muškát* (Geranium, 1976), *Vilma* (1979) confronted the collective memory of historical events with their subjective interpretations. The publication of Šikula's trilogy was followed by a debate that was one of the few culturally productive events in the literary life of that period.[5] Ladislav Ballek's *Pomocník* (The assistant, 1979), which depicted the rise and fall of a small-town butcher during the postwar period, also deviated from the established norms of historical fiction by filtering controversial events through a subjective perspective. This work built on Ballek's locally focused, emotionally inflected, and innovatively structured collection *Južná Pošta* (Southern mail, 1979), which was followed by the genre collage *Agáty* (Acacias, 1981).[6]

Contemporary Slovak historical fiction varies in its approaches to reimagining the past, but most of the writers tend to use archival sources in their rewriting of history after 2000. Several historical novels have been popular among readers, including Pavol Rankov's *It Happened on the First of September (or Some Other Time)* (*Stalo sa prvého septembra (alebo inokedy)*, 2008, trans. 2020) and *Matky* (Mothers, 2011), Silvester Lavrík's *Nedeľné šachy s Tisom* (Sunday chess with Tiso, 2016) and *Posledná barónka* (The last baroness, 2019) as well as Viliam Klimáček's *Námestie kozmonautov* (Astronauts' square, 2007), *The Hot Summer of 1968* (*Horúce leto 68*, 2011, trans. 2019) and *Vodka a chróm* (Vodka and chrome, 2013). The common denominator of these texts is an interest in Slovak national history either in the broader historical context of the twentieth century (from the era of the Austro-Hungarian Empire until 1989) or with a narrower focus on the Second World War and the Slovak state. The brief period of illusory autonomy under the fascist regime is the focus of both Lavrík's and Rankov's novels. Whereas Lavrík's *Posledná barónka* draws on local archival work, Rankov's *It Happened on the First of September* approaches the complex historical period through the romance involving three male friends and a young woman. Both novels are set in carefully localized settings, which contribute to the appeal and plausibility of the narratives. Klimáček, who is also a playwright and a theatre director, filters historical events through seemingly banal situations and characters, exposing instances of individual heroism but also failures, suffering, and naivete. *The Hot Summer of 1968*, originally written as a stage play and expanded into a prose text, is based on the recollections of real-life Slovak immigrants to Canada.

In Slovak historical fiction published after 2000, the essence of the historical era or event is not depicted in broad epic chronotopes but in the intimate spaces of individual and communal lives. Such an approach to the rewriting of history leaves room for the reader's active role in the reconstruction of the past. This chapter offers interpretations of three novels that represent different types historical fiction that nevertheless share the common interest in archival materials and filter the past through individual or family memory: *The House of the Deaf Man* (*Dom hluchého*, 2012, trans. 2014) by Peter Krištúfek, the novella *Konvália* by Denisa Fulmeková, and the memoir series by Alta Vášová *Ostrovy nepamäti* (The islands of unforgetting), which includes "Úlety" (Flights) and "Dolety" (Arrivals), and *Odlety* (Departures) published between 2008 and 2019. These novels illustrate radically different approaches to subjectivity and the archive in postmillennial Slovak historical fiction, yet they share a common feature: Instead of rewriting history to align with new ideological imperatives, they self-consciously explore history as a continually shifting process, the tenuous nature of memory, and the complicated connections and discrepancies between words and images.

PETER KRIŠTÚFEK'S HISTORICAL KALEIDOSCOPE: MEMORY AS AN ARTEFACT

Peter Krištúfek, the youngest author covered in this chapter, whose career was prematurely ended by a tragic accident, was a multi-talented artist: a novelist, a film director, a playwright, and a screenwriter. His novel *The House of the Deaf Man* has been published in two editions in Slovakia and abroad in translation. The novel is a saga involving multiple generations of a single family with a sweeping historical scope from the interwar period to the present. The account of its first-person narrator freely moves between the present and loosely chronologically ordered periods of his family history. The autobiographical premise for the novel is framed with a passing reference to the writer's family archive, but otherwise the novel features clearly fictitious characters and settings. The visual imagery of the novel draws on Krištúfek's experience as a filmmaker. Although the novel calls attention to the artificial aspects of historical narratives, its representation of history is not imaginary or illusory but grounded in the author's archival work of collecting, reading correspondence, and search for material evidence. Although the use of specific evidence and references to artefacts create an impression of authenticity, it also fragments the narrative and skims the surface of historical events in a way that does not allow for a deeper exploration of their significance. The ambitious historical framework of the novel also produces some confusion about the relationships among the characters and the different temporal planes.

The protagonist's investigation of his family's past is driven by the discovery of bones buried in the garden of his father's house in the fictitious town of Brežany. Although the novel begins as a murder mystery, the corpse or its killer are never identified. Instead, the bones are emblematic of the family's "skeleton in the closet," for Adam Trnovský eventually discovers that his father, Alfonz, a medical doctor and a respected citizen, was an ŠtB (Secret Service) agent, who betrayed his Jewish uncle during the Second World War and reported on the activities of the father of Adam's best friend, Vojtech Roško. He is the deaf man of the title who gradually loses his hearing in a physiological process that reflects his refusal to listen to others, his focus on survival, and his desire to be left alone during critical periods of political conflict and turmoil.

The structure of the novel, which heavily relies on visual imagery throughout, is organized around a visual framework. The eight sections of the novel open with images from Francisco Goya's "Black Series" of murals painted during the last years of his house while he lived in the House of the Deaf Man, an inspiration for the novel's title. The overall effect of the novel can be best described as kaleidoscopic, structured around configurations of visual images that highlight how historical narratives shift in response to different ideological perspectives and political imperatives. Krištúfek explicitly refers to the kaleidoscope in a scene that highlights how Alfonz Trnovský prefers to "watch the world go by" while "staring at the stained glass in the ceiling" of the Stag Hotel: "He once told me that he liked the design because it reminded him of a kaleidoscope filled with multicolored fragments of glass and mirrors that rearrange themselves into dazzling new patterns every time you move it."[7] The image of the kaleidoscope underscores the central function of visual images as shorthand for the complexity of historical events as well as the novel's emphasis on the artificiality and relativity of history. The movement of the kaleidoscope merely shifts the configurations, not the substance of institutions and individuals, and histories are rewritten to serve new imperatives. Vojtech Roško's father produces different stories of his career as a Second World War pilot in order to survive under different regimes. Parallel celebratory accounts on the USSR and the USA ironically comment on Slovakia's change of allegiances. Adam's brother Peter converts from a fanatical communist to a fervent nationalist. However, the kaleidoscopic effect can also mean that readers merely skim the surface of history. Ornamental stereotypes, which accumulate in recurring images throughout the novel, both illuminate and obscure the complexity of landmark historical events. The following examples of the novel's kaleidoscopic effect represent three pivotal moments of Slovak history: the establishment of the Slovak state (1939), the end of the Second World War (1945), and the fall of the communist regime (1989).

In 1939, Alfonz Trnovský is pressured by the local priest to participate in a Catholic procession. Even though he does not share the faith or the values that Catholicism comes to represent in the fascist state, he agrees out of fear because he is married to a Jewish woman and feels vulnerable under the new regime. The description of the procession draws on anti-Catholic stereotypes that caricature the priest and his flock while also forecasting Trnovský's tendency to go with the flow and passively adapt to different regimes in order to survive:

> At the head of the procession a canopy swayed gently in the breeze and the whole throng echoed its rhythm. Dean Peterský, decked out in lavish vestments, walked below the canopy, sheltered from the sun. Everyone watched the fat nape of his neck and imposing back with fascination, keenly following every gesture of his massive arm. I noticed at times Father got carried away by the atmosphere. He allowed himself to be swept away by the current, his movements became automatic, just like those of sheep gently jingling their little bells. He would then come out of his daze and wipe the sweat from his brow, only to lose himself again in the natural flow of the collective rhythm. In his trance he failed to notice that it was now cold and the sky had turned the dark colour of rotting fruit. A gust of wind played havoc with the dean's vestments, exposing the large hairy calves of his legs. There was a clap of thunder and the canopy toppled first to one side, then to the other, until eventually the procession was scattered by a heavy downpour.[8]

Dean Peterský's physique is reminiscent of Jozef Tiso, the priest president of the Slovak state, and his grotesquely abundant flesh and hair suggest deficient spirituality. The imagery underscores the collective fanaticism of the supporters of the Slovak state with explicit references to "sheep," "collective rhythm," and "the current" that carries Alfonz Trnovský toward his shameful future as a collaborator and ŠtB agent. The iconography of the scene is recognizable to readers who are familiar with the film treatment of the Slovak state in socialist-era films, which contributes to the novel's popular appeal. However, there is very little exploration of the psychological motives of the supporters of the regime and collaborators such as Trnovský, which was the focus of the arguably best film depicting the Slovak state, the internationally acclaimed *The Shop on Main Street* (dir. Ján Kadár, 1965).

Adam Trnovský becomes a documentary filmmaker employed at the Slovak Television, and his narration explicitly references film techniques.

The following account of the limbo between the departure of the German troops and the arrival of the Red Army is once again conveyed as a series of film images. In this instance, the evocation of commonplaces and stereotypes borrowed from documentaries and films on the Second World War has a defamiliarizing effect:

> A handful of Jewish survivors are wandering around town in their tattered camp rags. People cross over to the other side of the street, trying to avoid their emaciated faces. Father Savický, surrounded by children carrying bouquets of flowers, burst into the hospital eager to find a wounded hero, any hero. He is humming a brand new partisan song.
>
> An inexperienced, high-pitched voice drones from the loudspeaker:
>
> "*Citizens ... The Local National Committee and the People's Militia request that all items of furniture and valuables looted from the manor house and its adjoining properties prior to the arrival of the Red Army be returned under threat of the death penalty!*"
>
> So all the stuff is being carried back, as in a film that's being rewound. And it's the film negative, because while looting took place in the middle of the day, people are creeping back to the manor house under the cover of night. Few are willing to return the loot in broad daylight. Fearing house searches, politically conscious citizens hurl furniture over the walls and fences. Vases that used to decorate drawing rooms end up in the stream that flows through the park, only to be invaded by fish and the nymphs of caddisflies.[9]

Although the passage begins with stereotypical images of Jewish concentration camp survivors, it also subverts the readers' facile consumption of such stock images. The inhabitants of Brežany, who took advantage of the vacuum between the presence of German and Russian soldiers and looted valuable items from the manor, are forced to reverse their choices under the threat of the local authorities. The narrator, who is also a filmmaker, visualizes their action as a film that is being rewound and converted back to the negative. The burlesque scene reminiscent of silent film comedies also conveys a serious message, reminding readers that history (as presented in documentaries, for example) is a construct, but also a result of individual choices at any given moment in time.

The final example of the novel's use of visual images as shorthand for pivotal historical moments is a passage related to the regime change in the fall of 1989. The narrator describes the destruction of the memorial dedicated to the first communist president of Czechoslovakia, Klement Gottwald, whose repressive policies and tactics were parallel to Stalin's. The passage draws on the iconography that was used to symbolize the dissolution of the Soviet Bloc in the aftermath of the Cold War. Several seminal books on the wave of revolutions that brought down the totalitarian regimes in Central and Eastern Europe used images of defaced or toppled statues of communist idols, especially those of Lenin, and their titles evoked gothic images.[10] Later, museums of communism, which catered mostly to Western tourists, deployed similar gothic tropes. In the following passage, which presents Adam Trnovský's account of the incident, Krištúfek both exploits and subverts the tropes and stereotypes associated with the fall of communism:

> The former Gottwald Square in Bratislava was deserted. One day the oversized statue depicting the permanently drunk and syphilitic president and his pals was blown up by persons unknown. Unfortunately, I've only seen amateur footage on Austrian ORF TV, shot by a bystander from the entrance to the Technical University. The statue was no great loss, although perhaps the raw materials could have been put to some more sensible use. But it's the same conundrum as with Ceauşescu – when he was shot, should his body parts have been used for organ transplants? Or would they have retained his thoughts and emotions? Wouldn't Gottwald's past have remained carved in the stone? The swelling of the aorta, the alcohol-soaked nights after signing a few more death sentences, the vagina of an infected prostitute, the dread of the bewhiskered man from the Caucasus, whom he eventually followed on his last journey, having caught up with him in the antechamber of communist Heaven (instead of St Peter, I imagine Lenin himself met him at the gate in all his five-foot glory, with his shiny bald pate and a red star on his brow, holding an allegorical sickle in one hand and a metaphorical hammer in the other, mobbed by eager cherubim with young pioneer scarves), the smell of vodka and red carnations, flowery speeches on equality and justice ... These were the thoughts going through my head.[11]

The opening sentences of the passage once again reference film and emphasize the second-hand nature of the narrator's account. Instead of witnessing the incident, he paradoxically received the news from a Western report, the most accessible source of alternative news for the residents of the capital during the socialist era. For example, following the explosion of Chernobyl, Slovaks first learned how to protect themselves against potential exposure to radiation from ORF. The reference to ORF evokes the eyewitnesses' sensation that the events of November 1989 were so hard to believe that they appeared unreal as something seen only on the screen. The graphic depiction of Gottwald's diseased body and the reference to Ceauşescu draw on the stock gothic imagery used to represent the revolutions of 1989 in Western media and books, further underscoring the mediated nature of history. The narrator's fantastic image of a communist heaven involves a catalogue of stereotypes that once again appeal to popular notions of the socialist era. Having experienced the Revolution in his youth, Krištúfek draws on personal memories rather than research in this passage. Yet, paradoxically, even an event that happened in his hometown and during his lifetime is presented as a tableau rather than a witness account, foregrounding the tendentious and constructed nature of historical accounts.

The House of the Deaf Man presents history as a sequence of interchangeable situations that leave their traces in symbols and material artefacts. History is a process of continual beginnings, costly attempts at improving the human lot, and repeated catastrophes. The narrator, and thus the implied author, rely on irony to maintain emotional distance from historical events that can be traumatizing, and, as a result, privilege a postmodern account of history as a process of endless variability and change instead of a morally inflected existential account or a quest for the truth. As companion and a postscript to his historical novel, Krištúfek later published *Atlas zabúdania* (The atlas of forgetting, 2013). The book contains a collection of texts, documents, maps, and images associated with different periods of Slovak history covered in *The House of the Deaf Man*. The lavish reproduction of these artefacts highlights the writer's interest in the history of material culture and his preferred role as a curator or collector, which helps explain the kaleidoscopic character of the novel.

DENISA FULMEKOVÁ'S "SMALL SCENE" FROM THE GREAT HISTORY: MEMORY AND EMOTION

On the spectrum of historical fiction, Fulmeková's treatment of family history in *Konvália: Zakázaná láska Rudolfa Dilonga* (Konvália: The forbidden love of Rudolf Dilong, 2016) occupies the opposite end from Krištúfek's grand historical epic. This documentary novel depicts the secret relationship of the author's grandparents, a Catholic priest, poet, and a prominent cultural representative during the period of the Slovak state, Rudolf Dilong and Valéria Reiszová, a much younger woman of Jewish descent. During the period of the fascist republic, Dilong repeatedly intervened on behalf of his lover and their young daughter in order to protect them from internment in a concentration camp. Immediately following the war, he left them and emigrated first to Italy, then to Argentina, and finally to the United States, where he died in 1986.

The genre of the book overlaps with the memoir, and the author draws on emotional memory and personal involvement with the subject. The objective of Fulmeková's writing is a quest for identity through the recovery of family history. Historical fiction with a focus on family history is rare in Slovak literature, which stems from the lack of anonymity in a small nation and Slovakia's heterogeneous and ruptured cultural identity. Writing a personal history as a shared cultural experience requires a sense of correspondence with national history, which is difficult to achieve in the case of Fulmeková's protagonists. The writer fully realizes that as a witness and an observer of the forbidden love and complicated destiny of her grandmother, she enters an intimate space that nevertheless challenges established historical narratives. Her grandmother's first love for Rudolf Dilong was a very risky business during the era of the Slovak state, which persecuted the Jewish population. The narrative follows Valéria through the birth of her daughter and life after the end of the Slovak state, during the totalitarian communist regime of the 1950s, through the "thaw" of the 1960s until her death that follows the death of her husband. Fulmeková wrestles with the problem of subjectivity in a narrative that probes the troubling aspects of her grandmother' emotionally compelling and complex story. Her intentionally discontinuous narrative of "three human destinies and love" is organized into 167 sections of uneven length that consist of fragments, scenes, and pronouncements. In the introductory chapter she mentions that she has found "to her surprise, a growing compulsion to tell the story": "I have contemplated this material for many years, but I have just started to compile it several months ago, following the funeral of the last protagonist, which has definitely concluded the story. The fact that I share my protagonists' genes binds me, even constrains me. It forces me either to zealously distance myself from the fact that I am a part of this story, or to laborious reconstruction of what exactly the ones I write about said and felt. However, no matter how hard I try, my narration will not and cannot be completely objective."[12] The traces of Fulmeková's generational memory, which provide the starting point for the historical reflection, are tied with a family story that the author unveils gradually and cautiously because of its forbidden and controversial aspects. The "small scene" of the love story involving Valéria Reiszová, Rudolf Dilong, and Jozef Krivda is a literary version of the stories of three actual historical figures whose faces appear in the photographic illustrations for the book taken from the family album and whose lives intersect with a broader and complex collective history. The story involves human failure, compromises, and betrayal during the era of the Slovak state in the local context of the persecution of the Jewish residents in the western Slovak town of Malacky. The strength of Fulmeková's narrative is that it leaves the reader with a lingering emotion without certainty about the validity of any perspective as "objective truth." The interpretation is open to the individual reader, who has the opportunity to draw their own conclusions on the historical legacy of the book's "small scene" of history.

The story involves several resolutions and decisions made by Rudolf Dilong, who was not a historically and culturally neutral figure. After 1946, while he lived in exile, his life journey was determined by his profession and mission as a priest. He maintained sporadic contact with Valéria and her daughter Dagmar, the author's mother. His destiny was complex, but not comparable with the story of Valéria following the war, when she experienced great uncertainty and precarity without any contact or information about the father of her child: "The days turned into weeks, weeks into months. Valika started to realize, even if it does not mean that she accepted this bitter truth, that Dilong probably emigrated and she was left alone with her child. Yet she could not be sure of anything ... In short, she understood that he was gone, but she teetered in the constant uncertainty about his fate."[13] The reflective and empathetic narrative passages such as this quoted example alternate with recovered images of a photogenic, carefree, and talented girl not yet touched by the trials of life: "She glows in the photographs from early youth. Light brown hair styled into waves reminiscent of actresses in interwar Czechoslovakia, a modern city dress, thin eyebrows, a pretty symmetrical face. She always looks into the lens of the camera proudly, with a consciousness of her charm and beauty. She does not have an aura of a wallflower but quite the opposite. There is something modern, mature, and at the same time carefree about her."[14] The literary "photography" of the period and evocative fragments of dialogue are integral to Fulmeková's characteristic and effective narrative strategy in the book, which also includes an account of fated love that follows the conventions of film romance: "The fateful moment is near. They will meet in a moment; I can see them. She, a nineteen-year-old beauty in love with poetry and her young life, and he, a thirty-one-year-old charismatic man with prominent dark eyes. Slovak literary history will categorize him as one of the leading figures of Catholic modernism."[15]

Fulmeková's textual collage is not equally picturesque or photogenic in all its "scenes" of mediated memory. The small historical scene of a forbidden love ends with the passing of all three protagonists. The story of *Konvália* is concluded as narrated trauma, which provokes emotions induced by memory that are transferred to the reader. In addition to conveying an engaging story, this type of writing mediates a structured, compellingly layered phenomenology of memory, which, as it turns out, is never merely a private event. This type of fictionalized biography punctuated with documentary evidence presents an innovative contribution to Slovak historical fiction, one that connects play with genre (one can read the book as a parody of romance), personal memory, and documentary evidence. Moreover, there is an existential element to the story, which processes traumatic family memories. The protagonists cannot control the large forces of history that rule their destinies. In spite of the gesture toward the focus on genre in its subtitle, "The Story of a Forbidden Love," the book has an existential dimension that points to love, courage, and loyalty as ways of compensating for the damaging impact of historical events on individual lives.

ALTA VÁŠOVÁ'S "UNFORGETTING" OF MEMORY

Alta Vášová's writing is preoccupied with the recording of memories but also with reflection on the nature of memory, its endurance and fragility, as well as on the imperative of not forgetting the past.[16] Her memoir writing constitutes a thoroughly conceptualized and complex project, which presents history not only as a subject of the narration but also as a narrative process that tends to be fragmentary. Vášová gained critical attention with her collage of four texts entitled *Ostrovy nepamäti* (The islands of unforgetting, 2008). Three of the texts that comprise the book, "Sestričky" (Little Sisters), "Úlety" (Flights), and "Dolety" (Arrivals), are autobiographical. The fourth, entitled "With Božena," is her first experiment with so-called "parallel mental autobiography," in which she enters a transcendental dialogue with the nineteenth-century Czech writer Božena Němcová. Vášová later concludes the work of remembering with *Odlety* (Departures, 2019). The primary feature of Vášová's treatment of history and memory is free movement in time and space, and the secondary feature is her reconstruction of the time-space of historical experience as a subjective account that touches on collective destiny. However, memory is always unique, singular, and irreplicable; it contradicts and constructively subverts presumably "objective" facts in Vášová's texts. Even though such facts register in the narrator's consciousness, Vášová subjects them to a form of cultural autopsy that shifts in response to the individual personal timeframes of adolescence, maturation, and aging.

"Úlety" can serve as an example of these principles. The title deliberately emphasizes flights of the imagination and thus the autonomy, singularity, and non-transferability of individual memory. The book is organized retrospectively and records the narrator's process of remembering from the age of fifty-five to the age of thirteen. The narrative strategy functions as a meta-dialogue with the reader and with herself, and therefore with her own memory. In the introduction to the narrative, the writer points to the teleological and pragmatic aspects of personal memory as continual self-construction: "You choose from your surroundings ... you continually add, exchange what is worn out, continually renew, improve ... You become increasingly embodied in matter shaped into an accidental human, limited by the initial code – message, which is transmitted from the first cell, a tiny life saddled by you."[17]

In Vášová's conception, memory is a vital component of the human reproductive principle of spiritual being. She does not directly operate with metaphysical or theological concepts, but her perspective on the world as a shared entity combines the approaches of the natural sciences and humanities. The metaphysics of faith and respect toward the spiritual aspect of being are organically integrated in her narrative construction of the self. Nevertheless, Vášová's treatment of history continually challenges the understanding of history as teleological movement with intelligible causality. She understands history as consisting of individual moments such as meeting other humans or participating in micro events involving close family circles or broader social groups. Vášová's conception of history appeals to a generation that was educated to perceive historical events as reflecting a story of social progress and teaches them to understand history as consisting of small-scale, fragmentary, and existential events. It is therefore understandable that some of the central preoccupations of this kind of historical reflection include language, imagery, narrative perspective, and dialogue, and the focus varies among her texts. Whereas in "Flights" the author balances historical and personal time-space with frequent references to events relevant to collective memory and national history (the book is implicitly dedicated to the revolutionary changes that took place in November 1989), *Odlety* (Departures) is situated in the time-space of remembering through correspondence or archival records, which the narrator frequently refers to as "notebooks."

Vášová's autobiographical narration stages remembering as a performative act that not only explores the meaning of history, but also one's own personal participation in the historical experience through a repetitive process of self-construction: "You barely recognize them because of your unforgetting. The lines hidden in notebooks similar to this one. You are weighed down by the seriousness – the burden – the irrevocability of the spare sentences. They do not seem hopeless, but often resigned and sad. You meet with the person who thought – perceived – pronounced. Some woman, you realize ... You finally also realize that it is real. You recognize what is former, past, but has nevertheless left a trace. And you continue. In self-opening."[18] The aim of Vášová's narrative strategy is to cultivate "unforgetting," which constitutes the author's reflection on memory as a constitutive element of one's individual and unique process of self-construction. The narrator's dialogue with her own capacity for remembering and reflection includes a fragmentary and ruptured record, the discontinuity of narration, selectiveness, as well as pauses and silences.

The narrative speaks for a whole suppressed and silenced generation of people with a lost potential to think and feel freely. Even though

Vášová does not foreground this motif of shared generational experience in her autobiographical writing, there is a palpable undercurrent of implied responsibility and social engagement. After all, Alta Vášová had been a writer with articulated attitudes and opinions even before 1989. It is therefore not accidental that her autobiographical records are framed by political events. In "Flights," Stalin's death presents a milestone in the narrator's developing worldview; in "Sisters," the division of the Cold War also separates the two sisters, one of which stays home and the other opts for emigration. In "Arrivals," Vášová's narrator is a keen and engaged observer of politics and historical developments that shape the whole text. The "arrivals" of the title represent the traces of attachment to people close to and remote from the narrator, to authors or artists whom she admires or feels connected with (in addition to Božena Němcová the author references Marguerite Duras), as well as to public and political events that may appear innocuous but are potentially harmful. The text is marked by the need for living memory, unforgetting, and regulation of life in all its threatening forms.

Odlety more explicitly reflects on the narrator's own life story, as well as on the need to conserve it in time, which is running out. The author's preoccupation with unforgetting becomes more pronounced, pragmatic, and disciplined. The fragmentary records are framed with meta-reflection on earlier writing ("Flights" and "Arrivals") and develop the existential theme as a connection between recent and distant past, as well as a gradual loss of free imaginative memory: "Something has happened. The freedom, spontaneity, drawings and doodles – you move toward the direct ground for Departures, as if time has become the key player. To have everything ready, while your mind works. You transcribe it while it's fresh! ... You record what is worth saying and select, sort out records from recent years. In an almost parallel fashion. You have two notebooks! In the first one you are free – you don't have to weigh, complete, conclude. You work like a camera: the images are first fuzzy, then sharp. The first notebook has remained free."[19] The author's writing oscillates between the focus on the phonetic properties of speech and the visual pictures as different ways of recording memory. This oscillating movement contributes to the dynamic rhythm of the narrative, which opens spaces for the reader to co-create the past and compare their perception of it with the author's. Vášová's approach to autobiographical writing is radically different from autobiographical fiction and continually subverts the pragmatic function of language, which the author liberates not only from ideological frameworks, but from any tendencies to manipulate reality itself. She treats language and meaning in this way in order to explore the boundaries of language in response to the sensory perception of the world, which exists in the consciousness of the writer before it is translated into a literary sign or a medium of an ideology.

Vášová's method is particularly relevant today. In a dramatically altered situation brought on by the COVID-19 pandemic, the author's potential to anticipate the coming change is evident in the text, not in its political ramifications, which have not yet become apparent, but in its hidden correlations, which unsettle every creative and open consciousness that recognizes how human nature operates throughout the ages. She emphasizes the importance of freedom and creativity in the treatment of memory. In the history of small nations that did not contribute to global developments, the free manipulation of history has always been limited. Vášová takes full advantage of the potential to approach the past differently after 1989. Her work corresponds with the opening of new possibilities for Slovak historical fiction, biography, and memoir in the last twenty years. Historical experience has been reconceptualized with a focus on individual and singular events and values, which has broadened the aesthetic and generic possibilities for rewriting history and provided space for an exploration of the ontological aspects of individual human memory. Another key change is the separation of remembering as an individual endeavour from history as a presumably objective body of knowledge. Historical fiction focuses on the freedom of perception and choice on the part of the protagonist or the narrator, who functions as a small, negligible, or insignificant mediator of historical events in Slovak culture.

CONCLUSION

Despite its temporal distance from the turbulent events of the two world wars, post-millennial Slovak historical fiction continues to process the traumas of the twentieth century. However, the interpretation of history changes and the perspective is less polarizing, in some instances complicating and in others relativizing values and facts. The evolution of historical consciousness thus moves toward more pluralized assessments of pivotal historical events. This chapter has outlined three types of postmillennial historical narrative. Two of the texts focus on the Second World War and the Slovak state. Whereas Krištúfek, although initially inspired by his family history, creates a large-scale, ornamental, and stylized narrative that foregrounds the constructed and ideologically driven aspects of national history, Denisa Fulmeková moves in the opposite direction, even though she challenges official histories in parallel ways. She exposes an aspect of her family history associated with the wartime Slovak state, the deportations of Jewish population, and the Slovak version of clerical-fascist ruling power. She depicts this historical milieu through a story, in which, despite numerous losses and tragedies, the life force of her grandmother eventually prevails. Vášová's fiction represents the most radical approach to fictional representation of memory and the complexity of history. She foregrounds the fragmentary, discontinuous, and unreliable aspects of "unforgetting," and her fiction suggests that self-construction is predicated on not forgetting, since it is systematically preoccupied with continual classification and evocation of ambiguous past events. Paradoxically, the focus on self-development through learning about the past in Vášová's accounts of "unforgetting" conveys the most emphatic message on the relativity of historical experience. Those of us who spent at least half of our lifetimes in the twentieth century can relate to the author's continual reassessment of history, even while our faces are turned toward new developments that evoke the darker aspects of the past.

NOTES

1 The exception to this, as I demonstrate later in this chapter, is the work of Alta Vášová, who belongs to an older generation of writers but whose memoir fiction was published in the new millennium.

2 Merleau-Ponty, *Institution and Passivity*, 208–9.

3 Lipták, *Slovensko v 20. Storočí*, 7.

4 Novosád, *Zostrihy II: Témy-problémy-dilemy*, 197–9.

5 See Pynsent, "Mythopoeic Mythoclasm."

6 For more on Ballek as a writer of the borderland region, see chapter 7 by Passia.

7 Krištúfek, *The House of the Deaf Man*, 294.

8 Ibid., 60.

9 Ibid., 172.
10 For example, David Remnick's *Lenin's Tomb: The Last Days of the Soviet Empire* (1993) and Robert Kaplan's *Balkan Ghosts: A Journey through History* (1993).
11 Krištúfek, *The House of the Deaf Man*, 465.
12 Fulmeková, *Konvália*, 7.
13 Ibid., 64.
14 Ibid., 16.
15 Ibid., 18.
16 Alta Vášová is a Slovak writer, an author of prose texts as well as screenplays and scripts for film, television, radio, and theatre. She started writing in the 1970s, and prior to 1989, was primarily known as an author of scripts for musicals. In the new millennium, she turned her focus to autobiographical prose.
17 Vášová, *Ostrovy nepamäti*, 113.
18 Vášová, *Odlety*, 73.
19 Ibid., 7–8.

BIBLIOGRAPHY

Fulmeková, Denisa. *Konvália: Zakázaná láska Rudolfa Dilonga*. Bratislava: Slovart, 2016.

Krištúfek, Peter. *The House of the Deaf Man*. Translated by Julia Sherwood and Peter Sherwood. Cardigan: Parthian Books, 2014.

Lipták, Ľubomír. *Slovensko v 20. Storočí*. Bratislava: Kalligram, 1998.

Merleau-Ponty, Maurice. *Institution and Passivity: Course Notes from the Collège de France (1954–1955)*. Evanston, IL: Northwestern University Press, 2010.

Novosád, František. *Zostrihy II: Témy-problémy-dilemy*. Bratislava: IRIS, 2019.

Vášová, Alta. *Ostrovy nepamäti*. Bratislava: Knižná edícia časopisu Fragment, 2008

– *Odlety*. Bratislava: Knižná edícia časopisu Fragment, 2019.

Passia, Radoslav and Ivana Taranenková, eds. *Hľadanie súčasnosti. Slovenská literatúra začiatku 21. storočia*. Bratislava: Literárne informačné centrum, 2014.

CHAPTER FIVE

Poetry and Social Engagement

Viliam Nádaskay

Literary critics often assume that writers represent the collective consciousness of a nation, embody its values, and symbolize its condition.[1] As the early twentieth-century Czech critic František Xaver Šalda observed, "Politics cannot be readily excluded from poetry, just like anything that excites and arouses people in their lives. Whatever happens in life is entitled to disturb poetry as well, every wave rising steeply and passionately is entitled to beat at the gates of poetry and demand entry. But of course: such an appeal of life is too murky, too passionate, too naturalist, too external."[2] In Slovakia, such assumptions about the public role of the writer emerged during the period of Romanticism and the so-called Springtime of Nations in the nineteenth century and evolved in response to the historical events of the twentieth century. Ideas about writers' social engagement were revived and appropriated during the communist era of Czechoslovak coexistence, whether in support of the Leninist theory of reality mirroring, in the infamous Stalinist credo of writers as "the engineers of human souls," in the privileging of writers and explicitly equating them with technical and manual laborers, or in the service of the common trope during normalization that the writer ought to "look life straight in the eye." Poetry under state socialism was expected to promote a vague, yet strict set of values, to communicate interest in the current world (and sometimes domestic) events and phenomena within the preferred ideological framework, often under the guise of straightforward humanism.

Reading through Slovak literature of the 1990s and discussions around it, one might encounter an almost palatable distrust towards the social engagement of writers. The resistance to engagement is not difficult to understand, as at the time writers were no longer expected or needed to fulfil the role of the national conscience and social elites. The critical debates on literature in the latter half of the 1980s show that the young generation of writers had no ambition to attain any sort of moral or ethical merit, nor did its representatives aspire to become politically active figures. This generation eschewed topics seen as socially engaged in favour of new topics and individual aesthetic programs.

The desire of writers to break with the perceived communist and socialist-realist tradition was strong, and the public no longer looked up to them for moral guidance. Indifference towards the social role of writers was only one symptom of the radically changed situation in literary culture and its relation to society and politics. As Ivana Taranenková asserts, literature found itself in creative freedom and "suffered a shock" due to its sudden marginalized position and the loss of its social prestige, including the importance of its institutions and literary journals.[3] However, as Vladimír Barborík noted in a contemporary discussion, the 1990s were also a unique time when the established literary scene was finally disintegrating, declining, slowly withering away, and paving the way for something different, all without any institutional power quelling it.[4]

It is safe to say that after the undoubtedly restricting conditions of normalization, except for a short period that reflected the transition from socialism to democracy and capitalism, post-1989 poetry mostly abandoned social engagement to stress individual identity, personal interests, beliefs, and values, and leaned toward (postmodernist) literary deconstruction. Nevertheless, for a certain part of the younger generation of authors debuting from the late 1990s onward, engagement gradually became an integral part of their poetry, once again fulfilling its social function. The ambition to be a critical voice meant relating to society instead of ignoring it or rebelling against it from a radically individual perspective. Such ambition might, on the one hand, signal a shift towards accessibility, and, on the other hand, reflect an interest in voluntarily serving the role of a "conscience," but one no longer mandated by the state. Socially engaged writers openly embodied or critiqued certain values and responded to social and political issues, whether simply in their poetic work or by using their social position to express opinions in more accessible forms (press or social media). While engagement in art can produce multiple forms and outcomes, my understanding is traditional, simplified to accommodate authors who openly voice their concerns with certain social events or phenomena.

It is thus worth mentioning that the Czechoslovak dictionary of literary theory, *Slovník literární teorie* (Dictionary of literary theory, 1977), defines engagement in a circular fashion as party-mindedness. While engagement is "essentially the same as party-mindedness or tendency of literature; conscious inclination towards certain ideology and according intentional artistic work," party-mindedness of literature is "an aesthetic category of Marxist literary criticism, based on the work's engagement."[5] Poetry of engagement may be understood in its simplest terms as poetry through which an author openly assumes social or political stances, be it critical or affirmative of the status quo. The *Penguin Dictionary of Literary Terms and Literary Theory* approaches the issue through the lens of commitment, stating: "A committed or engaged writer (or artist) is one who, through his work, is dedicated to the advocacy of certain beliefs and programmes, especially those which are political and ideological and in aid of social reform."[6] Advocating political and ideological beliefs and causes would then be at the core of engaged poetry. However, engagement is closely tied with the social role of writers, with their personas, and their public activities beyond creative writing.

This chapter outlines the evolution of the concept of social engagement and its perception from socialist through post-socialist to current situation. My choice of writers and texts is determined by the simple fact that their poems are available in English translations. Fortunately, the translated poems also fittingly represent some of the most progressive and influential strands of contemporary Slovak poetry, demonstrating that poetry can serve a social function without resorting to being one-dimensional, unnecessarily straightforward, or mediocre.

POST-SOCIALIST ENGAGEMENT

Since engagement in socialist literature was usually presented as a category equal to aesthetic merit of a literary work and integral to the writer's social role, it was generally rejected with disregard once the era of state socialism was over. Miroslav Válek, a seminal Slovak poet and long-time socialist minister of culture, published his extensive poem *Slovo* (The word) in 1976. This resulted in an ecstatic, universal acclaim from media, critics, readers, and the political establishment. Thanks to the book, infamously dedicated to the communist party, Válek came to embody a socially and politically engaged writer, a devoted intellectual and versatile politician during the era of normalization.[7] To this day, the book continues to perplex readers as a controversial element in Válek's otherwise highly regarded oeuvre. The critical controversy merits a separate discussion, but the main issue is that Válek's position both as a poet and a politician, an idiosyncratic celebrity, and a representative of the highest cultural and moral values, was an emblematic example of how writers and intellectuals were perceived as representatives of collective identity, national or socialist. Or at least that is how they themselves often wanted to be perceived and affirmed.

Of course, there were writers who viewed their role as public figures and intellectuals as quite the opposite to frantic engagement in current affairs and within the boundaries of the status quo. They instead argued for individual freedom and sensibility against the abuse of power, as did Dominik Tatarka and Ivan Kadlečík, or opposed the grand narrative of socialism by depicting the "small histories" of their fictional characters within the ruthless "great history" of society, as did Pavel Hrúz or Martin M. Šimečka.[8] And then there were those who seemingly never aspired to hold any high moral ground, unwilling to conform to the image of writer as an ideologically "conscious" and committed public figure.[9]

For Slovak literary scholarship, engagement – or commitment – was and still is a vague and problematic term. Before 1989, it was not seen in dimensions described for example by Jean-Paul Sartre as writers' responsibility to society, or by Theodor Adorno as an attribute of art opposed to apathy, uniformity, and subordination to utilitarian aims.[10] Both thinkers attributed engagement mainly to the public role of writers or their critical stance towards the establishment. In socialist Czechoslovakia, it was mostly seen as another word for party-mindedness or its components. In addition to the somewhat compulsory allegiance to the Union of Slovak Writers, social engagement was often associated with writing on a specific range of topics, referencing typical communist imagery, national history, or contemporary (world) events and lifestyle. Only a small number of authors were critical of these topics, and virtually none directly challenged the basis of the communist regime. Under the disciplinary pressure of the state during the era of normalization, what was seen as social engagement in poetry was in most cases motivated by largely enforced social duty and a blatant display of social capital. As some literary scholars would observe, this pressure would often cut a divide in one's poetry, creating a dualism between the "real," socially valid and engaged, and the "ideal," private, socially unusable, pseudo-real.[11] For example, many authors would write in two modes: personal (tackling topics such as love, relationships, home, or nature), and social (speaking out on contemporary topics of global importance such as the Vietnam War, East-West animosity, the threat of nuclear war, technological progress, or very often on national history). This would often manifest in the way the authors composed their books, devoting separate sections to the respective topics. Although some poets might have written socially engaged verse with legitimate internal motivation such as the fear of nuclear apocalypse, rejection of limited, yet rising consumerism, or authentic support for the narrative of Slovak nationhood, their efforts almost always harmonized with the social and political climate, or even official policies. It is then easy to understand the resentment towards the notion of social engagement that was derivatively reproduced during normalization and was one of the key reasons why socially engaged poetry failed to spontaneously find fertile ground after 1989.

From today's point of view, only a handful of authors publishing during state socialism would be seen as socially engaged. Except for those indirectly portraying the bleak existential situation of an individual, most poets stubbornly wrote about their own inner or private lives with minimal relation to social reality or through marked eroticism and sexuality in their texts. The so-called civic poetry of normalization – the poetry seen as engaged in social criticism – had been mostly affirmative or critical of relatively benign topics, far removed from the actual everyday social reality of Czechs and Slovaks. However, under the new social and political circumstances in the late 1980s, poetry shifted towards a more critical worldview, allowing for open civic engagement on a broader variety of issues.

Post-socialist Slovak literature is often characterized by terms such as plurality, heterogeneity, fragmentation, differentiation, or integration.[12] Each term points towards the fact that poetry was no longer officially bound to a common principle: communist party-mindedness. All the attributes that traditionally made the writer "engaged" were mostly abandoned after 1989 in favour of individual creative freedom.

This is not to say that writers completely abandoned their perceived position as a part of the social elite and their image of moral authorities in the 1990s. On the contrary, a significant number of writers entered organized politics in the new democratic, yet still ambiguous social situation. There are obvious and prolific examples of Czech dissidents entering top-level politics, embodied most famously by the playwright and first post-socialist Czechoslovak (later Czech) president Václav Havel. Slovak dissent, much smaller in size and influence, entered the political scene for a very brief transformational time through the civic initiative and political movement *Public against Violence*, along with a larger portion of artists and culture professionals. After the division of Czechoslovakia in 1993, the populist Movement for a Democratic Slovakia led by Vladimír Mečiar started to dominate Slovak politics (and continued its presence well into the 2000s) and most of the engaged artists and writers retreated from political life. There are, however, numerous cases of literary professionals committing themselves to institutional politics, whether within the leading party, such as Dušan Slobodník and Ivan Hudec (two controversial ministers of culture), or in opposition to it, such as the literary critics Peter Zajac and Rudolf Chmel (the latter also serving as a minister of culture) or the writers Ladislav Ballek and Peter Jaroš.[13] It is worth noting that none of these figures were poets (contrasting with the two highest-ranking officials at the ministry of culture in the previous regime, Miroslav Válek and Pavel Koyš) and all of them were born before 1950. The younger generation, which was largely disillusioned by the transformation and content with its newfound radical individualism, turned away from politics. However, as I have mentioned above, many of the so-called individualist poets still remained indirectly within the confines of the political system by publishing under state patronage.[14]

Jaroslav Šrank has described four distinctive types of post-1989 poetry respectively characterized by private experience, spiritual focus, radical individualism, and experimental-deconstructive form.[15] Poetry of engagement is missing from the list, in part because the term is often still remembered for its association with the previous regime's literary culture and by extension political system, but also because engaged poetry itself was rare, occasional, or most often diffused among all four types. Instances of poets reacting to social and political shifts are thus sparse and derive mostly from the turmoil of the transformational period and Mečiarism. Most notable are the handful of authors who wrote socially engaged poetry programmatically. Authors such as Daniel Hevier, Ján Štrasser, or Ľubomír Feldek all had a certain history of writing socially engaged verse before 1989, aimed at the contemporary lifestyle, a bleak vision of the future, Slovak mentality and history, and humanity in general. These topics were still relevant after 1989, although in different socio-political configurations.

In 1990, Hevier published *Psí tridsiatok* (Gone to the dogs). Although thematically and formally varied and most probably written before 1989, it features a large portion of satirical poems, aphorisms, and short wordplays that poke fun at the early years of the beginning transition and the atmosphere of the last years of communist regime. Although playful in nature, the book features, as its title suggests, themes or modalities that became common for reflections on post-socialist transformation: feelings of its unrealized potential, resignation, and bitterness. Štrasser is notable as a lyricist for the satirical cabaret TV program *Večer Milana Markoviča* (Evening with Milan Markovič), which ran for several years starting in 1993 on national television and often clashed with the political establishment). His lyrics, published in 1994 and 1995 under the titles *Ples núl* (Ball of zeroes) and *Babky demokratky* (Democratic grannies), lampooned the Slovak political scene, namely Mečiar and his party, as well as the painful post-socialist transformation of Slovakia, its relationship with Western and Eastern Europe, and its national myths and stereotypes. In 1992, Feldek, by that time a well-known and critically acclaimed author and translator, published *Odzemok na rozlúčku a 19 jarmočných piesní* (Farewell odzemok and 19 market songs)[16] that heavily satirizes contemporary Slovak nationalism, tensions between Czechs and Slovaks within the federative state, Mečiar, as well as topics like Slovak religious conservativism, alcoholism, or backwardness.[17]

These versatile, accomplished poets reserved verses of biting satire or political commentary for forms that are not traditionally associated with the "high canon." Using the form of popular songs, performed in a cabaret on national television, short poems with readable word play and juicy punchlines, and ironical allusions to folk genres was, on the one hand, a way of delimiting oneself outside of the "official" canon and state-approved culture, previously largely devoid of such devices and now looked upon with a certain distrust.[18] On the other hand, it was a perfect way to gain more readers – commenting on fresh political issues attracts attention, especially in provocative or accessible form. That is not to say that reflections on the transitional period in Slovakia were absent from high-canonical poetry of the central publishing circle: Ján Šimonovič criticized the period as deviating from traditional values in his book of poems *Skepsa* (Skepticism, 1995), Erik Groch tackled the issue with an allegory of evil and immorality in his book *Baba Jaga: Žalospevy* (Baba Yaga: Elegies, 1991), and younger poets such as Kolenič, Urban, or Lehenová reflected upon the period as a time of unbound freedom, yet depressingly aimless and meaningless.

Poetry that would strive to engage in a dialogue with the reader, express political opinions, and critique social circumstances was a rather short-lived occurrence in the 1990s. Thus, maybe atypically, the zeitgeist of the era is better characterized by the absence of social engagement in literature, where the self and literary deconstruction played a major role. History did not end, as in Francis Fukuyama's famous prediction, yet a glance at Slovak literary production from the mid-1990s until mid-2000s would definitely tempt the reader to think otherwise.

In 2014, the literary journal *Romboid* (2014) conducted a survey regarding socially engaged poetry. Some respondents welcomed the renewed presence of poetry of engagement, some seemed to be genuinely perplexed as to its re-emergence, keeping in mind its old social function, and some simply took it into account in a rather sober, if uninterested manner. What all of the respondents did, in their own ways, was to acknowledge its existence and its new function – not to conform to a certain status quo, not to affirm generally accepted values, but to express doubts about current circumstances through poetry independently of any social and political demand or to bring poetry to wider audiences by tackling issues that resonate in the public space.

Poetry of engagement is a rising phenomenon in Slovakia, diverging into various forms and modes. The poetry of Michal Habaj draws a line from the "tradition" of the deconstructionist works of the 1990s, the voice of Katarína Kucbelová is markedly sarcastic and ironic, yet anxious and concerned, and the poems of Mária Ferenčuhová are deeply and subtly existential, relating to many spheres of human life. What all three share is a confrontation with the issue of identity: lacking one, having too many, or having a deformed one. However, identity is not national, nor of any group – it might be individual, existential, gendered, but the poetry of engagement usually relates individual identity to social and civilizational issues.[19]

MICHAL HABAJ (1974)

The status of the poetry of engagement as an occasional, marginal form persisted roughly until the 2010s, when the generation of authors born in the late 1970s and 1980s and growing up in the 1990s became the centre of attention. The all-pervading principle of individuality eliminated the will and incentive for collective efforts – the two major post-1989 entities that can be called literary groups (or at least groups with a certain common platform) were the so-called Barbarian generation and the text generation (sometimes called "anaesthetic" due to their cool, detached poetics). The latter was represented most consistently by Peter Macsovszky, Michal Habaj, and Peter Šulej, founder of the publishing house Drewo a srd, which was instrumental in the rise of experimental and unconventional poetry in Slovakia.[20] This generation operated strictly independently and not only most radically revitalized Slovak poetry towards and beyond postmodernity, published provocative experimental works, and received widespread critical attention, but it also continues to serve as a seminal reference point for literary development, providing important literary inspiration.

It might seem paradoxical that the poetry of social engagement was reanimated by authors whose form was initially oriented towards hermetic textual experimentation. Habaj debuted with a collection of experimental conceptual poems, *80-967760-4-5* (1997), referencing its own ISBN code in the title. His early works are abundant with intertextual allusions, the incorporation of literary classics and various popular discourses, later transformed into general diffusion and deconstruction of the self, references to both the past and the future, blending the line between irony and sincerity, pathos of "high art" and vernacular abrasiveness, and tense emotionality and stoic rationalism – essentially embodying the postmodernist pastiche principle as formulated by Fredric Jameson (1998). However experimental, unconventional, and hermetic his early poems may seem, they are not strictly removed from their social situation. For example, the debut addresses rampant consumerism and the newfound role of literature as a commercial product, referencing media, advertising, and pop culture discourse and lingo.[21] More importantly, it deems the author unimportant, more concerned with reconstructing his own subjective identity and metaphysical and ontological categories of the self. The issue of identity became the focal point of his work. Many of his poems feature fluid subjects, stylized for example as an impersonal voice, an adolescent schoolgirl, a cyborg, going as far as even publishing two whole collections of poems as a fictitious Russian poetess under the moniker Anna Snegina (in reference to Sergey Yesenin's famous work), with himself listed as a mere editor of "her" books. However, all of this is not a simple game of cat and mouse with the reader, nor a self-serving mystification to expose literature and its reception as a sham. As Zoltán Rédey has pointed out, Habaj's stylizations as a cyborg in his fifth book *Básne pre mŕtve dievčatá* (Poems for dead girls, 2004) manifest a turn in cultural and civilizational identity. While the poets of the older generation viewed commercial, technocratic, and consumerist post-industrial society at the turn of the millennium as profane, senseless, or dehumanized, poets such as Habaj viewed the same situation as rather positive, progressive, anticipating future technological and spiritual development into post-humanoid overcoming of human characteristics. This leads to what Rédey calls a romantic-utopian image of current civilizational reality.[22]

Habaj's work eventually evolved and started, though sparsely, addressing social circumstances directly, notably beginning with his poetry collection *Michal Habaj* (2012) that references, for example, a mass shooting in the USA, the Holocaust, and Slovak national identity and mentality. He expanded this line of his work in his most recent collection *Caput Mortuum* (2015), which includes one of his better-known poems, "Letter to a Developer":

LIST DEVELOPEROVI

vážený investor,

ako si práve zistil,
v tejto obálke
sa nachádza list,
nie nábojnica.

keďže nie som držiteľom
zbrojného pasu,
podobné gestá
by mali iba symbolickú platnosť.

ja som však priaznivcom
akcie, pokiaľ možno, priamej,
práve tak ako ty,
ktorý strpčuješ životy

mne, mojim spoluobčanom, nášmu mestu.

vyzývam ťa preto
k bezodkladnému zastaveniu
stavebných prác
na projekte Podkolibská Rezidencia
na projekte Panoráma Koliba
na projekte Uptown Koliba
na projekte Belaria
na projekte Areál Koliba.

v opačnom prípade
očakávaj najhoršie:

jemné posuny v chápaní
celkom konkrétnych
pojmov a skutočností:

pokoj, bolesť, život, smrť.

môj básnický projekt
sa ohlási raz na svitaní,
so spevom prvých vtákov,
predtým, než sa pohnú žeriavy,
udrú kladivá, zavrčia frézy a vŕtačky.

vygoogli si prosím tieto mená:
Villon, Byron, Baudelaire, Rimbaud, Lautréamont,
Whitman, Marinetti, Majakovskij, Tzara, Breton,

Habaj
teraz už vieš, čo mám na mysli, keď hovorím
o relatívnosti

dobra a zla
lásky a nenávisti
života a smrti

chcel by som vidieť tvoje oči
rozšírené poznaním pravdy.
je to iba okamih, ale večný.

to je výsadou poézie:

na rozdiel od tvojich stavieb z betónu,
nikdy nestráca pozornosť,
striehne ako dravý vták,
až kým nepolapí svoju korisť.

nikdy už nebudeš v bezpečí
pred básňou,
ktorá bola napísaná pre teba.

neprežiješ túto báseň,
tvoja stavba neprežije túto báseň,
tvoje meno zapadne prachom.

táto báseň si ťa nájde,
živého alebo mŕtveho,
na Bahamách alebo na Cypre,
s bankrotom či bez.

ale nemaj strach,
čas ortieľa a veštby sa naplní
dávno potom
ako žeriavy naposledy otočia svojím dlhým krkom,
frézy zaspievajú rekviem,
kladivá zatlčú posledný klinec do rakvy.

hrám sa tu s klávesmi,
zatiaľ čo ty tvrdo pracuješ.
na začiatku bolo slovo: skurvysyn,
na konci báseň,

ďakujem ti za inšpiráciu,
ó investor, ó developer, múza.

nevyspytateľné sú cesty božie,
vravel som ti:
dobro a zlo sú relatívne.

a táto báseň?
je len prejavom božského vedomia,
univerzálnej múdrosti,
centrálnej inteligencie vesmíru.
dnes dláždi cestu môjmu hnevu,
zajtra tvojej pokore, keď ráno

vstaneš, rozdáš majetok, vstúpiš
do kláštora, s modlitbou na perách,
radostne obcujúc s večnosťou.

teraz už vieš, že som ťa chcel varovať:

si taký istý Buddha ako ja.

tak vidíš:
si investor,
si múza,
si buddha,
a za to všetko vďačíš mojej básni.

teraz si však mŕtvy
a zostáva ti
znovu sa zrodiť.

sprevádzam ťa bardom beznádeje,
pozor si dávaj
na obrazy rezidencií, krásne ženy,
drahý alkohol, naopak, upriam
svoju pozornosť na túto báseň.
jej brány sú ti otvorené dokorán,
stačí vojsť

a skočiť z posledného poschodia.

poď,
prikryjem ťa bielou plachtou,
bielym listom papiera
s básňou,
čo ťa priviedla až sem.

bola to krvavá investícia,
hodná vykúpenia.[23]

LETTER TO A DEVELOPER

dear investor,

as you have just learned,
this envelope contains a letter,
not a cartridge.

since I am not the holder
of an arms certificate,
any such gestures
would have only symbolic force.

I do however favour
action, direct where possible,
precisely like you, who are making life bitter
for me, my fellow citizens, our city.

I call on you therefore
to halt forthwith
the construction works
on Koliba Hillside Residence.

in the opposite event
expect the worst:
mild shifts in the understanding
of quite specific
concepts and realities:

peace, pain, life, death.

my poetic project
will announce itself one day at dawn
with the song of the first birds,
before the cranes are stirring
or hammers strike, or drills and iron-cutters snarl.

google, please, these names:
Villon, Byron, Baudelaire, Rimbaud, Lautréamont,
Whitman, Marinetti, Majakovskij, Tzara, Breton,

Habaj

now you know what I mean when I speak
of the relativity
of good and evil
love and hatred
life and death

I'd like to see your eyes
widened by knowledge of truth.
it's just a moment, but an eternal one.

that's the advantage of poetry:
unlike your precast concrete
it never loses concentration,
it lurks like a bird of prey
till it catches its kill.

you will never be safe
from the poem
that's written for you.
you won't survive this poem,
your building won't survive this poem,
your name will crumble in dust.

this poem will find you
dead or alive,

in the Bahamas or Cyprus,
bankrupt or not.

but have no fear,
the time of judgment and prophecy will be fulfilled
long after
the cranes for the last time turn their scraggy necks,
the cutters sing their requiem,
the hammers drive the last nail into the coffin.

here am I playing with keyboards
while you're hard at work.

in the beginning was the word: whoreson,
in the end a poem,
thank you for the inspiration,
O investor, O developer, muse.
inscrutable are the ways of God,
I have told you:
good and evil are relative.

and this poem?
it is only an expression of divine awareness,
of universal wisdom,
of the central intelligence in the cosmos;
today it lays the path for my anger,
tomorrow for your humility, when in the morning
you'll rise, distribute your wealth, enter
a monastery with a prayer upon your lips,
joyfully communing with eternity.

now you know that I wanted to warn you:
you're the same Buddha as me.

so you see:
you're an investor,
you're a muse,
you're a buddha.

and all this you owe to my poem.

but now you are dead
and it remains for you
to be born again.

I accompany you as a bard of despair,
beware of images
of residences, beautiful women,
expensive alcohol, and instead focus
your attention on this poem.
its doors are open wide to you,
you need only go in
and jump from the highest storey.

come,
I'll cover you with a white sheet,
a white leaf of paper,
with the poem
that has brought you thus far.

it was a bloody investment,
worthy of redemption.[24]

Habaj takes on the implicit role of a poet, a citizen, and a resident of Bratislava, and criticizes the uncontrolled gentrification and construction of expensive villas in the lucrative residential neighbourhood Koliba. The poem is stylized as a letter, implying the act of official communication that carries a certain weight. The fact that it is published in a book makes it a peculiar open letter – which is exactly the genre often used to address civic affairs, to draw public attention, to initiate debate and provoke reactions. The poem opens with a presumption that the addressee, the developer, would automatically expect a weapon, a threat, albeit symbolic – he is instead greeted with a poem, described by Habaj as a more powerful display of disagreement and force, highlighting its durability, power, and omnipresence. The addressee is subordinate to the voice of the author, reduced to a mere inspiration for a poem. It deliberately and rather explicitly contrasts the construction of buildings with writing, both in terms of the spirit of their creation and longevity of their products.

The poem is structured carefully around subtle shifts in modalities. It starts out with an angry, accusatory tone, going as far as calling to halt the construction. The high-brow sentiment signals that the poet is aware of the spiritual and, more importantly, social value of his creation, and turns to an almost prophetic, preaching tone. He describes the developer's spiritual journey, even rendering him dead and ready to be reborn, in an ironic mode in relation to the poem itself as a means of his demise, threatening him with "mild shift in the understanding of quite specific concepts and realities," and urging him to "jump from the highest storey." However, the speaker, somewhat equated with the author, also remains serious in his threats, genuinely presenting the literary work as the only way of achieving eternity for the developer and presenting himself as his saviour of sorts.

The speaker's clear intention is to openly appeal to the developer. Also, being a poem published in a book, obviously intended for the supposed reader, it appeals to the reader to take notice and react. Habaj's work thus functions as a concrete act of social engagement. The lyrical subject with a very fluid identity constructs itself, and here it shows one of its many possible faces, mirroring effects of civilizational development, ambiguous, contradictory, and picaresque self, unable to speak directly. The issue of personal identity is once more crucial – Habaj implies himself as the lyrical subject. Within this poem, his identity, though multi-layered, is clear – he is a concerned and self-assured poet, truly himself, while "the developer" remains an enigmatic figure, general and stereotypical, desperate in his finiteness, and representing no "higher" values. It is not surprising that Habaj was, in relation to this poem and to the book as such, compared to a medieval clown, one who does not fear to speak the uncomfortable truth aloud.[25] The personal identity of the poet then merges with his perceived obligation to point out any social injustice and wrongdoing.

In this way, Habaj openly takes issue with his environment and social circumstances through poetry.[26] Although the so-called anaesthetic poetics had strong influence on Slovak poetry throughout the 2000s, after this approach to poetry reached its pinnacle with Habaj's eponymous book, it not only overstepped its normalized boundaries but also signalled a slow return to social engagement, along with several other authors around 2010. Slovak poetry, with its apparent resentment towards the social function of literature, started facing the reality of the highly globalized neoliberal world.

KATARÍNA KUCBELOVÁ (1979)

Katarína Kucbelová belongs to the same generation as Habaj, and, along with other, younger peers, developed a style that stemmed from the experimental poetics fully explored in the 1990s and early 2000s. Detached, anaesthetic, and ironic poetics that eschews the personal lyrical narrator, drawing largely on the postmodern situation of literature and society, played a surprisingly crucial role in re-establishment of socially engaged poetry in Slovakia. And like Habaj, Kucbelová is mostly concerned with identity in (post)modern society – she explores what identity is in essence and how one's identity interacts with society, masses, and other individuals.

To date, Kucbelová has written five collections of poetry, *Duály* (Dualities, 2003), *Šport* (Sport, 2006), *Malé veľké mesto* (Little big city, 2008), *Vie, čo urobí* (Knowing what to do, 2013), and *K bielej* (Towards the white, 2022), as well as two novels, *The Bonnet* (Čepiec, 2019, trans. 2024) and *Modroslepost'* (Blue-blindness, 2023). Since her third book, Kucbelová started tackling various social issues both in her poetry and prose, most explicitly and programmatically in *Vie, čo urobí*, with topics such as xenophobia, sexism, nationalism, intergenerational and interpersonal conflicts, ecology, consumerism, intolerance, institutional violence, destructive collective mentality and, at the same time, extreme individualism. A prime example is a fittingly entitled poem which best demonstrates Kucbelová's voice, her detached and often sardonic tone, and one of the most prevalent motifs of her work, uncontrollable growth:

SKLENÍKOVÁ BÁSEŇ

v tom plesnivom dome sa kvetom darí
majú tú správnu tropickú vlhkosť

cudzokrajné rastliny neprestajne kvitnú
veľkými jedovatými kvetmi
nečakane menia farebnosť

v obrovskej obrazovke sa prekrikujú prostredia
a plnia dom instantnými tropickými vôňami a príchuťami
kontrasty sa otupujú, dôvera rastie, okná sa rosia
farby už stratili schopnosť vypovedať
tóny zanikajú v domácej rapid montáži

izbové rastlinstvo vyráža do výšok a plazí sa
po kopách nepotrebných vecí
ako para z jedál
zmäkčuje rohy, zahladzuje kontrasty, vytvára prekážky a
nečakané úkryty
na hranie

zo schodiska sa ozýva krik paviána
vo vedľajšej izbe zhodila liana osvetlenie

vonku splýva suchá krajina so sivohnedým brizolitom
ale len na necelú sekundu[27]

A GREENHOUSE POEM

flowers do well in that mouldy house
it has the right tropical humidity

exotic plants are in bloom all the time
their big poisonous flowers
change colours all of a sudden

environments on the huge screen mingle
and fill the house with tropical perfumes and flavours
contrasts are dulled, trust grows, windows mist up
colours have lost their ability to signify
tones cease to exist in the rapid home montage

the indoor vegetation rises into the heights and creeps
up the heaps of useless things
like cooking steam
it softens the corners, effaces the contrasts, builds barriers and

unexpected hiding places
to play in

a scream of a baboon can be heard from the staircase
in the next room, a liana has flung the lighting to the ground

outside, the dry land blends with the grey-brown roughcast
but only for a little less than a second[28]

There are several noticeable contrasts and shifts in imagery. The title refers to the well-known greenhouse effect, responsible for rising temperatures on the earth's surface; it also refers to a house itself as a home. It is apparent from the wild, colourful imagery and humid, tropical atmosphere that it takes the term greenhouse quite literally.[29] Juxtaposing a greenhouse and a home is the first example of the blurring lines between natural and human-made environments, between complete helplessness in the face of uncontrollable mechanisms of nature and a strong sense of control in every aspect of life. The spaces of the poem shift from a greenhouse, through a literal (green) house, to virtual reality represented by a "huge screen," and finally to a bleak vision of the "outside" world.

Let us first consider the poem from the ecocritical point of view, which is clearly one that Kucbelová herself uses throughout her work. Consider one of the principles of ecology: "If we cannot know everything, if we cannot control the effects of our actions, if even the smallest human interference can cause massive natural destruction, then the only way to keep something important is to preserve it."[30] As if in conjunction with the modern ecocritical view that removes humans from the pinnacle of environmental hierarchy, the poem features no readily discernible subject; it simply relates certain sensual stimuli. Those would normally imply the presence of a subject; however, it is not mentioned in any way, creating a detached, impersonal, and somewhat generalized speaking voice.

There is a rather ironic stance towards natural conservation in the poem, since nature, its colours, noise, smells, flavour, and vigorous activity, all qualities that are traditionally seen as noble, worthy, and even untouchable, shift to a very vivid representation in a "different" reality, possibly on TV. Television, or any such technological medium, becomes a means of conserving stereotypical exotic images, far removed from the real experiences of an average Slovak (or European and simply Western) citizen. They are in fact too vivid for human senses to handle, and lose their meaning, while the outside world is implied to be as barren as roughcast, as if reality were flashing through for a second. After decades of controlled emotional exaltation, such desensitization that resulted from distaste towards traditional poetry was far too common in the 1990s, signalling a retreat to intellectual and often self-referencing literary experiment. Kucbelová, however, reacts with detachment and loss of sensory perception to wholly different phenomena: excess of stimuli and alternative and augmented realities. Isolation, fear for one's safety, and loss of contact with other people, nature, and even reality, are prevalent themes of the book, often aiming to criticize overly individualistic and egotistical thinking. She scrutinizes the problems of identity and its formation, whether it involves superficial identification with emotionally charged nationalist concepts or substitution of personal identity with one provided by the consumerist lifestyle. "A Greenhouse Poem" presents a "non-subject" with no sense of self; it is a mere "viewer" of the scene, hardly living and identifying with its surroundings.

The non-subject passively receives all kinds of stimuli, but does not react to them in any way, not even intellectually. It is subject to nature's conscious influence, taking on the active role and, as if being aware, reshaping the environment and even attempting to play. The language is sterile – apart from "heaps of useless things" and "unexpected hiding places," there is virtually no indication of a human, subjective view. On the one hand, the environment is dramatically altered as opposed to what is expected of a home or of nature in the European climate; on the other hand, the passive stance of the "viewer" implies resignation in the face of the uncontrollable force of nature as well as certain fascination with its exotic character. The poem is presented as a "rapid home montage," a device usually used to connect and juxtapose unrelated components. This structure implies a loss of unity in favour of discontinuous life and experience – just as the home itself is a montage, an amalgamation of "useless things," the natural order becomes grotesque, out of joint, dangerous, with the image of a baboon and liana inside the house. But there is one mention of a trait one might call humane (and that humans still share with animals, but not with flora), although described impersonally and rather abruptly: the growing trust. However, this trust is not an expression of a positive influence; it merely eases the non-subject into numbness, stagnation. Where there is unconditional trust, there is no need to be aware, responsive, and responsible.

The poem features a rather apocalyptic vision, flashing for a second through hallucinogenic images that border on simulation. The expansion of nature that overwhelms humankind and forces it into disarray is also a recurring theme in Kucbelová's book. The civilizational conflicts and chaos contrast with the individual turmoil that is being numbed. Her poems epitomize the famous quote of Fredric Jameson that "it is easier to imagine an end to the world than an end to capitalism."[31] She readily embraces such an apocalyptic vision and begins to imagine it in a way that seems to have no ideological connotations, yet in line with ecocriticism it can be read as a state of numbing complicity: "in ecology, the replacement of centers with networks is closely connected to … the complicity of the human observer. We can't do anything without causing lots of side effects because everything is connected, nothing is isolated."[32] In this vein, Kucbelová criticizes human activity, both its destructive effects and retrospective attempts to remedy these effects. The struggle for survival leads to conservation that leads to inactivity, allowing for the roles to reverse and nature to take over. It is not an entirely hopeless vision, but it is certainly not a hopeful one for humankind.

MÁRIA FERENČUHOVÁ (1975)

Belonging to the same generation as the previous authors, Mária Ferenčuhová's work is formally rooted in the already mentioned post-modernist "anaesthetic" poetics but tackles issues that are either openly personal or subtle social commentaries. Ferenčuhová debuted in 2003 with her collection of poems *Skryté titulky* (Hidden subtitles) and followed with *Princíp neistoty* (The principle of uncertainty, 2008), *Ohrozený druh* (Endangered species, 2012), *Imunita* (Immunity, 2016), and *Černozem* (Chernozem, 2020). A detached view, resembling the eye of a camera, allows Ferenčuhová to decompose her world into fragments, eager to find sense and connection, one unifying principle. She meanders between rationality and emotionality, personal relationships and bigger civilizational picture, and motifs of life naturally intertwining with those of death.

In her third book *Ohrozený druh*, Ferenčuhová covers the themes of ecological catastrophe, destructive influence of human activity on nature, inevitable end of human civilization, and the eventual reversal of roles between people and animals. Her rising social engagement continues in *Imunita*, which covers similar topics under one leitmotif: death. The book documents the author's struggle with cancer, but it is not centred on her. Although it certainly features poems in the first-person perspective, it is not simply the perspective of the author. She lends her voice to those who have no voice: terminally ill patients pushed out into the social periphery. The poems are laden with anxiety, despair, and a sense of the end. Even when it comes to the death of a six-year-old boy, painted as entirely senseless in the poem "Meteor," the boy's perspective and his questions are universal, as evidenced by the poem's closing lines:

> Posledné úvahy šesťročného:
> Kto vystrihol slnko,
> aj keď páli,
> kto nám ho neúnavne
> ponad hlavy posúva?
> Kto si po oblohe púšťa meteory?
> Je svet taký, aký ho vidím?
> Som naozaj tým,
> kým si myslím, že som
> bol?[33]
>
> The last reflections of a six-year-old:
> who cuts off the sun,
> even when it's burning,
> who never gets tired
> pushing it over our heads?
> Who drifts meteors
> across the sky?
> Is the world so, as I see it?
> Am I really
> who I think I
> was?[34]

Ferenčuhová often writes in a hyper-realistic style, aiming to describe even the slightest details and derive sense from them. When the vision of the world as an entity that may be described in any objective terms fails, questions such as those posed by the boy become in fact relevant, although unanswerable. The author disintegrates her world into small particles, in conjunction with the general disintegration of the world around her, whether it involves humanity, Earth, nature, or personal death. The cold stare of the camera's eye becomes an anxious stare, eye-to-eye with the "big unknown." The questions asked might seem grotesque in a way a person faced with their imminent demise might seem grotesque to someone not particularly aware of their mortality.

The situation in the poem "Profile Picture" is similar. It also introduces a terminally ill person faced with their potential end. The final question posed by the boy in the previous poem, resonates here as well, in the speaker's confrontation with the changes brought on by a disease:

PROFILOVÝ OBRAZ

V nemocničnej izbe
zdanlivo nie som sama:
na monitore slová podpory.
Od dojatia
        takmer nedýcham
Tekuté kryštály v očiach.
Ani zem by viac vody nevpila.

Posledná fotka,
kde sa moja tvár
stáva akvaparkom,
        priesvitné trubice tobogánov
        vychádzajú z nosa,
        iné sa zabárajú do žíl,
bude naveky aktuálna,

ak si ju trúfnem
        zavesiť,
ak ešte vôbec
vládzem
pohnúť
prstom.[35]

PROFILE PICTURE

In hospital seclusion
apparently I'm not alone.
On the screen words of support.
I almost don't breathe from emotion.
Liquid crystals in my eyes,
and in my lungs it constantly rains.

Not even the earth could drink in more water.

The last photo,
in which my face
becomes an aquapark
(transparent tubes for toboggans
emerge from my nose,
others sink into my veins,)
will be relevant forever.

if I dare
post it online,
if I were just
able to move a finger.[36]

The lyrical subject is stylized as a woman lying on a hospital bed, secluded, yet not alone, alluding to the fact that the hospital is filled with people with conditions similar to hers. Here, the topic of seclusion of the terminally ill that pervades the book is merely a setting.[37] The title signals the intention: the difference between public appearance and private vision, exemplified by an extreme case of a serious illness. The poem opens with the lonesome woman looking at her phone, noting she is apparently not alone and reading words of support. The technological aspect of her experience is crucial. On the one hand, while she is sentenced to seclusion, the phone provides her with at least some, though detached, contact that keeps her spirits up and occupies her, figuratively keeps her alive; on the other hand, she is literally kept alive by medical machinery. There is a distinct, grotesque accord between the woman's emotional and physical reactions. She cannot figuratively breathe from emotion, has metaphorical crystals in her eyes, is unable to move her finger in reluctance – yet all these can (and must) be taken literally from the perspective of real physical disability due to her illness.

Most of us know profile pictures as photos on social media, as portraits, or any pictures with a certain personal significance used to create the desired first impression in the online world, to represent a person. The profile picture, a photo that the ill woman contemplates posting online, is not traditionally representative, but it certainly represents her in her current state, unfiltered and frank. Ferenčuhová almost makes it seem that the picture does not actually represent a real person anymore, likening the woman's face to a mere series of tubes resembling something so light-hearted, almost childish, as an aquapark or toboggan. Furthermore, a profile can be understood as a list of traits – the sole fact that the woman is ill becomes her defining character trait. And last but certainly not least, a profile, as a perspective, indicates a surface view of a person that obscures a substantial part of them. In this case, it also creates a feeling of the reader's more direct involvement, as if sitting by the hospital bed, looking at the woman from the side.

A profile implies that something is unseen. This is precisely the sentiment Ferenčuhová aims to formulate – that society generally tends to marginalize people with terminal illnesses, and they still exist and carry on with their lives, although with deepened sense of their own finiteness. The author shows that there are dramatic differences among the social stereotypes, the public image, and the self-image of the terminally ill. The "reluctance" of the woman stems from the important fact that the photo she prepares to post online might be her very last likeness. In the world of social media that favours fast consumption, it would hardly be relevant forever, but metaphorically it is, because that is how she could be eventually remembered. Posting the photo would then mean admitting: "this is me," or even "this was me." However, it is not only her alleged reluctance that stops her from posting the photograph – it is also her physical disability. The body effectively prevents her from coming to terms with her appearance, her faltering state, her identity reduced to that of a patient, an object receiving support from the others. The contact with the outside world then has two sides: it provides support yet raises a dilemma whether people would be supportive even if they saw the woman's unhealthy and grotesque appearance.

Ferenčuhová's matter-of-fact mode of writing is used here for a different effect – not to signal desensitization, but sensitivity towards the fate of a terminally ill person.[38] In an extreme example of this approach, Ferenčuhová incorporates parts of several medical records within her poems, even including as a separate poem a verbatim medical record of a person who succumbed to heart disease. Such an approach may seem detached, but it exemplifies a principle that was identified by literary critics as documentary and, as to her apparent social engagement, cautionary.[39] Ferenčuhová's perceived earnestness in translating her first-hand experience with a life-threatening disease into poetry was often positively mentioned in reviews. It also made her into a relatively well-known representative of contemporary Slovak poetry, who routinely gives interviews in large newspapers and, notwithstanding her book's aesthetic qualities and its well-portrayed world of a marginalized social group, even wins high-profile awards. Ferenčuhová thus came to embody the image of a new type of engaged author that has developed since the 2010s – engaged not only in her literary work, but also as a public figure, not tied to a political party, yet prominent in voicing a liberal worldview, not radically challenging the status quo, but distinctly hinting at its faults.[40]

ENGAGED WRITERS OF TODAY

In a reciprocal fashion, as long as poetry still carries a certain symbolic function in society, social engagement is an integral part of poetry. In Slovakia, the character of the social function of poetry was heavily determined by social and political movements of the past, but its main contemporary concern has been the issue of identity. Social engagement channelled through poetry often meanders between expressing spiritual and secular, national and transnational, individualistic and collective identities, whether affirming the status quo, criticizing it, or downright rejecting it.

So, what is the conclusion as to social engagement in contemporary Slovak poetry? Where does it stand in these terms? The works presented in this chapter showcase some contemporary Slovak poetry that consciously embraces its potential function as social commentary. Contemporary Slovak poetry continues to confront the question of public engagement with newfound force, whether it is Habaj's search for identity in the post-postmodern mode, Kucbelová's sardonic and sarcastic criticism of uncontrollable human activity, or Ferenčuhová's deeply anxious and existential voice of all-human concern. Interestingly, social engagement as a poetic principle grew from a seemingly unexpected place – from deconstructionist poetry that eschewed any relations with the outside world and society. But even that mode of writing retained its critical function, aimed at the phenomena amplified by globalization such as consumerism, detached and dysfunctional interpersonal relationships, or loss of one's individual identity.

Today's young generation of Slovak writers do not hesitate to fulfill poetry's social function. The authors born in the 1980s and later differ from the authors discussed in this chapter (and their generational and aesthetically close peers such as Nóra Ružičková) in that they naturally and openly interact with social issues and zeitgeist of Slovak society, whether it be through radically formulated stances in biting satirical tone and in the distinct shock value of their poetry, or through more toned down critique of certain social issues. What still connects all of these contemporary Slovak poets, regardless of their poetics and opinions, is their refusal – sometimes implicit, sometimes explicit – to speak on behalf of any higher entity, institution, or official state ideology. They relate to or oppose certain ideological positions and their possible branches such as transnationalism, feminism, and humanism.

For a small country with a long tradition of literature intersecting with politics and social movements, which has often been concerned with its national identity, its significance on the European and global scale, and its relationship to larger nations, the state of engaged Slovak poetry in the last thirty years might seem a bit deficient. But although writers of today refuse to perform the role of officially designated conscience, to be committed, they no longer seem to mind being engaged, including moral and ethical messages in their work that are necessary for poetry to be engaging as well. Just as in F.X. Šalda's previously quoted remark from almost a century ago, politics cannot be removed from poetry. It is promising to see that Slovak authors, prone to mistrust and individualism after decades of mandated conformity to their state patrons, have finally started to transcend the distinction between engaged poetry and "authentic" poetry, and openly share their concerns about social issues with their audiences.

NOTES

1 For few general notes on the myth of the national writer and the role of Central and Eastern European intelligentsia in the society and especially national revival, see the chapter "The Writer as National Hero," in Wachtel, *Remaining Relevant after Communism.*

2 Šalda, "Několik myšlenek na tema básník a politika," 85.

3 Taranenková, "Premeny poetík?," 76.

4 "Literatúra 90. Rokov – výnimočná alebo svoja?," 30.

5 Vlašín, *Slovník literární teorie*, 21, 361.

6 Cuddon, *Penguin Dictionary of Literary Terms and Literary Theory*, 161.

7 *Slovo* indirectly relates to the poem *Vila Tereza* (1963) by the prominent leftist poet and intellectual Ladislav Novomeský (1904–1976), who stayed loyal to the communist cause even after being sentenced in the 1950s to life imprisonment by the same system he had helped build. He was later pardoned, joining the regime as a devoted intellectual who successfully endured the hardships of the twentieth century.

8 It should be noted that all four of these writers were either prose writers or essayists.

9 As for poets, see the case of Taťjana Lehenová in chapter 6 of this volume, and the more ambiguous cases of Ivan Kolenič and Jozef Urban, fellow poets of Lehenová's generation.

10 See Sartre, *"What Is Literature?" and Other Essays*, and Adorno, "Commitment," 87–8.

11 Mikula, *Na zapadákove nič nového*, 14–15.

12 Šrank, *Individualizovaná literatúra.*

13 Šrank, *Aktéri a tendencie literárnej kultúry na Slovensku po roku 1989*, 27–31.

14 This would produce paradoxical situations in the 1990s, such as when authors collectively known as the Barbarian Generation (Kamil Zbruž, Ján Litvák, and Andrijan Turan, by extension also Ivan Kolenič, Robert Bielik, and Jozef Urban), renowned for their shocking, provocative, and sometimes offensive poetry and lifestyle, would publish their books with financial support from the controversial state-mandated fund Pro Slovakia through which the Mečiarist system used to discriminate against "disloyal" writers (Šrank, *Aktéri a tendencie literárnej kultúry na Slovensku po roku 1989*, 29–30).

15 Šrank, *Individualizovaná literatúra.*

16 The odzemok was traditionally a shepherd's dance or a robber's "weapon dance," which includes vigorous jumps and squats with a *valaška*, a

characteristic Slovak axe, or with various other tools, performed in moderate tempo to basically any folk song with a repetitive motif. It is often a part of certain ceremonies and was originally meant to showcase the agility and strength of the dancer.

17 The same year, his satirical poem *Dobrú noc, moja milá* (Good night, my dear) was published in *Telegraf* and resulted in a lawsuit, filed by Slobodník against Feldek. The poem mentions a figure who was simultaneously a Nazi officer and State Security agent, alluding to Slobodník's past according to his memoirs. The lawsuit was settled in 2001 in the European Court, with Feldek as the ultimate winner (see *Rozsudek Evropského soudu*).

18 Feldek's and Štrasser's books were published by Archa, a publishing house founded by the dissident Martin M. Šimečka, and Champagne Avantgarde, an independent publisher. Hevier's book was published by the state publishing house Slovenský spisovateľ (privatized in 1992) in an edition devoted to satire. Hevier would later found his own publishing house, which became rather large and successful in the 1990s.

19 The most frequently cited names in the 2014 *Romboid* survey were Habaj, Kucbelová, Ferenčuhová, Marcela Veselková, Nóra Ružičková, Vlado Šimek, Mirka Ábelová, and Eva Tomkuliaková.

20 These experimental trends in Slovak poetry are covered in more detail in chapter 6 of this volume.

21 This form of implicit, yet marked social engagement is also present in the work of Peter Macsovszky, in the composition of his books and intertextual communication signalled through gradual repetition, sprouting of form and erosion of meaning – that among other things suggest environmental concern. See Hostová, "Of Ecosystems and Translations," 78.

22 Rédey, *Súčasná slovenská poézia v kontexte civilizačno-kultúrných premien*, 68–71.

23 Habaj, *Caput Mortuum*, 72–6.

24 Habaj, "Letter to a Developer," 86–9.

25 Urbanová, "Báseň Michala Habaja *List developerovi* zo zbierky *Caput Mortuum* (2015)," 141.

26 Jareš, "Být sám sobě šaškem," 62–4.

27 Kucbelová, *Vie, čo urobí*, 16.

28 Kucbelová, "A Greenhouse Poem," 269.

29 This is true for English – in Slovak, the original word is "skleník," which would literally translate as "glass house." Nevertheless, the connotations of humidity, heat, and enclosed space are still valid, though subtler.

30 Campbell, "The Land and Language of Desire," 131.
31 Jameson, "Future City."
32 Campbell, "The Land and Language of Desire," 132.
33 Ferenčuhová, *Imunita*, 30–1.
34 Ferenčuhová, *Tidal Events*, 53.
35 Ferenčuhová, *Imunita*, 27.
36 Ferenčuhová, *Tidal Events*, 92.
37 In another poem *Premeny* (*Changes*), this seclusion is addressed not only socially, but also spatially – it draws on the fact that several trolleybus lines in Bratislava terminate at (or did when the book was published) hospitals, other medical facilities (such as National Institute of Heart Diseases or National Oncological Institute) and even a cemetery, often located outside of the wider city centre. As such, the public transport lines become a metaphor for life's journey – not only does the terminus become a literal "terminal station" of life, the public transport lines transform the matter of life and death into a fairly everyday affair, traveling between the metaphorical stations.
38 Rácová, "Imunizáciou k scitlivovaniu," 136–7.
39 Ibid. See also Šrank, "Básnická zbierka Márie Ferenčuhovej Imunita medzi dokumentárnosťou a reflexívnosťou."
40 Another fine example of a woman poet as a public figure of sorts in Slovakia would be Mirka Ábelová. Although her poetry is often received with mixed feelings by academic literary critics, it is rather popular among a general readership. Her poetry evolved from expressing individualistic rebellious stances with clear shock value to reflections on relationships, social roles, and the unseen side of motherhood, still with a head-on approach and certain shock value.

BIBLIOGRAPHY

"Angažovaná poézia." *Romboid* 49, no. 9–10 (2014): 9–36.

Adorno, Theodor. "Commitment." *New Left Review* 1 (1974): 87–8. https://newleftreview.org/issues/i87/articles/theodor-adorno-commitment.

Campbell, SueEllen. "The Land and Language of Desire." In *The Ecocriticism Reader: Landmarks in Literary Geology*, edited by Cheryll Glotfelty and Harold Fromm, 124–36. Athens and London: University of Georgia Press, 1996.

Cuddon, J.A. *The Penguin Dictionary of Literary Terms and Literary Theory*. London: Penguin Group, 1999.

Ferenčuhová, Mária. *Imunita*. Kordíky: Skalná ruža, 2016.
– *Tidal Events. Selected Poems*. Translated by James Sutherland-Smith. Bristol: Shearsman Books, 2018.
Habaj, Michal. *Caput Mortuum*. Bratislava: OZ Vlna/Drewo a srd, 2015.
– "Letter to a Developer." Translated by John Minahane. In *Slovak Literary Review 2015*, 86–9. Bratislava: Centre for Information on Literature, 2015.
Hostová, Ivana. "Of Ecosystems and Translations: Some Ways of Translating Non-traditional Texts." *World Literature Studies* 8, no. 1 (2016): 74–85. http://www.wls.sav.sk/wp-content/uploads/WLS1_2016_Hostov%C3%A1.pdf.
Jameson, Fredric. "Postmodernism and Consumer Society." In *The Cultural Turn: Selected Writings on the Postmodern 1983–1998*, 1–20. London and New York: Verso, 1998.
– "Future City." *New Left Review* 2, no. 21 (2003). https://newleftreview.org/issues/ii21/articles/fredric-jameson-future-city.
Jareš, Michal. "Být sám sobě šaškem." *Romboid* 48, no. 8 (2013): 62–4.
Kucbelová, Katarína. *Vie, čo urobí*. Bratislava: Artforum, 2013.
– "A Greenhouse Poem." Translated by Ivana Hostová. *Poem: International English Language Quarterly* 4, no. 2 (2016): 269.
"Literatúra 90. Rokov – výnimočná alebo svoja?" RAK 1, no. 2 (1996): 19–32.
Mikula, Valér. *Na zapadákove nič nového*. Bratislava: Kalligram, 1999.
Rácová, Veronika. "Imunizáciou k scitlivovaniu (Mária Ferenčuhová: *Imunita*)." *Romboid* 51, no. 10 (2016): 133–9.
Rédey, Zoltán. *Súčasná slovenská poézia v kontexte civilizačno-kultúrnych premien*. Nitra: Filozofická fakulta Univerzity Konštantína Filozofa v Nitre, 2005.
Rozsudek Evropského soudu pro lidská práv z 12.7.2001 ve věci Feldek proti Slovenské Republice. Accessed 11 June 2022. http://spcp.prf.cuni.cz/judikat/es-feldek.htm.
Sartre, Jean-Paul. *"What Is Literature?" and Other Essays*. Cambridge, Massachusetts: Harvard University Press, 1988.
Šalda, František Xaver. "Několik myšlenek na tema básník a politika." In Šaldův zápisník, 84–110. Praha: Otto Girgal, 1933–34.
Šrank, Jaroslav. *Individualizovaná literatúra*. Bratislava: Cathedra, 2013.
– *Aktéri a tendencie literárnej kultúry na Slovensku po roku 1989*. Bratislava: Univerzita Komenského, 2015.
– "Básnická zbierka Márie Ferenčuhovej Imunita medzi dokumentárnosťou a reflexívnosťou." *Platforma pre literatúru a výskum* 30, no. 4 (2017). https://www.plav.sk/node/55.

Taranenková, Ivana. "Premeny poetík? (Niekoľko poznámok k reflexii slovenskej literatúry po roku 1989)." *Slovenská literatúra* 56, no. 6 (2009): 72–9.

Urbanová, Eva. "Báseň Michala Habaja *List developerovi* zo zbierky *Caput Mortuum* (2015)." *Fraktál* 2, no. 1 (2019): 141.

Vlašín, Štěpán. *Slovník literární teorie*. Praha: Československý spisovatel, 1977.

Wachtel, Andrew. *Remaining Relevant after Communism: The Role of the Writer in Eastern Europe*. Chicago, IL: University of Chicago Press, 2006.

CHAPTER SIX

Subversion and Experimentation in Contemporary Poetry

Ivana Hostová

In the atmosphere of cultural liberation in the 1990s, Slovak poets started exploring verse as a means of intimate self-expression and a means of voicing a rebellious attitude towards societal expectations. With the dissolution of state control over the cultural field, established institutions governing cultural politics lost their legitimizing power, and critics, editors, and newly established or restructured literary magazines played a crucial role in curating the production of literary artefacts and forming new cultural hierarchies. With the onset of radical individualization and the emergence of the entrepreneurial self in post-socialist countries, authors and small presses as the producers of literary goods also actively participated in reshaping the literary scene.[1] A natural source of inspiration for those who welcomed the opportunity to embrace creative freedom was the original and translated literature produced during the "golden sixties": the poetry of the Beat Generation, post-Second World War avant-garde, and a general spirit of mixing of the high and low (genres, language, ethos). The late 1980s and 1990s witnessed a surge in Czech and Slovak translations of the Beat Generation authors (William S. Burroughs, Allen Ginsberg, Jack Kerouac) and of poets writing in a similar vein (especially Charles Bukowski). Their countercultural ethos, visionary poetics, and radically free heroes appealed to many young aspiring Slovak poets. The first wave of writing that visibly broke free of the expectations of the former-regime's literary gatekeepers strongly resonated with the free-spirited ethos of Beat culture.

By the middle of the 1990s, a movement consisting of a group of authors leaning towards various forms of non-traditional and innovative writing procedures, critical theory, and deconstruction started gaining momentum. Their deconstructive-experimental approach to writing – rarely before had anything so radical appeared in Slovak poetry – caused numerous literary scandals, provoked literary wars, and attracted significant attention of critics and the following generation of poets.[2] With a large proportion of young (but also established) poets employing experimental and conceptual approaches to writing and modifying them according to their own vision since the early 2000s, the use of variously modified non-conventional and conceptual writing techniques became less a subversive gesture aimed at dismantling past models of the literary and more the mainstream means of poetic expression. The current landscape of Slovak poetry is lively and diverse as to expressive means and topics. Poets seek inspiration in all areas of life and arts, and with national support for the arts and literature, the sphere attracts talented young poets, critics, editors, and publishers, despite the admittedly dwindling audiences.

In this chapter, I highlight key Slovak poets who adopt deconstructive-experimental approaches in Slovak poetry, ones that I would argue have most intensely engaged with the "now" of a national culture positioned in a globalized world since 1989. These poets seek inspiration in contemporary world poetry, twentieth and twenty-first-century theory, science, and the world's spiritual systems and often touch upon global issues such as environmental crises, social differences, or political polarization. I will first provide a short discussion of the landscape of Slovak poetry in the 1990s and subsequently introduce the formally most innovative and inspiring works of the past two decades, during which experimental poetry increasingly reflects globalizing trends in Slovak culture. These texts employ a host of experimental approaches that often verge on poetic research and frequently transgress the boundaries of media, arts, and literary and academic writing.[3]

THE SUBVERSIVE AND EXPERIMENTAL POETIC GESTURES OF THE 1990S

The 1990s provided an opportunity for poets to test creative freedom and explore poetry as a means of authentic, radically individual, and intimate self-expression. The generation of poets of this period born in the 1960s pioneered intimate and socially transgressive writing, while also opening or dissolving established traditional poetic forms. The collections of poetry by Jozef Urban (1964–1999), Ivan Kolenič (b. 1965), and Taťjana Lehenová (b. 1961) expressed the spontaneously rebellious attitude of the young generation towards the mainstream society and institutions.[4]

One of the poems that illustrates this trend is Taťjana Lehenová's "Malá nočná mora" ("A Little Nightmare Music"). The sexually explicit text written in free verse – a combination that epitomises a radical shift in what poetry could be and do – is a joyful and humorous investigation into the linguistic handling of erotic love from the perspective of the female persona: "I want it. / I want you to be big and strong. / I want you to be a king."[5] It was first published in the literary periodical *Slovenské pohľady* in 1988 and on its inclusion in the poet's debut *Pre vybranú spoločnosť* (For the chosen few, 1989) caused a literary scandal. The discussions it provoked revolved around both its sexual content and its aesthetic qualities, which were perceived to be transgressing the established notions of literariness. The underlying impulse that fuelled the scandal, however, was the fact that a text carrying such content was written by a female author.[6] The book was the subject of over ten reviews, and the polemics it started spread across several issues of the literary magazine *Literárny týždenník* (Literary weekly).[7]

The wide critical response the publication elicited sprang from entrenched assumptions about the function of literature, which had been organized, orchestrated, and monitored under state socialism. The controversy also illustrates the exalted position that poetry still held in Slovak society during the period of transition from the totalitarian regime to liberal capitalism and democracy. Poems and reviews were still regularly published in several daily newspapers, literary "wars" were not completely isolated from the wider public debates, and poetry as a genre enjoyed a relatively large readership. Another important factor in play was that after a long period during which restrictions on topics, ethos, literary devices, and established notions of literariness kept poetry within rather narrow limits, transgression was not only still possible, but could also be perceived as extreme. This can rarely be said about the contemporary literary landscape.

By the mid-1990s, however, most of the poets who introduced the authentic subversive poetic gesture into Slovak literature stopped publishing poetry. This kind of writing, verse based on excess and expressing radical individual experience that broke taboos associated with such topics as intoxication or sex, was paradoxically embraced by poets who conformed to the political establishment. These writers quickly adapted to the post-1992 political circumstances, in which the regime of Vladimír Mečiar (who served as prime minister from 1992 to 1998) tried to control the cultural sphere by allocating resources based on the political allegiance of individual artists.[8] Their poetry of excess (which by the end of the 1990s turned to non-Christian spirituality) was retrospectively recognized not as a striving for literary excellence, but as a calculated step that secured for them the role of the writer and state funding.[9] State patronage in the period of populist "Mečiarism" was granted to cultural agents who were politically loyal to the cultural policies aiming at strengthening national cultural identity.[10] The seemingly transgressive authenticity of these poets created an apparently harmless illusion of radically free possibilities of poetic expression and, by extension, could serve as a demonstration of the regime's democracy. In reality, the state once again wished to uphold a patriarchal position towards culture and society that it had occupied during state socialism.[11] In contrast with the previous regime, this time there were no persecutions or censorship. The attempted manipulation of culture was solely orchestrated through the state's funding mechanisms. The distribution of funds aimed at supporting non-commercial literature was officially based on decisions of committees composed of specialists. Their rulings, however, were frequently disregarded; committee members would frequently be chosen based on their political inclinations, while funds for authors and publishers who openly showed their lack of sympathy with the political regime would be cut.[12]

Those agents active in the literary field who fully embraced the newly gained creative freedom sought alternative ways of financing their activities – they set up small presses, published books using their own resources, approached commercial sponsors, and applied for grants provided by various foreign foundations that were interested in aiding the democratic cultural development of the freshly post-socialist country. In the field of poetry, the most promising groups of writers embraced poetically subversive gestures leaning towards various forms of non-traditional and innovative writing procedures where shock and radical break with conventional literariness was an essential element. Key poets writing in this vein and making their debuts in the 1990s include Peter Macsovszky (b. 1966), Peter Šulej (b. 1964), Michal Habaj (b. 1974), and Nóra Ružičková (b. 1977). The next section briefly introduces their early writing, and I touch on the further development of their individual oeuvres in the following discussion of Slovak poetry in the new millennium.

It was Peter Macsovszky's widely reviewed first collection of poetry, *Strach z utópie* (Fear of utopia, 1994), which he published in the small press Drewo a srd founded by Peter Šulej, followed by the collection *Ambit* (1995), that accelerated the emergence of the freely associated group of non-conventional poets.[13] Macsovszky drew inspiration from a multitude of sources, including visual arts, Hungarian and Anglophone poetry, twentieth-century philosophy, and religious studies. The opening text of his first book of poetry illustrates some of the characteristic features of his poetics – its subversive potential, the poet's interest in institutional critique, conceptual writing, and minimalism.

THIS IS A REAL THING

Toto je viazaná reč básnického prejavu.
Označuje stupeň textovej viazanosti,
usporiadanie textu v jeho tvarovej podobe.
Vzťahuje sa skôr na formu ako na obsah.
Jej prednosť je v stručnosti.

Toto tu je základná jednotka
básnického rytmu, spravidla jeden riadok.
Vyznačuje sa zvukovým usporiadaním.

Doteraz povedané sa v plnej miere
vzťahuje aj na toto zoskupenie
základných jednotiek básnického rytmu
na základe spoločnej rýmovej schémy
a uplatnenia
rovnakého metrického pôdorysu.

Najmenšou strofou je dvojveršie.

Ak sa schéma v texte sústavne mení
a nepodlieha pravidelnosti,
vzťahuje sa skôr na obsah ako na formu.[14]

THIS IS A REAL THING

This is the regular speech of poetic discourse.
It denotes a degree of textual regulation,
arrangement of the text in its formal shape.
It relates to form rather than content.
Its merit is brevity.

This here is the basic unit
of poetic rhythm, usually one line.
It is characterized by a phonic structure.

What has been said so far fully
applies also to this grouping
of basic units of poetic rhythm
on the basis of a common rhyming scheme
and application
of the same metrical plan.

A couplet is the smallest stanza.

If the scheme in the text constantly changes
and is not subject to regularity,
it relates to content rather than form.[15]

The poem, composed from selected entries appropriated from a canonical Slovak dictionary of literary terms, demystifies the sterility of poetic conventions and opens a gap between the signifier and the signified in a way which was previously unexplored in Slovak poetry.[16] The novelty of this kind of writing, its intricate and clever philosophical charge, and the sheer bold impertinence of its gesture resulted in the book becoming an event that marked the beginning of contemporary Slovak poetry.

Equally important in 1994 was the fact that Peter Šulej set up his press Drewo a srd and published his debut collection of poems, *Porno* (Porn), and that both he and Macsovszky continued writing with great vigour and actively grew their network. Peter Šulej's poetry leans towards dynamic, joyfully subversive play investigating new developments in technologies and results in a sort of flashy verbal and visual disco. His collections of poetry employ collage and pastiche to juxtapose fragments of pop culture, references to music, science, geographical places, and eroticism, and both revitalize and develop an impressively wide array of experimental writing techniques. Šulej is also one of the pioneers of generative poetry in Slovak – in 1989, he generated a poem in the computer language Modula 2, which worked with a database of sixty adjectives, sixty nouns, and sixty verbs.[17] Its refrain was published in *Porno* as "Erotický fragment" ("Erotic Fragment").

EROTICKÝ FRAGMENT

Rozrušená príliš hustým rastrom
zelenej trávy
Prestáva vnímať okolie
Voniam lístky mäty v tvojom náručí
Zasypem jamy prvotných výbuchov

EROTIC FRAGMENT

Excited by excessively thick grid
of green grass
She stops registering the surroundings
I smell mint leaves in your arms
I'll fill in the pits of primary explosions[18]

Michal Habaj's debut *80-967760-4-5* (1997) was strongly influenced by the writing of Peter Macsovszky. However, beginning with his second collection *Gymnazistky. Prázdniny trinásťročnej* (Grammar school girls: Holidays of a thirteen-year-old, 1999), the poet started developing his unique style based on play with fragments of pop culture, advertising, sci-fi, cyberpunk, and a wide range of Slovak and world poetry. The poem "Čo zostalo z toho všetkého" (What remained of all that) was published in his third collection *Korene neba. Básne z posledného storočia* (The roots of heaven: Poems of the last century, 2000).

ČO ZOSTALO Z TOHO VŠETKÉHO

odchádzajú: zanechávajúc za sebou spúšť: horiace
kone: mŕtve tanky: meče a klávesnice: uťaté ako ruky
krvavé: v tráve a tŕstí: nahé chrastie tiel: už malé a
neviditeľné robotické systémy: bzučia a vzlietajú:
mechanické muchy digitálne lienky: ozbrojené vzdušné
sily: nové bombardéry: kto v nich sedí a riadi z kokpitu
hlávky smrtonosné stroje času? bojím sa: že už nikdy
tvoja dlaň v moju sa neschúli: keď odumierajú nám
spomienky: na krásu nahého tela: hlboko pod skafandrom
väzneného: pod novými a novými vrstvami hmoty:
nepočujem tvoje srdce: nepočujem tvoju krv: *hlboko*
hlboko: ďaleko ďaleko: na mŕtvych planinách:
sa potácame: dve amorfné bytosti objímajúce sa
cez vrstvy spomienok: zo všetkých strán: prichádzajú
bojové systémy: kam sa schovávame pred nebezpečenstvom
ak nie do svojich sŕdc?[19]

WHAT REMAINED OF ALL THAT

they depart: leaving behind them a dustbowl: burning
horses: dead tanks: swords and keyboards: chopped like bloody
hands: in grass and thicket: bare brushwood of bodies: now small and
invisible robot systems: buzz and become airborne:
the mechanical flies the digital ladybirds: armed aerial
forces: new bombarders: who sits there and guides from the cockpit
the death-bringing warheads the engines of time? I fear: that never
more will your hand huddle in mine: when our memories
are dying away: of the naked body's beauty: deep under the spacesuit
of the prisoner: under more and more layers of matter:
I do not hear your heart: I do not hear your blood: *deep*
deep: faraway faraway: on the dead plateaux:
we grope: two amorphous beings embracing
through layers of memories: from all sides: arrive
the fighting systems: where shall we hide from danger
if not in our hearts?[20]

The poem combines several emblematic motives of Michal Habaj's writing, layering the sentiments of courtly love, romantic exultation, decadent aestheticism, and the desensitization brought about by advanced technologies and cool, detached capitalist relationships. Cybernetic motives are, in the vein of cyberpunk aesthetics, set in a post-apocalyptic, post-human world. Nostalgia, a longing for a long-lost chivalric world of warm human touch and genuine emotion, is the dominant mood in this poem as well as in much of Michal Habaj's writing in general. The speaker is often stylised as a cyborg – a role that, however, as the critic Zoltán Rédey asserts, only serves to highlight the nostalgic effect which gives the charm of the lost non-technological old world greater gravitational force.[21] The tone of Habaj's writing, constantly balancing between irony and genuine longing, traps the speaker in what the German sociologist Ferdinand Tönnies termed *Gesellschaft* – "a world which is haunted by an escapist nostalgia for the eternal verities of nature," inhabited by divided selves "consisting of a private personal core and a social front or image" so typical of the late twentieth century.[22] Connected with the element of nostalgia is the portrayal of gender identities and erotic love in the post-apocalyptic atmosphere. The imagined female addressee, present only as an absence, as a memory of a beautiful object, is an embodiment of the lost world of courtly love.

As Michal Habaj's take on erotic love in this poem suggests, the changes in society, towards which this poetry is acutely attuned, radically disrupted all sorts of orders and identities, including the assumed gender roles (and their literary representations). Critical inquiries into gender identities, mainly mediated by the feminist magazine *Aspekt* founded in 1993, were also defining prisms through which the transforming Slovak culture of the 1990s was rethinking itself. Poetry as an expression of the zeitgeist reflected this as well. One of the first young women poets accepted into "contemporary" Slovak poetry – i.e., the writing nested in the specific circumstances of the 1990s – was Nóra Ružičková. Her debut collection of poems, *Mikronauti* (Micronauts, 1998) was not closely connected with Macsovszky's, Šulej's, or Habaj's writing in a poetological sense, but was nevertheless published by Šulej's Drewo a srd. Ružičková's work draws on feminist thought, philosophy, psychoanalysis, critical theory, and employs the techniques and concepts of intermedia art and conceptual writing. In *Mikronauti*, she combines her background in the visual arts, feminisms, and poetry with an accent on the speaking persona's self-scrutiny used as a tool for a situated investigation of the world, language, and the possibility of understanding and conveying messages.

FROM *MIKRONAUTI*

Jediným odkrytím ucha
sa odhalila nahota
o vykradnutí obrazu slovami

V obojstrannej ilúzii priestoru
bolesť v tvare lievika

V uvedomení si seba ako úbežníka
protikladná ilúzia pozorovateľa

Jediné odkrytie úlohy
skrylo obojstrannosť nahoty

FROM *MICRONAUTS*

A single uncovering of the ear
revealed the nudity
of the image robbed by words

In the two-sided illusion of space
funnel-shaped pain

In the realization of the self as the vanishing point
a contrary illusion of the observer

A single uncovering of the task
concealed two-sided character of nudity[23]

The poem introduces some of the main themes of Ružičková's poetic research: a keen interest in effects of perception and materiality of signs, an emphasis on the physical experience as an opportunity to scrape off the sediments of cultural codes, and the deconstruction of the body and its reflection in the visual culture.

Thanks to the vigorous energy propelled by the sudden freedom of movement and speech as well as the admirable social and intellectual skills and persistence of these early initiators of experimental approaches, this strand of writing quickly gained a strong momentum. By the turn of the millennium, its practitioners had built an extensive infrastructure of small presses, events, periodicals, critics, and poets, and became involved in various international network-building projects.

SLOVAK POETRY IN THE GLOBALIZED PRESENT

In the new millennium, the integration of Slovakia in international political structures including the EU and NATO has also shaped the country's cultural policies, which have become less nationally oriented and increasingly open to global impulses. These circumstances have made it possible for innovative writing to move from grassroots forms into institutionally sanctioned ones. With the stability of state patronage and established status on the literary scene, the functions of this strand of poetry shifted as well. Gradually, the use of variously modified and often downplayed conceptual and avant-garde techniques came to be perceived as mainstream rather than subversive. With Slovak culture as a whole striving to forge an identity on the international scene, poets started looking at representing national identity and entering transnational cultural spaces. Among other venues, this breaking out of the national space has been facilitated by the nodal formats of festivals that invite intermedia and collaborative works. Most poets wishing to enter the field in the new millennium have taken the experimental and conceptual approaches into account and modified them according to their own talents and understanding of the function of poetry in contemporary culture.

Among the poets of the new millennium, Katarína Kucbelová (b. 1979) and Mária Ferenčuhová (b. 1975), who both made their debuts in 2003, emerged as key figures that would help shape the face of Slovak poetry. New innovative writing techniques, especially concerning electronic literature, were introduced by Zuzana Husárová (b. 1983), who published her first collection of poetry (*Liminal*) in 2012. Since Slovakia took a neoliberal turn, poetry has been pushed to the periphery of public attention. New poetry is rarely discussed or published outside the literary scene, and the readership size of newly published contemporary poets does not exceed a few hundred readers. Nevertheless, the sphere continues to attract young poets, critics, editors, and publishers. Recently, several promising poets have intensely engaged with current social and political issues and problems associated with non-normative or marginalized identities in their writing. The most noteworthy of the poets publishing their first collections of poetry after 2015 are Michal Tallo (b. 1993), Ivona Pekárková (b. 1988), and Dominika Moravčíková (b. 1992).

A significant part of critically acclaimed contemporary Slovak poetry considers the complex circumstances in which it is positioned on the trans-local and trans-national level. Instead of enclosing itself in its own marginality and replicating it, it aims to engage with the present and actively builds the infrastructure of the field (through readerships, publishing houses, literary magazines, poetry readings). These endeavours can broadly be grouped in two (somewhat overlapping) approaches. The more traditional approach remains mostly text- and book-bound and uses the expressive means that are most readily accessible to readers of genres other than poetry (fiction, journalism, etc.). The other approach, which is especially relevant to this book's focus on how Slovak literature engages with the world and the one I outline in the rest of this chapter, can be characterized as experimental writerly practice, often the result of collaboration, one that crosses linguistic, geographical, and media borders, abandons the compartmentalization of arts, humanities, and sciences, and interacts with new technologies. This poetry explores the creative possibilities offered by trespasses and cross-pollinations and most readily widens its audiences to include people interested in other arts and in the technosphere.

THE SANCTITY OF INTRUSION, OR THE BEAUTY OF REPETITION WITH VARIATION

Peter Macsovszky: Santa Panica *(2014)*

As the poem discussed in the previous section shows, Peter Macsovszky's writing is inherently subversive and critical. It intensely examines institutions, prejudice, and preconceived ideas on all levels, from the physical through the psychological to the ideological. His text-based conceptual book, *Santa Panica* (2014), introduces a compositional experiment that is modelled on a pattern legible in mathematical, musical, psychological, and environmental terms. It combines a gradual – viral and organic – disintegration of a strictly applied method using an Internet search engine. A major part of the book can be thought of as a fractal whose parts gradually become the nurturing ground for the subsequent growth of the text.[24] The starting point of the collection is a phrase from a book on karma. The method consisted in the author entering the words of the sentence one by one into a search engine. For each, he associatively picked a phrase that suited his intentions and arranged the sentences into a stanza in the order defined by the first verbal chain on karma. Then the first sentence generated in this way served as the impulse for the second stanza, which was then generated in the same way as the first one. The process continues and spreads over various poems until the regular pattern gets broken by the intrusion of the lexeme "panic." Increasingly, the text behaves more erratically as the poems start to spring from the corresponding paragraphs and are partly infected and disintegrated by this corrosive element. Thus the flow of the text models the way panic functions on the psychological and social level, as an element bringing chaos into the structure and logic, but at the same time, by its repetitive obsessive behaviour, it creates a new (pseudo)logic, a new structure that organizes elements into new patterns that can no longer be attributed to a rational construction of the world.

STRACH Z PANIKY

Rozhovor je aj to že jeden rozpráva. Nepíšem
literatúru a už vôbec nie hodnotnú. Byť tlmenou
neznamená byť šedou myškou. Viem že nemám
tvár anjela. Tieto čísla odrážajú rastúci záujem.

Rozhovor je panika. Aj to že jeden rozpráva je panika.
Nepíšem je panika. Literatúru je panika. A už vôbec
je panika. Nie hodnotnú je panika. Byť tlmenou je
panika. Neznamená je panika. Byť je panika. Šedou
je panika. Myškou je panika. Viem je panika. Že je
panika. Nemám je panika. Tvár je panika. Anjela je

panika. Tieto je panika. Čísla je panika. Odrážajú je
panika. Rastúci je panika. Záujem je panika.

Strach z posudzovania inými. Vyhýbanie sa situáciám.
S nízkou sebadôverou. A strachom z kritiky. Prejavujú sa
ponosami. Červenanie. Trasľavosť rúk. Nutkanie na
močenie. Daktorý z týchto javov bude prvoradým
problémom. Príznaky sa môžu stupňovať do náporov.

FEAR OF PANIC

Even one person talking is a conversation. I don't write
literature certainly not valuable literature. Being discreet
is not the same thing as being mousy. I know my face
is not angelic. These numbers mirror a growing interest.

Even one person talking is panic. A conversation is panic.
I don't write is panic. Literature is panic. Certainly not
is panic. Valuable literature is panic. Being discreet is panic. Is not
is panic. The same as thing is panic. Being is panic. Mousy is panic.
I know is panic. My is panic. Face is panic. Is not angelic is panic.
These is panic. Numbers is panic. Mirror is panic. A growing is panic.
Interest is panic.

Fear of being judged by the others. Evading situations. Low
self-confidence. And fear of being criticized. Symptoms
include complaints. Blushing. Shaky hands. Urge to pee. One of
these is the primary problem. Symptoms can escalate into attacks.[25]

Peter Macsovszky: Sarcangelium *(2018)*

In his most recent works, Macsovszky has effectively blurred the boundaries between poetry, prose, and academic essay into a cross-genre resembling a treatise. Its stylistic and compositional character smooths out the staccato character of his verse and vertically segments his prose writing. *Sarcangelium* (2018), together with *Breviár pre posledných psychológov* (Breviary for the last psychologists, 2019) and *Babylonské epitrofie: Zlomky zo sympózia mágov* (Babylonian epitrophies:

Fragments from a symposium of magi, 2021) form a theoretical-fictional-poetic trilogy that combines the appropriative technique – selective and consciously imprecise – with creative authorial writing and provide a satirical and critical reading of world mythology, religion, and philosophy. The multiplicity of voices in *Sarcangelium*, springing from various backgrounds – canonical texts of Western religion and philosophy, non-Western mythology, Internet blogs or discussions, and esoteric thinkers – relativize and negate each other and primarily function as distancing forces aimed at the critique of ideological bases of Western civilization and at uncovering repressed areas of knowledge.[26] The complex handling of the world's spiritual and mythological tradition that destabilizes hierarchies in *Sarcangelium* is coded in its very title, which layers the evangelium or "gospel" with "sarcasm," as well as the Hungarian words *szarka*, "magpie" (equalled with "thief" in Slovak phraseology), and *szar* "excrement." Extracts from *Sarcangelium*'s sixteenth section question and reconfigure several sets of culturally ingrained hierarchies:

FROM *SARCANGELIUM*

Pasus 16

17: Ako toľko iných žien, aj táto žena, Valentína Vladimirovna Tereškova, si musela od mnohých veľa vytrpieť. Napchali ju do skafandra a nútili zotrvávať v priestore, kde bolo sedemdesiat stupňov.

...

23: Tri dni nejedla, a keď vystúpila z rakety, vrhla sa na jedlo, ktoré jej priniesli kazašskí pastieri. Naštvala tým bádateľov, lebo vraj zničila časť cenného materiálu, čiže črevnú mikroflóru.

24: Ale písané je, že človeka nepoškvrňuje to, čo do neho vchádza zvonka, ale to, čo z neho vychádza.

25: Táto jednoduchá žena ponúkla svoje telo, svoje zdravie i svoj um. Všetci dávali zo svojho nadbytku, ale ona dala všetko, čo mala.

...

45: Pascal vraví, že Ježiš sa odlúči od svojich učeníkov, aby čelil agónii, a my sa tiež musíme odtrhnúť od svojich najbližších príbuzných a najdôvernejších priateľov, aby sme ho mohli nasledovať.

...

48: Keď sovietska kozmonautka vystúpila z kabíny a uvidela zástup zvedavcov, ktorí pribehli z neďalekej dediny, zľutovala sa nad nimi. Lebo boli ako ovce bez pastiera.
49: Rozdala im svoje zásoby kozmonautského jedla a potom sa spýtala: Koľko máte chlebov? Potom už s chuťou prežúvala čierny chlieb, tvaroh a cibuľu k tomu.

Passus 16

17: Like many other women, this particular one, Valentina Vladimirovna Tereshkova, was also made to suffer a lot. They shoved her into a spacesuit and made her stay in a room that had a temperature of 70 °C.
...
23: She didn't eat for three days and when she came out of the spacecraft, she wolfed down the food Kazakh shepherds offered her. This angered the researchers, who claimed she destroyed part of the precious material, i.e., her intestinal microflora.
24: But it is written that one does not get tarnished by what gets inside, but by what comes out.
25: This simple woman offered her body, her health and her mind. Everyone gave from what they have extra, but she gave everything she had.
...
45: Pascal says that Jesus parted from his disciples to face agony, and we, too, must separate from our nearest and dearest and closest friends to follow him.
...
48: When the Soviet cosmonaut came out of the cockpit and saw the crowd who'd run there from the village nearby, she felt sorry for them. For they were as sheep not having a shepherd.
49: She gave them her supplies of cosmonaut food and then asked: How many loaves have ye? Not a moment later she was munching with relish on black bread, cheese and onion.[27]

The text escapes generic boundaries by mixing the biblical narrative (Gospel of Mark) with scientific discourse and ordinary speech (from an online discussion forum) resulting in a hybrid textual product, a sort of essay-poem. It takes the historical figure of the first woman in space, Vladimira Tereshkova, as the focal point. The cosmonaut serves as a complex sign that allows for decentring, questioning, complicating, and subverting symbolic hierarchies (Western/Eastern, male/female, high/low, etc.) that govern much of our everyday orientation in the world. The fragments from which the text is built are composed in such a way as to constantly shift and question stock evaluative stances. The text oscillates between a detached, ironic/sarcastic tone and sombre criticism. By intimately intertwining such topics and motives as messianic sacrifice (also in the name of scientific progress) and the traditional roles of women, it layers and rewrites cultural-historical prisms that form the basis of current globalised, though always situated, frames through which the world is conceptualized.

NEXUS OF KIN

Peter Šulej: Rotácie (Rotations, 2020)

Peter Šulej has played a key organizational role in the Slovak poetry field since the mid-1990s, by publishing poetry collections in his presses Drewo a srd and *Vlna*, discovering new poets, organising poetry festivals, and connecting agents across individual arts, as well as through the magazine *Vlna* he co-founded with Ján Šimko, Zuzana Očenášová, and Beata Jablonská in 1999. His own poetry can be thought of as a written counterpart of his off-page activities. It sketches out a wide range of new experimental techniques, joins institutional and cultural critique with a sort of poetic coverage of a life in which the boundaries of the private and public are virtually non-existent. He was also one of the first contemporary poets who challenged the traditional format of the poetry reading and introduced elements of other arts, mainly performance and dance (usually collaborating on the projects with his spouse, the dancer, choreographer, and director Petra Fornayová) to public presentations of poetry in the early 2000s.

Lately, Šulej's poetry has taken the form of fuzzily composed and complicatedly interlinked collages of fragments in which glimpses of commentaries, overheard phrases, encounters with places, people, and music are intertwined with personal, regional, and national history. The position of the subject recording and filtering these impulses is internal (participant) and external (observer) at the same time, and the poetic discourse is radically critical towards both domestic and foreign impulses. This interplay of distancing and familiarizing techniques can also be observed in his latest collection of poetry, *Rotácie* (Rotations, 2020). An example of these can be seen in the poem "viii. (prišli odišli)" (viii. (they came they left)), which is a sort of personal registry listing births, marriages, and deaths in a family that bears factual likeness to the poet's own extended family (Fig. 6.1). The notional and repetitive tone of the piece shields off the emotional contents connected not only with memories of these events, but also with the motif of one's own death. The patterned cacophony and irregular rhythm of the repeating influx and outflow of personas has a mesmerizing quality, and the poem can be thought of as a script containing solely stage directions.

However, as was also the case in his previous recent books, this collection equally introduces the element of the contemporary human situation into its motivic structure. The final lines of the poem express uncertainty as to the continuation of the "enter" – "exeunt" chain and mention "machines." In this way, the poem subtly hints at the paradigmatic shifts regarding the living conditions (ecology, digital colonization, etc.) humankind will be facing in the near (transhuman) future. The first half of the poem, due to the combination of repetition, variation, restricted vocabulary, and a fascination with genealogies, reminds the reader of the writings of Gertrude Stein and authors inspired by her, including the Slovak poet Milan Adamčiak (1946–2017). The other half (Fig. 6.1) is written in Hindi and activates several modes of reading. The least probable of these is that it expects the reader to be able to decipher it on her own. Since there are very few Slovak speakers of Hindi, the text in this positioning would be directed at a geographically very removed audience. On the one hand, such a gesture can be interpreted as a symptom of nostalgia about the fact that poetry as an art form is severed from its greater outreach in a world dominated by other means of aesthetic communication. On the other hand, the text may also function as a utopian space in which the poetic crosses the boundaries of languages and is able to communicate in an abstract, almost musical way. Another, more viable direction to which it points is the need to technologically enhance the reading process using OCR (optical character recognition) software and machine translation. With the help of these tools, the impenetrable, exoticizing, and visually pleasing other of the script that – by virtue of being placed in a book of

Slovak poetry both makes the boundaries between the East and the West visible and challenges them – reveals its verbal semantics to be a list of Hindustani kinship terms. Their precise order as presented here might not be that important – even with up-to-date advanced machine translation technologies, the result is still often only approximate. What matters, however, is that these terms are much more intricately structured than in Slovak (or English) and as such become a critique of superficial, low-context individualistic Western cultures. What is more, the poet had in fact been studying Hindi and wrote the passage himself, instead of copying it from a webpage or book resource.[28] The attention, time, and deep engagement with another culture that learning a foreign language requires, provide a sharp contrast to easy commodification of others and becomes an appeal for (re)building closeness and compassionate understanding as alternatives to objectification.

VIII. (THEY CAME THEY LEFT)[29]

संबंधी नातेदार रिश्तेदार माँ-बाप माता-पिता माता माँ मौसी मौसा पिता बाप पति पत्नी बापू
भाई-बहन भाई भाभी भतीजा भतीजी भानजा भानजी बहन बहिन जीजा बाबा आजी दादा दादी
नाना नानी ताऊ ताई चाचा चाची मामा मामी बुआ फूफा फूफी बीबी साला सलहज साली साढ़ू
ससुर सास दामाद जामाता पुत्रवधू जेठ जेठानी देवर देवरानी ननद ननदोई बाल बच्चे पुत्र बेटा·
पुत्री बेटी पोता-पोती पोता नाती नवासा पोती नातिन नवासी चचेरा भाई मौसेरा भाई फुफेरा भाई
ममेरा भाई चचेरी बहन ममेरी बहन मौसेरी बहन फुफेरी बहन सौतेली माँ सौतेला बाप वाग्दत्ता मंगेतर
दुलहिन वधू दुल्हन वर दुल्हा प्रेमिका प्रेमी संबंधी नातेदार रिश्तेदार माँ-बाप माता-पिता माता माँ
मौसी मौसा पिता बाप पति पत्नी बापू भाई-बहन भाई भाभी भतीजा भतीजी भानजा भानजी बहन
बहिन जीजा बाबा आजी दादा दादी नाना नानी ताऊ ताई चाचा चाची मामा मामी बुआ फूफा फूफी
बीबी साला सलहज साली साढ़ू ससुर सास दामाद जामाता पुत्रवधू जेठ जेठानी देवर देवरानी ननद
ननदोई बाल बच्चे पुत्र बेटा पुत्री बेटी पोता-पोती पोता नाती नवासा पोती नातिन नवासी चचेरा
भाई मौसेरा भाई फुफेरा भाई ममेरा भाई चचेरी बहन ममेरी बहन मौसेरी बहन फुफेरी बहन सौतेली
माँ सौतेला बाप वाग्दत्ता मंगेतर दुलहिन वधू दुल्हन वर दुल्हा प्रेमिका प्रेमी संबंधी नातेदार रिश्तेदार
माँ-बाप माता-पिता माता माँ मौसी मौसा पिता बाप पलि पत्नी बापू भाई-बहन भाई भाभी भतीजा
भतीजी भानजा भानजी बहन बहिन जीजा बाबा आजी दादा दादी नाना नानी ताऊ ताई चाचा चाची
मामा मामी बुआ फूफा फूफी बीबी साला सलहज साली साढ़ू ससुर सास दामाद जामाता पुत्रवधू
जेठ जेठानी देवर देवरानी ननद ननदोई बाल बच्चे पुत्र बेटा पुत्री बेटी पोता-पोती पोता नाती नवासा
पोती नातिन नवासी चचेरा भाई मौसेरा भाई फुफेरा भाई ममेरा भाई चचेरी बहन ममेरी बहन मौसेरी
बहन फुफेरी बहन सौतेली माँ सौतेला बाप वाग्दत्ता मंगेतर दुलहिन वधू दुल्हन वर दुल्हा प्रेमिका
प्रेमी संबंधी नातेदार रिश्तेदार माँ-बाप माता-पिता माता माँ मौसी मौसा पिता बाप पति पत्नी बापू
भाई-बहन भाई भाभी भतीजा भतीजी भानजा भानजी बहन बहिन जीजा बाबा आजी दादा दादी
नाना नानी ताऊ ताई चाचा चाची मामा मामी बुआ फूफा फूफी बीबी साला सलहज साली साढ़ू
ससुर सास दामाद जामाता पुत्रवधू जेठ जेठानी देवर देवरानी ननद ननदोई बाल बच्चे पुत्र बेटा
पुत्री बेटी पोता-पोती पोता नाती नवासा पोती नातिन नवासी चचेरा भाई मौसेरा भाई फुफेरा भाई
ममेरा भाई चचेरी बहन ममेरी बहन मौसेरी बहन फुफेरी बहन सौतेली माँ सौतेला बाप वाग्दत्ता मंगेतर
दुलहिन वधू दुल्हन वर दुल्हा प्रेमिका प्रेमी संबंधी नातेदार रिश्तेदार माँ-बाप माता-पिता माता माँ
मौसी मौसा पिता बाप पति पत्नी बापू भाई-बहन भाई भाभी भतीजा भतीजी भानजा भानजी बहन
बहिन जीजा बाबा आजी दादा दादी नाना नानी ताऊ ताई चाचा चाची मामा मामी बुआ फूफा फूफी

Fig. 6.1 | Peter Šulej. From *Rotácie* (Rotations).

WHAT TIME IS NOW

Nóra Ružičková: Súčasnosti (Contemporaneities, 2021)

In the new millennium, Nóra Ružičková's work has been increasingly conceptual, intermedia, and collaborative, examining and transgressing the boundaries of the page, language, gallery, sound, image, art, poetry, and criticism. Her latest collection of poems, *Súčasnosti* (Contemporaneities, 2021), explores the discursive manipulation by and of the concept of the new and now, over the past hundred years. The poet continues her critical investigations into the gaps between the material reality and language that traps us in narratives, including the Jamesonian "return of narrative as the narrative of the end of narratives."[30] The multi-layered text of the collection was composed from variously adapted fragments appropriated mainly from persuasive journalistic contributions on various topics, including art and literary criticism, agriculture, reproductive and cultural politics, and the role of women in society. The poet's archival research provides glimpses into modifications and repetitions of discursive constructions of presents positioned between the verbally created pasts and futures. The textual ecosystem can be entered through several strands of intercommunicating topics. One of the ways to read the collection is to see it as a guide through Slovak cultural history from the end of the First World War to the present, illustrating the key turns in its politics and economy: the authentic socialist optimism of the 1920s and 1930s, the communist coup of 1948 and the totalitarian cultural politics that followed it, the revolutionary spirit of the 1960s, the normalization period and the creeping onset of state-controlled neoliberalism of the 1970s and 1980s through to the fully neoliberal capitalist present with its lack of vision. The book can be read both as a leftist feminist commentary on the globalized shift from utopian new worlds to the neoliberal obsession with new commodities, and as a melancholic satire on the naïve attempts to engineer and project a culture and society. At the same time, it is a web of stimuli that invites the reader to engage with philosophical handlings of temporality as such. However, these abstract notions are not presented through a transparent language; the materiality and figurative force of the fragments of speech as carriers of verbal jouissance violently, sensually intervene into the cognitive handling of individual pieces.

FROM *SÚČASNOSTI*

dozrel čas premeny
sústava nahlodaná vnútornými rozpormi je v rozklade
nová kultúra otvára široké horizonty do budúcnosti
približuje odveké sny o slobode, šťastí a trvalom mieri
v novej spoločnosti sa úlohy umenia rozširujú
centrom záujmu je pracujúci človek
umenie mu chce urobiť život krajším
a učiť ho vidieť novým spôsobom v známej skutočnosti
umenie tým spolutvorí aj novú skutočnosť
lebo ju nielen odráža, ale aj pretvára
ak má nové umenie zasluhovať svoje meno
forma musí v ňom byť adekvátna novému obsahu
utváranie nového slohu a nového umenia
bude tvorivým procesom
vyznačeným novými umeleckými objavmi
tento proces nepoprie
všetko, čo sa doteraz utvorilo
ale nájde svoje východisko
v doterajšej tvorbe a bude
jej organickým pokračovaním

1948

spojenie medzi ekonomikou a kultúrou
dnes už chápu aj politici
kreativita sa v dnešnej spoločnosti
stáva motorom inovácií
dnes už môžeme napočítať
celý rad ekonomických ukazovateľov
od samotnej ceny diela
či vstupenky
až po známe multiplikačné efekty
ktoré kultúrni manažéri
v prípade potreby
vysypú z rukáva

2012[31]

FROM *CONTEMPORANEITIES*

the time is ripe for change
the system eroded by internal struggles has decayed
new culture opens wide horizons into the future
brings abiding dreams of freedom, happiness, and permanent
peace closer
in the new society the mission of art broadens
the worker has become the centre of attention
art strives to make his life more beautiful
and teach him to see the familiar reality in a new way
in this way art participates in the creation of new reality
it does not just reflect it, but also remodels it
if the new art is to be worthy of its name
its form has to resonate with its new contents
the creation of the new style and new art
will become a creative process
marked by new artistic discoveries
this process will not dismiss
all that has been created before
but will build on
the art of the past and become
its organic continuation

1948

nowadays even politicians are aware of
the connection between economy and culture
in present-day society creativity
has become the engine of innovation
nowadays we can count
a whole host of economic indicators
from the price of the work itself
or the ticket
up to known multiplier effects
which cultural managers
know by
heart

2012[32]

The two poems, which react to different periods in the history of Slovak culture, testify to two contrasting visions and justifications of the arts. The first one, set in 1948, the year which saw a dramatic change in the organization of Slovak society, invests art with the force to create reality and bring happiness and peace. The latter, set in the contemporary world of 2012, insists that art be a source of economic profit. In both cases, however, art is treated as a tool meant to enhance the dominant ideologies. By carefully selecting and arranging the textual material, the poet also draws attention to the constructed nature of both the past and the present paradigms.

A PORTRAIT OF THE POET AS A YOUNG ALGORITHM

Zuzana Husárová and Ľubomír Panák: Liza Gennart: Výsledky vzniku (Outcomes of origin, 2020)

The poetry of Zuzana Husárová explores various media, technologies, and creative methods. Her works, which can be thought of as materializations of artistic research, are usually collaborative, and she often participates in collective projects or projects conceptualized by other artists. In 2020, she and the sound artist and software developer Ľubomír Panák published *Liza Gennart: Výsledky vzniku* (Liza Gennart: Outcomes of origin), an AI-generated collection of poetry. The duo used GPT-2, the most advanced natural language-processing technology at the time, and trained it on a large corpus of contemporary and older Slovak poetry. The concept was devised by Husárová, who also made the selection of generated poems to be included in the book and edited them in a non-intrusive way. As experiments suggest, GPT-2 human-in-the-loop generated poetry in English, i.e., poetry with a human agent participating in the process of editing or selection of the outputs, can be virtually indistinguishable from poetry written by human authors.[33] However, the texts included in the collection, as is also stated in the book's paratext, intentionally contain remnants of unnatural language. These elements may spring from the inflected character of the Slovak language, but also from the specific features of the database used for training the algorithm – an appreciable portion of contemporary Slovak poetry employs appropriative techniques and occasionally computer-generated language; therefore, it does not always adhere to the rules of grammar.

The collection invites the readers to ponder on the shifting and messy boundaries and relationships between the human and the machine, the inhumanness of natural language as such and on the posthuman condition in general.[34] Readerly attitudes that activate these interpretational fields are triggered by the book's paratextual framing as well as by its textual content, which was edited in such a way as to create a linguistic strangeness and detachment from natural speech. In effect, a close reading of the book turns the reader into a player of a paranoid game in which she questions the extent to which any text available for reception is a projection of one's expectations of a coherent meaning.

The alien, eerie, convoluted world Liza has created by virtue of the seamless, non-metaphorical blending of the ordinary and knowable with the non-realizable, which is much stranger than Lautréamont's meeting of a sewing-machine and an umbrella on a dissecting-table, poses the question of *who* sees the world like this, *whose* is this immaterial world made of language. Liza as a learning algorithm is a sort of alien child with no access to sensory perception, blind, deaf, unable to touch, taste, or smell – an entity that cannot really understand the language she speaks. This, however, also leads to the questioning of human (and, increasingly, technologically enhanced transhuman) engagement with the world and our own limitations regarding the access to its materialities and meanings.

FROM *LIZA GENNART: VÝSLEDKY VZNIKU*

Miscelánea
4.

Vstupuješ do tohto sveta?
Ani v spálni sa nedá nič robiť, také nešťastie, že sa dáš v mozgu odstáť, a možno to robíš aj kvôli mne. Ale kvôli mne.

* podvečer
* lebo to vyzerá ako výčitka
* ale súhlasíš, že to vyzerá ako bezfarebný kľúč
* lebo za oknami sa vznášajú vlhké slová
* pripomína to, že kľúč v okne nie je priveľmi drahý
* vietor

* ako v papieri, keď sa v bezvetrí zbierajú pálenky
* ako v našich bytových vlasoch, keď sa v dome nevie vypnúť
  na chodník, ale v ráme, ktorý nie je v našom svete
* a vietor, ktorý má povahu, je bezfarebný
* ktorý nedá celý vlastný stav, bezfarebný ako
  v papieroch, keď nedá celý vlastný stav
* a vietor, ktorý má povahu, je bezfarebný
* a vietor, ktorý nie je v našom svete, je v poriadku
* a vietor, ktorý nie je v poriadku, je bezfarebný

FROM LIZA GENNART: OUTCOMES OF ORIGIN

Miscellanea
4.

Do you enter this world?

There's nothing to do. Not even in the bedroom, such misfortune, you leave it soak in the brain and perhaps you also do it for my sake. But for my sake.

* late afternoon
* because it doesn't sound like a reproach
* but you agree: it resembles a colourless key
* because wet words float out the window
* it reminds – the key in the window isn't too dear
* wind
* like in paper when the windlessness gathers liquors
* like in our apartment hair when in the house it can't turn off over the
  pavement, but in a frame that is not out of our world
* and wind with a personality is colourless
* which doesn't give an own complete state, colourless like in paper
  when it doesn't give an own complete state
* and wind with a personality is colourless
* and wind not out of our world is all right
* and wind that is not all right is colourless[35]

The poem comes from the section of the collection that the algorithm generated without human input in the form of keywords. In an aesthetic mode of reading, the attention of the human recipient gravitates towards clusters of words that allow for a more coherent sense-making. Phrases and strings of words like "colourless key," "windlessness gathers liquors," or "wind not out of our world" create an unsettling, melancholic atmosphere of an absence, an emptied space of a world that is not "ours." The human longing for meaning (once we account for the origins of the poem) can only be frustrated by a text that lacks any sort of depth, since neural networks cannot be said to create, understand, or have intentions of any kind, and the synthetic text they produce is invariably flat. However, in cases where the text hints at voids, lacks, and negations in an aesthetically pleasing way, it appears to address this irreconcilable vacuum of meaning and provides a fertile ground for deliberations on human-machine relations.

WHO IS TO EXERCISE POWER?

Nóra Ružičková and Marianna Mlynárčiková: Cvičenie s monografiami *(*Exercise with Monographs, *2016)*

Nóra Ružičková's creative projects can be thought of as temporal and material nodes in a single, albeit layered and intricately branched, ongoing research project. One such strand of her work can be entered through the bilingual Slovak-English chapbook *Cvičenie s monografiami* (*Exercise with Monographs*, 2016; translation into English by John Minahane). Ružičková co-authored it with the artist Marianna Mlynárčiková, with whom she has been collaborating since 2004. The pamphlet is part of a series involving a cooperation with the actors Dana Snopková and Miriam Kujanová from the community City Theatre Divadlo z Pasáže in Banská Bystrica, the only stage in Central and Eastern Europe that allows actors with mental health disabilities to be involved in professional theatre and express themselves through performance. By the very composition of the working collective, individual works as outcomes of this collaboration cross the boundaries of individual arts and transgress the confines of social exclusion. This participatory, institutionally critical, and activist project that works with literary and social texts aims at making visible the established hierarchies of power and the degree of access to legitimization and knowledge to variously positioned subjects.[36] It includes videos, such as *Bouvard a Pécuchet bádajú na poli*

Fig. 6.2 | Nóra Ružičková and Marianna Mlynárčiková. From *Exercise with Monographs* (2016). Pictured are Dana Snopková and Miriam Kujanová. Used with the authors' permission.

slovenského umenia (Bouvard and Pécuchet explore the field of Slovak art, 2014) and *Falomonografická veža* (Phallomonographic tower, 2016), the book of conceptual poetry <*-abc-*> (2018), as well as the bilingual Slovak-English *Exercise with Monographs*, which combines photography with text.

The intertwining of two discourses and their visual counterparts in *Exercise with Monographs*, which contains instruction, history, the theory of physical education, and canon-building academic writing on art, invites readers to participate in research into power structures of Western scientific and (art) historical narratives and investigate and critique them through bodily experience. Through intertextual work and complex dialogue woven between the verbal and non-verbal elements of individual pieces, the pamphlet builds a network of subversions of power relationships in which humour plays a crucial role. The visuals, in which big, heavy, glossy canon-building art history books are handled as material objects – weights and other sporting equipment – by subjects usually excluded from art communication or from deeper access to knowledge and knowledge-creation, lend the work an air of the grotesque which, however, does not ridicule the models qua trainees, but rather the obsession of academia with erecting monuments to selected agents in the field. The element of spontaneous joy in the faces of the models/trainees encourages the audience to dismantle barriers between the producers and users of knowledge in a non-violent, playful way.

The textual element consists of excerpts from art history books and exercise instructions appropriated from various publications and adjusted to be executable with books as gym equipment. Sometimes, these function as captions, at other times, e.g., in "XVI." (Fig. 2), the visual compositions contradict them. The contradiction in "XVI." is also "exercised," since the trainees are basically instructed to shake their heads. In the light of its caption, "sketching nudes he never wished to sketch allegories," the photograph gives the impression of a reproduction of an allegorical painting. The heavy, deep wine-red velvet draperies with the intricate play of dark and light tones in their folds, half-covering an old stone wall together with potted plants that underscore the artificial, arranged, and makeshift character of the scene, form the background of the image, which is contrasted with its figures dressed in bright-coloured sports clothes. The facial expressions of the models/trainees – one of them appears concerned, the other amused – can be read as commentaries on the composition. In a literal reading, they express their momentary feelings concerning the shooting process, reflecting their concentration on the physical task at hand. In an allegorical reading, the expressions can be interpreted as postures that signal the complex structure of the work.

The composition of the individual pieces and the whole project are partly calculated and rational, partly produced by chance encounters with the specificities of the site and the used materials. The draperies in the background are part of the set used by the theatre for rehearsals and are meant to give the impression of a curtain; the use of the potted plants in the shots was inspired by the visuals in one of the socialist-era workout handbooks that also sometimes suggested that the trainees use books as equipment, since specialized sporting goods were scarce.[37] Allowing objects and spaces to speak for themselves in this way also reveals and softens the violence of artistic representation inflicted on objects and materials.

CONCLUSION

Since the 1990s, experimental writing techniques and texts saturated in critical theory have attracted a growing network of artists. In the new millennium, innovative and radical poetics have come to dominate Slovak poetry. Over the past decade, Slovak poetry has been drawing on diverse sources of domestic and foreign inspiration, and its current landscape is populated by talented authors of all generations. However, the trend that aspires to engage with the present in the sense of being consciously positioned in a globalized world is often either manifestly formally innovative or, at least, draws on the innovative and subversive methods and techniques that sustained the vitality of Slovak poetry in the twentieth century and found free expression during its last decade.[38]

NOTES

1 See Šrank, *Individualizovaná literatúra.*

2 Experimental-deconstructive poetry is one of four types of poetry typical of the 1990s and early 2000s as described by Jaroslav Šrank in his *Individualizovaná literatúra* (the other three being the poetry of non-conformist individualism, spiritual poetry, and poetry focusing on the poet's private life).

3 I would like to thank the authors of the works presented in the second half of the chapter for providing me with publicly unavailable digital forms of their projects. I would also like to thank all authors and translators for kindly allowing me to reproduce samples of their work in this chapter.

4 Šrank, *Individualizovaná literatúra*, 175.

5 Lehenová, "A Little Nightmare Music," 266.

6 Bokníková, "Žena ako autorka," 24–52.

7 For a bibliography and discussion of the polemics, see Bokníková, "Žena ako autorka."

8 Vladimír Mečiar's party was called "Movement for a Democratic Slovakia" – the illusion of democracy was, thus, part of the government's strategy.

9 See Valér Mikula, *5 x 5 a iné kritiky*, 120, and Šrank, *Individualizovaná literatúra*, 79.

10 See Lefevere, *Translation, Rewriting, and the Manipulation of Literary Fame.*

11 See Havelková and Oates-Indruchová, eds, *The Politics of Gender Culture under State Socialism.*

12 Šrank, *Aktéri a tendencie literárnej kultúry na Slovensku po roku 1989*, 29–30.
13 Šrank, *Nesamozrejmá poézia*, 74–5.
14 Macsovszky, "This Is a Real Thing," in *Strach z utópie*, 7.
15 Macsovszky, "This Is a Real Thing," in *Poetry Reaching Out*, 9–10.
16 Šrank, *Nesamozrejmá poézia*, 112.
17 Husárová, "Slovenská elektronická literatúra," 70.
18 Šulej, *Porno*, 11. English translation by Ivana Hostová.
19 Habaj, *Korene neba*, 16.
20 Habaj, "What remained of all that," 13–14.
21 Rédey, *Súčasná slovenská poézia v kontexte civilizačno-kultúrnych premien*, 70.
22 Tönnies, *Gemeinschaft und Gesellschaft*, 64. See also Haiman, *Talk Is Cheap*, 80.
23 Ružičková, *Mikronauti*, 42. English translation by Ivana Hostová.
24 See Hostová, "Of Ecosystems and Translations," 74–85.
25 Macsovszky, *Santa Panica*, 43. English translation by Ivana Hostová.
26 Foucault, "*Society Must Be Defended*," 7.
27 Macsovszky, *Sarcangelium*, 93–6. English translation by Ivana Hostová.
28 Šulej, Facebook message to author.
29 Šulej, *Rotácie*, 65.
30 Jameson, *Postmodernism, Or the Cultural Logic of Late Capitalism*, 6.
31 Ružičková, *Súčasnosti*.
32 Ružičková, "From *Contemporaneities*."
33 See Köbis and Mossink, "Artificial Intelligence versus Maya Angelou," and Goldenfein, "Algorithmic Transparency and Decision-Making Accountability," 41–61.
34 For the theoretical concepts underpinning this collection, see Paul De Man, *The Resistance to Theory* and Craig Dworkin, *Reading the Illegible*.
35 Gennart, *Výsledky vzniku*, 84–5. English translation by Ivana Hostová.
36 Mlynárčiková, *Intertextualita ako nástroj inštitucionálnej kritiky*, 6.
37 Ružičková, email to author.
38 The research for this chapter was supported by grant funding from VEGA 2/0009/23 Creative Experiments with Text from the Perspective of Critical Posthumanism: Poetic, Artistic and Translation. Readers interested in learning more about contemporary Slovak poetry are encouraged to consult the appendix to this volume with its bibliography of English translations of poets covered in this chapter and in chapter 5, "Poetry and Social Engagement."

BIBLIOGRAPHY

Andričík, Marián. "Slovak Poetry in English Anthologies." *Bridge* 2, no. 1 (2020): 19–36. https://www.bridge.ff.ukf.sk/index.php/bridge/article/view/1/33.

Bokníková, Andrea. "Žena ako autorka – žena ako téma v slovenskej poézii od šesťdesiatych rokov po súčasnosť." In *Studia Academica Slovaca* 29, edited by Jozef Mlacek, 24–52. Bratislava: Stimul, 2000.

Bourdieu, Pierre. *The Field of Cultural Production: Essays on Art and Literature*. New York: Columbia University Press, 1993.

Davenport, Thomas H., and John C. Beck. *The Attention Economy: Understanding the New Currency of Business*. Boston: Harvard Business School, 2001.

De Man, Paul. *The Resistance to Theory*. Minneapolis University of Minnesota Press, 1986.

Dworkin, Craig. *Reading the Illegible*. Evanston, IL: Northwestern University Press, 2003.

Foucault, Michel. *"Society Must Be Defended." Lectures at the Collège de France, 1975–1976*. Edited by Mauro Bertani and Alessandro Fontana. Translated by David Macey. New York: Picador, 1997.

Gennart, Liza. *Výsledky vzniku*. Bratislava: Vlna/Drewo a srd, 2020.

Goldenfein, Jake. "Algorithmic Transparency and Decision-Making Accountability: Thoughts for Buying Machine Learning Algorithms." In *Closer to the Machine: Technical, Social, and Legal aspects of AI*, edited by Cliff Bertram, Asher Gibson, and Adriana Nugent, 41–61. Melbourne: Office of the Victorian Information Commissioner, 2019. https://papers.ssrn.com/sol3/papers.cfm?abstract_id=3445873.

Habaj, Michal. "What Remained of All That." In *Poetry Reaching Out: New Slovak Poetry in Translation*. Translated by John Minahane, 13–14. Bratislava: Ars Poetica, 2012.

– *Korene neba*. Banská Bystrica: Drewo a srd, 2000.

Haiman, John. *Talk Is Cheap: Sarcasm, Alienation, and the Evolution of Language*. Oxford and New York: Oxford University Press, 1998.

Havelková, Hana, and Libora Oates-Indruchová, eds. *The Politics of Gender Culture under State Socialism: An Expropriated Voice*. London and New York: Routledge, 2015.

Hostová, Ivana. "Fissuring into Existence. The Visceral, Sculptural, and Textile-Textual in the Poetry of Maggie O'Sullivan and Nóra Ružičková." *Studi slavistici* 16, no. 1 (2019): 49–65.

– "Of Ecosystems and Translations: Some Ways of Translating Non-traditional Texts." *World Literature Studies* 8, no. 1 (2016): 74–85.
– "Slovak Poetry in English Translation after the Collapse of State Socialism: Tracing the Trajectories of Internationalisation." *Meta* 68, no. 1 (2022): 159–79.
– "Temporalities – Technologies – Transgressions: Notes on Contemporary Slovak Poetry." *Porównania* 2, no. 27 (2020): 313–24.
Husárová, Zuzana. "Mainly Love." Accessed 11 June 2021. https://husarova.net/2017/09/07/mainly-love/.
– "Slovenská elektronická literatúra." *World Literature Studies* 8, no. 3 (2016): 57–77.
Jameson, Fredric. *Postmodernism, Or the Cultural Logic of Late Capitalism.* Durham, NC: Duke University Press, 1991.
Juhásová Jana. "Prayer in Contemporary Slovak Poetry: Current Genre Tendencies." *Religious and Sacred Poetry: An International Quarterly of Religion, Culture and Education* 2, no. 2 (2014): 115–40.
– "From Symbol to Latency: Two Forms of Spiritual Discourse in Contemporary Slovak Poetry." *Zeitschrift für Slawistik* 58, no. 4 (2013): 444–61.
– "Herbert as a Method: Eschatological Issues in the Poetry of Contemporary Slovak Spiritual Poets." *Zeitschrift für Slawistik* 60, no.1 (2015): 83–112.
– "Pilate's Wife: Involvement in Women's Poetry and Its Spiritual Dimension." Świat i Słowo: filologia, nauki społeczne, filozofia, teologia 23, no. 2 (2014): 257–70.
– "Reduction and Aesthetic Attitude in the Poetry of Rudolf Jurolek." *Religious and Sacred Poetry: An International Quarterly of Religion, Culture and Education* 4, no. 1 (2016): 177–96.
Köbis, Nils, and Luca D. Mossink. "Artificial Intelligence versus Maya Angelou: Experimental Evidence That People Cannot Differentiate AI-Generated from Human-Written Poetry." *Computers in Human Behavior* 114 (2021): 106553. https://doi.org/10.1016/j.chb.2020.106553.
Lefevere, André. *Translation, Rewriting, and the Manipulation of Literary Fame.* London and New York: Routledge, 1992.
Lehenová, Taťjana. "A Little Nightmare Music." In *One Hundred Years of Slovak Literature*, edited by Stanislava Chrobáková, 266–7. Bratislava: The Union of Slovenian Writers and the Association of Organisations of Slovak Writers, 2000.
Macsovszky, Peter. "This Is a Real Thing." In *Poetry Reaching Out: New*

Slovak Poetry in Translation. Translated by Marián Andričík, 9–10. Bratislava: Ars Poetica, 2012.
– *Santa Panica*. Bratislava: Vlna/Drewo a srd, 2014.
– *Sarcangelium*. Bratislava: Vlna/Drewo a srd, 2017.
– *Strach z utópie*. Banská Bystrica: Drewo a srd, 1994.
Mikula, Valér. *5 x 5 a iné kritiky*. Levice: LCA, 2000.
Minahane, John. "Bitter Truths." *Dublin Review of Books* 6, no. 25 (2012). http://www.drb.ie/essays/bitter-truths.
Mistrík, Erich. "Kultúrna globalizácia Európy a súčasná civilizačno-kultúrna situácia na Slovensku." In *Demokracie a Evropa v době globalizace*, edited by Marta Goňcová, 203–11. Brno: Masarykova univerzita, 2003.
Mlynárčiková, Marianna. *Intertextualita ako nástroj inštitucionálnej kritiky*. PhD diss., Akadémia umení v Banskej Bystrici, Fakulta výtvarných umení, 2016. https://opac.crzp.sk/?fn=detailBiblioForm&sid=114493DC47550B5639EE60A58B86.
Rédey, Zoltán. *Súčasná slovenská poézia v kontexte civilizačno-kultúrnych premien*. Nitra: Univerzita Konštantína Filozofa v Nitre, 2005.
Ružičková, Nóra. "From *Contemporaneities*." *Asymptote* 12, no. 43 (2022). Accessed 11 August 2022. https://www.asymptotejournal.com/poetry/contemporaneities-nora-ruzickova.
– *Mikronauti*. Banská Bystrica: Drewo a srd, 1998.
– *Súčasnosti*. Kordíky: Skalná ruža, 2021.
Ružičková, Nóra, and Marianna Mlynárčiková. *Cvičenie s monografiami/Exercise with Monographs*. Translated by John Minahane. Bratislava: tranzit.sk, 2016.
Somolayová, Ľubica. "Since the Velvet Revolution." *Poetry Wales* 41, no. 2 (Autumn 2005): 40–4.
Šrank, Jaroslav. "Field Notes: New Developments in Slovakian Poetry." Accessed 11 June 2021. https://www.full-stop.net/2015/02/26/blog/jaroslav-srank/field-notes-new-developments-in-slovakian-poetry/.
– *Aktéri a tendencie literárnej kultúry na Slovensku po roku 1989*. Bratislava: Univerzita Komenského, 2015.
– "Book Culture in Slovakia after the Year 2000." *Perspektywy Kultury* 22, no. 3 (2018): 21–42.
– *Individualizovaná literatúra*. Bratislava: Cathedra, 2013.
– *Nesamozrejmá poézia*. Bratislava: Literárne informačné centrum, 2009.
Šulej, Peter. *Porno*. Banská Bystrica: Drewo a srd, 1994.
– *Rotácie*. Bratislava: Vlna/Drewo a srd, 2020.
Tönnies, Ferdinand. *Gemeinschaft und Gesellschaft*. Leipzig: Fues's Verlag, 1887.

CHAPTER SEVEN

Regional Writing and National Identity in the Borderlands

Radoslav Passia

Despite the small size of its territory, Slovakia is a country of great regional differences, both in terms of culture and economic development. This diversity stems from both historical causes and geographical features related to the country's location at the meeting point of various languages, ethnic groups, and land formations. Most of the Slovak territory consists of mountainous areas that present natural obstacles to the development of infrastructure and transportation. The uneven development of the country originated in the political and economic system of Hungary, which formed the modern Slovak nation. The Hungarian administrative organization of the Slovak territory into districts also contributed to the isolation of certain regions and varied rates of development.[1] This trend was reflected in the great diversity of dialects and folklore, which still constitute a distinct aspect of Slovak national identity.

The uneven economic development of certain regions continues today and contributes to the differences between the values of the provinces and the capital. During the 1990s, these regional differences bolstered the success of Vladimír Mečiar's politics and their appeal to the mostly illiberal political orientation of the rural areas that still make up about 47 per cent of the Slovak population. After 1989, these regions faced a problematic social situation following the transformation of the socialist, centrally planned economy into a market economy, which resulted in rising rates of unemployment and a set of associated social problems. The ideological foundation of "Mečiarism" was nationalism, and, therefore, following the election of 1998 and the formation of a pro-Western government, new opportunities to reflect on the problems of Slovak cultural, ethnic, linguistic, and geopolitical identity opened in the cultural sphere. These topics had been largely discredited because of their exploitation by the nationalist political discourse of Mečiar's government. It is, therefore, not surprising that literary reflection on the theme of national identity was also pushed to the background, even though it had been one of the central preoccupations of Slovak culture in previous decades. For example, the themes of cultural and national identity had resonated in Slovak society in the 1960s, when Slovakia's leading political and cultural representatives pushed for the federalization of Czechoslovakia, which was established in 1969.[2]

Slovak literature continued to reflect on these issues during the 1970s and 1980s in the work of prominent writers such as Vincent Šikula, Peter Jaroš, or Ladislav Ballek. Following the revolution, these topics were addressed in a reactionary fashion by the conservative nationalist faction of Slovak culture, which expressed their xenophobic views and insufficiently distanced themselves from the authoritarian regimes of the past. In some cases, this faction even openly attempted to rehabilitate such regimes in the nation's collective memory, particularly the Second World War-era Slovak state and the communist regime.

However, the problem of Slovak national identity is not merely the legacy of the turbulent Central European history of the twentieth century; its roots are much older and associated with its geographical position on the borders of the Latin West and the Byzantine East, as well as with the non-existent historical tradition of Slovak statehood.[3] As the historian Dušan Škvarna puts it, "Slovak society had absorbed its own history in a vacant and distorted form. A long and continuous thread of deformed perspectives on this past, beginning in the nineteenth century and ending in 1989, perceived as a continuum of humiliation and insignificance, inevitably left its mark on the mental, cultural, and moral outlook of Slovak society."[4] From a comparative perspective, it is significant that the canon of Slovak literature of the nineteenth and twentieth centuries contains hardly any texts set in the borderland regions of contemporary Slovakia, that is, in the regions that were not perceived as self-evidently Slovak due to their multi-ethnic character.

During the 1990s, in response to "Mečiarism" and to the postmodern rejection of grand narratives, most Slovak writers avoided stories that touched on controversial or even traumatizing aspects of collective memory and a shared linguistic, national, and regional identity. Some of this vacuum was filled by publishing texts by the older generation that could not appear for ideological reasons before 1989. The traditional tangle of problems associated with what is sometimes described as the "Slovak question" was brought back under literary scrutiny by the "millennial" generation which had spent most of its life in a democratic and open society. The focus of this chapter is a group of writers who address the questions of cultural, linguistic, and ethnic identity in prose that is thematically and spatially anchored at "home" in Slovakia, particularly in its variously conceptualized peripheries, not only in the diverse borderland regions inhabited by minority groups, but also on the margins of society.

There is also another group of predominantly women writers who reflect on questions of national and cultural identity through the subjective perspective of characters who reside abroad for social and personal reasons.[5] The goals, perspectives, and poetics of such contemporary women's writing are the focus of the next chapter, but a brief description of this trend should be included here before turning to the perspectives of regions and social margins.

In the first two decades of the new millennium, the literary works that highlighted the expat experience attracted critical and popular attention because their themes coincided and intersected with the broader social experience. During this period, the tendency toward "opening the windows to Europe," which had shaped Slovak culture during the interwar period in the newly established democratic Czechoslovakia, was once again replicated in a more widespread and dynamic form in response to Slovakia's integration in the European Union. These texts examine how the identity of their expatriate women protagonists develops against the backdrop of linguistically and culturally distinct Western Europe or, in some cases, more remote foreign settings, which impact the protagonists' perceptions of gender roles and national affiliation. Their Slovak identity is not founded on grand national narratives or the subject of detached intellectual reflection; it stems from concrete situations, from privately and intimately experienced otherness in foreign environments.

INNOVATIVE ASPECTS OF NEW REGIONALISM

Alongside the more popular and medialized expat literature, regional literature develops as its complementary and less recognized twin, which thematically draws on domestic space, works with a different type of opposition or tension, and bears some characteristics of the so-called minor literature as defined by Gilles Deleuze and Félix Guattari as "that which a minority constructs within a major language."[6] The poetics of this prose are more focused on social contexts, regional details, and linguistic and cultural specifics of a narrowly limited geographical space, while also foregrounding space as a category. The main opposition is not between the world and a (Slovak) character, but a newly conceived heterogeneous Slovak identity, since these texts thematically draw on the tensions produced by the mixed identity of regions shared by the Slovak majority and other ethnic groups. It is worth noting that some of the regions depicted in these texts had not been widely represented in Slovak literature in earlier periods. From the geographical point of view, this type of writing focuses primarily on two peripheries: the Slovak-Rusyn-Roma area of the Carpathian Mountains in northeast Slovakia and the Slovak-Hungarian borderland in southern Slovakia. These regions are also marked by the historical presence of other, now lost cultural and linguistic elements, particularly German and Jewish.[7]

The innovative features of these aim to make minorities visible and shape their image in the eyes of the majority population. They also enrich literature written in Slovak by contributing motifs and themes that had only sporadically appeared before 1989, and even then, mostly in literature written in minority languages. There are several reasons why this heterogeneous but also integrating perspective on national identity has only recently become more prominent in Slovak literature. The key reason is the traditionally defensive character of the literature of a "small nation," whose attributes were fully formed only with the emergence of an independent state in 1993. According to the Czech historian Miroslav Hroch, smallness is "a characteristic that is not quantitative but situational. It describes European nations that emerged through the process of national movements and were the result of their success."[8] The spaces for the emergence of national self-definition since the period of the Slovak National Awakening in the nineteenth century were the core or central territories with a majority Slovak population, which primarily consisted of the north-western districts of Upper Hungary. Even the capital Bratislava, previously dominated by a German- and Hungarian-speaking population, began to function as a seemingly natural and neutral space for producing Slovak culture only after its Slovak population increased in the 1920s and 1930s, and it finally became Slovakia's cultural centre following the Second World War.

Tara Zahra's concept of "national indifference" touches on problems of ethnic identification in the mixed borderland areas of Central Europe. She calls attention to the pressure put on citizens by the individual successor states of Austria-Hungary, which was driven by the idea that nations had a natural right to self-determination, to choose a single nationality: in the case of Czechoslovakia, primarily (Czecho-) Slovak. As she explains, the collapse of the empire "marked the demise of the nationally indifferent or neutral state in east central Europe. The Czechoslovak, Polish, and Yugoslav governments all forcibly classified citizens, hoping to boost the legitimacy of their states domestically and internationally by reducing the number of people counted as members of minority groups."[9] Zahra's national indifference is particularly pertinent to this chapter because it attempts to conceptually grasp national relations in Central Europe, especially in several borderland regions of the Austro-Hungarian Monarchy. Zahra does not consider such "indifference" to be a self-identifying category of particular groups; on the contrary, it is a concept that is primarily negative and nationalist: "Indifference only existed as such in the eyes of the nationalist beholder. Ironically, however, this imaged noncommunity was brought to life and institutionalized through nationalists' own persistent efforts to eradicate it."[10] National indifference, which was a distinct characteristic of the linguistically and ethnically diverse borderland areas, took on various forms in the Slovak literature of the twentieth century, which was conditioned to assume positions of defensive ethnocentrism.

ABSENT IMAGES OF THE BORDERLANDS IN THE SLOVAK CANON

The most evident sign of the national indifference of the borderland regions is their absence from the canonical core of Slovak literature of the nineteenth century and most of the twentieth century. It was not a result of an intentional and active exclusion, but the absence of concrete representations of certain social and geographical spaces rendered them practically invisible in Slovak culture. There are no texts in the broadly conceived Slovak literary canon from the period of the national revival or the modern period set in the north-eastern or eastern borderlands of contemporary Slovakia, or the territories that had historically manifested a high degree of national indifference toward assimilatory pressures on the part of the dominant groups (first Hungarian, then Czechoslovak and Slovak). Thus, in a sense, the eastern border presented an open problem for Slovak literature since its beginnings. Zahra mentions that the indifference of borderland territories is not necessarily merely a relic of the premodern past that will inevitably be "wiped out by the forces of modernization, state building, and modern mass politics,"[11] but also a reaction to the modernizing political conceptions that posited a teleological development toward nationally monolithic states.

In the rare instances when the above-mentioned borderland region appeared in Slovak literature, the representations involved fantastic, fictionalized, or even dystopian elements, which the nationally oriented literature used to overcome the undesirable national indifference of these regions. These approaches can be explained with reference to Baudrillard's concept of the simulacrum, or the image of a non-existent reality which becomes more real than the original itself: "The simulacrum is never that which conceals the truth – it is the truth which conceals that there is none."[12] This mode of depicting the cultural, ethnic, and linguistic situation in the territories can, even when statistical data is taken into account, be considered largely nationally indifferent.[13] It was used, for example, in regional novels such as Anton Prídavok's *Svitanie na východe* (Sunrise in the east, 1928) and Jolana Cirbusová's *Cez zatvorenú hranicu* (Through the closed border, 1929). Prídavok captures the destiny of the cultured and nationally conscious Janiga family who live in the eastern Slovak town of Prešov. The marriage of their daughter Viera and the Czechoslovak legionnaire Havran is a reward for their long-term fidelity to the Slovak national cause. At the centre of Cirbusová's novel is an eastern Slovak family of a squire named Oravský, whose estate is severed by the newly created border between Czechoslovakia and Hungary. In this case, fulfilled partner love also functions as a sweet reward for those who embrace the Slovak national cause. Such literary representations of the positions and relationships among nationalities in eastern Slovakia are significantly idealized, since the (Czecho-)Slovak national cause was not in fact nearly as popular in this area as the novels would suggest. However, almost a century after the publication of these novels, the initially idealistic patriotic visions of the writers have become actualized in eastern Slovakia if we consider that the originally much more diverse ethnic map of the region and its multiple identities have become much more homogeneous.

Nevertheless, the problem of regional and national identity in Slovakia's borderlands is still acute for contemporary artists, particularly writers. Since the turn of the millennium, we can even speak of its noticeable revitalization. In popular culture consumed by a broader mass audience, the revival of regional and national identities is reflected in the increased popularity of folk art. For the American sociologist Joseph Grim Feinberg, for example, contemporary Slovakia serves as a case study of "how folklore was reformulated in response to a context where most overt expressions of nationalism – along with many concepts that were associated with nationalism – became politically illegitimate."[14] Regional themes also appear in contemporary prose. Regional literature focuses primarily on the peripheral parts of Slovakia inhabited predominantly by ethnic minorities: the Rusyns, the Roma, and the Hungarians. Each of these minorities enters the majority cultural space with a different cultural and historical background and distinct representations in contemporary Slovak literature, which feature their own specific thematic and narrative elements.

THE EASTERN CARPATHIANS: LITERARY IMAGES OF RUSYN IDENTITY

The difficulty of integrating the space of the Eastern Carpathians (which includes parts of eastern Slovakia, Poland, and Carpathian Ukraine) in a monolithic national narrative has gradually become a distinct topic in the intellectual self-reflection of the minorities that inhabit this region. Their complicated ethnic, linguistic, and cultural predicament often resulted in complete adaptability to new environments, or, in other words, voluntary assimilation. For example, the artist Andy Warhol was born in Pittsburgh to immigrants from the Rusyn village of Miková in northeastern Slovakia in 1928.[15] However, when commenting on his ethnic and cultural roots, Warhol made the frequently cited statement: "I come from nowhere."[16] As his biographer Bob Colacello explains (with some factual inaccuracies):

> Like very many American stories, Andy's really began in the "Old Country."
>
> "I come from Nowhere," Andy once said. And, for once, he wasn't lying. Ruthenia, the Eastern European land of his parents and grandparents, *was* nowhere. It can't be found on any maps – it's in the Carpathian Mountains, just north of Transylvania, at the point where the present-day boundaries of Poland, Czechoslovakia, Hungary, Romania, and the Soviet Union meet. Its rulers – the Austro-Hungarian Empire until World War I, Czechoslovakia and Russia [*sic*] since then – have systematically denied the identity of its people as a distinct nationality. (The Hapsburgs liked to think of their Ruthenian subjects as "Highlands Hungarians," the Czechs called them "Eastern Slovaks," and the Russians called them "Western Ukrainians" or "Little Russians.") It has always been somebody else's backyard, in constant danger of disappearing into the cracks between clashing powers and cultures, and its people were always made to feel like aliens in their own country. As one of Andy's relations put it, "In Europe, the Ruthenians were the poorest of the poor. We never even had a flag."[17]

Paul Robert Magocsi similarly conveys the history of "the excluded ones" through the metaphor of "people from nowhere."[18]

The Greek Catholic Church has historically been an important keystone of Rusyn identity and functioned as a mediator between Roman and Orthodox Christianity, but in recent years its potential has been weakened by the secularization of Slovak society as a whole. The revitalization of the Rusyn national movement in Eastern Slovakia after 1989, which had mainly consisted of the cultivation of traditional folklore up to that point, was closely tied to the establishment of professional institutions, particularly the Theatre of Alexander Duchnovič in Prešov, and to the codification of the standard Rusyn language in 1995. The increased cultural activity in this period, which Magocsi describes as the third national revival, has been impeded by geopolitical limitations.[19] Rusyns live on the peripheries of several Central European countries, their language is not unified, and they do not have any shared political representation or a standardized school system. However, by asserting an autonomous literary voice they aim at audiences broader than their national community in order to counteract what might be described as colonizing and even orientalist perspectives that were used to represent their cultural space in literature written in other languages, particularly Hungarian and Czech, in the past.

The Slovak-American writer Andrew Krivak presents a combination of external and internal perspectives on the Rusyn community in his novel *The Sojourn* (2011), which is partly set in the Eastern Carpathians. He draws on a typical literary figure for the region: a modern, civilized, or otherwise different outsider, who is confronted with the conservative rural environment. In this case, the outsider is also a former insider, the Slovak immigrant Josef Vinich, who returns from Colorado to what was then Upper Hungary with his father following a family tragedy, the death of his mother. Krivak draws on the western motif of the frontier, which in this case is represented by the Carpathian Mountains, and the sojourn in this environment is a part of the young man's initiation. The ethnic features of this space are captured in the following scene that depicts the father's and the son's departure: "All this time, we spoke in English. The first day he hoisted me into that saddle and we led the herd away from Pastvina, the last he spoke of any Slavic language was to those same Rusyn peasants who greeted him as they took to the fields in Lent with 'Slava lsusu Khristu,' to which he responded, 'Slava na viki,' and then ceased to say a word comprehensible to me, until, by the end of the summer, I knew – and could respond to – the language that was to become our own there in the mountains, and which he insisted I never speak when we went back to the village, where everyone spoke Slovak, or Rusyn, or Hungarian to outsiders."[20] In the mountains, Josef Vinich develops new skills as a shepherd and hunter and gains life experience that he later applies on the battlefields of the First World War. Following the war, he returns to Pastviny, but the death of his father makes him decide to return to the United States. The dynamic and ambiguous relationship between adaptation and assimilation on the one hand, and the distancing from one's origins on the other, manifests as a battle between the call of the blood and desire for life in the modern world, which is passed from generation to generation. Josef leaves "the old" and departs for the New World just like his father before him, whose attempt to emancipate himself from "nowhere" had failed. He returns to the Carpathians, but he does not become a part of them, and he speaks English with his son in order to mentally free himself from the burden of the environment in which his native language originated.[21]

Only in the new millennium has Slovak literature begun to address this sense of being uprooted and threatened with the loss of minority identity more directly. Around this time, this theme has also begun to appear (although in a somewhat exoticized fashion) in other literatures, perhaps most distinctly in the travel narratives of the Polish writer Andrzej Stasiuk. It became evident that the revitalization of the cultures and languages of minorities, which began after 1989, was constrained by economic and social limits. The processes of assimilation may have slowed down, but remained irreversible. Maroš Krajňak's novel *Carpathia* (2011) is a unique example of a literary reflection on the fate of Rusyn culture and the legacy of Rusyn history. The author is an ethnic Rusyn but wrote the novel in Slovak; initially inspired by his work as a guide for US immigrants of Rusyn origin visiting the homeland of their ancestors after 1989. Krajňak's narrator repeatedly travels through areas that he calls the Zones. These consists of multiple parts and create one whole, which the reader can gradually, based on geographical clues in the text, identify as the Polish part of the Eastern Carpathians, the adjacent Carpathian area of eastern Slovakia, and the Carpathian Ukraine.

The category of space is central to Krajňak's book, which is reflected in its active engagement with cultural and historical geography. Real and fictitious place names are combined following a logic stemming from the obvious autobiographical framework of the text. Although the narrator no longer lives in the Zones, he is bound to them through close ties with not only family and friends, but also with local history and broadly conceived culture. The narrator is an amateur explorer of his nation's history, genealogist, photographer, tourist, and a local expert with intimate knowledge of the land of his childhood, who repeatedly registers its lamentable current state and skeptically forecasts its future, which is detectable in the views of the people and the state of the language that they speak.

The temporally fragmented first-person narration is thematically anchored in the period of the Second World War and its aftermath. The references to the war take various forms: military artefacts and other material traces, retrospective scenes that depict events related to the borderland witnessed by the narrator's close relatives, as well as a depiction of the deportations of Polish Rusyns in the so-called Operation Vistula, which was organized by the Polish government in 1947: "Two years have passed since the war. Strange, fearful people begin to appear in the neighborhood. They speak the language of the Zones and arrive alone or in groups. They seek distant relatives or just aimlessly wander through the villages and plead for help. They speak of Zone 0, from which they have come as a space in which whole villages burn and where the army deports all living people and animals. They want to stay here, in the Carpathians. They beg for food, for permission to sleep in the barns, for the chance to stay and live in them. Some of them manage to stay, but most of them disappear."[22] The book is populated with various episodic characters, but at the centre of the story is the narrator himself and his homeland with its turbulent history, symbolically divided into Zones, and its vanishing language. However, the author does not mention the Rusyns explicitly, but describes them only indirectly as the inhabitants of the Zones and refers to the Rusyn language as the "language of the Zones." He also includes symbolic references to Rusyn culture, for example by mentioning a bear who seems to have "stepped out of the flag of the Zones" (the Rusyn flag features a red bear).[23] This ethnicity can also be identified synecdochally through references to real-life people of Rusyn origin incorporated into the text, such as Andy Warhol.

Krajňak's topographic prose is closely tied with the twentieth-century Rusyn history of this region. The author evokes images of old times and nostalgically parts with the vanishing nation and its language.[24] The regional elements are also evident in the narrative, which draws on the genre of the so-called *moritát*, a horrifying folktale. Krajňak's tales are not set in a distant past like the more traditional types of moritát but draw on the events of the Second World War, the subsequent ethnic deportations, and the political divisions of the territory inhabited by the Rusyns (when most of Ruthenia, formerly part of interwar Czechoslovakia, became a part of Soviet Ukraine).

The narrator adopts various forms of self-fashioning: the place name "the zone" explicitly alludes to the film *Stalker* by Andrei Tarkovsky: "I am like a real Stalker who has returned to the Zones after a long absence, and now with the impending sleep I pass through my earlier perceptions so that the long dead Tarkovsky can enter me."[25] Carpathia, thus, starts from the same narrative point as Tarkovsky's *Stalker*: the narrator lives outside of the Zones but possesses unique expertise as a guide to this mysterious, vanishing territory.

Beside the acknowledged inspiration taken from Tarkovsky's *Stalker*, the place name, the Zones, evokes an image of a forcefully partitioned whole (for example, in connection with the recurring motif of the Second World War, the occupied zones of the allies in defeated Germany), and, in connection with the Carpathians, the Hungarian writer Ádam Bodor's novel *The Sinistra Zone* (*Sinistra körzet*, 1992, trans. 2013), in which the zone also represents a mysterious country governed by its own laws that are incomprehensible to outsiders. The work consists of two strands that represent two types of travel narrative: an abstract one resembling that of *Stalker* and moving toward a discovery of universal human values, and a concrete one anchored in culture and history, which represents specific events and personalities of the region and Rusyn history. The literature of the Eastern Carpathians also shows some typological connections with magic realism. This derives not so much from the Latin American writers whose work has entered Slovak culture through translation since the 1960s, but a secondary transfer made possible by the similar cultural traditions of several closely related literatures in the Carpathian region, which are particularly connected through the reception of the classical and modern Ukrainian short story.[26] Several key Eastern Slovak writers were inspired by the balladic and social dimension of Ukrainian prose, its mythologizing tendency, and its overall close affinity with folklore.[27] In the 1990s, literary critics discussed the connections with magic realism in the writing of authors such as Václav Pankovčín, who presents local mythology and folktale fantasy in the form of anecdotal short stories. Although his literary production was limited by his premature death, Pankovčín created a unique literary world of the Eastern Slovak borderland area, in which its specific geography is interspersed with fantastic and magical features.

THE ROMA: BETWEEN STEREOTYPES AND AUTHENTIC VOICES

The Slovak Roma minority faces unique social, economic, educational, and cultural problems and often suffers from segregation and social exclusion. Víťo Staviarsky is another regional writer preoccupied with the cultural and linguistic diversity of Eastern Slovakia, but his fiction focuses on the social peripheries and particularly on the relation between the Slovaks and the Roma. However, Staviarsky does not opt for engaged social criticism, even though his poetics are based on personal experiences and knowledge of the Roma community. Instead of reflecting on broader social contexts, he privileges intimate stories about relationships that probe the lives of people on the margins. His "Roma cycle" consists of the debut *Kivader* (2007), the novels *Kale topánky* (The black ["kale" in Romani] shoes, 2012), *Rinaldova cesta* (Rinaldo's way, 2015), and the short story collection *Kšeft* (The deal, 2019). The characteristic features of Staviarsky's writing are ethnic and social stereotypes in characterization and a tragicomic mode. His situational humour stems from linguistic defamiliarization (through the Roma language and dialects) and from the clash between the actions of the Roma characters and the radically different value system of the majority. The plot, genre, and language of the author's "Roma prose" draws inspiration from popular literature for adults, particularly from the updated proto genre of the folktale in its original function as a narrative for adults. His stories of everyday experience capture the dark aspects of contemporary life, its spontaneity, roughness, and even animality. These are the characteristics that the majority tends to connect with the Roma.

Although Staviarsky often chooses themes from the semi-criminal environment on the social margins, his narrative perspective is fundamentally sympathetic, but also exoticizing. This signals the strategy of self-colonizing, a term used by Alexander Kiossev "for cultures having succumbed to the cultural power of Europe and the west without having been invaded and turned into colonies in actual fact."[28] In Staviarsky's case, he intentionally evokes certain stereotypes held by the Slovak majority toward not only the Roma but Eastern Slovakia in general, which tends to be perceived through exoticizing perspectives by outsiders. This approach can be contrasted with the radically different poetics of Agda Bavi Pain's story collection *Koniec sveta* (The end of the world, 2006), which was inspired by punk subculture. In his representation of the linguistic diversity of the social periphery in Košice, Pain adapts the genre of the gangster story to a regional setting. He captures the original urban language that had not previously appeared in Slovak literature, which originates in the confrontation of spoken Slovak, Hungarian, and Romani, and various social idiolects.

Although both Staviarsky and Pain are connoisseurs of the local social and linguistic contexts, their voices belong to the majority. As Charles Sabatos has observed, "although the Roma are one of the largest minority groups in the Czech and Slovak republics, literary depictions of their culture, especially by writers of Romani origin, are still quite rare when compared with minority literatures in major world languages."[29] The literary works produced by Slovak Roma writers are generally traditional with respect to their modes of expression and use the generic forms of folktale: oral history and autobiography. Fiction by key Roma writers focuses on the themes of the Roma holocaust (*porajmos*) as well as other conflicted aspects of the past, particularly during the era of socialist Czechoslovakia, which brought social benefits but also institutional disrespect for the Roma cultural identity. For example, the writings of Ľudovít Didi, especially his episodic family saga *Príbehy svätené vetrom* (Stories sanctified by the wind, 2004) and *Róm Tardek a jeho osud* (Tardek the Rom and his destiny, 2013), use traditional narrative approaches to map the life of the Roma community and Slovak-Roma coexistence from the end of the Second World War to the present. Didi shows how the need to adapt to the social framework of the majority shapes his protagonist Tardek's character: "Tardek wasn't like the other Roma. He had an enormous desire to climb higher, to obtain something, to fight for something. Even though life knocked him down on his knees again and again, it did not break him. The more life crushed him, the more he struggled to get higher, even come out on top of the white man."[30]

Elena Lacková is one of the few Slovak Roma writers who has reached international attention. Lacková's debut was the play *Horiaci cigánsky tábor* (The burning Gypsy camp, 1946), which focused on the status of the Roma, primarily in Eastern Slovakia, during the Second World War. In her subsequent work, she continued to represent this theme in the Roma language as well as in Slovak, which was in line with her lifelong mission as a social activist and cultural worker. In her case, the Czech cultural environment played an important role in the promotion of her work through the critical attention it received. Lacková became one of the few established Roma writers of this era partly due to her unique personal accomplishments and circumstances. She resided in the Czech lands where the level of social exclusion of the Roma was lower than in Slovakia and became the first Roma woman in Czechoslovakia to earn a university diploma, graduating from the prestigious Charles University. Her position as a Slovak Roma writer is also unique because her collection of "Roma tales" written in Slovak has been translated back into Romani.

Lackova's best-known book, published in Czech as *Narodila jsem se pod šťastnou hvězdou* (I was born under a lucky star, 1997), originated as a transcription from oral narration predominantly in Romani, which was translated into Czech by Milena Hübschmannová, the leading specialist of Roma studies in the Czech Republic. It was published in English translation as *A False Dawn: My Life as a Gypsy Woman in Slovakia* (2000). Lacková's autobiography is an important literary document, which consists of multiple layers. It presents a picture of the Romani community from the era of interwar Czechoslovakia, through the period of the Slovak state, and until the end of the socialist regime. Hübschmannová's recorded interviews with Lacková, which were concluded in 1986, provide an authentic testimony on the forms of Romani folklore and everyday culture. At the same time, it is a case study that captures the struggle of an exceptional woman and social activist to live authentically in the rigidly patriarchal environment of a traditional Roma family under several regimes, which subjected the Roma to various levels of control, paternalism, and exclusion. From the literary perspective, the strongest moments of the book are those that creatively adapt oral folklore and idiom:

> When they buried Grandpa on the third day, that night Mother strewed ashes on the ground in the sitting-room. We didn't have a floor, only the compacted earth. Every Saturday we mopped it with yellow loam, and it shone like the sun. No one in the settlement had a floor. "We'll be able to tell if Grandpa will come," said Mama, "by the footprints in the ashes." You see, a dead person can turn into a cat, a dog, a bird, a nightmare, into anything he wants. Depending on what it is, he leaves the footprints of a cat, dog, or a bird. Or a human being. He can even come back to earth in his own form, only you can't see his face. All Roma believe this. Well, and Mama said that in the morning she found two footprints in the ashes. Human ones! Grandpa had come to see us in his own form. That meant he was a good person, worthy, and that he didn't have to turn into a dog.[31]

Alongside their search for origins, or the unique constitutive elements of the Roma way of life, Roma authors also turn to escapist motifs, which appear to be opposed to the intention to develop and strengthen their own culture, which is often invisible in the eyes of the majority. In her foreword, Hübschmannová interprets this "protective mimicry of *gadžo* ways" (whiteness) as an attempt to distance oneself from the segregated Roma community and gain the acceptance of the majority through voluntary assimilation.[32] This phenomenon not only describes the authorial intention of Roma literature or the actions of the specific literary characters, but is also reflected in the attitudes of Roma elites outside of literature.[33] Hübschmannová comments on this tendency in connection with Lacková:

> It seemed unbelievable to me that, contrary to her lifelong efforts and activity, she would sometimes deny that she was a Rom. Of course, from my side it was simply an unbelievable lack of comprehension, an inability to empathize with the situation of a Rom who did not steal, did not burn the floors, did not change money on the black market, who sent her children to school, worked, and yet read in the newspapers day after day that Gypsies and Roma stole, robbed, changed money illegally, destroyed flats, and did not go to work; of a Rom, who at every step on the street, felt the disdainful glances of "white" people, who on every street corner read "Death to Gypsies."[34]

The reasons for such strategic distancing of Roma elites from their ethnic origin doubtlessly stem from their desire for broader social acceptance, but the problem is also related to the larger context of interethnic relations in the borderland regions of Central Europe, where this pragmatic strategy is often employed in multi-ethnic communities. In the case of the Roma, it is used more frequently because of the continuing social segregation of their communities.

THE IMAGE OF THE SLOVAK-HUNGARIAN BORDERLANDS IN CONTEMPORARY PROSE

The decisive factor that shapes the representation of Hungarians in Slovak literature is the complicated shared history of the two nations in the multi-ethnic Austro-Hungarian Empire prior to 1918, when the Hungarians gained the status of a ruling nation with state identity, and the Slovaks were in the position of a minority that suffered discrimination. Another painful period of the shared history was the Second World War, which was preceded by the loss of Czechoslovak territory to

Hungary, exchanges of borderland minority populations between Slovakia and Hungary, and the forced post-war deportation of Hungarians from this region to the Czech lands in 1945–47. Today, most of the Hungarian minority in Slovakia lives in a territory that stretches from east to west alongside the 650-kilometre border between Slovakia and Hungary.[35] However, literary representations of this population and landscape have mainly focused on the southern part of Central Slovakia and the fertile lowlands called Žitný ostrov in western Slovakia.

According to the cultural historian Ivan Halász, southern Slovakia was "the last large region of Slovakia that became an integral part of Slovak literature after World War II," but the "literary incorporation of southern Slovakia actually occurred as late as the 1960s and the 1970s."[36] The most influential writers who helped create the image of the Slovak-Hungarian borderlands in modern Slovak literature were Ladislav Ballek and Ivan Habaj. These authors were also representative with respect to the geographical settings of their short stories and novels. Ladislav Ballek's *Južná pošta* (The southern post, 1974), a collection of stories set in south-central Slovakia during the Second World War, illustrates the unique properties of the southern border as described by Vladimír Barborík in his commentary on Ballek's stories: "In contrast with the natural border of mountains in the north, the southern border is more open (its relativity is confirmed by continual shifts), and it is crossed not only by smugglers but also by cultural and linguistic influences. The mixing of cultures and languages is given by the urban character of the prose as well as by historical framework of the chaotic transitional period, during which vanishing social structures and traditions clash with the new order that is not yet fully established."[37] Ballek's narrative is centred around the fictional Palánk, based on the actual town of Šahy. In his novels *Pomocník* (The assistant, 1977) and *Agáty* (Locust trees, 1981), Ballek expands his depiction of the region and its people. In his stories and novels, small, individual, and family histories react to and intersect with the history of Czecho-Slovak-Hungarian political relations and the "grand" Central European history of the twentieth century. Whereas Ballek's and Habaj's fiction is peopled with concrete characters, their families and lines, the dominant perspective is a collective one that promotes the Slovak nation and state. This perspective is evident in Ballek's central set of characters: the protagonist of five of the stories is Ján Jurkovič, the son of a member of the fiscal guard, which is tasked with the protection of the state border.

Ivan Habaj uses a similar strategy in his novel trilogy *Kolonisti* (The colonists, 1980, 1981, 1986), which literary historian Rudolf Chmel describes as "a collectivist social-political novel."[38] Habaj's novel focuses on the families and lives of the "colonists," or the original inhabitants of the "Slovak North," who came to the "Slovak South" following the founding of Czechoslovakia, a territory that had been inhabited predominantly by ethnic Hungarians up to that point, in order to establish agricultural settlements and cultivate the land allotted to them by the state. The novel focuses on the history and the politics of this process, and its poetics are shaped by the writer's geopolitical vision of this space:

> The southern borderlands, the territory above the Danube River, which has been the crossroads of various cultures for ages, but also a territory that has been unsettled, turbulent, fluctuating, and soaked with the blood of many human generations for centuries, the site of military clashes of various opposing powers, a land that has enjoyed very little peace, where the settlers had to constantly fight somebody, ardently defend their bare lives and modest dwellings, repel attacks, ambushes, and raids. Here, at the crossroads of roads and interests, people have walked on shaky ground, always becoming a hurdle or standing in in someone's way or being pushed out of the fertile lowlands into the narrow valleys of the mountains in the north.[39]

The numerous individual destinies of Habaj's characters primarily serve as illustrations of the author's interpretation of the "grand" history, which is organized around the metaphor of return. As the quote from Habaj's novel illustrates, his version of history emphasizes that the "ousted" – meaning original – inhabitants of the Slovak South had been forced to leave for the mountainous north and, following the establishment of Czechoslovakia, they merely returned to their originally Slavic homeland. Historical milestones also determine the overarching temporal framework of the plot. For example, the first part begins with the founding of Czechoslovakia and ends with the Vienna Arbitration of 1938, in which Nazi Germany and fascist Italy forced Czechoslovakia to hand over its southern territories and the Carpathian Ukraine to Hungary.

At the beginning of the twenty-first century, Ballek and Habaj were still the names primarily connected with literary representations of Slovak-Hungarian relations and southern Slovakia in the broader public consciousness. However, the topic was also addressed in Hungarian minority literature originating in Slovakia. Starting in the second half of the 1980s, the work that reached a broader cultural awareness was that of Lajos Grendel, a Slovak Hungarian writer influenced by postmodernism, whose work was published in both Hungarian and Slovak by the bilingual Bratislava publisher Kalligram. At the turn of the millennium, Grendel published three novels depicting the fictitious town and district New Hont in south-central Slovakia: *Tömegsír/Masový hrob pri New Honte* (The mass grave by New Hont, 1999), *Nálunk, New Hontban/U nás doma, v New Honte* (At our home in New Hont, 2001), and *Mátyás király New Hontban/Kráľ Matej v New Honte* (King Matthew in New Hont, 2005). Grendel's novels, which were also published in Slovak under the common title *Newhontská trilógia* (The New Hont trilogy, 2016), were remarkable in their adaptation of the established tradition of "regionalist" literature – for example, the work of Kálmán Mikszáth, who wrote about the mixed Slovak and Hungarian regions in the nineteenth century. Grendel's literary treatment of Central European historical tribulations features a wide range of characters and narrative approaches, ranging from affectionate humour, through parody and irony to satirical poses. Another depiction of the destinies of a small town in this region by a minority Hungarian writer appears in Péter Hunčík's novel *Határeset/Hraničný prípad* (The border case, 2008/2011). Hunčík also opts for a panoramic point of view, in which the small lives of the characters are impacted by the "grand" twentieth century, and uses child narrators, fragmented narration, and elements of alternative history to convey the oblique perspective of the Hungarian minority.

In the years immediately following the 1989 revolution, Slovak literature tended to avoid the topic of the Slovak-Hungarian borderlands. To a certain degree this silence was associated with the fact that questions of Slovak-Hungarian relations, especially ones related to the rights of the minorities, were the subject of intense debates in other public spaces, becoming a painful topic in Slovak political and media discourse as well as a source of diplomatic conflicts. Daniela Kapitáňová's *Samko Tále's Cemetery Book* (*Samko Tále: Kniha o cintoríne*, 2000, trans. 2011) points to the simplification and vulgarization of the political discussion on these topics through Samko Tále, a narrator with a mental disability, who introduces various secondary characters and issues through micro-narratives and commentaries.[40] The comic and parodic force of the narration stems from Samko's distortion of individual words and their meaning, from his mechanical repetition of phrases and language constructions, as well as from their socially inappropriate uses. Thus Samko, who is an unreliable narrator from the narratological perspective, constructs a tragicomic metaphor for Slovak society. Samko lives in Komárno, a town inhabited by a predominantly Hungarian population, and although the regional problem of Slovak-Hungarian relations is not Kapitáňová's primary focus, the commentary on ethnic coexistence during this period becomes a key source of situational comedy. For example, the "idiot" Samko accurately recognizes and reproduces the Slovak nationalist rhetoric that pervaded the private and public spheres:

> Otherwise there aren't many Germans in Komárno, just lots of Hungarians and Gypsies and also some Vietnamese, especially in the Market Place but the Vietnamese are nice because they don't push other people around and they don't speak Vietnamese. I mean they do speak Vietnamese but only among themselves. But Hungarians speak Hungarian even when they are not among themselves.
>
> But people forgive the Vietnamese for speaking Vietnamese because we have never been suppressed by them. And that's why they are allowed in Slovakia. We have always been suppressed by the Hungarians and that's why we will never forgive them. That goes without saying, right?[41]

Samko Tále's Cemetery Book captures the contemporary problems inherent in Slovak-Hungarian relations, which had accumulated during the 1990s and presented a threat of more significant conflict, at the level of language (vocabulary and idioms). Following the trend of critical and parodic reflections on nationalism, Slovak literature began to emphasize new approaches foregrounding multiculturalism and more positive aspects of history, in which Slovak-Hungarian relations functioned symbiotically rather than antagonistically.

The southern borderlands also appear in popular works appealing to a broader readership, such as Pavol Rankov's novel *It Happened on the First of September (Or Some Other Time)* (*Stalo sa prvého septembra (alebo inokedy)*, 2008, trans. 2020), in which the town of Levice serves an integrating function by connecting characters with varied national and social backgrounds. Like Ballek and Habaj (who knew the Slovak South from within as residents), Rankov structures the temporal frame of his novel around important historical milestones, but in contrast to them, he conceptualizes the diverse space of interwar Levice as a backdrop for a historical fiction that illustrates and celebrates Slovakia's ethnic heterogeneity. His primary objective is not to capture the unique atmosphere and the stories of the Slovak South; on the contrary, he is interested in following the evolution of characters with a certain social and ethnic background in the "greater" world and in depicting how their destinies unfold against the backdrop of key historical events in twentieth-century Slovakia and Central Europe.[42]

Literary representations of the Slovak-Hungarian borderlands typically capture a relatively limited geographical space in south-central Slovakia. The youngest generation of writers who purposefully reflect on the space of the Slovak South include two authors from Lučenec, Peter Balko and Jakub Juhás, who confirm that the image of this space in Slovak literature has been dominated by the chronotope of childhood and initiation. The choice of this established chronotope also tends to be associated with the characteristic mode of fragmented narration of a child narrator, who is usually unreliable from the narratological perspective, and, therefore, the narratives tend to contain imaginative and fantastic elements.

Peter Balko claims to be inspired by the imaginative, "magic realist" strand of modern Slovak prose (represented, for example, by the above-mentioned work of Václav Pankovčín). In his debut, the fragmentary novel *Vtedy v Lošonci* (Once upon a time in Lošonc, 2014), he explores generational themes, in which youthful "research" of personal, linguistic, cultural, and social identities plays a central role.[43] For Balko, his native town is in this respect an important space of initiation: "I saw my town, my Lošonc, which expelled me from its foundations and threw me out into the world naked and unprepared."[44] Space is an essential component of Balko's prose, yet its function is ambivalent. On the one hand, the positive relationship with the multicultural and bilingual town and its immediate surroundings is an integral part of the author's and his child protagonists' personalities. On the other hand, in most instances this relationship is presented through the lens of ironic rhetorical hyperbole: "Red pepper and Leviathan. The children of the South. Comrades, blood brothers. The best friends in Novohrad, whom nothing will separate, not even the third world war. We stood in the heart of Lošonc and both suspected that this was not the end."[45]

Juhás's prose debut *Novoročný výstup na Jaseninu* (The New Year's ascent of Jasenina, 2016) provides specific geographical data that places the narrative in the mountain range Slovenské Rudohorie, more precisely approximately between the villages Lovibaňa and Kokava nad Rimavicou, so, therefore, practically in the centre of Slovakia, but at the same time in its depopulated, socially frustrating periphery. Juhás's book can be categorized as a lyrical-reflective topography, which, against the backdrop of a thirty-one-kilometre hike during the transition from autumn to winter, evokes dark images of poverty, spiritual emptiness, and various forms of decay, while also offering a dim hope associated with the narrator's return to his native land. From a formal perspective, *Novoročný výstup na Jaseninu* consists of two generic forms. The first one consists of a formal experiment. From the thematic use of abstract categories (decay, cold, emptiness, space) in its mise-en-scène sequences and fragments, the book moves toward more concrete images that shift Juhás's poetics toward dimensions that reflect a human, living, intersubjective world that reflects spiritual apathy and the poverty of the social periphery. The other generic form of Juhás's prose is more traditional, following the conventions of the genre of the travelogue of initiation that includes the cathartic moment of returning home. The narrator returns to his native land, searches for his roots, and resumes communication with the region and his ancestors, which the author signals by dedicating the book to his grandfathers. In his style and poetics, Juhás presents an alternative regional variation of Krajňak's approach. However, whereas Krajňak's moralizing narratives of north-eastern Slovakia aim at enlightening readers, since the narrator presents himself as an expert chronicler of the Rusyn microcosm within a certain historical timeframe, Juhás does not anchor his pilgrim, traveller, or tourist in the depth of social history.

The historical context of the Slovak-Hungarian borderlands does not adopt gestures and positions associated with national indifference as frequently as texts representing the ethnically mixed regions of eastern Slovakia. Cultural identities are more clearly defined and more firmly anchored in history in this space, and literary criticism and cultural history use more traditional terms such as multiculturalism or "biliterariness" to describe them. Thanks to pioneering writers such as Ballek and Habaj, the Slovak-Hungarian borderlands became a part of the Slovak literary imagination in the second half of the twentieth century, and regionalism was established as one of the key productive strands of Slovak prose. This development was undoubtedly also determined by extra-literary factors and associated with the continued evolution of Slovak national identity, for the self-definition of which Hungarian culture and society had historically served as a negative counterpoint. Contemporary Slovak prose depicting the Slovak-Hungarian borderlands no longer displays such ethnocentric ambitions, but several of the writers included in this chapter nevertheless continue to emphasize the category of space, which remains a key element of self-identification on the part of the "southern" narrators.

NOTES

1 These divisions were known in Slovak as župa, in Hungarian as *varmegye*, and in Latin (still used as an administrative language in nineteenth-century Hungary) as *comitatus*.

2 On the tensions between nationalism and "Czechoslovakism," see Benko-Hudek, "Ideológia čechoslovakizmu."

3 See for example Žeňuch, *Medzi východom a západom*.

4 Škvarna, "Koncepty slovenských dejín," 216.

5 This group of writers includes Ivana Dobrakovová, Zuska Kepplová, Michaela Rosová, Svetlana Žuchová, and more recently Barbora Hrínová and others. For a more detailed discussion of expat writing, see chapter 8.

6 Deleuze and Guattari, *Kafka: Toward a Minor Literature*, 16.

7 Slovakia is more ethnically diverse than the neighbouring Central European countries such as the Czech Republic, Poland, or Hungary. According to the official census of 2021, ethnic minorities, the largest of which are Hungarian, Roma, Czech, and Rusyn, comprise over 16 per cent of the population. Furthermore, 5.6 per cent of the Slovak population also chose the option to include a secondary nationality on the census form. From the perspective of the ethnic and cultural identity of minorities and their assimilation, it is interesting that more people claimed Roma and Rusyn nationality as secondary than primary. See www.scitanie.sk. (The current ethnic map of Slovakia has been markedly affected by the wave of refugees that have arrived following the Russian invasion of Ukraine in the spring of 2022.)

8 Hroch, *Hledání souvislostí*, 244.

9 Zahra, "Imagined Noncommunities," 101.

10 Ibid., 105.

11 Ibid., 98.

12 Baudrillard, *Selected Writings*, 166.

13 Drawing on a case study of Košice, Ondrej Ficeri demonstrates the facile changes in the ethnic affiliation of the large part of the population in response to the changes in national regimes during the first half of the twentieth century. See Ficeri, *Potrianonské Košice.*

14 Feinberg, *Paradox of Authenticity*, 14.

15 The Andy Warhol Museum of Modern Art (which presents some originals of Andy Warhol's work on loan from the Andy Warhol Foundation for Visual Art in New York) was established in the small town of Medzilaborce, near Miková, in 1991.

16 Colacello, *Holy Terror*, 11.

17 Ibid.

18 See Magocsi, *People from Nowhere.*

19 See Magocsi, "The Third Rusyn National Revival."

20 Krivak, *Sojourn*, 32.

21 The novel has not appeared in Slovak, but it was published in Czech translation under the title *Dlouhý návrat.*

22 Krajňak, *Carpathia*, 17.

23 Ibid., 70.

24 For an analysis of the nostalgic dimensions of Krajňak's prose, see Gephardt, "Productive Uses of Nostalgia."

25 Krajňak, *Carpathia*, 98.

26 See Passia, "Východokarpatský magický realizmus?"

27 The reception of literature in translation led to the appearance of parallel creative attempts in the literary circles of Eastern Slovakia. (For example, this is evident in the Ukrainian modernist Vasyl Stefanyk's influence on the contemporary prose writer Stanislav Rakús.)

28 Kiossev, "The Self-Colonizing Metaphor."

29 Sabatos, "Finding a Voice," 181.

30 Didi, *Róm Tardek a jeho osud*, 44.

31 Lacková, *False Dawn*, 27.

32 Hübschmannová, "Foreword," in Lacková, *A False Dawn*, 7.

33 For example, Arne B. Mann's *Rómsky dejepis* (*The History of Roma People*) drew media attention because of the protests of several prominent figures who were included in the book as positive examples of Roma personalities in the cultural and social life of contemporary Slovakia, even though they did not identify with the ethnicity themselves.

34 Lacková, *False Dawn*, 7.

35 According to the official 2021 census of inhabitants, houses, and apartments in the Slovak Republic, about 422,000 people claimed Hungarian nationality, which is 7.75 per cent of the Slovak population.
36 Halász, *Južné Slovensko v literatúre*, 162.
37 Barborík, "Výchova pamäťou," 520–1.
38 Chmel and Habaj, "Kolonisti," 91.
39 Habaj, *Kolonisti I*, 29.
40 The book was translated into twelve languages, including the English translation by Julia Sherwood, and is one of the most widely translated Slovak books published after 2000.
41 Kapitáňová, *Samko Tále's Cemetery Book*, 92.
42 In the coda section of this volume, Magdalena Mullek reflects on her process of creating the English translation of Rankov's novel, which was published by Slavica in 2020.
43 Losonc is the Hungarian name of his native town, Lučenec.
44 Balko, *Vtedy v Lošonci*, 185.
45 Ibid., 178.

BIBLIOGRAPHY

Ballek, Ladislav. *Južná pošta*. Bratislava: Slovenský spisovateľ, 1974.

Balko, Peter. *Vtedy v Lošonci*. Levice: KK Bagala, 2015.

Barborík, Vladimír. "Výchova pamäťou." In *Sondy. Interpretácie kľúčových diel slovenskej literatúry 20. storočia*, edited by Peter Zajac, 508–25. Bratislava: Kalligram, 2014.

Baudrillard, Jean. *Selected Writings*, edited by Mark Poster. Stanford: Stanford University Press, 1988.

Benko, Juraj, and Adam Hudek. "Ideológia čechoslovakizmu a slovenskí komunisti." In *Čechoslovakizmus*, edited by Adam Hudek, Michal Kopeček, and Jan Mervart, 281–309. Prague: NLN, 2019.

Chmel, Rudolf, and Ivan Habaj. "Kolonisti." In *Slovník diel slovenskej literatúry 20. Storočia*, edited by Rudolf Chmel, 90–3. Bratislava: Kalligram and Ústav slovenskej literatúry SAV, 2006.

Colacello, Bob. *Holy Terror: Andy Warhol Close Up*. New York: HarperCollins, 1990.

Deleuze, Gilles, and Félix Guattari. *Kafka. Toward a Minor Literature*. Translated by Dana Polan. Minneapolis: University of Minnesota Press, 1986.

Didi, Ľudovít. *Róm Tardek a jeho osud*. Bratislava: Slovart, 2001.
Feinberg, Joseph Grim. *The Paradox of Authenticity: Folklore Performance in Post-Communist Slovakia*. Madison: University of Wisconsin Press, 2018.
Ficeri, Ondrej. *Potrianonské Košice. Premeny etnických identít obyvateľov Košíc v medzivojnovom období*. Bratislava: Veda, 2019.
Gephardt, Katarina. "Productive Uses of Nostalgia in Contemporary Slovak Fiction: Veronika Šikulová's and Maroš Krajňak's Experiments with Generational Memory." *Canadian Slavonic Papers* 60, no. 3–4 (2018): 548–70.
Habaj, Ivan. *Kolonisti I*. Bratislava: Vlna – Drewo a srd, 2020.
Halász, Ivan. *Južné Slovensko v literatúre (Stereotypy a interetnické súvislosti)*. Komárno: Univerzita J. Selyeho, 2018.
Hroch, Miroslav. *Hledání souvislostí. Eseje z komparativních dějin Evropy*. Prague: SLON, 2016.
Juhás, Jakub. *Novoročný výstup na Jaseninu cez Horné Fafáky, Sebedinú, Sedlo Prieraz, Šutovu jamu a Brložno*. Prague: Rubato, 2016.
Kapitáňová, Daniela. *Samko Tále's Cemetery Book*. Translated by Julia Sherwood. London: Garnett Press, 2011.
Kiossev, Alexander. "The Self-Colonizing Metaphor." *Atlas of Transformation* retrieved 15 June 2022 from http://monumenttotransformation.org/atlas-of-transformation/html/s/self-colonization/the-self-colonizing-metaphor-alexander-kiossev.html.
Krajňak, Maroš. *Carpathia*. Bratislava: Trio Publishing, 2011.
Krivak, Andrew. *Dlouhý návrat*. Prague: Odeon, 2013.
– *The Sojourn*. New York: Bellevue Literary Press, 2011.
Lacková, Ilona [Elena]. *A False Dawn: My Life as a Gypsy Woman in Slovakia*. Translated by Carleton Bulkin, foreword by Milena Hübschmannová. Hatfield: University of Hertfordshire Press, 2000.
– *Narodila jsem se pod šťastnou hvězdou*. 2nd edition. Prague: Triáda, 2002.
Magocsi, Paul Robert. *The People from Nowhere: An Illustrated History of Carpatho-Rusyns*. Uzhhorod: V. Padiak Publishers, 2006.
Mann, Arne B. *Rómsky dejepis*. Prague: Nakladatelství Fortuna, 2001.
Passia, Radoslav. "Východokarpatský magický realizmus? Rekonštrukcia cesty 'magického realizmu' do slovenskej literatúry východu." [Carpathian Magic Realism? Reconstruction of the Journey of "Magic Realism" into Slovak Literature from the East]. *World Literature Studies* 8, no. 2 (2016): 29–39.
Rankov, Pavol. *It Happened on the First of September (or Some Other Time)*. Translated by Magdalena Mullek. Bloomington: Slavica Publishers, 2020

Sabatos, Charles. "Finding a Voice: The Slovak-Roma Woman Writer in Irish and Czech Fiction." *Romani Studies* 30, no. 2 (2020): 181–200.
Škvarna, Dušan. "Koncepty slovenských dejín a deformácie historickej pamäti." In *Kontakty literatúry*, edited by Magdalena Bystrzak, Radoslav Passia, and Ivana Taranenková, 191–216. Bratislava: Veda, 2020.
Zahra, Tara. "Imagined Noncommunities: National Indifference as a Category of Analysis." *Slavic Review* 69, no. 1 (Spring 2010): 93–119.
Žeňuch, Peter. *Medzi východom a západom*. Bratislava: Veda, 2002.

CHAPTER EIGHT

Expatriate and Cosmopolitan Writing

Tamara Janecová

The social changes associated with the opening of borders in Central Europe led to the emergence of expat literature that builds on the legacy of emigrant literature while also introducing new themes and dilemmas. New authors from the millennial generation, predominantly women in their thirties, depict their experience of living abroad, capitalizing on the novelty of this type of international experience. This trend is part of a broader development related to the changed attitude toward the subject in postmodern literature. In addition to the strengthening of subjective narration in autofiction, expat writers revitalize the opposition of home and the world and focus on issues related to identity. An emigrant or expat protagonist's journey into the unknown is driven by various motives: to learn a foreign language, to make money, to gain new experiences, or to get a fresh start. The primary obstacle is the fact that by crossing the border of their home country (not only a geographical but also a cultural and mental one), the protagonists of emigrant and expat fiction find themselves in a foreign space governed by different social codes, in what Vilém Flusser has called an "ocean of chaotic information."[1] Without a cultural compass, the subjects cannot orient themselves, and are forced to "transform the information whizzing around into meaningful messages, to make it livable." In this case, the need to "process the data ... is a question of survival."[2] Their confrontation with the world leads not only to a realization of their own identity, but to its creative refashioning.

As Vladimír Barborík notes, the subject and their relationship with home and memory is the starting point for the exploration of identity in expat literature.[3] These texts literalize the "return" of the subject in order to mediate authentic experiences, which include the experience of living in the West and the processing of the experience following the narrator's return home. The writers emphasize the confrontation with other cultures and the psychological impact of leaving one's home. Dana Hučková explains that expats "offer a view from outside and an opportunity to make comparisons first and foremost with their own personal identity ... Home and the world come together, join and overlap, but it always depends on the individual what place they give to space in their perception of reality."[4] Expat writers highlight moments of crisis in which the opposition of home and abroad challenges the protagonists' sense of identity. The cultural clash may destabilize the protagonists' sense of self, but also lead them to construct new identities. Zygmund Bauman characterizes this process as "a series of 'new beginnings,' experimenting with instantly assembled yet easily dismantled shapes, painted one over the other; a palimpsest identity."[5] He emphasizes that the art of forgetting is as important as the art of remembering in this process.

The emerging genre of expatriate writing builds on the theme of emigration (whether due to economic or political circumstances), which is well established in the history of Slovak literature. Economic emigration, particularly to the United States, was widespread among Slovaks during the oppressive period of Hungarian rule during the nineteenth and early twentieth centuries, as documented by writers such as Thomas Bell.[6] During the interwar Czechoslovak Republic, often characterized by the phrase "opening the windows to Europe," works such as Ivan Horváth's collection *Vízum do Európy* (Visa for Europe, 1930), set in various foreign cities, reflected the increased contact with the continent. This era was recalled nostalgically in the socialist era by writers like Dominik Tatarka, whose *Prútené kreslá* (Wicker armchairs, 1963) draws on the experience of the author as a student in Paris shortly before the Nazi occupation of Czechoslovakia in 1939. In the context of the 1960s, the novella's intimate love story highlighted the universality of human relationships in the face of ideological and geopolitical divisions.

After the Second World War, emigrants left Slovakia in several waves, particularly following the communist takeover of power in 1948 and the Warsaw Pact invasion in 1968, but when compared with the situation in Czech literature, relatively few major Slovak writers chose to emigrate to the West. The reestablishment of democracy after the Velvet Revolution in

1989 and the founding of independent Slovakia in 1993 changed the character of migration abroad. Emigration was no longer a response to political repression but a free choice involving economic opportunities for some and education for others, especially among the middle and upper classes, who were motivated by the quest for better knowledge of the world and the self. Globalization accelerated the process of opening borders, which led to increased freedom of movement after Slovakia joined the European Union in 2004, entered the Schengen Area in 2007, and adopted the Euro in 2009. This process of integration provided new opportunities for traveling, working, and studying abroad for a new generation of young people born in the late 1970s and early 1980s, who were young children in 1989 and were shaped by the more open and democratic Slovak society after of the Velvet Revolution. When confronted with foreign environments, they were better prepared to redefine themselves and their cultural identities.

In this sense, the journey from the border crossing to the translation of the new world into the protagonists' own comprehensible code is a test of adaptability, which involves adaptation to a specific place regardless of the destination. The protagonists find themselves in so-called "non-places" as understood by Marc Augé, ones that cannot be categorized in relation to history or identity.[7] These are temporary or provisional places of transition such as airports, hotels, hostels, leisure parks, large retail outlets, as well as cable or wireless networks. In these non-places, as Augé states, "solitude is experienced as an overburdening or emptying of individuality, in which only the movement of the fleeting images enables the observer to hypothesize the existence of a past and glimpse the possibility of a future."[8] Emigrant and expat literature uses such spaces to intensify and expand the protagonists' sense of loneliness.

The prose of emigrant writers from the 1968 generation who have continued to publish after 1989 explores the psychological repercussions of exile. Even though travel became much easier after the reopening of the borders, the writers' increased contact with home may reinforce feelings of nostalgia. In contrast with expat writing, emigrants are particularly concerned with the problem of naming and processing experience in a second language. In order to illustrate the emigrant experience in the aftermath of the Cold War, the first section of this chapter focuses on two writers who left Czechoslovakia in 1968: Jaroslava Blažková, who emigrated to Canada as an already established writer, and Irena Brežná, who left with her family in her late teens and settled in Switzerland. Both authors seek to find a middle ground between the excesses of nostalgia and the pressures to assimilate. They are also keenly aware of their struggles as emigrants in the broader global contexts of migration and cross-cultural contact.

The challenges of adapting to new conditions and constructing a new identity are also introduced but rarely resolved in expat prose. The resolution of the conflict may involve a return or escape to one's home country. Regardless of the fulfillment or failure of the expat's original plans, such as starting a new life, educating oneself, or making money, the journey is usually represented as meaningful because it serves as a means of gaining self-knowledge and refashioning one's identity. The second section of this chapter focuses on two expatriate writers, Ivana Dobrakovová and Zuska Kepplová, whose fictions are representative of the psychological depth and intercultural awareness that characterizes the expat fiction produced by their generation.

Emigrant and expat prose are shaped by different social and political circumstances. Emigrants are more preoccupied with language and resist stereotypes in the process of constructing their new identities since their location is more fixed than in the case of expats. Nevertheless, when considered in terms of literary and narrative conventions, emigrant and expat prose share many common features. Both emigrant and expat texts foreground the inner lives of subjects and, thus, involve a certain narrowing of the narrative perspective. In terms of narrative structure, both types of texts involve meandering or mosaic-like *syuzhets* that reflect the fragmentation of human identity in response to life abroad. The timelines tend to contrast the present and the past, which correspond with the foreign (now) and domestic (then) layers of experience. Both emigrant and expat texts also highlight the problem of borders, both literal and metaphorical, and involving a range of cultural, mental, linguistic, political, and geographical meanings. The themes of departure and arrival tend to not only frame the narrative, but also to symbolize the inner journey.

EXILE, NOSTALGIA, AND LANGUAGE: EMIGRANT WRITERS' RESISTANCE TO ASSIMILATION

Slovak emigrant, exile, and expat literature typically foregrounds the experience of individuals who struggle with the fact that most people they encounter abroad do not know their small country of origin. The protagonists are depicted in situations that involve persistent contrasts between the East and the West, and they reflect on these cultural tensions from the perspective of their Central European identity. Their predicament involves intense experiences and a sense of exclusion, or an existence on the margins, or in between. Émigré and expat prose also highlights images of everyday life, especially the material aspects of life abroad: food, sleeping arrangements, and hygiene. Paradoxically, despite their apparent banality, such mundane scenes anchor the exceptional phases of the protagonists' life journeys. The contrasting background of daily life resonates with the more profound challenges of expat life such as questions of identity, the search for one's place in life and the world, and the relationship with home, which is ever-present in emigrant and expat literature. As Radoslav Passia puts it, "the theme of home is often highlighted through its absence, whether through temporal distance (often involving childhood memories), or spatial distance, or a combination of both."[9]

Jaroslava Blažková is a cosmopolitan author; her interest in other people and cultures becomes, in Dobrota Pucherová's terms, "a means of transforming herself: the identity of her narrators is not shaped by confrontation with alterity but by its acceptance. This type of attitude toward foreigners and the foreign is a political position on Blažková's part. After her disappointment with the socialist systems of East Central Europe, she rejects any form of exclusive community and envisions a democracy that encompasses all."[10] While she was a leading figure in the generation of Slovak novelists who emerged in the 1960s and gained notoriety for her novella *Nylonový mesiac* (Nylon moon, 1963), Blažková's books were denied republication and excluded from library collections following her illegal emigration. She started publishing again after a long pause around the time when the expat authors of the younger generation started appearing on the Slovak literary scene. Her recent works share the focus on the subject and autobiographical elements with expat prose. *Happyendy* (Happyends, 2007) is an epistolary novel that focuses on the emigrant experience of living between two cultures and not belonging to either one of them. The solution of Blažková's narrator is to create her own private inner world. Her protagonist is emotionally and morally connected with the world of Slovakia because it shaped her perspective on life and moral values, yet her stories are anchored in Canadian settings. The book explores themes of alienation and nostalgia, but also reflects the narrator's persistent quest for home, which requires an understanding and acceptance of a foreign culture.[11]

The autobiographical narrative of *Happyendy* consists of thirteen chapters, each containing of a letter written to a friend in Slovakia. The narrator describes her life in Canada through observations and reflections, putting focus on mundane details of everyday life. The storyline is fragmentary and follows the passing of seasons from spring to fall, which indirectly contrasts with the narrator's preoccupation with aging and with the waning strength of the body and the mind. While taking care of her gravely ill husband, the protagonist complements her daily routine with the recording of minor incidents, which mostly involve walks in the neighbourhood or observations on nature. The descriptions of her meetings with neighbours showcase her wit and attention to nuances of psychology. She describes seemingly mundane experiences with gentle irony, which connects the tragic and comic aspects of life, and this light touch extends even to heavy topics such as illness, aging, and death. Letter writing combines literary creativity and a sense of humour, while also serving as a form of scriptotherapy. The narrator signs her letters in ways that reflect her current sense of self. For example, in the following passage, she explains to a visiting friend that she conducts long conversations with a spider who keeps her company at home:

> "'Do you know who you are talking to?!"
> "What's wrong? With whom?"
> "With a shriveled fly! There's a dead fly caught in the spider web!"
> I picked up my strongest glasses, climbed up on a chair to take a closer look and indeed – a fly! My beautiful spider has gone who knows where, and I've been keeping company with a mummified fly.[12]

In the end the narrator signs this letter, which harmoniously blends themes of loneliness and sadness with comic incidents, with a self-ironizing gesture: "Yours fantastically / amazingly irresistible / owner of a menagerie / a shepherdess of spiders."[13]

In the monotonous flow of time the narrator discovers small jobs: she finds pleasure in plotting how to protect the tulip bulbs from squirrels and bashfully welcomes the blooming of lilacs. Her descriptions of nature highlight the lyric dimension of her writing. In such moments her prose becomes static and aesthetic, radiating joy and passion, as for example while collecting plants and recalling their (Slovak) names: "In the depths of the park I discover additional gems: German chamomile, deschampsia, common silverweed, and common sage all spring to life there. In the meadow then, the first daisies, cockscombs, morning glories, bellflowers, fern-leaf dropworts, wood anemones, and look – locust trees."[14] The passage synesthetically blends different senses; the catalogue of plant species evokes a visual image of flowers and their various colours, shapes, and fragrances. The names of plants in the original Slovak text are carefully selected to create euphonic effects involving alliteration, paronomasia, long resonant vowels, and at the end a pause emphasized with a dash, followed by the name of a tree. Blažková's pictures of nature do not merely serve a conventional or descriptive function; they poetically express the narrator's appreciation of the beauty of everyday experience and her artistic worldview.

The passages that focus on life in Calgary and reflections on Canadian customs (such as an extended section devoted to Halloween), art and literature, including numerous references to writers (Samuel Beckett, Rudolf Sloboda, Ján Johanides, etc.), are interspersed with memories of the author's youth in Bratislava, scenes of married life, and her departure from Czechoslovakia in 1968. The accounts of life abroad and memories of home are also subtly contrasted. The narrator's affinity for literature, and her love of language as a means of capturing the world, become a source of suffering after she loses her linguistic mastery in exile: "It was clear to me that this new language will never flow from my tongue, that I will never use it to create jokes, puns, flights, sparks, fireworks of the imagination as I had used to at back at home."[15] Thus the narrator's limited language fluency affects her sense of identity in Canada.

However, Blažková does not depict Canadian society as a monolith. She lives in an ethnically diverse community and highlights the varying lifestyles of its members. Multi-culturalism, cultural identity, and subjective experience are the focal themes of Blažková's story "Na svadbu do Kalifornie" (A wedding in California, 2012). The plot is minimalistic, and the central storyline focuses on the event itself, which functions as an apt metaphor for connecting the dissimilar. The first-person narrator describes the wedding of her granddaughter, a Canadian with Slovak and British roots, to Jasim, an upper-class Indian man. At first, Jasim's mother is not happy with the potential bride because she does not meet her racial, cultural, or religious standards. The wedding preparations bring the families of the couple together and bring to light cultural misunderstandings and mutual suppressed prejudices. The narrator registers them in surprised and questioning looks, pauses, or other signs of embarrassment.

Blažková's sense of humour and awareness of grotesque details are evident in this text. She lightens the tension using self-irony and witty commentary. For example, she observes that even though her role in the wedding is that of a venerable matriarch (there is only one representing each side of the family), she spatters food on her clothes, moves less than gracefully while she climbs the hill to get to the site of the wedding, and loses all inhibition while dancing. Although there is a touch of pathos in the narration, the narrator always questions and lightens it through descriptions of the wedding atmosphere and drinking, which elevates her spirit: "Both of us, us 'venerable' ones, realized the wonder of the accident that brought her from the thousands-of-miles-away tip of the Indian subcontinent and me from the thousands-of-miles-away city on the Danube, here under the roof of the pavilion in the Californian town of Berkeley, to witness that her grandson and my granddaughter become suddenly, out of the blue – one body. 'Now we ARE family!,' declares the old matriarch."[16] The conclusion of the story completes the leitmotif of connection, unity, and fulfillment. The protagonist is one of the last guests to leave and while she waits in the dark for her son to pick her up, she looks up at the stars and experiences an almost mystical sense of fulfillment and happiness, claiming that she touched eternity with her little finger.[17] Blažková once again draws on her autobiographical experience and uses lyrical images of nature. Whereas in *Happyendy* such passages provided a contrast between the colourful flora and the grey monotony of daily experience, in "A wedding in California," the peaceful contemplation of plant life and the heavens provide a respite from the turmoil of the wedding party.

Irena Brežná, who moved to Switzerland as a young adult, focuses on the different challenges of negotiating adaptation and assimilation in Western Europe. While Blažková continued to write in Slovak in North America, Brežná writes in German, although most of her works have been published in Slovak translation. Her autobiographical novel *The Best of All Worlds* (*Die beste aller Welten*, 2007) depicts her personal family story against the backdrop of official history.[18] Based on the author's childhood in socialist Czechoslovakia and the events that eventually led to her emigration, the novel presents this era through the first-person perspective of the eleven-year-old protagonist Jana, using the filter of childlike naivete to unmask the perverse rules of a world subject to political ideology. For most of the novel, Jana's mother is imprisoned for an attempt at illegal emigration, and the narrative is framed by this absence of the mother; from the very beginning, it functions as a trigger point and a traumatizing experience. The time span of the story is about one year, the duration of the mother's absence. The rest of her family does not provide adequate consolation: Jana does not get along with her brother, her father (a former lawyer now considered a "bourgeois element") is forced into manual labour, and her grandmother hides the fact that her native language is German. Nevertheless, her relationships with her mother and grandmother are formative for the protagonist, and on the last page of the novel, her mother returns home. Jana's world of ideas includes what she is taught in school about five-year plans, proletarian brotherhood, and the bourgeoisie, and the ideological terms that pepper her speech have a grotesque and tragic effect, leading to an internal struggle and emotional confusion.

Jonny Johnston has described "the politics of the school-room" in Brežná's novel as "a space in which nation/citizen-building and anti-capitalist socialist discursive positions are distinctly privileged."[19] On the one hand, Jana gradually internalizes the socialist narratives and values, which are systematically reinforced by her schooling. On the other hand, she realizes the inevitable dichotomy of a life radically divided into private and public spheres: "Mama didn't steal anything or kill anyone. Maybe the word got her put in prison. In our country, words are dangerous. I'm afraid that it was my words that did it. Sometimes I forget Mama's warning: You can't say the same things at school that we say at home. In my head I built a wall – my family words live on the right and school words live on the left. They are two worlds and two languages, and I go back and forth between them every day like a secret agent."[20]

The novel is composed as a sequence of associations, consisting of everyday events, the small joys and problems of childhood, and reflective passages, in which Jana processes the material she learns as school and interprets it in her own way. When she follows the "big truths" to their logical conclusions, she exposes their fallacies. For example, she concludes that perpetual progress requires the construction of an increasing number of chimneys, because a developed socialist country must need a lot of chimneys and dirty rivers, while backward countries have clean rivers. In a similar fashion, her reflections untangle other ideological knots, such as the communist conception of religious faith as an instrument for manipulating people. Jana subjects her social environment to the same kind of implicit but precise critique, with an emphasis on the conceptions of femininity and masculinity embodied in her grandmother's conservative views. For example, she points out the different norms for girls and boys: she must behave well and never get angry but she can cry, while her brother is not allowed to cry but can express his anger. The novel is thus a critique not only of totalitarian but also of gender ideology. *The Thankless Foreigner* (*Die undankbare Fremde*, 2012) is inspired by Brežná's experience of immigrant life in Switzerland.[21] The protagonist must come to terms with her departure from the homeland, her inner struggle in response to the foreign culture, and problems of identity. The first-person narration begins with an account of the border crossing and describes a scene in which an official writes down her surname and adapts it to Swiss conventions, an act that has symbolic dimensions:

> In the barracks we were interrogated by a captain with several speech defects. He couldn't roll his *r* or pronounce any of the letters ž, ľ, ť, dž, ň and ô and he stressed the wrong syllable on our surname, so I hardly recognized myself. Writing it on a form, he stripped off all the hats and wings.
>
> "You don't need all those twiddly bits here."
>
> He also struck off my rounded, feminine ending, giving me my father and brother's surname. What was I supposed to do with this masculine version, stripped bare? I shivered.[22]

The account of the border crossing and the short stay in a refugee camp serves as an introduction to the central theme of the novel, which is a reflection on the protagonist's relationship with her new home. The novel alternates two narrative perspectives, graphically accentuated with different types of font, each of which emphasizes the problem of assimilation abroad and nostalgia for home: In one storyline, the protagonist focuses on a subjective, intimate reconstruction of her own story; in the other, she records the emotionally charged stories of other immigrants applying for asylum from her point of view as a professional interpreter.

The problematic adaptation to the new environment is expressed through the personification of the country. While traditionally a homeland or *patria* is represented by the feminine figure of a mother, the protagonist perceives her new home as an alienating manifestation of patriarchy: "I felt like an object my mother had installed in a strange house, like an underage bride, thrown back a hundred years, married off to a country like an austere old man. I was supposed to love and respect him, get along with him for a lifetime ... I remained obstinate, refusing to be grateful for my forced marriage to the host country."[23] The protagonist considers Switzerland traditional, "cold" and organized in contrast with Czechoslovakia, which represents an irrational yet fervent approach to life. She realizes that Switzerland represents the freedom of the developed world, but also experiences feelings of loneliness, rootlessness, and alienation; it does not seem possible to start over. Her inner crisis, refusal to adapt to the new environment, and deep nostalgia for home correspond with Vilém Flusser's observation that "whoever loses his home, suffers. He is bound to his home by many threads, most of which are secret threads beyond his consciousness. If the threads tear or are torn, then this tear is experienced as a painful surgical incision into his most private self."[24] For Brežná's protagonist the loss of home is a violation of her personal integrity, and in describing this predicament, the narrator uses a metaphor similar to Flusser's: "Back home everything was permeable, the doors in public toilets didn't lock, we were all one single, indivisible body. And I had been amputated from that body."[25] Both Flusser and Brežná use a surgical metaphor to compare the loss of home with bodily injury – the separation from home is manifested as physical pain.

In her job as a translator, the protagonist negotiates the tension between her obligation to maintain a professional distance and her empathy with human stories. Every day, she has to confront refugees on the borderline of poverty and in desperate physical and mental states. She faces emotionally tense situations while interpreting during a delivery or a gynecological exam, in prison or in a psychiatric hospital. These passages serve as contrast or even a parallel to the narrator's own retrospective story of emigration. On the one hand, her living conditions are better than those of the people for whom she interprets; on the other hand, she shares their feelings of loss and inner disintegration. She also points to the relationship between the language and the body: "I like that moment when they stand before me and the language is revealed. I often guess the language a few seconds earlier. I can tell which combination of sounds has shaped their mouth."[26] In this novel, language does not serve merely as a means of communication, but also represents a whole set of issues related to identity and cross-cultural understanding.

The protagonists of Brežná's and Blažková's autobiographically inspired novels must adapt to their new countries yet resist assimilation in their countries of exile. Their central theme is coming to terms with nostalgia for home through two perspectives. The first one consists of a reconstruction of memories of arrival and gradual, albeit problematic adaptation to the new environment. The second one consists of reflections on the emigrant experience that is related to the authors' opportunity to revisit Slovakia after 1989. Both authors emigrated to the West in 1968, and their fiction focuses on the consciousness of the socialist past as a cultural burden carried by the protagonists. They pay attention to language as one of the central components of cultural identity, which undergoes a crisis in response to foreign cultures and languages. Whereas Blažková wrestles with the challenge of life in Canada through writing in her native Slovak, Brežná writes in German, filtering the emigrant experience for her Swiss compatriots. Their return to the homeland highlights their realization that their home has been lost not only in space, but also in time.

GLOBALIZATION, MOBILITY, AND HYBRID SELVES: FLUID IDENTITY IN EXPATRIATE WRITING

The protagonists of expatriate literature face moments of crisis and alienation, but in contrast with those of emigrant authors, their transformation is contingent on a revision of their personality, ethnic, and social traits. The subject of expatriate literature undergoes a process of self-definition or liberation from markers of identity determined by citizenship, nationality, ethnicity, sexual orientation, cultural affiliation, or tradition. In particular, ethnicity is a central category that decisively influences the subjects' identity formation, even as they move toward a realization of their freedom. According to Andreas Hoeschen, a person identifies with a particular ethnic group and thereby integrates within a cultural, historical, or linguistic space, thus defining their place in the world. Ethnicity is an essential prerequisite for human existence, since every individual is anchored in an ethnically specific cultural context.[27] In expatriate literature, symbolic attributes associated with one's homeland are often subjected to ironic re-evaluation. However, a conscious erasure of collective memory weakens identity, which induces feelings of loneliness and social exclusion.[28] The unique characteristics of Slovak expat prose have been shaped by the predominantly female authors who have published fiction inspired by their experiences abroad. For example, Michaela Rosová's *Dandy* (2011) features a heroine who ends up in Germany after she breaks up with her partner in Britain. Her new relationship with a young German, Ole, is a catalyst for exploring her complicated sense of "being closer to home, but nevertheless not home."[29] Her existence in a transitional "non-place" confronts her with traumas of her past and a sense of alienation from her surroundings. Svetlana Žuchová's *Zlodeji a Svedkovia* (Thieves and witnesses, 2011) focuses on characters who move to neighbouring Austria for economic reasons, continually move between two worlds, and use storytelling as a means of self-preservation. The book presents a mosaic of expatriate destinies and shows how the quest for a better life can involve obstacles, crime, and disappointment.

The expat fiction of Ivana Dobrakovová and Zuska Kepplová, the main focus of this section, also explores such psychological and social dimensions of the expat experience. While Dobrakovová uses the foreign European setting as a catalyst or backdrop for an exploration of her central characters' psychology, Kepplová is particularly interested in how the discrepancy between the idea and the reality of life abroad and culture shock lead to different forms of maladjustment. These authors have developed a gender-specific set of themes including women's perception of embodiment and an emphasis on family ties. Their liberation from the more conservative home environment creates space for the questioning of gender and sexual identities as well as LGBT issues.[30] The increased mobility of Slovaks in the era of globalization has led writers to explore more fluid themes of identity.

Yet contemporary expat prose reflects an awareness of the persistent borderline dividing Europe even decades after the fall of the state socialist regimes in 1989. According to Boris Buden, the differences between the East and the West have not persisted as much in the political or economic spheres, but "only the conceptual space of differentiation has changed, becoming exclusively cultural. Culture has completely absorbed everything that used to be our social, political, or historical experience and dominates almost an entire space of our everyday life."[31] Therefore, it is essential to consider how emigrant and expat prose represents cultural conflicts and how the protagonists respond to them. One of the consequences of the persistent cultural division of Europe is the protagonists' inability to assimilate to foreign cultures or their rejection of assimilation and negotiation of feelings of nostalgia and homesickness.

Expat prose features interactions among people who are foreign to one another, and, as Bauman points out, these contacts are fundamentally different from meetings among close people and friends: "It is, by comparison, a mis-meeting. In the meeting of strangers there is no picking up at the point where the last encounter stopped, no filling in on the interim trials and tribulations or joys and delights, no shared recollections: nothing to fall back on and to go by in the course of the present encounter. The meeting of strangers is an event without a past. Often, it is also an event without a future (it is expected to be, hoped to be, free of a future), a story most certainly 'not to be continued,' a one-off chance."[32] Expat texts tend to expose the ephemerality of such relationships, which is pervasive in our globalized world.

Ivana Dobrakovová has drawn on her own experience of living abroad, beginning with her debut collection *Prvá smrť v rodine* (The first death in the family, 2009), and continuing with *Bellevue* (2010, trans. 2019) and *Toxo* (2013). The characteristic feature of her prose is a focus on protagonists who suffer from psychological problems such as obsessive-compulsive disorder, paranoia, and anxiety. The unfamiliar space presents additional, specific challenges that lead to a deterioration of the characters' mental health. Dobrakovová focuses on the interior lives of her female heroines, showing how their dysfunctional or inadequate home lives contribute to the disruption of their identity and psychological integrity. This theme is evident in her first collection, for example in her story "Klbko hadov" ("A snake pit"), which is set in a multi-ethnic volunteer camp in France. The author uses second-person narration, which is unusual in Slovak literature and reinforces the subjectivity of the account. The "you" address paradoxically creates the impression that the narrator-protagonist is engaged in a monologue primarily addressed to herself. The author typically writes long and syntactically complicated sentences, which blur the perspectives of the narrator and the characters: fragments of direct discourse are integral to the narrator's account, which further accentuates its subjectivity. At the same time, the second-person narration draws the reader into the story and creates the illusion that the writing relates to the reader's own lived experience:

> On Saturday we had planned to go to Puy-en-Velay for a day trip, but during breakfast Olivier helplessly threw up his hands and announced, I am truly sorry, kids, but the railways workers are on strike, what am I supposed to do?! We will go to Ivray instead; there is another camp there, and I think they are fixing some bridge there or what, don't stare at me like newborn calves and eat, rapido, rapid, the vans will be here in ten minutes. Cédric dipped his baguette with jam into coffee and remarked that it was a pity because in Puy-en-Velay we could see Gargantua's shit, and when you laughed and spurted coffee on to the table cloth, Cédric frowned, Marcela, you are such a pig, and don't laugh, it happens to be true, why don't you tell her, Olivier.[33]

The "you" address is a strategic choice, since Dobrakovová depicts an experience shared by her generation: volunteer work abroad provided popular opportunities for cheap travel and acquisition of foreign language skills for young people after 2000. The protagonist of the story finds herself in an international community of young people, which leads to emotionally charged experiences of otherness. The latent conflict of the story involves an opposition of the introverted narrator and the collective life of the camp, raising issues related to privacy, physical intimacy, social anxiety, language, and cultural barriers. The narrator perceives these challenges as a threat, hence the title – a pit of snakes.

Dobrakovová further explores this theme of the threatened subject in her novel *Bellevue*, whose protagonist also travels to the south of France, but engages in a different kind of work, taking care of patients with physical disabilities in a sanatorium called Bellevue. As Donald Rayfield puts it in his review of the English translation, "What eventually emerges is a picture, faintly reminiscent of a Camus novel, of a northerner's alienation in a southern landscape, as well as a plausible portrayal of the carer's dilemma: how to protect oneself from the mood and even the fate of those you care for."[34] Blanka's mental illness deteriorates in response to her confrontation with the disabilities of the patients, and the resulting interpersonal conflicts eventually force her to return home with a fragmented sense of self.

The collection *Toxo* extends the established set of the author's themes with a focus on pregnancy, pregnancy loss, and motherhood. The stories foreground the body as a source of anxiety or even repulsion. Against the backdrop of life abroad, the author broadens the exploration of borders beyond those associated with nationality or psychology and explores social and bodily boundaries. The foreign is manifested more broadly through the Italian setting, "being foreign becomes an external sign of existential alienation, which makes Dobrakovová's heroines, pulled into the world of human, parental, or partner demands, fatally insecure and in continual need of ways to escape."[35] The narrator and protagonist of one of the stories, "Rosa," is a vulnerable, anxiety-ridden young Slovak woman named Blanka (like the protagonist of *Bellevue*), who lives with her Italian partner Luigi and strives to adapt to life in Italy. She obsessively reflects on her own thought processes and even mundane daily activities (eating in public, a visit to the doctor) make her anxious. Although she tries to rationalize the situations, irrational fear often prevails, and her inability to control the situation, despite her highly developed intellect, deepens her frustration and leaves her paralyzed by continual self-analysis. To others she appears as an introverted, intelligent, and impractical woman, whose polar opposite is the grotesque character of her housekeeper Rosa, a hot-blooded middle-aged Italian woman whom Blanka finds both fascinating and repulsive. Her perpetual presence in the apartment disrupts Blanka's fragile but at least partially stabilized private space; she embodies an aggressive life force that overpowers the protagonist. Rosa is verbally and physically dominant, always addresses Blanka by random first names, thus signalling a kind of disregard for her as a foreigner from "the East," and tries to teach her "how to be a woman," emphasizing care for one's appearance and domestic skills. Blanka's fascination with Rosa is partly associated with her latent, suppressed, but stirring bisexuality, presenting a reference point for her own bodily awakening and self-awareness. She reacts to Rosa's physicality with hypersensitivity:

> Blanka was both attracted and repulsed by that body, which was hard to admit not only to Luigi, but also to herself. And the body was perpetually present, exposed bit by bit, day after day, look Alessia, can you

> feel how my knee has swollen? And Rosa is already rolling up her pant and guides Blanka's hand over her knee, can you feel, this is fluid, I will have to have it drained. And here, on the wrist, Ilenia, can you see these two bumps ... Within a couple of months, Blanka was acquainted with all of the bruises, burns, scrapes, scars, birth marks, warts; she could admire, assess, touch. Rosa was not stingy, Rosa bestowed herself, Rosa wanted to share her body with everyone.[36]

As this example shows, this story also smoothly alternates between the narrator's and the character's points of view, frequently using free indirect discourse – a single sentence may intersperse Blanka's thoughts with those of secondary characters. This narrative strategy emphasizes the subjectivity as well as the authenticity of the narrative; the reader is positioned as a front-row spectator to Blanka's mental deterioration, or the disintegration of the expat subject.

Whereas Dobrakovová tends to focus closely on a particular character's psychological response to the foreign environment, Zuska Kepplová filters the experience of living abroad through multiple perspectives of different characters. The narrators in her debut *The Moon in Foil* (*Buchty švabachom*, 2011, trans. 2023) are four young women and one man, all of whom are trying to change their lives and make a fresh start, but whose ambitious plans tend to fail. The book consists of two parts: the first novella, "You Can Be Not Afraid," consists of five stories set in London, Paris, Helsinki, and Budapest, while the second novella, "Trianon-Delta," portrays a lesbian relationship as a part of a complicated love triangle.[37] As Kepplová has acknowledged in an interview, this work is partly autobiographical: "The magic of this book was that it was not too ostensibly literary. The material was not too fictionalized, which made it more readable for a broader audience."[38] Kepplová also depicts the physical effects of language in terms similar to Brežná's in *The Thankless Foreigner*: "Her fellow traveller was explaining her theory of the connection between the body and mind. Our facial muscles take on their shape based on how we use them in our native language. When we learn another language, our face changes. The muscles gently add new layers, new ligaments stand out around the mouth, the corners of the mouth move in new ways, we breathe differently between words, and we blink differently. Thus when people who have lived abroad for a long time come back, their faces look different."[39]

The characters in *The Moon in Foil* experience loneliness induced by separation from home and inability to find their place abroad. The "buchty" or sweet buns in the original Slovak title of the book serve as a synecdoche for the warmth of home, but also for a specifically Slovak (or Slavic) cultural burden. They are mentioned at one point when a character jokingly vows to have the word "buchty," as an emblem of home, tattooed on his stomach in the German Gothic script, which evokes book learning, seriousness, and high culture.[40] This also alludes to Slovak folktales in which the hero sets out on a journey with a bundle of sweet buns, since Kepplová's protagonists set out on similar journeys. As Věra Eliášová has noted, "the familiar tastes of sweet rolls symbolically provide the only safety and comfort when all else is open and prone to transformation. But even this comfort, the familiar sweet taste, must finally change."[41] Thus, the title corresponds with the central themes of the journey and nostalgia for home.

Kepplová's characters react to their situations differently. For example, in the story set in Paris, Natália compensates for her sense of uncertainty and ephemerality with brief erotic encounters. This evokes Baumann's concept of so-called "fluid love," "which as a new-style partnership with its fragility of marital contract ... spawns much misery, agony and human suffering and an ever-growing volume of broken, loveless and prospectless lives."[42] The protagonists leave the provincial routine of their homes in Slovakia, but once their enthusiasm wanes, they fall into a similar routine of daily work and social problems that is not any less frustrating than the one they faced at home – on the contrary, perhaps more so. The financial stresses are higher than at home, the work conditions are demanding, and the protagonists do not have the support of close-knit bonds with other people. They are perpetually stressed because on the one hand, they are fulfilling their dreams, but on the other hand, they face a prosaic and gritty reality. Their confrontation with the foreign complicates their sense of identity.

Although their generational experience as millennials is radically different from that of their parents, Kepplová's protagonists still confront the legacy of the Cold War era, when Slovakia was a part of the Soviet Bloc. The borders have changed and become more porous, but they are still present. One of Kepplová's protagonists is surprised "how everyone assumed that Slovaks had one foot in Russia. He knew nothing about Russia, except for the names of a few authors he hadn't read."[43]

Petra, a Slovak woman working in a Paris hotel, trains a new Albanian employee who says: "If we stopped serving them, they'd have no one to cook for them, do their laundry, or take care of their children, wouldn't you say?"[44] The reference to the vague "them," a collective antagonist, reminds Petra of her mother, who embodies a blend of patriotism and nostalgia for socialism in the story. These are precisely the trends that Kepplová's protagonists resist. They are confronted with incidents that make them feel that the "old Cold War divide has survived – as a boundary between two identity blocks, the West and the East,"[45] but they are left behind in a liminal space in between. They do not belong and do not want to belong to one "camp" or the other (Eastern or Western). One of the characters also differentiates between the emigrant experience of the socialist era and the new expat experience: "We hadn't packed up our suitcases in the middle of the night, we hadn't swum across the Danube, nor had we climbed over barbed wire. We were simply doing what everyone else was talking about: 'Nowadays you can travel, go to good schools, meet people, and speak with them in a foreign language.' We wanted to be a part of it, to engage with the world. To eat it with a big spoon. To break our teeth on it."[46]

The story of Anka in London is a type of *Gastarbeiter* blues. She finds herself in an anonymous, continually changing community of workers from Eastern Europe, suffers from intense loneliness, and her mental state is aggravated by conflicts with the hostile environment. A representative example is a scene from the employment office, where Anka finds a job after a prolonged effort. This destination for people with social problems is an apt setting for showing the types of conflicts expat workers face. After one of the arguments, Anka "sat down at her desk and tried to carry on as usual. Red veins were scribbled across the whites of her eyes, her voice trembled, and her Slavic accent became stronger. The words softly stuck together, she could not meter them correctly. She had to repeat every sentence. On the phone someone said angrily: 'Am I the fucking last British person on Earth??' In the evening she opened her umbrella and walked out onto the street. A large Black woman sitting on the steps outside the building hissed at her: 'You Polish crap!'"[47] The narrator focuses attention on the physical symptoms of Anka's anxiety (red eyes, shaky voice). When she loses control over her body, she also loses her confidence in her foreign language skills. In a moment of crisis, an "older" Slovak identity overshadows the "new" identity painstakingly constructed in England. Kepplová places Anka in two successive negative confrontations, which also heightens her sense of crisis.

Kepplová also explores different forms of sexuality, particularly in "Trianon," whose title brings attention to the border-crossing relationships it portrays.[48] The main storyline consists of first-person narration by the main protagonist Juliana about her Romanian lover Cristina. While developing their relationship, the two women are also still involved in side relationships with men: Cristina is in a long-term relationship with a compatriot, while Juliana has trouble letting go of her ex, and gets involved in a potential relationship with a man from Sarajevo. The first part of the story is set in the international space of a university in Budapest. The specific scenes of student life (intellectual debates, book reading, rich social life) are underscored with feelings of ephemerality and the resulting sadness. The life journeys of different people with their dreams and ambitions intersect in this space. The grant system that allows only for temporary stays eventually divides the lovers. Juliana flies to Romania to spend time with Cristina at the delta where the Danube flows into the Black Sea, which takes on symbolic dimensions as a site of paradise, a place of connection between the two characters, in contrast with the earlier love triangles. The novella is structurally more unified than the other stories in *The Moon in Foil*. Contrasting the structures of the three texts, Ivana Taranenková writes that "while in the first part Kepplová composes a fluid, multi-voiced mosaic consisting of different characters' stories, the second part focuses on the relationship between the narrator and her lover. She constructs her narrative in a way that parallels the protagonist's effort to unify her world through the love that she experiences."[49] "Trianon-Delta" is, thus, a reflection on personal, cultural, and sexual identity, while also advocating for various forms of otherness.

In *57 km od Taškentu* (57 kilometres from Tashkent, 2013) Kepplová explores expat themes from an opposing perspective that presents post-socialist Slovakia through the eyes of Americans. The book consists of two novellas. The first novella, entitled "Sl__boda" ("Fr__dom") is structured like a mosaic. The structure resembles that of *The Moon in Foil*, but with the added elements of epistolary fiction. The narratives of individual characters are contained in short chapters, and the protagonists address their accounts to one another. The protagonists are a married couple, Henry and Vera, and a teacher of English, Mick. Finding the "exotic" Eastern Europe attractive, they come to Bratislava shortly after the opening of the borders with a shared cultural mission, which Henry describes in this way: "Mick and I were discussing the country in which we live and which we help transform; he spoke of a generation of kids that grows up watching MTV clips and the series *Beverly Hills 90210*, and they see their future in them, of parents who confuse business with ruthless street fighting. 'They don't have any civic consciousness!' He whacked the bar countertop with a newspaper. I argued that they had lost their sense of trust and belonging; their morality begins with hospitality and ends with bribery."[50] The American characters in the novella represent the outsider perspective; Rafał Majerek describes the cultural dynamic as "a model confrontation between the centre and the periphery that follows the pattern of cultural conquest."[51] The insider Slovak perspective is represented by the character of a painter who emigrated before the Revolution and returned in the 1990s. He views the country as existing in a state of vacuum, weightlessness, and therefore emptiness, as well as in anticipation of change.

In her novel *Reflux* (2015), Kepplová further explores the impact of living abroad on the returning expat's sense of identity. The protagonist, Eva, is a student of African literature who returns home from the United States to a small Slovak town in order to take care of her grandmother who suffers from Alzheimer's disease. In a fragmented narrative, the third-person narrator describes the period that preceded Eva's departure from home. They define the departure as a concrete (destined) moment, when Eva decided that "she has to do something, something has to happen, a milestone that will separate the old form the new, one from the other."[52] The study of a non-traditional subject serves as a means of her radical life transformation. The motivation in selecting her course of study is a mystery to the protagonist herself, but between the lines we can infer that it was a gesture of rebellion against her parents and home. There are also a few fragments connected with Eva's stay in a university town located somewhere "in the middle of a cornfield,"[53] where she experiences a failed romance with an Indian named Kumar. When Eva returns to Slovakia, she meets a Roma worker named Milan, who reminds her of Kumar, while riding a bus. Both men are complete opposites of Eva; their attitude to life is spontaneous and carefree.

Hostility toward the Roma is a central theme of the book. It appears in the speech of the characters, such as a woman Eva overhears at the market saying that "they [the Roma] stick together like a pack, they would gladly tear me to pieces!"[54] This xenophobic language associates the Roma with animal imagery. When Eva rebukes others for such attitudes, she is told that she does not understand because she does not live in Slovakia anymore.[55] In *Reflux*, the protagonist clashes with the Slovak reality, which she perceives and analyzes with increased sensitivity. She notices that the built environment is not adequately accessible to people with disabilities, encounters xenophobic attitudes at every step, and senses the surprise and disapproval of others when she is not satisfied with a dish and wants to send it back at a restaurant. Eva does not get along with people closest to her. As a hyper-analytical subject, she reflects on abstract topics as well as on her own sensory perceptions, for instance, while kissing: "The cigarette burnt out in her hand while she squeezed his shoulder with the other. The skin was surprisingly soft and smooth. She would savour the touch if at the same time she did not have to wonder if he found her skin to be surprisingly stiff and rough."[56] Eva could not find her place in the United States, but she cannot find it in Slovakia either. On the contrary, her feelings of loneliness and alienation only intensify at home. These feelings are aggravated by the generational conflict in her family and by Eva's ruptured relationships with her mother and grandmother. The subtitle of the book, "Someone Strange Is in the House" underscores this situation. The title, *Reflux*, has a dual function – it points to a hereditary disease that runs in Eva's family, the return of food from the stomach to the mouth as well as to the return of a person home from abroad that is accompanied with "sour" feelings. The book is characteristic of one of the types of Slovak expat prose, the so-called "texts of return," in which the authors of this generation reflect on their returns and explore the ways in which home, both the country and their domestic circle, has changed during their absence.

CONCLUSION

Expatriate fiction has begun to appear alongside books by the older generation of emigrant writers, and the two types of texts share some intersecting characteristics. They present intimate accounts of female subjects severed from their home linguistic ties and relationships, in which personal experiences of living abroad reinforce their sense of rootlessness in the world. Moreover, these texts reflect how the protagonists still confront the remnants of the Iron Curtain abroad, no longer on the political but on the cultural level, which confirms that the processes of European integration that began in 1989 are still active and unfinished.

A key part of the journey beyond the borders of one's home country is the subject's self-actualization through contact with the other and individual adaptation to what is initially foreign in an open multicultural world.[57] Although the concept of identity is central to expat prose, the texts provide perspectives on the unstable and questionable aspects of identity instead of providing answers. Who then are the protagonists of expat fiction? Zuska Kepplová's narrator in "Trianon-Delta" characterizes these nomads of the new era as follows: "We're nomads who speak the Latin of our times. When the money runs out, we move on. We find new friends. We build new routines. We change lovers. We put the sad face of Picasso's clown at the bottom of our suitcase."[58] This short passage encapsulates the dominant themes of expat prose: the journey, ephemerality, autobiographical elements, and especially the focus on the subject. These are also the features expat literature shares with emigrant prose, even though emigrant prose is more preoccupied with language, the past, and nostalgia for the homeland. The emphasis on personal experience abroad, the themes of identity and loneliness, gendered perspectives, and the personal focus of the narration link expat and emigrant prose with contemporary Slovak autofiction and women's writing.

NOTES

1 Flusser, *Writings*, 104.

2 Ibid., 104.

3 Barborík, *Literárnokritická reflexia*, 50.

4 Hučková, "Finding One's Own Path," 3.

5 Bauman, *Postmodernity and Its Discontents*, 24–5.

6 Thomas Bell (1903–1961), the descendant of Ruthenian emigrants from eastern Slovakia, is particularly remembered for the novel *Out of This Furnace* (1941). For a discussion of Bell's use of the immigrant experience as an inspiration for his writing, see Charles Sabatos, "Between Two Worlds," 74–88.

7 Augé, *Non-Places*, 77–8.

8 Ibid., 87.

9 Passia, "Domov, cesta a skúsenosť s iným."

10 Pucherová, "Jaroslava Blažková," 112.

11 Ibid., 102.
12 Blažková, *Happyendy*, 138.
13 Ibid., 142.
14 Ibid., 156.
15 Ibid., 185.
16 Blažková, "Na svadbu do Kalifornie," 13.
17 Ibid., 16.
18 The Slovak translation by Jana Cviková was published under the title *Na slepačích krídlach* (On chicken wings), but Janet Livingstone's English version (although translated from Slovak) uses the original title. So far only an excerpt from the English translation has been published, in the online journal *Body*.
19 Johnston, "Critical of Swissness," 185.
20 Brežná, *The Best of All Worlds*. This quotation from the unpublished English translation by Janet Livingstone is cited with the translator's permission.
21 The Slovak translation *Nevďačná cudzin/k/a* by Jana Cviková appeared in 2014, the English translation by Ruth Ahmedzai Kemp was published in 2022. The original *Fremde* involves a play on words between "foreigner/stranger" and "abroad" which is captured in Slovak by adding "k" to "cudzina" (abroad) making "cudzinka" (foreigner), but this nuance cannot be rendered in English.
22 Brežná, *The Thankless Foreigner*, 3–4.
23 Ibid., 16, 34.
24 Flusser, *Writings*, 92–3.
25 Brežná, *The Thankless Foreigner*, 34.
26 Ibid., 7.
27 Hoeschen, "Etnicita," 207–8.
28 Czaplinszky, "Kontury mobilności," 29.
29 Rosová, *Dandy*, 32.
30 The Slovak expat writer Andrea Salajová, who lives in Paris, also explores themes of gender and sexual identity in such novels as *Eastern* (2015), whose original title is in English although the novel is in French.
31 Buden, *Transition to Nowhere*, 45.
32 Bauman, *Liquid Modernity*, 95.
33 Dobrakovová, *Prvá smrť v rodine*, 51.
34 Rayfield, "Madness and Misanthropy."
35 Passia and Taranenková, eds, *Hľadanie súčasnosti*, 64.
36 Dobrakovová, *Toxo*, 31–2.

37 The structure of Kepplová's multi-city text is reminiscent of Ivan Horváth's *Vízum do Európy* (Visa for Europe, 1930), mentioned above.
38 Kepplová, "Rodiny sa nedá striasť" (interview with Katarína Sedláková).
39 Kepplová, *The Moon in Foil*, 40–1.
40 Eventually the protagonist gets this tattoo.
41 Eliášová, "The New Europe's Brave New World," 419.
42 Baumann, *Liquid Modernity*, 90.
43 Kepplová, *The Moon in Foil*, 47.
44 Ibid., 8.
45 Buden, *Transition to Nowhere*, 37.
46 Kepplová, *The Moon in Foil*, 162.
47 Ibid., 20.
48 The Trianon agreement, signed in Versailles after the First World War, radically altered the ethnic map of Central Europe. Hungary lost two thirds of the territory that it ruled as a part of the Austro-Hungarian Empire.
49 Taranenková, "O nostalgii nomádov."
50 Kepplová, *57 km od Taškentu*, 42.
51 Majerek, "Doświadczenie migracji we współczesnej prozie słowackiej," 42.
52 Kepplová, *Reflux*, 13.
53 Ibid., 52.
54 Ibid., 55.
55 Similar situations occur in the recent book *The Bonnet* (*Čepiec*, 2019, trans. 2023) by Katarína Kucbelová. When the protagonist from the capital travels to Central Slovakia, she confronts the local Slovaks' hostility toward the Roma, and they retort: "But here we have to live with them, you know." See Kucbelová, *The Bonnet*, 98.
56 Kepplová, *Reflux*, 51.
57 Passia, "Domov, cesta a skúsenosť s iným."
58 Kepplová, *The Moon in Foil*, 138.

BIBLIOGRAPHY

Augé, Marc. *Non-Places. Introduction to an Anthropology of Supermodernity*. London and New York: Verso, 1997.

Bakhtin, M.M. *The Dialogic Imagination*. Translated by Caryl Emerson and Michael Holquist. Austin: University of Texas Press, 1981.

Barborík, Vladimír. *Literárnokritická reflexia slovenskej literatúry 2008*. Bratislava: Ars Poetica, 2009.

Bauman, Zygmunt. *Postmodernity and Its Discontents*. Cambridge, Oxford, and Boston: Polity Press, 1997.

– *Liquid Modernity*. Cambridge, Oxford, and Boston: Polity Press, 2006.

Blažková, Jaroslava. *Happyendy*. Bratislava: ASPEKT, 2007.

– "Na svadbu do Kalifornie." *Romboid*, 47, no. 9 (2012): 3–16.

Brežná, Irena. "The Best of All Worlds" (excerpt). *Body*, 19 May 2013. https://www.bodyliterature.com/2013/05/19/irena-brezna/.

– *Na slepačích krídlach*. Bratislava: ASPEKT, 2008.

– *Nevďačná cudzinka*. 2nd ed. Bratislava: ASPEKT, 2016.

– *The Thankless Foreigner*. Translated by Ruth Ahmedzai Kemp. London, New York, Calcutta: Seagull Press, 2022.

Buden, Boris. *Transition to Nowhere: Art in History after 1989*. Berlin: Archive Books, 2020.

Czaplinszky, Przemysław. "Kontury mobilności." In *Poetyka migracij*, edited by Przemysław Czaplinszky, Renata Makarska, and Marta Tomczok, 9–42. Katowice: Wydawnictwo Uniwersytetu Śląskiego, Katowice, 2013.

Dobrakovová, Ivana. *Prvá smrť v rodine*. Bratislava: Marenčin PT, 2009.

– *Bellevue*. Translated by Julia Sherwood and Peter Sherwood. London: Jantar, 2019.

– *Toxo*. Bratislava: Marenčin PT, 2013.

Eliášová, Věra. "The New Europe's Brave New World: Writing Migration in Zuska Kepplová's *Sweet Rolls in a Tattoo*." *European Journal of Women's Studies* 21, no. 4 (2014): 415–30.

Flusser, Vilém. *Writings*. Edited by Andreas Ströhl. Minneapolis and London: University of Minnesota Press, 2002.

Hoeschen, Andreas. "Etnicita." *Lexikon teorie literatury a kultury: koncepce, osobnosti, základní pojmy*. Edited by Ansgar Nünning, Jiří Trávníček, and Jiří Holý, 207–8. Brno: Host, 2006.

Hučková, Dana. "Finding One's Own Path." *Slovak Literary Review* 1, no. 1 (2013): 1–3.

Johnston, Jonny. "Critical of Swissness, or Critically Swiss? Recent Autobiographical Fictions of Irena Brežná." *German Life and Letters* 68, no. 2 (2015): 171–89.

Kepplová, Zuska. *The Moon in Foil*. Translated by Magdalena Mullek. London, New York, Calcutta: Seagull Books, 2023.

– *57 km od Taškentu*. Levice: Koloman Kertész Bagala, 2013.

– *Reflux: niekto cudzí je v dome*. Levice: KK Bagala, 2015.

– "Rodiny sa nedá striasť" (interview with Katarína Sedláková)." *Pravda*, 18 May 2014. https://kultura.pravda.sk/kniha/clanok/317889-zuska-kepplova-rodiny-sa-neda-striast/.

Kucbelová, Katarína. *The Bonnet*. Translated by Julia Sherwood and Peter Sherwood. London, New York, and Calcutta: Seagull Books, 2024.

Majerek, Rafał. "Doświadczenie migracji we współczesnej prozie słowackiej (na przykładzie tekstów Zuski Kepplovej)." *Studia Litteraria Universitatis Iagellonicae Cracoviensis* 14, no. 1 (2019): 29–41.

Mikula, Valér. "Panoptikum." *Romboid* 43, no. 4 (2008): 49–51.

Modrovich, Mária. *Lu & Mira*. Levice: Koloman Kertész Bagala, 2011.

Moxey, Keith. "The History of Art after the Death of the Death of the Subject." *Invisible Culture: An Electronic Journal for Visual Studies* 1 (Winter 1999). https://www.rochester.edu/in_visible_culture/issue1/moxey/moxey.html.

Passia, Radoslav. "Domov, cesta a skúsenosť s iným. Premeny vnímania domova v slovenskej próze." *A2*, no. 2 (2012). https://www.advojka.cz/archiv/2012/2/domov-cesta-a-skusenost-s-inym.

Passia, Radoslav, and Ivana Taranenková, eds. *Hľadanie súčasnosti: slovenská literatúra začiatku 21. storočia*. Bratislava: Literárne informačné centrum, 2014.

Pucherová, Dobrota. "Jaroslava Blažková: Pohľady z kanadskej emigrácie." In *Pohled odjinud*. Edited by Michal Sýkora, 99–113. Olomouc: Univerzita Palackého, 2014.

Rayfield, Donald. "Madness and Misanthropy." *Literary Review*, October 2019. https://literaryreview.co.uk/madness-misanthropy.

Rosová, Michaela. *Dandy*. Levice: Koloman Kertész Bagala, 2011.

Sabatos, Charles. "Between Two Worlds: Slovak Language and American Identity in *Out of This Furnace*." *Comparative American Studies* 11, no. 1 (2013): 74–88.

Taranenková, Ivana. "O nostalgii nomádov." *Pravda*, 21 September 2011, https://kultura.pravda.sk/kniha/clanok/39967-kniha-tyzdna-o-nostalgii-nomadov/.

CHAPTER NINE

Women's Writing and Social Change

Rafał Majerek

INTRODUCTION

Before the political and cultural changes of the 1990s, the canon of Slovak literature was almost exclusively associated with male authors. The apparently marginal participation of women in literary life was evident in dictionaries, publications on literary history, textbooks, and other texts contributing to the canonical view of Slovak literature that was ingrained in the collective cultural consciousness. *Slovník diel slovenskej literatúry 20. storočia* (The dictionary of Slovak literary works of the twentieth century, 2006) is a representative example of this trend. This publication includes key terms related to poetry and prose, which the team of contributors – literary scholars from the Slovak Academy of Sciences and several other research institutions – considered to be the most valuable and essential works of Slovak literature during the period of 1901–2000. Only twelve out of the total of 117 authors who produced the texts included in the publication are women. Although there is not yet a publication of this type covering the period since the beginning of the twenty-first century, we can assume that its gender-based representation of included authors would look different. We can make conclusions about such a shift based on recent scholarship, developments in the literary market, and the recipients of prestigious literary awards, which are reliable indicators of the trends in the field of literature. The Anasoft Litera Prize for the best prose book of the year, considered the most important Slovak literary award, attests to the increasing participation of women in literary life, the rise in the prestige of women authors, and the appreciation of their importance in the production of symbolic value. The ratio is not quite equal – from the establishment of the award in 2006 until 2021, fifty men and thirty women were nominated. Ten awards went to male authors and six awards to women authors, but the trend indicating the growing importance of women authors is evident and indisputable.

Even in the absence of a critical consideration of the term "women's writing," these developments in the representation of women writers in publications and awards reflect one of the key changes in Slovak literature following the Velvet Revolution and the subsequent political and social democratization. The status of women authors has been changing since the 1990s, and concurrently with the process of post-communist transformation, Slovak women writers have been moving from the margins to the centre and becoming more influential in the development of Slovak literature. This process cannot be measured primarily by a quantitative growth in the number of published books authored by women; their numbers were quite high even before 1989. The increased visibility of women in Slovak literary life has been made possible by the gradual development of innovative approaches and ways of assessing texts, more openness, and more dynamic conceptions of literariness and the function of literature, which introduce new perspectives in discussions of literary quality. As a result, women's voices are more distinctly audible and recognizable in recent Slovak literary production, and thanks to these voices, the thematic range of literature and the diversity of artistic approaches have broadened. Issues that have been systemically suppressed and tabooed gain cultural representation, women authors question gender stereotypes, and women's writing sparks discussions about value in literary history and literary criticism. Recently published works by women make manifest what has been veiled by neutral or universal constructions. Literature becomes a means of liberalization, production of critical and subversive narratives, and examination of questions that had formerly been excluded from official discourse. The changed status of women's writing, which is evident in comparison with the recent past, reflects a gradual re-evaluation of cultural paradigms and a degree of "democratization" in the area of identity politics. The monologic model of culture, which was a legacy of communist power as well as of traditional culture, with its associated systems of prohibitions and obligations, especially in the area of gender relations, gradually disintegrated after 1989. The new model of culture based on dialogue and pluralism facilitated and invigorated the search for different forms of identification and conceptions of cultural value. These new circumstances make it possible to examine questions of human and civil rights, and public discourse becomes permeated with alternative conceptions of the relationship between the individual and the collective. New forms of self-actualization become possible in the private as well as public spheres. Although traditional cultural models remain relatively strong and contribute to the reproduction of power relations, new forms that do not fit these models emerge and deliberately resist or deviate from tradition.

WOMEN IN SLOVAK LITERARY LIFE: HISTORICAL AND CULTURAL CONTEXTS

Only a few women writers managed to gain visibility in Slovak literary life before 1989, and their output was often subjected to stereotyping in critical assessments.[1] The reasons for this state of things can be traced to the specific aspects of the development of Slovak culture as well as the broader patriarchal distribution of power. The first phase of emancipatory efforts, which began in the late nineteenth century and concluded with the access to basic civil rights, especially the right to vote in 1919, took place in the context of the struggle for the preservation of the Slovak national identity and culture. The political and social conditions in Slovakia – the lack of autonomy, colonial Hungarian policies that aimed at a forced denationalization of Slovak population and suffocated any form of national life – made it imperative that all cultural activity serve national interests. Women's activities in the area of culture and literature were acceptable if they related to the struggle for Slovak identity, which was directed and shaped by Slovak national activists. Any attempts on the part of women writers to formulate their own critical positions on social conditions or to independently explore their own literary themes and approaches were less acceptable, especially if they could potentially deviate from the national agenda and traditional roles. Dana Hučková comments on the problems associated with the open discussion of women's rights that affected literary life: "The opponents of women's emancipation considered women's abandonment of passive roles and their interest in expressing their own views, which included calls for a re-evaluation of gender roles, however mildly and non-aggressively formulated, an expression of immoral and anti-Christian (irreligious) ideas. In their view, such ideas clashed with social and cultural customs as well as with human nature, as evidenced by the biologically determined differences between the sexes. They appealed to common sense, urging people (women as well as men) not to succumb to the fads of their era that disrupted traditional ways of thinking."[2] The broader context of traditional patriarchal culture led to increased vigilance and agitation in reaction to women's writing and called for supervision or means of correction on the part of editorial offices of magazines as well as literary critics. Women's writing was considered a kind of excess, a disruption of the established order, and transgression beyond the private sphere assigned to women. Women's writing could be justified as a contribution to the national effort, or by its confinement to popular literature that, albeit considered contemptible, at least contributed to the preservation of the Slovak language.[3] The prevailing attitudes toward women's writing (and more generally toward women) are evident in the characteristic rhetoric of reviews, in which describing a text as "unwomanly" or attributing "manly courage" to its author is considered praise. This is how critics responded to the work of Božena Slančíková Timrava, a prominent realist writer, implying that "determination and originality remained – in spite of the sex of the given author – specific to men and their world."[4] However, Slovak women writers of the nineteenth and early twentieth centuries overcame a multitude of obstacles and "without any expectation of appreciation during these unfavorable times managed to assert and support *the feminine element* that had been suppressed for various reasons" and without which "Slovak culture would have been incomplete."[5]

During the interwar period in democratic Czechoslovakia, the conditions for the development of Slovak culture and literature changed dramatically. In an independent state both men and women writers could turn their attention away from extra-literary obligations, and, free of this burden, could explore new themes and artistic approaches. In the new state, women finally gained political rights; they had the opportunity to pursue university education and actively participate in the various forms of cultural life. Realist writers continued to publish; new names of women poets and prose writers appeared on the literary scene. Some of them gained recognition and a stable position in literary life quickly, as for example Margita Figuli, who is considered one of the leading authors of so-called lyricized prose. However, when we consider Slovak literature of this period more comprehensively, it is evident that its gender-based composition did not substantially change and that women writers remained on the periphery of literary life. The reasons for this state of things arguably stemmed from the inertia that perpetuated stereotypical and normative ideas about the possibilities for women's self-actualization, as well as from the conviction regarding the inferiority of women's voices and their perception of the world perpetuated by the patriarchal system. Women internalized these prejudices during the process of socialization, and only exceptionally talented and confident women managed to overcome such internal and external barriers.

This pattern of slow and vigilant opening of the literary scene to women writers continued during the following periods of the Slovak state, which was subordinate to Nazi Germany during the Second World War, and socialist Czechoslovakia after 1948. Important new voices emerged, and the number of women writers increased significantly in contrast with the previous periods, especially in the second half of the twentieth century. Their visibility, the degree of which was determined by literary criticism, was still only partial and fragmentary. This situation reflected the unequal social relations, systemic discrimination, and exclusion, as well as the perpetuation of a set of prejudices and stereotypes in the social consciousness. Obligations and prohibitions, even though they might not have been explicitly stated, still limited women writers' freedom of expression. The controversy that followed the publication of Jaroslava Blažková's story "Poviedka plná snehu" (A short story full of snow) in 1964 provides a symbolic example of the continued scrutiny of women's writing. The protagonist of the story wants to pursue her own idea of freedom despite social and cultural conventions. The polemic surrounding the literary text soon turned into a discussion of the author's morals, showing that while nobody kept women from writing, there were limits to their self-expression, which was subject to cultural control. Blažková's text was considered to be potentially dangerous from a moral standpoint, since according to the critics, it did not fulfil the required didactic function, but on the contrary, could lead young people to follow negative models of behaviour. The reception of the text reflects the residual idea that the primary function of literature written by women should be education and entertainment. The central problem, however, was the story's erotic theme, which clashed with the cultural tabooization of women's erotic and sexual expression.

The fact that women are present in contemporary literature at an unprecedented scale does not mean that women's literary talents have suddenly flourished. This trend is associated with a set of factors that are connected and related. The opening of a pluralist cultural space after 1989 meant that various forms of expression came to be more widely accepted than in the earlier periods. Literary criticism and the cultural community gradually became more willing to accept the representation of different kinds of experiences and more open to texts that deconstructed dominant narratives, including the patriarchal ones. The opening of the cultural space also meant that various forms of censorship and self-censorship had lesser impact on writing and publication of literary works. The increased openness and adoption of new approaches to the examination of various questions, including gender issues, in literature, were also influenced by free contact with foreign cultures, especially with the West, which had been strictly regulated during the socialist era. Of course, these factors were not an immediate and natural consequence of the movement toward democracy in Slovakia, but the greater degree of freedom created the essential conditions for the process of change in literary life.

DEMOCRACY, FEMINISM, AND LITERATURE

During the period of post-communist transformation, the most frequent buzzwords of official social and political life emphasized human rights, freedom, equality, and justice. However, in practice such ideals were confined to the realm of myth-making or wishful thinking, and the new democracy perpetuated inequalities such as the ones caused by gender-based prejudices and stereotypes. Reflecting on twenty years of transformation in Slovakia, Jarmila Filadelfiová and Zora Bútorová write: "Whereas 'the gender-based divide' between the private and public spheres has been mostly dismantled, the gender inequalities within these spheres persist."[6] They also mention that during the period of transformation, "new inequalities and problems were added to the 'traditional' ones. The threat of poverty and social exclusion increased for large groups of women ... There were repeated attempts to limit reproductive rights."[7] Gender-based inequality in different areas of social life became the focus of feminist organizations, which began to emerge in the 1990s. They initiated debates on the systemic social and cultural causes of the inequalities between women and men, endeavoured to expose these problems, and work toward their solutions in the public sphere. Feminist activities, however, were hindered by various obstacles, and were sometimes considered to be useless, rebellious, and potentially dangerous.

The resistance to feminism can be explained with reference to historical contexts, particularly the fragmentary and discontinuous emancipatory movement in Slovak culture. Discourse related to women's rights never had the opportunity to develop continuously and freely. Before 1918 the territory of Slovakia was a part of Austria-Hungary, and as already mentioned, the so-called "woman question" was secondary to national interests under the unfavourable political conditions of this period. During the two decades of the interwar Czechoslovak Republic, several pro-feminist initiatives developed, but the period was too brief for them to bring about a substantial change in the understanding of the status of women in society. The socialist system, which officially promoted ideas about the equality of women, provided increased educational and work opportunities, but it did not eliminate inequality in other areas of life.

After 1989, feminism did not gain significant political support even in leftist or social-democratic political parties, which usually include women's rights in their programs in stable democratic countries. Issues related to gender rights were dismissed as trivial, or the examination of questions related to gender equality was postponed to an unspecified point in the future, to be addressed once the so-called "essential" problems of the young democracy would have been solved. There were also more critical responses to feminism as a "foreign" extravagance that clashed with the national tradition. It was caricatured as an anti-men, Marxist, and dogmatic ideology, which could lead to the disintegration of family and society, and therefore elicited various negative emotions.[8]

Despite these challenges, the backlash, and the unfavourable atmosphere, feminist thought began to develop in Slovakia starting in the 1990s, especially thanks to the women's association ASPEKT founded by Jana Juráňová and Jana Cviková in 1993. Its principal objective was to increase the awareness of gender issues in Slovak society through educational and research projects, while also promoting different theoretical approaches to feminist reflection. Starting in 1994, the organization also published the journal *Aspekt*, which featured translations of classic feminist studies, original theoretical works, literary texts, essays, and informative articles that mapped the position of women in Slovakia and other post-communist countries.[9] The activities of the association connected and overlapped with the missions and objectives of academic and socio-political feminisms; the academic discourse was engaged and focused on achieving real-life social change. The thematic issues of the journal, for example, "The Myth of Beauty," "Motherhood," "Feminisms," "Women and Power," "Lesbian Experience," "The Personal Is Political," or "Patriarchy," can be interpreted as a map of problems that were considered important, ones that called for theoretical grounding and political intervention. Collections of essays on issues such as the participation of women in politics, violence against women, or reproductive rights were published with similar objectives. The projects and activities of the association were collaboratively created and led by representatives of different fields and various areas of culture and art, and occasionally also resulted from a broadly conceptualized international cooperation. One of the important features of Slovak feminism on both the theoretical level and in social activism was the merging of features characteristic of second-wave feminism, which could not be expressed under totalitarian conditions, and post-feminism. For this reason, questions related to gender differences and anti-essentialist conceptions of problems associated with the heterogeneity of female subjects were examined in a parallel fashion. Alongside attempts at a reconstruction and analysis of women's experience and presence in the history of Slovak culture, which are central to women's studies, scholars pursued projects focused on cultural construction of gender and gender performance. The 1990s thus present a decade of accelerated development in Slovak feminist thought, which included the adoption of the concepts of world feminism, critical reflection on its heuristic potential, and attempts at applying selected theoretical approaches in the local context.

ASPEKT was not the only organization focused on the issues related to the status of women in society and culture. During the period of transformation, other associations were founded: the Alliance of Slovak Women (Aliancia žien Slovenska) in 1994, the Centre for Gender Studies (Centrum rodových štúdií) in 2001, and the Feminist Philosophers' Club (Klub feministických filozofiek) in 2002, but ASPEKT undoubtedly played the key role in increasing the visibility of women's issues. Even though, like in other cultures, feminism could not count on universal acceptance in Slovakia, at least some topics and questions related to gender issues began to surface in public discourse and had a degree of influence on individual consciousness.

Literature in its social and cultural contexts was one of the central areas of interest for *Aspekt*, which included studies and articles devoted to theoretical, historical, and critical questions. In 1996, the association started publishing a book series that presented Slovak literary texts, translations of important feminist texts, scholarly monographies, and literature aimed at young readers. The Slovak literature selections included mainly new texts, but the series also included representative texts from the older literary tradition. These were mainly texts by the few women authors who had been included in the literary canon, as well as those whose work had been forgotten or was little known. These publishing initiatives, along with the literary criticism included in the journal, contributed to the reconstruction of the Slovak tradition of women's writing and the recovery of its genealogy. The objectives of this new approach to literary history and of the new contextualization and re-interpretation of older texts were to recover the memory of the past experiences of Slovak women writers and thus build a foundation for the reflection on their status in contemporary literary life.

In the reconstructed tradition of nineteenth and early twentieth-century women's writing, realist writers were placed in the position of "founding mothers," since they consciously fought for their own subjectivity as women and creators, called attention to the problem of gender inequality, and used various strategies to bring about change. The most prominent of these figures were the abovementioned Božena Slančíková Timrava as well as Hana Gregorová, who is considered the most radical advocate for women's emancipation of this period. As a part of the genealogical investigation, scholars returned to the work of other first-wave feminist writers, Elena Maróthy-Šoltésová and Terézia Vansová, interpreting their editorial, social, and nationalist activities in new contexts. These writers had been a part of the literary canon, but feminist scholarship provided new perspectives on their writing, especially highlighting historical representations of gender issues. The revival of interest in these women's writers was also supported by scholarship that applied feminist and gender studies approaches to their writing and republished their selected works.[10] For example, the anthology *Potopené duše* (Drowned souls), which included a selection of works by women poets from the first half of the twentieth century, contributed to the recovery of women's voices that had been forgotten or excluded from literary consciousness.[11] Through its publishing initiatives, ASPEKT also tried to recover the memory of texts that the communist regime had attempted to erase from the cultural consciousness. One of the examples is the publication of selected works by Jaroslava Blažková, whose works were banned by the regime following her emigration to Canada in 1968.[12]

The abovementioned initiatives had educational value. Their contextualization of women's writing that was sensitive to gender provided a new perspective on the history of literature, and demonstrated how the prevailing distribution of power affected the status of women writers. In addition, these initiatives functioned as a performative gesture that recovered the tradition of Slovak thought on women's right to independence, self-actualization, and creative expression. They demonstrated that this tradition was important and already present in the domestic history of Slovak culture, which undermined the claim that feminism was a foreign and imported fad. Making phenomena that had been veiled or distorted visible also had an ethical dimension. The objective was not only to recover specific authors, but also to celebrate women who had been silenced in their time and whose experience and world views had not been recognized.

Contemporary texts by Slovak writers published by ASPEKT and other publishing houses vary both in their poetics and their themes. They also represent various positions on current ideological, social, and cultural issues. Therefore, the term women's writing, which I use as a general framework for a part of Slovak literary production following 1989, merits at least a brief theoretical contextualization.

THE TERM "WOMEN'S WRITING"

Slovak criticism has paid significant attention to the feminist line of contemporary literature that explicitly addresses political trends, often suggesting that such political elements negatively impact the artistic dimension of texts. Women's writing is a broader term because it also includes texts that are not overtly engaged with feminist politics.

In Slovak literary criticism, the term applies primarily to prose, even though some key women authors of poetry and drama also appeared after 1989.[13]

A precise definition of women's writing as a list of internal, poetic, or systemic characteristics is of course impossible and does not appear necessary. Some conceptions of women's writing (Hélène Cixous's well-known essay "The Laugh of the Medusa," for example) resolutely reject any attempts at theorizing or defining *écriture féminine*, which is considered an untameable, rebellious phenomenon that evades any form of conceptualization. In my view, women's writing can be considered analogously to how literarity is examined in the framework of poststructuralist theory. Jacques Derrida describes this correlation as follows: "Literarity is not a natural essence, an intrinsic property of the text. It is the correlative of an intentional relation to the text, an intentional relation which integrates in itself, as a component or an intentional layer, the more or less implicit consciousness of rules which are conventional or institutional-social, in any case ... The essence of literature, if we hold to this word essence, is produced as a set of objective rules in an original history of the 'acts' of inscription and reading."[14] This perspective supports the claim that in Slovak literature after 1989, thanks to the acts of inscription and reading, a contemporary form of women's writing emerges. This form of writing is characterized by an intentional approach to a certain group of texts, connected with a particular, although not always clearly defined conception of its key features.

This conception can be only partially reconstructed since it describes a plural and polyphonic space that continually changes. When we try to characterize its basic contours, it includes texts that share a focus on the problem of women's identity and experience explored in various contexts – psychological, social, or cultural. The most common themes include family and intimate relationships, negative experience (various forms of violence, including symbolic), embodiment, sexuality, relationship with nature, and sisterhood. Women's writing tends to use autobiographical approaches or quasi-autobiographical structures. The texts often include autofictional elements or meta-textual reflections. Literary criticism also mentions stylistic or compositional features such as loose structure, stream of association instead of a causally sequenced plot, emotional expression, reliance on metaphors, fragmentariness, avoidance of synthesis, and preference for mosaic-like images of reality.[15]

The texts of individual writers demonstrate idiosyncratic combinations of these approaches and themes, which are, of course, applied in various ways. With respect to its characteristically disillusioned or subversive character, contemporary women's writing functions as a counterpoint to texts that perpetuate prejudices, stereotypes, and power relations, such as formulaic romance novels, which were associated with women's writing in the past.

Conceptualized in these ways, women's writing can be considered one of the symbolic practices of contemporary Slovak literature. It contributes to the shift in cultural paradigms by facilitating self-expression for a marginalized group, giving its members the opportunity to participate in the creation of cultural values and in discussions concerning the functioning of society. What is at stake for women writers is not to proclaim and emphasize the "femininity" of their perspectives, but to be included in literary life based on the quality of their writing. At the same time, they expect that the critical assessment of their artistic approaches and their thematic focus will not be subjected to gender-based assumptions and prejudices.

WOMEN'S VOICES IN THE POLYPHONOUS SPACE OF CONTEMPORARY SLOVAK LITERATURE

The liberalization of Slovak literary life in the 1990s allowed for new themes and forms of expression, preparing the ground for the dynamic development of literature from the beginning of the twenty-first century, which was also associated with the appearance of new women writers. Although most of the works discussed in this section were published in the new millennium, their emergence was made possible by the socio-cultural transformation of the 1990s. The year 1989 was an important milestone in the development of contemporary women's writing by opening spaces for discussions on women's positions in public life and for the development of feminist thought. After the revolution, Slovak women's writing initially included authors who had published before 1989 alongside debut authors and was far from homogeneous, reflecting a variety of artistic approaches and thematic preferences. Although it is difficult to generalize about such a diverse set of texts, closer analysis and interpretation of individual texts and initiatives points to some dominant trends.

One of the most significant features of contemporary Slovak women's writing is its autobiographical focus. Whereas in the past autobiographical forms such as journals, memoirs, or letters provided space for women's self-expression and compensated for the restrictions on publishing, contemporary texts use autobiographical elements to foreground subjective perspectives. The focus on the subject serves not only to present individualized women's experience, but also to examine questions related to identity. Women writers adapt classic forms of autobiographical writing by building on them, stylizing them, and using quasi-autobiographical structures and other narrative strategies that highlight the intimate perspective of the subject. The texts tend to be fragmentary, heterogeneous, and far from straightforward, highlighting the process of writing and the construction of identity. The claim that autobiographical elements are a key characteristic of women's writing is evident in its recurrence in the prose of different generations, including, for example, the work of Jaroslava Blažková (b. 1933), Alta Vášová (b. 1939), Mila Haugová (b. 1942), Etela Farkašová (b. 1943), Jana Bodnárová (b. 1950), Stanislava Chrobáková Repar (b. 1960), Veronika Šikulová (b. 1967), Katarína Kucbelová (b. 1979), and Ivana Gibová (b. 1985). The modes of representing life experiences, thematic scopes, and reflections concerning individual identity take different, unique forms for each of these writers. The texts often emphasize family contexts (Farkašová, Šikulová) or foreign environments (Chrobáková Repar). The composition and style of the texts may reflect creative experiences from other fields, such as art (Bodnárová) or philosophy (Farkašová).

The work of women writers also tends to include meta-reflections on the process of writing, open search for the most suitable forms and devices, and reflections on how to name the emerging text. For example, the narrator of Farkašová's book *Po dlhom mlčaní* (After a long silence, 2001) considers several possibilities – a letter that is to be continued, a diary, sketches, notes, records, postcards from the self and to the self, but does not lean toward any of them. Šikulová subtitles her book *Tremolo ostinato* (2020) as "a non-novel." Such approaches, along with the rejection of linear plot lines, the emphasis on process, and the crossing of genre and discourse boundaries (for example literary and philosophical in the work of Farkašová), indicate that stable structures and forms are inadequate. Such structures and forms cannot capture the shifting, dynamic relations between the subject and other people and the world or the subject's understanding of their own identity. The search for literary forms is also reflected in experimentation with style and language, which may involve foregrounding the lyrical or rhythmical aspects of language, or exuberant use of association and wordplay, which is particularly pronounced in Šikulová's prose. In some cases, the experimentation involves visualization or imagery, which is evident in Bodnárová's writing, or can lead to the shattering of language structures characteristic of various, often very distant types of discourse and their mixing, which Inge Hrubaničová attempts in her book *Láska ide cez žalúď/dok* (The way to a man's heart is through his belly, 2007).[16] Even though they do not appear in the work of all Slovak women writers, I consider such open, creative, or even rebellious approaches to the questions of genre and traditionally conceptualized literariness a characteristic feature that establishes contemporary women's writing as a distinct category in Slovak literature.

The examination of gender issues is one of the key themes that preoccupy contemporary women writers. This trend is most evident in texts that are openly feminist in their critique of power relationships, prejudices, and stereotypes, highlighting their negative impact on the social status and personal lives of women and focusing on different types of negative experiences such as violence and cultural restrictions. For example, the process of socialization as a forced adaptation of girls to designated roles and the internalization of the conviction of their "natural" subjection and passivity are the central themes of Jana Juráňová's *Iba baba* (Only a chick, 1999), which conveys a potentially affirmative message through the main character, a young rebel. One of the key elements of this book is its subversive treatment of fairytales, which the author rewrites along feminist lines. Intertextuality as an instrument of critique is also evident in Juráňová's other texts, such as the book that includes two shorter prose texts, *Siete* (Nets, 1996), a new contextualization of well-known texts that exposes their oppressive aspects. The author also tends to focus on issues associated with discrimination against individuals, as well as with the recovery of historical figures, one that I return to later in this chapter.[17]

The family is another central theme in Slovak women's writing, most often represented without illusions as an environment in which the process of cultural "taming" manifests as a reflection of social power relations. The mother-daughter relationship tends to take centre stage in prose fiction that focuses on the theme of family. For example, Etela

Farkašová depicts this relationship as suffering from a lack of communication, emotional distance, excessive demands on the part of the mother, and a sense of guilt on the part of the daughter when she cannot meet these demands. The daughter nevertheless considers repairing the broken relationship with the mother after a period of estrangement. Farkašová's prose, particularly the novel *Stalo sa* (It happened, 2005) centres on a dying mother and examines the concept of a family story from a gendered perspective as a key aspect of one's personal identity. Unsentimental treatment of the theme of family as involving complicated and negative emotions is also evident in Bodnárová's prose *Insomnia* (2005), foregrounded in Monika Kompaníková's *Boat Number Five* (*Piata loď,* 2010, trans. 2021), and examined in relation to various forms of violence in Uršuľa Kovalyk's prose, which I will discuss in more detail later in this chapter.

Breaking taboos is one of the key strategies in the work of contemporary women writers. The taboos broken in their writing do not concern only the family environment and relationships with parents, but also issues related to the body and sexuality. Women writers open themes that have received only limited attention in Slovak literature, including various forms of female desire, erotic aspects of adolescence, perception of one's body, pregnancy, menstruation, pregnancy loss, etc. Women writers also raise awareness about mental illness, whether in the form of anxiety or trauma, which is another problem that has been suppressed and overlooked in Slovak society. This theme is prominent, for example, in the work of Ivana Dobrakovová, particularly in her debut collection *Prvá smrť v rodine* (The first death in the family, 2009) and in the novel *Bellevue* (2010, trans. 2019), or Ivana Gibová in her prose *Bordeline* (2014) and *Barbora, boch & katarzia* (Barbora, god & catharsis, 2016).

Women's writing also provides interesting perspectives on the contemporary transformations of intimacy. Relationships in their traditional form, such as marriage, are usually represented as dysfunctional and lacking in authentic emotional foundations and honest communication, or even depicted as traps that limit women and as barriers to their self-actualization. Informal relationships appear more acceptable, even though those also often turn out to be disappointing. The problem of intimacy becomes more multi-dimensional now that writers represent forms of intimacy that were avoided in the past. For example, non-heteronormative relationships are explored in Hrubaničová's abovementioned *Láska ide cez žaluď/dok* and in the short story collection *Jednorožce* (Unicorns, 2020) by Barbora Hrínová.

Although the thematic range of texts covered by women's writing is much broader than my brief introduction may suggest, the themes and narrative approaches that I have highlighted are predominant and shared among several texts. Nevertheless, individual authors' approaches to specific themes and their modes of contextualization and representation vary. Jana Juráňová's *Žila som s Hviezdoslavom* (literally "I Lived with Hviezdoslav," 2008), published in English as *Ilona*: *My Life with the Bard* (2014), and Uršula Kovalyk's collections of short stories *Neverné ženy neznášajú vajíčka* (Unfaithful women don't lay eggs, 2002) and *Travesty šou* (2004, selected texts published in English as *The Night Circus and Other Stories* in 2019), represent two particularly original approaches that have contributed to the development of the contemporary forms of women's writing.[18] The two writers share the feminist context, the conviction about the culturally and socially determining impact of gender roles, and the awareness of the systemic aspects of inequality. While their work intersects in the area of feminist politics, their narrative approaches and themes are different. Juráňová's prose attempts to recover and understand women's experience in a particular period and social context. She selects a story that can be considered paradigmatic and representative of the stories of other women who also suffered under historical constraints and gender-based inequalities. Kovalyk's stories reflect contemporary problems associated with various forms of violence, but also feature characters who reject the cultural preconceptions of "femininity" and seek other forms of self-actualization. The two writers' perspectives increase the visibility of historical and contemporary aspects of women's experience, while also reflecting the heterogeneity of the contemporary forms of Slovak women's writing.

JANA JURÁŇOVÁ'S *ILONA: MY LIFE WITH THE BARD*: RECOVERING A FORGOTTEN WOMAN'S STORY

The bard of Jana Juráňová's title, Pavol Országh Hviezdoslav (1849–1921), is considered one of the most significant personalities of Slovak culture. He was a poet, playwright, and a translator whose works are included in the Slovak literary canon, and memorial plaques and statues emphasize his indisputable status as a classic writer. His name is also connected with the preservation of Slovak national and cultural identity during the difficult period of Hungarian domination and forced Magyarization of Slovaks. Although his texts are generally not read outside compulsory school education and a narrow circle of literary scholars, Hviezdoslav's place in the Slovak cultural consciousness is associated with a certain type of reception that perpetuates the static idea of the great poet. Hviezdoslav himself contributed to this idea through self-mythologizing, including the allusions to "star" (hviezda) and "glory" (sláva) in his pen name, and Slovak literary historians have adopted and systematically perpetuated this idea. Thus Hviezdoslav is still present in Slovak culture, in Valér Mikula's words, as one "whose glory reaches the stars and whom the stars celebrate," a social myth and a cultural icon.[19] The canonized cultural text as constituted by the mythical idea of Hviezdoslav's life and work serves as a basis for Juráňová's novel, which uses it as a starting point for feminist interpretation of gender issues in Slovakia of the early twentieth century and for a broader reflection on patriarchal power relations.[20] Her approach shifts the reader's perspective on the writer by placing his wife, Ilona Nováková Országhová, at the centre of the story and focusing on her life, her thoughts, and her feelings. The author had used a similar approach in her play *Misky strieborné, nádoby výborné* (Silver bowls, excellent vessels, 1997), in which she recovered the stories of women of the Romantic period, the wives and muses of the national revivalists, who had previously been treated as mere accessories in the life stories of the male leaders of the movement and as figures without agency or voices of their own. Like this play, the novel on Ilona's life with Hviezdoslav continues Juráňová's preoccupation with the theme of silenced female experience and attempts to recover a story that had been excluded from official history and cultural consciousness. Juráňová draws on historical sources, particularly the poet's letters and information from biographical and historical works, which she weaves into the fictive memories of the protagonist.

The narrative time frame is clearly defined. In the first chapter, Ilona receives an invitation to the ceremonial unveiling of the bust of her husband in the Pantheon of the National Museum in Prague, and in the last chapter we find a brief mention of this event and the announcement of her death. The installation of Hviezdoslav's bust among the busts of other important personalities of Czechoslovakia, in the symbolic space to which the poet always wished to belong, appears to be the last task of the loyal wife, fulfilled with the same dedication that led her to stand by his side during his lifetime. The narration highlights the subjective perspective of the protagonist, her way of perceiving the world and her thoughts and emotions. Her memories, which are not chronologically ordered and are presented in a fragmentary fashion, focus on several key themes: her life with the famous poet, her understanding of her own position in family and social life, and reflection on gender issues, especially the education of women and their adaptation to compulsory cultural roles. It is interesting that in some passages the protagonist appears to censor her own thoughts, especially those that may lead her to question the official version of her life. For example, she shares a following reflection related to her photographs: "She recalled the fine afternoon when a man other than her husband had favored her with a glance, capturing her for eternity. A young man, an artist. In his presence she did not feel like a housewife ... Perhaps if the picture had been taken by her husband it would have come out very differently. A silly thought flashes through Ilona's mind, she is scared by her own thoughts. Perhaps there would have been an empty space in the photograph. A gray shadow in the shape of her silhouette. How could that idea have entered her head? Her husband loved her all his life. He couldn't have managed without her."[21] The internalized constraints that do not allow Ilona to freely articulate her own feelings and her reverence for norms that govern not only conduct but also ways of thinking tend to influence the form and style of her reflections. While her thoughts on the poetic greatness of her husband and accounts of everyday life are pronounced firmly and without hesitation, her consideration of other issues often takes the form of questions, suggestions, or hurried pronouncements that she subsequently scrutinizes.

Ilona's understanding of her own unequal position in the marriage as "natural," and the self-control such a position requires exposes the detrimental effects of internalized cultural norms and socially accepted forms of "femininity." Thus, the novel opens a set of questions related not only to the life of Ilona Országhová, but also to the gender inequalities prevalent in Slovakia during the nineteenth and early twentieth centuries. These questions primarily address the obstacles and restrictions in the area of women's education and the promotion of the ideal role of the wife as the only proper form of self-actualization. Ilona accepts such gender-based inequalities as self-evident: "When her brother, two years her junior, will be her age, he will still have his studies ahead of him. She is seventeen and her years of studying are over. There is nowhere else for a girl to go and no reason to go anywhere either. The goal is clear: to get married. Any other goal would be a failure."[22] The protagonist pursues a clear objective, emancipatory ambitions are foreign to her, even when she considers the choices of other women who deviate from the compulsory model. She remembers Hviezdoslav's sister Mária, who separated from her husband, an exceptional transgression that could be tragic for a woman who alters her destiny in such an unacceptable way. In the given social structure, there was no other option for Mária, who did not get the chance to get an education despite her talents, relegating her to social exclusion and to an unfulfilled life remote from her expectations. Ilona thinks of her sister-in-law with empathy, yet her reflections do not include the causes and circumstances that had such a negative impact on Mária's destiny: "Some women just don't seem to find their place in life. Is it because they don't fit in, because they miss their time? Perhaps life really is a kind of outline of an embroidery pattern? And what happens when a woman veers away from the pattern? She ends up like Mária, like that stranger Marína, like Lída, like ... but Ilona's life has worked out the way it was supposed to. Ever since she was a little girl she had the pattern in her mind. She knows it by heart, has followed it faithfully, very faithfully ... And whatever happened to all those women who have not followed the pattern? A chill runs down her spine. As if she had walked into a dead forest."[23] The unequal educational opportunities for girls and boys limited or even barred women's access to the public sphere, which included literary life. This situation mirrors the famous motif of Shakespeare's sister from Virginia Woolf's essay, which highlights how patriarchal culture commits symbolic violence against women, silences them, and renders them invisible.[24] Women who pursued self-actualization and creative activity despite such restrictions risked ridicule and criticism. If they decided to remain single, they also faced economic insecurity. Juráňová mentions Timrava as an example, citing her claim that "if she had got married and had children, she would never have become a writer."[25] Male writers did not have to face such dilemmas, since household tasks were performed first by their mothers and then wives, and they could more easily find their position in the public sphere thanks to a certain degree of homosocial reproduction.

Ilona's reflection on her own identity and social status leads her to contrast her experience with those of other women, but it is her relationship with Hviezdoslav that remains the focal point of her life. The picture of their life together that emerges from her memories suggests peace, regular rhythm, and balance that is disrupted only by occasional news of the deaths of loved ones and the difficult times connected with the period of the First World War. However, the everyday domestic routine dominates their life; they perform their own familiar gender roles, move along well-trodden paths, and complete their tasks. These roles and tasks are, of course, situated in different cultural realms. Ilona takes care of the domestic order, the garden, and solutions for everyday problems. The text problematizes the significance of the spheres each of them inhabits and thus challenges the primacy of the poet's status in cultural memory. On the one hand, Juráňová uses irony to expose Hviezdoslav's tendency to take offence at minor critical remarks on his texts, his narcissistic pomposity, and his inability to take care of himself. On the other hand, she affirms everyday life, elevating ordinary activities that are undervalued in culture, ones that seem invisible and do not leave any apparent traces, yet are essential to life. The attention that the text gives the domestic sphere, primarily associated with female activity, emphasizes its significance, which is not necessarily lesser than that of majestic and exceptional creative feats. The shift in emphasis recovers the character of Ilona from being dismissed as insignificant, or from the prevailing cultural treatment of the invisible work of women.

The protagonist's focus on day-to-day activities does not mean that Iona does not have other interests, ambitions, or desires. In the historical context of the significantly limited opportunities for women's education, she is relatively well educated and well read; she longs to see other countries and learn about other cultures. However, the clash between her aspirations and the conditions of her life brings her disappointment and leads to her return to the prescribed model of a wife. Her dreams are shattered by her husband's symbolic superiority:

> When her husband decided to go to the seaside she hoped she might accompany him. She wanted to see foreign countries with him, she wanted to see famous paintings in famous galleries with her own eyes ... Once, when they had visitors, he asked her suddenly: "Tell me, my dear wife, what should a good husband and wife be like?"

"One body and one soul," she was quick to respond.

"You see. And when I go to the seaside it's as if you were there with me."[26]

In the culture represented by Hviezdoslav, its unflinching guardian, a woman has a clearly determined place in the social and symbolic order, and her dedication to the keeper of the hearth should satisfy all her ambitions and needs. The protagonist is reconciled with this status quo, and even though she occasionally feels restless, she identifies with the compulsory ideal of a wife. She understands her own existence in correlation with the personality of her husband, his oeuvre, and his lofty cultural status. She accepts and conforms to cultural norms, even though it means suppressing her personal emotions and ambitions. She does not generally name the power relations that mould her but merely suspects their existence, and on occasions when she inadvertently or metaphorically refers to them, she quickly subjects her thoughts to self-censorship. Ilona is not a rebel, and the text suggests that she could not be in the context of her time, which makes Juráňová's examination of gender roles more realistic and compelling.

In what sense can we then speak of the feminist dimensions of the novel? The author presents gendered experience as an integral part of the broader cultural and social experience, in which women's lives are subjected to various restrictions, exclusionary practices, silencing, and symbolic violence. In the text these issues are explicitly addressed, suggested through various signs or identifiable by readers familiar with the historical context. Gender roles and social functions are based on a set of binary oppositions: high/low, active/passive, rational/emotional, public sphere/private sphere, official history/everyday life. Within these binaries the first, more positively valued quality is associated with masculinity. I understand the author's objective not as an attempt to mechanically invert such hierarchies, which tend to be considered self-evident and "natural" in cultural history. Instead, she exposes their artificial and constructed character and their share in the creation and reproduction of patriarchal power relations. The novel thus has an engaged and ethical dimension – it is an attempt at recovering and reconstructing the experiences and thought processes of multiple women who lived in the same period and the same environment as Ilona Országhová and whose voices were not recorded. The following fragment reflects Ilona's longing for such representation of contemporary women's voices: "Ilona has never written anything except for letters to her husband when he was away from home. The letters might be turned into a story of their ordinary life but they wouldn't amount to a novel. Secretly, she longs to read a novel of this kind. A novel that would tell of days all resembling one another. A novel that would tell how she gave each day solid shape. How she had always been available. How she had known when to be silent when silence was required."[27] Juráňová's book fulfils the wishes of her protagonist by building a bridge between the past and the present women's experience. The novel raises the question of the degree to which the restrictions presented in the text have been removed or maintained in cultural and social life. It is a documented fact that inequalities persist in certain spheres of Slovak life, and contemporary women writers explore such themes. What is important is that these issues can now be publicly discussed and women's voices have the chance to be heard. This points to a significant historical shift in cultural models for gender roles between the milieu of the protagonist Ilona and Juráňová's own time, which opened a discursive space for her novel of recovery.

THE VIOLENT WORLD AND FORMS OF RESISTANCE IN URŠUĽA KOVALYK'S FICTION

Critics tend to situate Uršuľa Kovalyk's writing in the context of feminist prose. Kovalyk depicts the oppressive world of patriarchy, violence that particularly impacts family and partner relationships, detabooizes issues related to the body and sexuality from the female perspective, and uses expressive language, including vulgarisms and other non-standard forms of communication. Her texts open themes that have been suppressed, critique gender-based prejudices and stereotypes, and expose hypocrisy and reluctance to develop systemic solutions to problems such as domestic violence and social exclusion. Kovalyk's texts can be considered socially engaged in the sense that her writing can be interpreted as an attempt to cultivate sensitivity and openness, or a reflection on the possible solutions for negative social phenomena, especially those that jeopardize human freedom and safety. Her rebellious approach, conscious violation of cultural norms of "literary civility," and emphasis on themes associated with the body and sexual urges connect Kovalyk's fiction with the context of écriture féminine.[28]

Kovalyk connects the negative experience of patriarchy, which is one of the central themes of women's writing, with the family environment and the figures of fathers, husbands, and partners. Fathers are represented negatively; they exercise their position of power through demands for obedience as well as emotional, physical, and sexual abuse. The impact of such upbringing on the lives of the characters is tragic and manifested as depression, suicidal ideation, and chronic anxiety. In situations that appear hopeless, fear and hatred toward the father is the dominant emotion, and his death seems the only possible solution, as in the story "Betrix a ja" ("Betrix and me") from Kovalyk's debut collection:

> My death was imminent. Death took on the shape of my perpetually drunk father, careening in the kitchen and screaming "I will kill all of you" ... I felt like a hounded animal. Every night I hoped that perhaps father would not come, or he would break his neck on the stairs somewhere. Everything was so hopeless, not a single light in the black tunnel, and I often thought of death. I imagined that he would find me in the bathroom grotesquely twisted by the white radiator, with slit wrists and a smile on my face. And that he would then go mad and be taken away to the madhouse. And that my mother would finally be free. I thought about this all the time, and in fact I could not think of anything else anymore.[29]

The traumatic events of the past impact the adult life of the character who replicates the model observed in childhood in her own relationship. She becomes a helpless victim of violence committed by her husband, who is another version of her aggressive father. Hatred toward a father can also be associated with the feelings of rejection and alienation, as in the story "Obyčajný mŕtvy otec" ("An Average Dead Father"): "I haven't seen him for ages. Because he had abandoned me. Denied me. Rejected me as soon as he and my mother were divorced. Now that I think of it he had ditched me a long time before that. Before I was even born. At the very moment of spurting his semen into my mother's womb to fertilise an egg, the moment he reached orgasm. That's when he abandoned me. He had never given a shit about me. Back then he must already have thought of me as just this weird, bothersome burden that had to be looked after and for whom he had to keep quiet at night. A screaming little kitten. He should have drowned me."[30] Only the death of the father finally allows the protagonist to overcome, at least partially, the traumatic sense of his absence. The transformation of the absent, but in some sense also desired person who remains present in the character's consciousness as "an average corpse"[31] is a form of liberation, which opens space for fantasy and creation of an ideal father who would meet her needs and expectations instead of a "a drunkard, an alcoholic, a brawler."[32] The narrative challenges the cultural norm according to which death, especially the death of a relative, requires self-censorship of the modes of remembering, the imperative to highlight positive character traits and suppress negative ones. The story violates this norm, and instead of the culturally mandated fiction, directly addresses the causes and consequences of trauma, which in turn allows for a degree of healing.

Subordination, emotional and physical abuse, or complete alienation and absence of communication also plague the existence of women characters in marriages and partner relations in Kovalyk's prose. An important theme in her stories that focus on these problems is sexual violence. Intimate relations involve the objectification of women, who serve as a means of satisfying men's sexual needs. In patriarchal culture, as feminist authors show, the main function of the woman, beside the role of the mother, is to serve as an object for sexual consumption, which needs to adapt to the expectations and demands of men. Her own sexuality and pleasure can only be considered if they contribute to greater male pleasure.[33] Kovalyk tends to present sexual intercourse as an obligation and a violent act, which is reflected in the imagery of her texts. In the story "Júlia" ("Julia") the situation of the woman is compared to the predicament of "an animal nearing a trap," and the man is described as "a large bird of prey."[34] The only form of resistance and imaginary escape that the protagonist can imagine in such a moment is emotional detachment, distracting herself through focus on unrelated objects that she can see or sounds that she can hear. The insensitive and brutal sexual act is depicted in several texts, including the story "Samovražda" ("Suicide"): "We're sitting on a bed and you are kissing me. It feels as if you're trying to bite all the birthmarks out of my body. I don't feel like making love but you take me by the neck and your hand, which brooks no resistance, undoes your flies. Oh yes you do, you say and I feel you thrusting your hard, hot penis into me. I lie back. Like a rag doll ... I have only a bit part in this play. Your sweat burns my thighs, your penis cuts me like a birthday cake."[35] The text also mentions sexual abuse by the father and the obliviousness of the mother, whose care for her daughter is limited to reflections related to her appearance. The story depicts the impact of coming of age in a dysfunctional family environment. The pictures of violence and distorted intimacy, limited to the mechanical movements and satisfied needs of only one of the parties, involve rather schematically portrayed male characters, a pattern that has been addressed in some critical responses to Kovalyk's texts. Certainly, the male figures in these texts are sometimes faceless and identified only by their repulsive behaviour and equally repulsive and only fragmentarily depicted appearance and clothes.[36] Nevertheless, I consider Kovalyk's approach to characterization a justifiable strategy that highlights the protagonists' feelings of alienation. These male characters reflect the objective of Kovalyk's critique, which does not target the individuals with such negative traits, but the cultural foundations that facilitate, or even justify violence. In Kovalyk's stories, the world is presented as a trap and a space of oppression, in which the fate of women is determined by gender inequalities and the replication of negative models, as a place lacking in forms of assistance and essential systemic solutions. Emancipatory tendencies are not presented as integral to the thought processes of the heroines; their escape from hopeless life situations is sometimes radical, which is reflected in thoughts of suicide or escape into dream worlds that provide alternatives to reality.

The most positive relationships involve women or men who do not conform to patriarchal role models and heterosexual matrices. Female alliances, which value spiritual support, responsibility, and mutual care above all else, provide alternatives to the world of restrictions and violence and serve as a form of escape as well as a form of resistance. The protagonists of the story "Staroba s Dušanou" ("Old age with Dušana"), from Kovalyk's debut collection, jokingly plan a common future after they bury their husbands – the "clowns": "I look forward to it, says Dušana, I will wander around the house naked, completely, now I cannot because he is repulsed by the view of my body, as if he looked better than me. And I will play music at the loudest volume and dance and grow grass in the garden."[37] Their close relationship is foregrounded against the backdrop of the characters of their husbands, a former dissident and a policeman who detest each other, and their projected future is presented through contrast with their current marital responsibilities, perpetual reproaches, and a sense of limited freedom. The mutual understanding of the women is evident in their honest conversations, in which they analyze their intimate relationships and openly discuss their problems, emotions, bodies, and sexuality without embarrassment. There is space for female dialogue, particularly in friendships, which is evident in the short story "Šelma" ("Predator") from the second collection of Kovalyk's short stories, but in some cases, it is also possible in family relationships. In the story "Tri ženy" ("Three Women") (in the same collection), three daughters meet by the bedside of their dying mother and remember her life. They do not avoid the topic of their mother's erotic life, which can be considered a violation of a certain taboo, but also a sign of honesty and mutual trust.

In some stories Kovalyk moves from a realist to a fantastic mode and includes imaginary elements in her texts. In connection with female alliances the concept of the femininity of God appears as a central theme in the text "Auto" ("The car"). It is significant that God, who represents everything, feels the most comfortable in the feminine form, in which she manages to save the protagonist, who has decided to commit suicide. The author adapts the familiar motif of divine intervention as the only form of help in a hopeless situation, but she interprets it in the light of feminist thought and thus deconstructs the patriarchal model of the world.[38]

The relationships between men and women are represented without illusion in Kovalyk's first two collections, in which any possibility of mutual understanding and trust appears unattainable. In these stories, the characters who represent the hegemonic type of masculinity undermine female subjectivity, deprive women of dignity, and abuse them. The only exceptions are male characters who do not conform to the hegemonic model and are equally threatened by real and symbolic violence. In the aforementioned story "Betrix and me," a gay cousin is the only person who is close to the heroine. The impact of cultural norms on the process of child rearing is reflected metaphorically and somewhat fantastically in the positive relationship between the protagonist and a mysterious being – "he looked like a child or a dwarf. In short, like a creature from another world"[39] – whom she finds in the street and takes home with her in the story "Dažďový Jo" ("Rainy Day Joe"). Their idyllic relationship radically changes after her ex, Eduard, begins to interfere in her life: "Eduard ... taught him everything he thought a real man ought to know. And I mean everything: from spitting down from the balcony to swearwords, which he claimed would come in handy at football games. Joe no longer wanted to wear ballerina dresses. He made me buy him the kind of clothes Eduard wore ... His face coarsened, he drank beer and spent all day watching TV with Eduard. He no longer danced. And he didn't amaze me any longer either. From time to time he would still cuddle up to my tummy, looking over his shoulder to check that Eduard couldn't see him."[40] The questioning of gender stereotypes, which is represented affirmatively in the first half of the story, and the disappearance of the character after his transformation into "a real man" at the end of the text signal a problem that is the focus of masculinity studies, which is the impact of gender constructs not only on women, but also on men. The intervention of a typical representative of the patriarchal order into the life of a hitherto happy couple causes damage, which emphasizes the feminist perspective.

Corporeality and sexuality are associated not only with negative experience and male violence in Kovalyk's fiction. Her texts also address other aspects of women's experience that are rarely represented in Slovak literature such as menstruation, delivery, breastfeeding, and aging. The author depicts these phenomena with a degree of openness that defies cultural norms and unequivocally problematizes feelings associated with the body and its various functions. She also portrays female sexuality free of shame and fear in ways that violate all cultural norms for women's involvement in erotic encounters. For example, she introduces Paula from the story "Predator," one mentioned above in connection with the motif of female alliances, through the perspective of her friend: "Not even a corpse could resist Paula's sex appeal. She isn't all that young or beautiful, not even particularly fit, but every time I see her I'm ensnared by her charm, like a fly falling into a pot of honey ... In fact, generally speaking, I'm not even attracted to women, except that Paula is not a woman, she's the quintessence of sex and it makes no difference what gender you are; she would seduce a sexless fly. She's a hunter, she has never let a man pick her up – she's always been the one who chose her man and she would always get the one she wanted."[41] She is aware that her attitude toward sexuality can be judged by men, remembers the words of one of her loves, who accused her of nymphomania, and comments on such judgements in generalizations of her own: "If you want to screw you're a nymphomaniac, if you don't, you're frigid."[42] She thus points to the familiar way of controlling women's sexuality through shaming. The protagonist's perception of her own body and eroticism, accentuated through ironic references to a massive clitoris, defies cultural expectations, since sexual potency is considered to be desirable only in men and is perceived as shameful and unacceptable in women. The open examination of questions related to female sexuality corresponds with some aspects of the concept of écriture féminine. Cixous's manifesto emphasized the need for decensoring the woman's attitude toward her own sexuality, which "will tear her way from the superegoized structure in which she has always occupied the place reserved for the guilty."[43] This affirmative aspect of women's writing is connected with the discovery of one's own voice as well as with the free construction of new forms of feminine identity.

With respect to Kovalyk's thematic range and her manner of portraying several serious social problems, particularly violence, injustice, and discrimination, we can classify her writing, as I mentioned above, as socially engaged. The author's choice of these themes is a sign of her conviction that making social phenomena visible and analyzing their causes in fiction is a step toward change. Kovalyk uses literary means to call attention to the same problems that women's associations and non-profit initiatives address through awareness raising and intervention. For example, during the first Slovak national media campaign to stop violence against women, which was conducted by seven women's non-governmental organizations at the turn of 2001–02, the organizers wrote: "The discrimination against women is a direct result of the unequal and unjust division of power between men and women. This injustice can be described in various ways – as traditional values, cultural heritage, the natural world order – but in fact it is still injustice that violates the rights and lives of women. It is the main cause of men's violence against women in private and in public ... We can recognize it, so let's have the courage to call it by its real name."[44] Kovalyk's texts tend to share this objective; she has the courage to openly name negative social phenomena and use fiction to depict them in compelling ways and point to their systemic contexts. In this way, "she transforms the existential into the aesthetic."[45] Other key motifs of her work can also be considered in the context of social engagement, such as her detabooization of female corporeality and sexuality, which can be interpreted as a call for the freedom of expression in a culture that privileges men. The author's writing thus convincingly and compellingly contributes to the gradual opening of a new pluralistic space in contemporary Slovak culture, in which the right to one's own voice should no longer be controlled and restricted by any power relations.

CONCLUSION

The degree of openness toward cultural representations of various forms of identity, experience, or value systems is a specific indicator of the state of a given society and its dominant cultural model in specific historical periods. The story of women's writing in Slovakia – the shifts of its position in literary culture: initially being ignored and silenced, then included in literary history in fragmentary ways, and finally being gradually liberated from stereotypes and recognized for its quality – can be interpreted as a story that reflects certain transformations of cultural paradigms, particularly ones concerning gender roles.

The visibility and audibility of women writers in contemporary literature is a sign of the fact that the traditional model of gender relations has been somewhat destabilized, or, to put it more precisely, it no longer appears as the only viable and acceptable one. The new approaches to the problem of gender in the social as well as in the literary contexts have been, without doubt, made possible by the transformation of the political system, which created a general framework for free discussion and facilitated an accelerated process of reflection on the causes and consequences of gender inequality that was inspired by the concepts of Western feminism. The key factor, however, was the willingness of women – activists, literature scholars, and writers – to take on the role of agents in different areas of democratization, to initiate such processes, and explain the need for change. The poet, writer, and literary scholar Stanislava Chrobáková Repar has captured the position of Slovak feminist activists: "Women have been – in the worlds of literature, art, and science – long deprived of their rights, which was justified by the differential logic of gender stereotypes. Therefore they must also defend and claim their rights as a collective subject of history (more precisely, as gender-based victims of essentialist definitions of identity and manipulation). That means that they must assert themselves in society and perform equally as those who – in contrast with women – are given advantages on the basis of gender; an activist dimension is in this case essential."[46] I recognize the literary manifestation of such an activist objective, which does not need to be superficial or explicitly expressed, in the writers' sense of freedom in their approach to creative activity and in their selection of the means of expression, themes, and issues. It is this sense of freedom that has often been suppressed and restricted as a prerequisite for publishing women's writing. The status of women's writing as an integral and significant part of contemporary Slovak literature confirms that earlier historical barriers and limitations have lost their power, the social and cultural consciousness has shifted, and forms of self-identification and self-reflection have become more open and courageous. This new context is reflected in literary production, while literature, as a symbolic cultural practice, also shapes and co-creates this context.

NOTES

1 Cviková, *Ku konceptualizácii rodu*, 137. The author points out that in interpretations of women's writing, critics tended to point out irrelevantly the ways in which the given writer fulfilled the traditional gender roles as a wife or mother. Another problem that Cviková identifies is the unjustified separation of women authors from the broader context of the literary production in particular periods. This type of purposeless separation is also evident in some criticism on contemporary literature. See Taranenková, "Paralelné vesmíry," 401.

2 Hučková, "Ženská emancipácia ako literárna téma začiatku 20. storočia," 19–20.

3 Marcela Mikulová offers an interesting perspective on this problem in connection with the works of Elena Maróthy-Šoltésová and Terézia Vansová: "The idea of writing engaging stories for women in Slovak and facilitating the development of *the habit of reading in Slovak* may appear to be very utilitarian and not sufficiently noble. Both writers entered literary life with such apparently small ambitions, and we must conclude that the success of their activities was greater than anticipated. The reasons for their success may be that both of these women writers showed *a lesser degree of prejudice* and a greater understanding for the needs of their time than the above-mentioned male authors." Mikulová, "Implicitné polemiky," 174. The male authors Mikulová refers to, Svetozár Hurban Vajanský and Jozef Škultéty, enjoyed a dominant status in the literary life of that time and had the decisive word on questions related to preferred models of literature.

4 Cviková, "Po boku muža," 76.

5 Mikulová, "Implicitné polemiky," 176.

6 Filadelfiová and Bútorová, "Sľubné začiatky," 366.

7 Ibid., 367.

8 One of the important sources of the distorted and negative ideas about the feminist movement, which started to appear in the media and partially influenced public opinion, were the critical reactions to feminism that were expressed in the former circles of dissident and exiled writers during the 1990s, still during the period of the shared Czechoslovak state. For example, Josef Škvorecký's series of articles entitled *The Adventures of American Feminism I–III* published in the journal *Respekt* had an impact on public opinion. Through tendentiously selected radical examples from the American environment, he caricatured and ridiculed feminism, presenting it not only as a senseless but also an aggressive ideology. See Filipowicz, "Szacunek bez szacunku," 74.

9 The last printed issue of the journal was published in 2004 (No. 1, 2003–04). Its tradition is continued by the feminist webzine *ASPEKTin* (http://www.aspekt.sk/aspektin/title).

10 The ASPEKT series, which included selections from the works of Hana Gregorová (2007) and Terézia Vansová (2011), was one of the products of a multi-year project called "The History of Women," which was dedicated to the discovery and recovery of Slovak women's cultural tradition. The title of the series, "The Reader," suggested that its main goal was to familiarize readers with the most important Slovak thought on the status and rights of women.

11 The book *Potopené duše. Z tvorby slovenských poetiek v prvej polovici 20. storočia* (Drowned souls: selected works of Slovak women poets of the first half of the twentieth century, 2017), which was also published as a part of the "The Reader" series, was edited and introduced by Andrea Bokníková. The selection includes published and unpublished poems by twelve women poets whose work is not generally referenced in literary histories, as well as selections from their other writing (non-fiction prose, letters, literary criticism, fragments) and information on their lives and literary destinies. This publication was an important foundation for the reevaluation of the history of Slovak poetry, as well as a contribution to the analysis of canon formation.

12 Blažková's emigrant writing is discussed in more detail by Tamara Janecová in chapter 8.

13 Ivana Hostová discusses contemporary Slovak women poets in chapter 6.

14 Derrida, *Acts of Literature*, 44–5.

15 The abovementioned features of women's writing appear in various theoretical works. See Kraskowska, "O tak zwanej 'kobiecości' jako konwencji literackiej," 202–3.

16 The pun does not directly translate into English, but Hrubaničová's title, which literally means "love passes through the stomach," plays on the overlap between the Slovak words "žalud" (head of the penis) and "žalúdok" (stomach). In the rendering above, "belly" might also hint at the slang term "willy."

17 Gender issues in private and social contexts as well as the persistent stereotypes that disadvantage women also take centre stage in Ivica Ruttkayová's *Marilyn miluje literatúru* (Marilyn loves literature, 2007) and works by other women writers, especially those whose books have been published by ASPEKT.

18 Both Juráňová's *Ilona* and Kovalyk's *The Night Circus* were translated by Julia Sherwood and Peter Sherwood, whose joint translation activities are discussed by Julia Sherwood later in this volume. *The Night Circus* includes twelve of the seventeen stories from *Travesty šou*, three from the book *Čisté zviera* (Pure animal, 2018) and one story that has been not published in book form.

19 Mikula, *Od baroka k postmoderne*, 56.

20 My interpretation of Juráňová's prose draws on my earlier research; see Majerek, "Odzyskiwanie historii zapomnianych."

21 Juráňová, *Ilona*, 118.

22 Ibid., 29.

23 Ibid., 106.

24 Farkašová, "Oživené," 5.

25 Juráňová, *Ilona*, 85.

26 Ibid., 64–5.

27 Ibid., 82–3.

28 In my interpretation of Uršuľa Kovalyk's fiction I draw on my previously published research; see Majerek, "Związki prozy Uršuli Kovalyk z feministycznym nurtem literatury."

29 Kovalyk, *Neverné ženy*, 7–8.

30 Kovalyk, *The Night Circus*, 55.

31 Ibid., 56.

32 Ibid., 58.

33 Walczewska, "Feminizm," 235.

34 Kovalyk, *The Night Circus*, 42.
35 Ibid., 29.
36 Uličianska, "Ako postaviť vajíčko na špičku," 134.
37 Kovalyk, "Neverné ženy," 51.
38 Součková, *P[r]ózy po roku 1989*, 385.
39 Kovalyk, *The Night Circus*, 9.
40 Ibid., 11–12.
41 Ibid., 1.
42 Ibid., 4.
43 Cixous, "The Laugh of the Medusa," 880.
44 Iniciatíva piata žena, "Vyhlásenie k začiatku kampane proti násilu páchanému na ženách," 8–9.
45 Gajdoš, "Review of *Neverné ženy neznášajú vajíčka*," 152.
46 Chrobáková Repar, *Bielym atramentom*, 20–1.

BIBLIOGRAPHY

Cixous, Hélène. "The Laugh of the Medusa." Translated by Keith Cohen and Paula Cohen. *Signs* 1, no. 4 (Summer 1976): 875–93. https://www.jstor.org/stable/3173239.

Chmel, Rudolf, ed. *Slovník diel slovenskej literatúry 20. storočia*. Bratislava: Kalligram, Ústav slovenskej literatúry SAV, 2006.

Chrobáková Repar, Stanislava. *Bielym atramentom. Feministická literárna kritika a gynokritika*. Bratislava: ASPEKT, 2019.

Cviková, Jana. *Ku konceptualizácii rodu v myslení o literatúre*. Bratislava: Ústav svetovej literatúry SAV, ASPEKT, 2014.

– "Po boku muža a národa." *Aspekt* 11, no. 1 (2003–04): 71–8.

Derrida, Jacques. *Acts of Literature*, edited by Derek Attridge. New York and London: Routledge, 1992.

Farkašová, Etela. "Oživené portréty" (Review of Jana Juráňová, *Žila som s Hviezdoslavom.*) *Knižná revue* 19, no. 4 (2009): 5.

Filadelfiová, Jarmila, and Zora Bútorová. "Sľubné začiatky a vzdialené horizonty rodovej rovnosti." In *Kde sme? Mentálne mapy Slovenska*, edited by Martin Bútora et al., 366–72. Bratislava: Inštitút pre verejné otázky, Kalligram, 2010.

Filipowicz, Marcin Łukasz. "Szacunek bez szacunku. Stan dyskursu feministycznego w Czechach i Słowacji w latach dziewięćdziesiątych XX wieku." In *Literatury słowiańskie po roku 1989. Nowe zjawiska, tendencje, perspektywy. Tom II. Feminizm*, edited by Ewa Kraskowska, 72–83. Warszawa: KOLOR PLUS, 2005.

Gajdoš, Martin. Review of Uršula Kovalyk, *Neverné ženy neznášajú vajíčka. Revue svetovej literatúry* 38, no. 3 (2002): 150–2.

Hučková, Dana. "Ženská emancipácia ako literárna téma začiatku 20. storočia." In *Modernizmus v pohybe*, edited by Michal Habaj and Dana Hučková, 18–58. Bratislava: Veda, vydavateľstvo SAV, 2019.

Iniciatíva piata žena. "Vyhlásenie k začiatku kampane proti násilu páchanému na ženách." In *Piata žena. Aspekty násilia páchaného na ženách*, edited by Jana Cviková and Jana Juráňová, 8–9. Bratislava: ASPEKT, 2001.

Juráňová, Jana. *Ilona: My Life with the Bard*. Translated by Julia Sherwood and Peter Sherwood. Philadelphia: Calypso Editions, 2014.

Kovalyk, Uršuľa. *Neverné ženy neznášajú vajíčka*. Bratislava: ASPEKT, 2002.

– *The Night Circus and Other Stories*. Translated by Julia Sherwood and Peter Sherwood. Cardigan: Parthian, 2019.

Kraskowska, Ewa. "O tak zwanej, 'kobiecości' jako konwencji literackiej." In *Krytyka feministyczna. Siostra teorii i historii literatury*, edited by Grażyna Borkowska and Liliana Sikorska, 200–12. Warszawa: Instytut Badań Literackich, 2000.

Majerek, Rafał. "Odzyskiwanie historii zapomnianych. Uwagi o prozie Jany Juráňovej Žila som s Hviezdoslavom." In *Zrozumieć Słowiańszczyznę. Prace poświęcone profesor Marii Bobrownickiej w dziewięćdziesiątą rocznicę urodzin*, edited by Maria Dąbrowska-Partyka, 133–40. Kraków: Wydawnictwo Uniwersytetu Jagiellońskiego, 2010.

– "Związki prozy Uršuli Kovalyk z feministycznym nurtem literatury." In *Z warsztatu współczesnego słowacysty. Studia słowacystyczne dedykowane pamięci Profesor Marii Honowskiej*, edited by Halina Mieczkowska, Aleksandra Hudymač, and Zbigniew Babik, 247–57. Kraków: Wydawnictwo Uniwersytetu Jagiellońskiego, 2010.

Mikula, Valér. *Od baroka k postmoderne*. Levice: L.C.A., 1997.

Mikulová, Marcela. "Implicitné polemiky a turbulencie v ženskom písaní." In *Konfigurácie slovenského realizmu. Synopticko-pulzačný model kultúrneho javu*, edited by Marcela Mikulová and Ivana Taranenková, 172–95. Brno: Host, 2016.

Součková, Marta. *P[r]ózy po roku 1989*. Bratislava: Ars Poetica, 2009.

Taranenková, Ivana. "Paralelné vesmíry." *Slovenská literatúra* 57, no. 4 (2010): 398–402.

Uličianska, Zuzana. "Ako postaviť vajíčko na špičku." Review of *Neverné ženy neznášajú vajíčka*, by Uršula Kovalyk. *Aspekt* 11, no. 1 (2003–04): 134.

Walczewska, Sławomira. "Feminizm." *brulion* 6, no. 19B (1992): 233–41.

CODA: TRANSLATORS AND TRANSLATIONS

Translating Politics and the Politics of Translation

Magdalena Mullek

Pavol Rankov's novel *Stalo sa prvého septembra (alebo inokedy)* (2008) is one of the most widely translated works of contemporary Slovak literature: it has been published in a dozen languages, including the English version titled *It Happened on the First of September (or Some Other Time).*[1] The novel has also won three major international awards: the European Union Prize for Literature in 2009, the Angelus Central European Literature Award in 2014, and the Prix de livre européen in 2020.[2] In this exploration of the contemporary politics of translation in the context of publishing Slovak literature in English, I draw on my translation of Rankov's novel as a case study. My account of the experience of translating the book focuses on the strategies that I used to clarify the politics of mid-twentieth-century Slovakia for a contemporary audience removed from the narrated events in language, time, and place.

Set primarily in the central Slovak town of Levice, Rankov's novel describes thirty years of Czechoslovak history from the verge of the Munich Agreement in 1938 up to the Warsaw Pact invasion that suppressed the Prague Spring in 1968, by following the lives of three friends, Jan, Peter, and Gabriel, who are infatuated with the same girl, Mária. Although *It Happened on the First of September* reads like a bestseller, it employs many complex literary devices including the linearization of history, fragmentation, pastiche, linguistic code-switching, allegory, mythopoesis, and intertextuality. The narrative is woven from many styles, both textual and discursive, and Rankov continually plays with the novel's genre. There are moments when the novel reads like a historical document, others when it reads like a fairytale, and others still when it is more like a popular romance novel. These stylistic masks together with the other devices make it clear that *It Happened on the First of September* is not simply a historical novel, as the text proclaims, but a *postmodern* historical novel, which uses history as intertext. Throughout the novel, Rankov questions the cultural memory of historical events and destabilizes it by freely intermingling real events with artistic inventions. He invents backstories for some of the most controversial events of the time, thus creating a new mythopoetic narrative of history. This leads to considerable challenges for a translator bringing the work into a different language and culture, as I show in my discussion below.

THE POLITICS OF TRANSLATION IN THE SLOVAK CONTEXT

The term "politics of translation" has appeared in many articles on translation with a wide range of meanings, and given its flexible nature, it may be useful to delineate its scope in this chapter. Among the many things it has been used to describe are translation approaches that pursue a particular agenda (feminist, postcolonial, etc.), the changing status of translation studies in the academic world, and the role of the translator in the translation process. My own use of the term "politics of translation" refers to the decisions, activities, and relationships that go into bringing a book from an original to a published translation, as well as about the roles of the various stakeholders in this process.

The obstacles involved in bringing *It Happened on the First of September* from a Slovak original to a published English translation are an exemplary case of the broader challenges facing smaller literatures in the global publishing marketplace. I first read Rankov's novel two years after it had been published in Slovakia and not long after it won the European Union Prize for Literature. Based solely on my own enjoyment of the text, I chose it as one of my projects for the Advanced Workshop in Translation at Indiana University. In October 2010, I read a short excerpt to a small audience at the American Literary Translators Association Conference in Philadelphia. After the reading, I was approached by the publisher of the now-defunct literary journal *The Dirty Goat* (Host Publications), who was interested in publishing an excerpt from the novel in his next issue. Thus, the first two chapters of *It Happened on the First of September* in English appeared in *The Dirty Goat* 24 in 2011, and then ... nothing happened. No publisher contacted me eager to publish Pavol Rankov's first novel in English.

In December 2012, I sent my translations of a short story by Rankov and an excerpt from his novel to the annual periodical *Two Lines*, and the chapter "1941" was published in their twentieth anniversary print issue, "Landmarks." Over the next few years, I kept translating more chapters, and I sent samples and book pitches to several publishers, to no avail. In the meantime, I had been invited to translate selections for the *Dedalus Book of Slovak Literature* (2015), edited by Peter Karpinský, which presented some of the best-known Slovak authors from the late nineteenth century to the present. Then Miroslava Vallová, the director of the Slovak Literary Centre in Bratislava, suggested that I compile an anthology of contemporary Slovak prose. After I pitched the idea to Slavica Publishers, they accepted it for their new imprint, *Three String Books*, resulting in the volume *Into the Spotlight: New Writing from Slovakia* (2017). Thanks to the relationship I developed with Slavica while working on *Into the Spotlight*, two years later I was able to bring them my English translation of *It Happened on the First of September*, which they published in 2020.

The path of *It Happened on the First of September* from Slovak novel to published English translation is not atypical. When it comes to translating Slovak literature into English, I have participated in or been privy to this process enough times to make two observations, which may also hold true for other language pairs: translators are frequently the ones selecting books for translation, and Slovak books are often published in English thanks to existing relationships with publishers. While it should not come as a surprise that personal connections are crucial in every aspect of life, it is a little more counterintuitive that so many translations from Slovak (as well as other smaller languages) are published as a result of the translator's selection. Why do translators hold so much of the decision-making power in this situation?

Since Slovakia has yet to produce an international bestselling author such as Stieg Larsson or Elena Ferrante who would bring publishers eager to get his or her books translated into English, it is safe to assume that no one expects to make large profits on the sales of Slovak books. Although in Slovakia there are local authors of mainstream fiction such as Táňa Keleová-Vasilková or Dominik Dán who sell thousands of copies, their titles get no traction in the English-language market dominated by US popular fiction. Bestsellers aside, there is also no literary board in Slovakia that decides which works are worthy of translation and which are not. Even if such a body existed, there is no guarantee that English language publishers would listen to its recommendations. Without international bestsellers or official lists of recommended titles, it may seem obvious that publishers themselves would select what to translate. The problem is that publishers are extremely busy and their offices are often understaffed, so they cannot be expected to familiarize themselves with every country's literature or to look for new writers in small literary journals (such as the ones where I have published numerous translations from Slovak). On the contrary, they are inundated with submissions and must discard most of them.

That is not to suggest that there are no other means by which books get selected for translation. There are rare publishers who read Slovak literature themselves, either in the original or through an intermediary language, and if a particular work catches their interest and they decide to publish it in English, they seek out a translator for the work. There are also organizations, such as the Slovak Literary Centre, which promote their selections of Slovak literature through publications such as *Books from Slovakia* and attend international book fairs, attempting to find publishers for these works, but they are competing against many other similar organizations from many other countries for the attention of a small number of translation-inclined publishers.

Without obvious external deciding factors such as bestseller status and without the publisher's ability to sort through the vast sea of available works, the translator is the next obvious candidate for the book selection process. The translator usually speaks the original language, is involved with the source literature, should have a well-developed knowledge of specific authors and books, and most importantly, has connections with publishers or a vested interest in developing them. All these factors make the translator a natural bridge between the world of Slovak literature and the English language publisher. Based on existing relationships, a publisher is more inclined to listen to a translator's next proposal.

It Happened on the First of September fits this pattern, and so do other recently published Slovak books in English, such as Julia and Peter Sherwood's series of translations for Jantar Publishing (*In the Name of the Father*, 2017; *Big Love*, 2019; *Bellevue*, 2019) and Parthian Books (*The House of the Deaf Man*, 2014; *The Equestrienne*, 2016; *The Night Circus and Other Stories*, 2019) and Janet Livingstone's work with Two Dollar Radio (*Seeing People Off*, 2017; *Away! Away!*, 2018). Perhaps the best recent example is the "Slovak List" published by the Kolkata-based Seagull Books, which includes books by several different authors and translators. Although the entire series was arranged by the diligent work of Julia Sherwood, the selections were made by the translators themselves. All of these are examples of how the relationship between translators and publishers is beneficial to getting Slovak literature out in the world. Translators are critical to the process of bringing Slovak literature into English as the main link between English-language publishers and Slovak-language books. They are responsible for much more of the selection process than any other group in the publication chain, and their relationships with publishers make them key players in the politics of translation.

TRANSLATING TWENTIETH-CENTURY POLITICS FOR TWENTY-FIRST-CENTURY READERS

Before giving specific examples from my own translation strategies, let me begin with a brief overview of the novel. The story opens at the Levice swimming pool on the first of September 1938, where the Czech Jan (aka Honza, Ján, Ian) Bízek, the Hungarian Peter Rónai, and the Jewish Gabriel (aka Gábor) Rosenberg, are in pursuit of the same Slovak girl, their classmate Mária Belajová. They realize that only one of them can end up with her, so they decide to have a swimming race to determine which one should court her first. The race ends with Gabriel nearly drowning, but it becomes a recurring motif in the novel as they vie for Mária over the next thirty years. The onset of the Second World War ends the protagonists' carefree youth. Honza (Jan) and his family flee to Brno, in the Protectorate of Bohemia and Moravia, Gabriel ends up in forced labour in Hungary, and Peter is sent to the front, where he deserts. Mária is the only one to remain in Levice. Her father is a member of the then-underground communist party, on whose orders he infiltrates the Hungarian Arrow Cross Party, only to be later accused of having been a fascist collaborator. Hardships notwithstanding, the friendship between the protagonists persists, and after the war, all of them end up in Levice again. Peter becomes an important city official and a dedicated communist, and his friends always turn to him for help with such issues as immigration papers, work and housing, as well as political protection. Ján is forced into collaboration with the Secret Police and ends up working at a secret army food research institute, but throughout the repressive 1950s his disillusionment with the system grows, and in 1956 he emigrates to the USA, where he is known as Ian. After years of experimenting with a top-secret recipe he had brought from Czechoslovakia, he wins a contract to supply the US Army with instant scrambled eggs and builds a successful instant foods business. He is unaware, however, that in 1957 Mária gives birth to their daughter, Katarínka. Gabriel survives tuberculosis, then spends years in the High Tatras working as an accountant, until he moves to Bratislava for work. Mária oscillates between the three men, first nearly marrying Peter, then being abandoned by Ján days before their scheduled wedding, and finally refusing to marry Gabriel, even after dating him for years. In 1968 Ján is finally allowed to visit his daughter and friends in Czechoslovakia, and the three men try to recapture their lost youth on a camping trip. As they and Katarínka happily roam through the mountains, Soviet tanks roll into Czechoslovakia in response to the reforms instituted by Alexander Dubček and others. As the Soviet Union re-establishes control of the country, Ján persuades Peter and Gabriel to emigrate, but despite his best efforts, Mária chooses to stay behind.

The lives of the characters in *It Happened on the First of September* are inextricably linked to the major historical events of 1938–68, including the Munich Agreement, the First Vienna Award, the Second World War, the deportation of Jewish people, the rise of communism, and many others, all the way to the Soviet invasion of Czechoslovakia in 1968. Ján, Peter, Gabriel, and Mária become part of the tapestry of history of this time period as they experience every political change "on their own hides," to borrow an expression from the novel's dedication.[3] Toward the end of the novel, Rankov aptly summarizes the link between the characters' lives and politics, using Mária as his mouthpiece, "It's where we've ended up. Not because of our own mistakes, because of politics. We weren't able to live our own lives; we had to live the way we were told to."[4] Indeed, politics act as the hidden driving force behind the characters' lives.

Given the novel's propensity for the political, my translation had to address a variety of issues related to the politics of the time period. At the same time, I had to keep in mind that the English language reader is distanced from these events not only in time, but also in language and culture. Throughout the translation process I had to balance authenticity and accessibility, staying true to the terms, slogans, and cultural idiosyncrasies of the time period, while making them understandable to their new audience. Among the decisions I had to make were how to represent period-specific terminology, such as names of political entities and their members (i.e., *ľudáci*, *szabadcsapatok*, *nyilas*), whether and how to translate a number of different languages spoken by different characters with various degrees of intelligibility to the Slovak reader, and how to deal with forms of address that include titles and names unfamiliar to the English-language reader.

One of the techniques I used in my translation of *It Happened on the First of September (or Some Other Time)* to help its readers grasp period-specific terminology is interpolation, the insertion of short explanations into the text. Throughout the novel, Pavol Rankov uses the original names for various political entities (in Hungarian, Russian, or other languages) rather than giving their Slovak translations. In part, this is likely because their original names would have been widely used and understood during the time period that is being described, and in part, it fits his overall strategy of using language as an indication of the prevailing political climate. In many such instances, I retained the original words, but I also inserted short explanations that would orient the English-language reader.

In "Episode 1939," Regent Horthy visits Levice after it has been reclaimed by Hungary, following the First Vienna Award. Rankov describes the scene preceding the regent's visit: "Výklady židovských obchodov, ktoré len pred pár hodinami roztrieskali *szabadcsapatok* [emphasis added, not italicized in original] a ďalší vlastenci, boli zakryté doskami a tie boli zasa prekryté Horthyho podobizňami, maďarskými štátnymi znakmi a potrétmi svätého Štefana."[5] In this sentence, Rankov chose to leave the term szabadcsapatok, which refers to volunteer militias, in the original Hungarian (which is not comprehensible to the average Slovak reader today). I could have simply provided a literal translation or used a word such as "partisans" or "guerrilla fighters," but in order to retain the author's use of a Hungarian term, I took the opportunity to insert a short explanation.

My translation of this passage is as follows [underlining added for emphasis]: "The windows of the Jewish shops, shattered only a few hours earlier by Hungarian paramilitary units known as *szabadcsapatok* and by other patriots were boarded up and plastered with images of Horthy, Hungarian state symbols, and portraits of Saint Stephen."[6] The words that are underlined in this passage are the additional explanation, not present in the original. In this way, I was able to keep the original term as well as help the reader understand its meaning and consequently, a little more of the political context.

I used a variation of this strategy with another Hungarian term, *nyilas*, which refers to a member of the Hungarian Arrow Cross Party. Nyilas and its plural and adjectival forms appear in the original text more than a dozen times, so giving the English-language reader an explanation gives a necessary clue to the political climate. Interestingly, Rankov educates the Slovak reader in its meaning as well. Before introducing the term nyilas, Rankov uses the full name of the Hungarian Arrow Cross Party in "Episode 1940," which reads: "A vraj sa pridal k Nyilaskeresztes Párt Hungarista Mozgalom." ("And rumor has it that he's joined the Hungarian Arrow Cross Party.")[7] However, the word nyilas itself does not appear until the next episode, five pages later: "Nezaoberali sa tým, že jej otec je nyilas."[8] Both sentences refer to Mária's father, who had supposedly joined this party. Rankov is counting on the context of the reference to the same person both times and hoping that the reader will remember the long party name, or at least its first part, and correctly deduce that a nyilas is a member of the Hungarian Arrow Cross Party. I did not feel confident that an English-language reader would follow the same connection over five pages for the unpronounceable Hungarian term Nyilaskeresztes Párt Hungarista Mozgalom. Instead, I opted for a strategy that avoids the party name, which would likely be skipped over by the reader, retaining the novel's more frequently used term for party member. I put the party and the party member on the same line, at their first mention in the novel. Thus my translation reads: "And rumor has it that he's a *nyilas*. He's joined the Hungarian Arrow Cross Party."[9] Adding the underlined explanation, "that he's a *nyilas*," creates an association between the foreign term nyilas and the Hungarian Arrow Cross Party. When Rankov's first reference to nyilas appears, I translated the sentence as follows: "They didn't care that her father was a nyilas."[10] Thanks to the initial interpolation of the term nyilas, all subsequent instances of the term do not require an explanation. Although I would not recommend interpolating every foreign term in a translated text, interpolation is a useful technique for providing the reader with some of the more obscure foreign terms or concepts, especially when footnotes would impede the flow. Interpolation helps retain authenticity while also improving accessibility.

Slovak critics have written about Pavol Rankov's use of multiple languages in *It Happened on the First of September (or Some Other Time).* Besides Czech and Hungarian, the novel's characters also frequently speak Russian, German, English, or Hebrew. Beyond the basic utility of language as a marker of nationality or location, Rankov also uses the various languages to indicate political change, be it because of changing borders, governments, or identities. Rankov's inclusion of these languages gives the novel documentary-style authenticity, especially when it comes to representing the co-existence of people of many nationalities and political persuasions in a small geographic area.

While trying to retain as much of the language diversity of the original as possible, I also considered what Umberto Eco and others have termed "functional equivalence," that is, creating the same world picture in the mind of the reader of the translation that would be created in the mind of the reader of the original.[11] In instances when a Slovak reader would have likely understood a given passage in another language, but an English reader would have been lost, I gave preference to recreating the experience of understanding the passage over retaining its original language. An example of such a removal of a foreign language to aid understandability can be found in "Episode 1956." Ján is attending a political workshop in Romania led by a Soviet political commissar. At the end of the day's session, the following exchange takes place:

> – Ako budeme žiť keď zanikne rodina, – spýtal sa.
>
> – Základnou bunkou komunistickej spoločnosti sa stáva výrobno-pracovný kolektív, – vyhlásil lektor.
>
> – *I ľubov, i polovaja žizň?* – spýtala sa Irina, blondínka zo Sojuzu, ktorú Ján zaregistroval hneď prvý deň.
>
> Politruk rozhodil rukami:
>
> – *Pri kamunizme vsjo budet, i vsevo budet mnoga.*[12]

In the original text, the lines I have italicized are in Russian, which most Slovaks of the time would have understood at least passively, but transcribed in Latin script, since many contemporary Slovak readers would not be able to read Cyrillic. At the same time, Rankov assumes that a Slovak reader will be able to figure out their meaning because of the common Slavic roots of many of the words. Both sentences in Russian are full of Slovak cognates such as I/A, ľubov/láska, i/a, polovaja/pohlavný, žizň/život, Pri/Pri, kamunizme/komunizme, vsjo/všetko, budet/bude, i/a, vsevo/všetkého, budet/bude, mnogo/mnoho. The purpose of having those lines in Russian is to create verisimilitude of the political workshop led by a Russian lecturer, with attendees from various countries, not to obscure what they said.

Consider the same passage in English, but with the Russian language phrases left blank, as an indication that there are no cognate words for English-language readers, apart from kamunizme/communism:

> "What's life going to be like after the disintegration of the family?" he asked.
>
> "The production work group will become the basic building block of communist society," said the lecturer.
>
> -------------------- asked Irina, a blonde from the Soviet Union whom Ján had noticed the first day.
>
> The political commissar spread his arms wide.
>
> ------------------------------.[13]

In this version, the entire joke of the latter part of the conversation would be lost on the English language reader, which would be a much greater loss than the lack of verisimilitude. From the attribution of the first line in Russian, the speaker is identified as being from the Soviet Union. Based on earlier information in the chapter, we also know that the political commissar is from the Soviet Union, therefore, we can infer that he too speaks Russian.

In the published translation, I rendered the passage entirely in English:

> "What's life going to be like after the disintegration of the family?" he asked.
>
> "The production work group will become the basic building block of communist society," said the lecturer.
>
> "What about love and sex?" asked Irina, a blonde from the Soviet Union whom Ján had noticed the first day.
>
> The political commissar spread his arms wide. "Under communism we'll have everything, and we'll have plenty of it."[14]

By recreating a functionally equivalent exchange, the translation shows that Irina is thinking about sex at a political workshop, which gives a clue to her character that plays out later in the chapter. The reader also gets to experience the typical bombast of communist propaganda that would have been presented at this type of political workshop, and almost anywhere else during the socialist period, when everything in the Soviet Union was officially proclaimed to be superior.

Although there are a number of instances where understanding the meaning of a passage is more important than retaining the original choice of language, there are also instances of intentional non-understanding, which were important to retain as such. The first one is from "Episode 1945." At the end of the Second World War, Gabriel joins a Soviet military unit that purports to hunt fascists in Hungary, and he becomes their Russian-Hungarian translator. After some time, Gabriel figures out that they are not hunting fascists, but czarist loyalists, and he runs away. During his escape, he barges into the home of a couple of unsuspecting Hungarian villagers in an attempt to obtain civilian clothing: "Gabriel turned into the first courtyard at the edge of the nearest village. He entered the house, and shouted at a frightened old man and woman":

> "*Davaj odezhdu!*"
> "*Nem értem,*" the old woman squealed.
> "Nem értem?" Gabriel tapped his holster. "I'll pull out my pistol and you'll change your tune to értem, értem!"[15]

Gabriel, the Hungarian-Russian translator, chooses to speak Russian to hide his own identity and to make it look like the incident is being perpetrated by Soviet soldiers, even though he speaks the language of the couple he is robbing. The Hungarians do not understand his request, but the threatening tone combined with Gabriel tapping his holster make it clear that he is making some type of a demand. The substance of it is much less important than the threat. Except for people who grew up under communism and studied Russian in school and those of Hungarian heritage or living in areas with large Hungarian populations, most Slovaks would not understand the phrases in Russian, Hungarian, or both. Of course, few English-speaking readers would understand the phrases in either language. Non-understanding is the situation the Hungarian characters also find themselves in, so leaving the phrases in their original languages allows the reader of the translation to experience the passage from the perspective of the Hungarian couple, just like most readers of the Slovak original would.

The second example of a passage in which non-understanding was the function of the original is from "Episode 1940," in which Honza catches his sister Jitka and several Germans having sex in their parents' apartment. The parents are at work, and Jitka kicks Honza out of the house under the pretense of making lunch and not wanting her younger brother underfoot. But Honza comes home early because it is raining, and he encounters the following scene:

> His hand was already on the doorknob when he heard unfamiliar voices speaking in German.
>
> "*Nochmal! Nochmal! Mit der Zunge!*"
>
> "*Stärker!*"
>
> Gestapo, Honza thought.[16]

Honza hears German, does not understand the words, and because this is happening during the Second World War, he immediately jumps to the conclusion that the Gestapo has come for their parents. The words being spoken are not important, but rather the fact that Honza does not understand them. Since a Slovak reader would most likely not understand what the German phrases mean either, it makes perfect sense to retain those phrases in German, allowing both the Slovak and the English reader to experience the passage from Honza's perspective, not from the omniscient narrator's perspective.

The non-understanding in the examples above also brings the reader into the political circumstances of the time period. In the first example, the reader is shown the clash of the Soviet liberators with the local Hungarian populace – while Gabriel simply takes advantage of the opportunity to disguise his identity, the Soviet soldiers had been capturing and mistreating Hungarians throughout the earlier parts of that chapter. In the second example, the reader is shown the fear of the German occupiers that is invoked by nothing more than a few words of German.

A more subtle, though no less pervasive, sign of the times than the use of different languages in *It Happened on the First of September* is the ubiquitous use of "Comrade" as a form of address. The novel is full of "Comrades," including such long versions as Comrade Teacher Mária

Belajová. To better understand the use of this and other similar constructs requires a bit of background in the way Slovaks have addressed one another, both historically and in the present. Slovak society has always been obsessed with titles such as "doctor" and "professor," which are used with great frequency in everyday interactions. (While in common English usage one may address someone as "doctor," "professor," or "reverend," the use of this type of address is reserved for a limited number of degrees and professional titles and is most frequently utilized in professional settings and formal interactions.) When addressing someone, frequently it is not only the title that is used, but also the honorific before it, thus producing forms of address such as "Mrs Doctor" (*pani doktorka*) and "Mr Professor" (*pán profesor*). In Slovak, this type of formal address also applies to a much wider range of titles, including "engineer" for people who have completed the equivalent university degree, as well as certain professions or positions, such as teacher (i.e., *pani učiteľka*) or director (i.e., *pán riaditeľ*). While this usage does not sound stilted at all in Slovak, it would be glaringly so in English.

During the communist period in Czechoslovakia, the use of Mr and Mrs was often replaced by the terms *súdruh/súdružka*, which are generally translated into English using the non-gendered term comrade. This form of address could be used on its own if the person's last name was not known, or it could be used with a last name, for example, *súdruh Dubček* (Comrade Dubček), instead of Mr Dubček. The *súdruh/súdružka* address could also precede titles, professions, or positions, producing forms of address such as *súdruh prezident* (Comrade President) or *súdružka učiteľka* (Comrade Teacher). Any of these forms of address could be further extended with a last name, resulting in phrases like Comrade Teacher Mária Belajová. In texts set in contemporary times, addressing someone as Mr Professor in English would come across as highly unnatural, bordering on rude, therefore, the substitution of Professor (perhaps with the last name) would create a better cultural equivalence. On the other hand, in the case of a text set during the socialist period in Czechoslovakia, removing all those comrades would lose something of the original setting.

Umberto Eco speaks to a similar issue in regards to translating a nineteenth-century French novel, where the word monsieur appears many times over, yet one encounters "Sir" in contemporary English with much less frequency. While he agrees that in a contemporary text one could and probably should omit some or all of the "monsieurs," in the case of a novel such as *The Count of Monte Cristo*: "the presence of all those *monsieurs* not only lends the story its 19th-century French tone, but brings into play the conventional conversational strategies that are essential if the reader is to understand the relationships between the real characters. This means that the French *monsieur* is not only a lexical item, but a sort of pragmatic operator, bound up with the customs of a society."[17] I would argue that the *súdruh/súdružka* of the socialist period is a similar pragmatic operator, inextricably linked to the Czechoslovak society of the time. Besides being the customary form of address, the various uses of *súdruh/súdružka* also indicate the linguistic distance representative of the social-political distance between members of the party and those who were not, the overall formality of relationships between employers and employees, and between most people in professional settings, which was the hallmark of the time period. While the repeated usage of Comrade X and Comrade Y may sound unusual to a contemporary English-speaking audience, it is part of recreating the cultural and political milieu of the text.

While the use of the title comrade ostensibly implied the equality of the interlocutors, paradoxically it became increasingly ironic, and sometimes condescending. This was particularly evident when someone would be referred to by their profession, but one which would not be typically used in a form of address or by the action they were engaged in at the given moment. An example of this type of usage can be seen in "Episode 1966." When Peter is driving across the border to Hungary, a customs official asks: "Where are you headed, Comrade Driver?"[18] Similarly, when Peter is speaking to the principal of an elementary school who is particularly pleased about how he demoted Mária to peeling potatoes in the school cafeteria instead of teaching first grade, he boasts: "What do you say to that, Comrade Journalist?"[19] In the former example, the customs official is indicating his superiority in the situation, in the latter, the principal is quite smug because of what he perceives to be justice. Whereas in English a customs official would have likely addressed Peter as "Sir" to indicate respect, what happens to Peter is precisely the opposite. The official addresses Peter as Comrade Driver to make clear Peter's subordinate position in the situation, and therefore, the address could not be translated as "Sir," because this dynamic would have been lost. And while the principal's smugness would have been clear from the actions he described regardless of how he had addressed Peter, his use of "Comrade Journalist" at the end of his rhetorical question not only reaffirms his smugness, but it also shows him to be a buffoon.

While all those comrades helped recreate a socialist era authenticity in *It Happened on the First of September*, all the foreign languages, including the ones not understood by the majority of readers in Slovak or in English, lent the text the documentary authenticity of different locations and changing political realities. Interpolation of some of the more obscure or frequently used foreign terms allowed me to leave them in their original language and gave the reader the necessary information to decode their meaning. All of these translation choices worked together to recreate the political environment of the novel and to make it more accessible to a contemporary English language reader.

NOTES

1 Rankov, *It Happened on the First of September.*
2 Rankov, *Stalo sa prvého septembra.*
3 Rankov, *It Happened on the First of September.*
4 Ibid., 234.
5 Rankov, *Stalo sa prvého septembra*, 19–20.
6 Ibid., 8.
7 Rankov, *Stalo sa prvého septembra*, 27.
8 Ibid., 32.
9 Rankov, *It Happened on the First of September*, 14.
10 Ibid., 18. Since this is the second appearance of the word *nyilas* in the translation, following the rules of *The Chicago Manual of Style*, the term is no longer italicized.
11 Eco, *Mouse or Rat?*, 48.
12 Rankov, *Stalo sa prvého septembra*, 212.
13 Rankov, *It Happened on the First of September*, 167.
14 Ibid., 167.
15 Ibid., 60.
16 Ibid., 15.
17 Eco, *Experiences in Translation*, 19
18 Rankov, *It Happened on the First of September*, 240.
19 Ibid., 141.

BIBLIOGRAPHY

Eco, Umberto. *Experiences in Translation*. Translated by Alastair McEwen. Toronto: University of Toronto Press, 2001.

– *Mouse or Rat? Translation as Negotiation*. London: Phoenix, 2004.

Rankov, Pavol. *It Happened on the First of September (or Some Other Time)*. Translated by Magdalena Mullek. Bloomington: Slavica Publishers, 2020.

– *Stalo sa prvého septembra (alebo inokedy)*. Bratislava: Kalligram, 2008.

An Interview with Translator Julia Sherwood

Prepared by Katarina Gephardt

In what ways does your emigrant background influence your work with languages as a translator?

My early experience as an emigrant provided the first trigger for my future work as a translator. I emigrated with my parents because of the relentless political persecution our family suffered. We arrived in Germany in 1978, ten years after the huge wave of emigration that followed the 1968 invasion of Czechoslovakia. I was surprised to find that during those ten years, so many émigrés had neglected their native Slovak and Czech, letting their language become contaminated by German. For them, the priority was to blend in, adapt to the new culture, but I never wanted to cut myself off from my roots and the culture I grew up in. Moreover, as someone who had always been interested in languages and spent the previous six years fighting for my right to study languages at university (it was the seven or eight rejections of my applications that really drove me to emigrate) I swore to myself that I would never let that happen to me. I made the conscious decision that whenever I came across a new German word for which I didn't know the Slovak equivalent, I would look it up in a dictionary, and, after settling in the UK and switching languages again, I continued doing that with English. When my daughter was born, I decided to raise her bilingually. She was born in January 1989, so at that time I still thought we would never be able to go back to Czechoslovakia and that she would be able to acquire, at best, a passive knowledge of Slovak. But to me even this was very important, not just as a way of keeping my native language up at home, but also because I wanted to instill in my daughter from an early age the understanding that there are different languages and therefore different ways of conceptualizing the world, so I only ever spoke to her in Slovak and my husband in English. Then November 1989 happened, and I started visiting Slovakia again, taking her along. And I am very proud to say that she is now fluent in Slovak.

If you try to juggle several languages, making sure the ones you use less don't get rusty is quite a challenge. In all those years of living abroad – more than half of my life by now – I have continued reading in Slovak as well as in Czech and have also done my best to keep up my German, Russian, and Polish by maintaining contacts and through reading. Since I started working as a translator, I have followed new trends in Slovak and Czech literature, reading as much as I could. But of course, I also need to read as much as possible in English since a firm grasp of the target language is what matters most in translating. For many decades it was an unchallenged dogma that one should only ever translate into one's native language, so when I started translating into English, I felt a bit like an impostor. The received wisdom has changed more recently as the world has opened up and people have been moving countries more freely and frequently, becoming competent in several languages. The whole concept of a "native language" is now being questioned and many prefer to speak of "first" and "second" languages. Having said that, I am aware of my limitations: after all, I was in my late twenties by the time I came to live in the UK, and there are some gaps I can never fill. That is why I prefer to translate into English jointly with my husband Peter, whose entire education has been in the UK and whose breadth and depth of knowledge, background in linguistics, and feel for literature guarantee that the final "product" is truly polished and idiomatic.

What does your process of collaborative translation look like, and how does your husband's own practice as a translator from Hungarian inform your collaboration? I am also curious how you reach consensus on the books that you choose to translate.

I am the one who starts the ball rolling since Peter does not read Slovak. This also means that I suggest a writer or text for us to translate, although we take the final decision jointly, based on several criteria: first and foremost, the quality of the text and the challenges it presents (we prefer more challenging works) and whether it feels right for us. This is as much an aesthetic as an ethical decision, as well as a question of whether we like the style and feel we can relate to the book's characters or setting (e.g., rural or urban; contemporary or historical). It certainly helps if the work has a dose of humour, and sometimes also if we have met the author and got on with them and find that we are on a similar wavelength.

The process we have developed and honed over the years is as follows: I do the first couple of drafts and may ask Peter's advice on the odd specific problem as I'm working on them. I then pass a rough draft on to him with some general guidance on what I feel is important about that particular text (style, register) or the kind of voice (or voices) we should be aiming for; sometimes I point out a specific problem in brackets and suggest several alternative solutions for certain words or phrases. Peter then revises the text and passes it back to me. I go over it again, generally accepting his suggestions or, occasionally, rejecting them and highlighting problematic words or passages that need further discussion. We may repeat this process once or even twice, depending on how demanding the source text is. Next, we print the text out, often changing the type and size of font to defamiliarize it, and read it again, writing any further corrections on the printed page. We complete the process by taking turns to read the translation out aloud to each other to make sure that it reads well in English. It is amazing how often a better, more natural, more idiomatic solution trips off our tongues almost automatically in the course of this reading.

Peter's contribution is important on many levels. He has a wider vocabulary and range of registers and can draw on many years' of experience of translating and teaching languages and linguistics as well as on his work as a lexicographer (he is the author or co-author of several Hungarian-English dictionaries). Finally, though Slovak and Hungarian are very different languages, centuries of shared Slovak and Hungarian history have left a deep imprint on the way their respective speakers perceive the world and express ideas and emotions. As a result, Slovak has many idiomatic expressions that are very similar or even identical to Hungarian (or German, for that matter).

Which of your literary translations from Slovak to English were the most challenging and rewarding and why?

Peter likes to say that if a text doesn't pose a challenge, it is not worth translating. Every book presents a particular challenge of its own. First and foremost, it is a question of finding the right voice, not just for each writer but also for each book, one that conveys or echoes the voice of the original as closely as possible – although, given the differences between Slovak and English and the difference in the cultural context, it can never be (and should not be) the same. However, as much of the flavour of the original as possible should be retained: a little bit like trying to make *bryndzové halušky* in the UK or the US, where many of the ingredients – *bryndza*, Slovak "ewe's cheese," or *slanina*, bacon, "lard," or "smoke-cured pork fatback" – are not available.

But I should really illustrate this with literary examples. When translating Balla's *In the Name of the Father* or *Big Love*, the challenge was recreating the author's style, characterized by sudden shifts of tone and register between the absurd and the realistic, humour and horror, colloquial and elevated language. Then there is Balla's syntax: very short, succinct sentences – sometimes consisting of just one or two words – alternate with extremely long sentences that can run to one or two pages. In the case of the short ones, when bringing the message across, it is not only the choice of the right words but also of the word order that matters. Probably the most challenging are his long sentences, with their brief asides and longer digressions, which develop a momentum whose cumulative effect can be highly comical. To maintain the same effect without sounding clumsy or obscuring the meaning in English we often revise a sentence many times, reading it aloud at the final stage.

Ivana Dobrakovová's books pose similar, though different, syntactical challenges. Her long sentences reflect her narrator's state of mind and, while they can also be inadvertently comical, the streams of consciousness of her protagonists in *Bellevue* and *Mothers and Truckers* reflect their memories of traumatic experiences or mental breakdowns. Dobrakovová aims to get inside her characters' heads and show what they are going through from their perspective, something she does particularly well in her novel *Bellevue*. Blanka, the book's narrator, gradually loses her grip on reality, and the author conveys this process masterfully through the text's gradually disintegrating, fragmented syntax and idiosyncratic punctuation. It proved to be an additional challenge to persuade the publisher that the peculiarities of the syntax and punctuation in both Balla and Dobrakovová's works are a hallmark of their style and must be retained in English.

Much has been written about the specific challenges of translating humour and that is something we have also faced in several of our translations. Pavel Vilikovský's writing combines his specific subtle humour and irony as well as his frequent use of puns, with a distinctive narrative voice. The pun in the title of his novel *Fleeting Snow* (the original, *Letmý sneh*, is a play on the similarity between the words *letmý*, "fleeting" and *letný* "summery, pertaining to summer") proved impossible to convey in English, so we took great pains to find the best possible equivalent for his gently ironic, colloquial yet highly polished narrative voice which the late author described to me, in his typical self-deprecating way, as *pokleslý hovorový jazyk*, "trashy, colloquial language." Since Vilikovský was himself a distinguished and experienced translator from English, we were quite nervous about how he would receive our rendition of his work. His words of appreciation ("*s hlbokou vďačnosťou za vynikajúci tvorivý preklad*," "with deep gratitude for an outstanding, creative translation") in my copy of his final book *Rajc je preč* (The thrill is gone, yet to be translated into English) are something I will treasure forever. Getting to know and work with great writers such as Pavel Vilikovský was a great privilege and a further rewarding aspect of this kind of work. I have come to think of several contemporary Slovak writers as friends, and touring the UK with Balla, Ivana Dobrakovová, and Uršuľa Kovalyk in 2019 was tremendous fun, an additional bonus for a "people person" like myself.

The cultural, political, and historical contexts for Slovak literature can be hard to understand for English readers. How have you dealt with that challenge in the process of translation?

The fact that Slovakia's culture and history are not well-known in the English-speaking world can indeed sometimes cause difficulties. There is no one-size-fits-all solution, and we have dealt with it in a variety of ways, depending on the nature of the book. However, there is one principle we have stuck to: we avoid footnotes at the bottom of the page, as we don't believe they have a place in a work of fiction. The simplest, most common way of dealing with unfamiliar terms is by inserting into the text brief, unobtrusive explanations, sometimes called stealth glosses. For example, when the narrator of Uršuľa Kovalyk's *The Equestrienne* mentions a pop-singer whose name would mean nothing to the Anglophone reader, we referred to him as "the disco star Michal David."

Our first book-length translation from Slovak was Daniela Kapitáňová's *Samko Tále's Cemetery Book*, a brilliant, dark satire on the dreary totalitarian Czechoslovakia of the 1970s and 1980s and the rise of xenophobia and nationalism that followed the fall of communism in 1989. Creating an English version of the narrator's idiosyncratic language – a mix of childish naiveté, officialese, and garbled idioms – without making Samko Tále sound like a foreigner who hasn't learned English properly was a major challenge. We employed various strategies to ensure that there would be no dissonant clashes within the narrator's distinctive voice. For example, in consultation with the author, we inserted quite a lengthy Samko-ish explanation of the ending – *ová* in Slovak woman's names, adding the italicized second half of the following sentence: "Seriously, I'm not making it up, she was a woman and her name was Timrava, not Timravaová, *even though a proper Slovak name for a woman is supposed to have ová at the end, like Darinka Gunárová, she's also called Darinka Gunárová with ová at the end because that's the law*." Also, the publisher, Donald Rayfield, suggested including a page of "guidance for the British reader" at the beginning of the book. It explains the temporal and geographical setting, the currency, the term *Spartakiad*, and also provides a guide to pronouncing the names of the characters.

Although *Samko Tále* was critically acclaimed when it was published in 2010, several people have told me more recently that they found many of the cultural, historical, and political references unfathomable, and that had diminished their enjoyment of the book. With hindsight I think we should have offered more detailed guidance, perhaps in the form of a translator's note. Based on this experience, when we were preparing the publication of Jana Juráňová's *Ilona: My Life with the Bard* – a book based on the life and work of Pavol Országh Hviezdoslav – we included a translators' note with a summary of his biography and significance, as well as five pages of endnotes on the late nineteenth and early twentieth-century cultural and political figures and institutions mentioned in the book. Similarly, two of our recent translations, Ján Johanides's *But Crime Does Punish* and Ján Rozner's *Seven Days to the Funeral*, provide endnotes on terminology, political figures, and events in Czech and Slovak twentieth-century history, which may not be familiar to Anglophone readers today.

How has the market for literary translation in the UK or in the broader context of Anglophone countries evolved since you first started translating Slovak literature into English?

The Anglophone book market's resistance to translations in general has been much written about, even if lately the proportion of translated books has gone up from the oft-quoted 3 per cent to about 5 per cent. However, this figure refers to translations from *all* languages into English, of which "lesser translated languages" such as Slovak, comprise just a tiny fraction. I'm not talking only about literatures of countries with populations of a size similar to or smaller than Slovakia, such the Czech Republic, Hungary, the Baltic countries, Slovenia, or Croatia, but also about languages with larger numbers of speakers, such as Arabic or the languages of the Indian subcontinent. Translations from these languages are barely visible in the English market.

On a more positive note, the problems faced by these literatures have gained increasing recognition in recent years, and the situation has been slowly improving. For example, from 2014 to 2016 researchers in Czech and Slovak, Portuguese, Scandinavian, and South Slav literatures from the British universities of Bristol, Cardiff, and University College London ran a project aimed at better understanding the ways in which European literatures written in less well-known languages, which depend on translation to reach the wider world, are trying to break through into the cultural mainstream. The resulting book of almost 300 pages, *Translating the Literatures of Small European Nations*, which was co-edited by Rajendra Chitnis, Jacoub Stougaard-Nielsen, Rhian Atkin, and Rhian Milutinovic and published in 2019, constitutes the most detailed and wide-ranging comparative study of the subject to date.

An active – or rather, activist – translator community has also been trying to improve the situation. For example, I am a member of a group of translators from lesser translated languages formed in early 2021 to seek ways of supporting one another and promoting literary works by authors from our respective source languages (currently Bengali, Finnish, Greek, Hungarian, Latvian, Slovak, Slovene, and Welsh). The special issue of the *AALITRA Review*, published in October 2022, entitled *Enriching the Global Literary Canvas: Celebrating Less Translated Languages*, is the first tangible outcome of our work.[1] Furthermore, literary journals focusing on translation, including online outlets such as *Words Without Borders*, *BODY.Literature*, and *Asymptote* have made accessible in English works by writers from across the world and in a wide range of languages, including Slovak. Several initiatives have helped raise the visibility of translators. The campaign #TranslatorsOnTheCover, launched in October 2021 by the author Mark Haddon and the writer and translator Jennifer Croft in collaboration with the UK Society of Authors, called for translators to be routinely credited on book covers and within a few weeks their open letter attracted 1,500 signatures. Several major publishers have since pledged to put translators' names on book covers. Looking specifically at translations of Slovak literature into English, great progress has been made since I first started translating in 2009. A list I have compiled shows that thirty-three books by Slovak writers (including prose, poetry, and children's books) appeared in English translation in the twenty-year period from 1989 to 2009. By comparison, in the course of the following fourteen years, from 2010 to 2024, seventy new translations from the Slovak were published. This wouldn't have been possible without the support of the Slovak Literary Centre (formerly Slovak Information Centre on Literature) and their efforts to promote Slovak literature abroad and, crucially, the SLOLIA grant administered by this agency. The grant system has encouraged publishers to take the risk and publish authors who are largely unknown in the English-speaking world (let's face it, despite all these achievements, most Slovak authors remain largely unknown). Slowly, the number of publishers willing to champion Slovak authors has also grown, a good example being Karolinum Press's recently launched Modern Slovak Classics series.

Whereas I felt quite isolated when I first embarked on translating Slovak literature, over the years, I have established contacts with fellow translators. Their number has also grown, so that I now feel a part of a community – not just of those who translate into English but also into other languages, such as Hungarian, German, or Polish. We can provide support to one another and share information on our projects as well as on publishers. More recently, many of us have benefited from the establishment of translator grants, allocated by the Slovak Arts Council (Fond na podporu umenia).

Summing up, I feel that Slovak literature is no longer a complete *terra incognita* but that it has established a few outposts on the map of the Anglophone world, and that it is being noticed by book reviewers in traditional print media as well as by bloggers. Some Slovak books have made inroads by stealth, so to speak: for example, reviews of Uršuľa Kovalyk's books have been trickling in two, or even three, years after publication, thus attracting new readers, with *The Equestrienne*, first published in 2016, being reprinted in 2021.

You have made significant contributions to the promotion of Slovak literature in the UK and the broader Anglophone world. What are the highlights of your activity in this role of a literary ambassador? What challenges have you faced?

The major challenge facing all translators of Slovak (as well as of other less translated languages) into English is finding publishers. It's been a real uphill struggle, as for some of the books I have translated, I had to wait several years to find a publisher or, to be precise, had to keep knocking on publishers' doors hoping against hope that one day some of them would open, even if there were moments when it seemed like a doomed Quixotic enterprise. But I'm not one to give up easily. Call it patience, or maybe sheer stubbornness, but eventually most of my dream projects have come to fruition, and it has been immensely gratifying to see more and more works by Slovak writers being published and recognized. There remain many authors whose works deserve to appear in English translation, but the situation is improving, with more and more publishers being prepared to take on Slovak authors.

As for the highlights, I am especially happy about the cooperation with a leading publisher of translated literature, the Kolkata-based Seagull Books, whose highly acclaimed publications are distributed throughout the Anglophone world and who have invited me to curate a Slovak list for them. Since the list launched in 2021, nine books have been published and a further four are scheduled to appear over the next couple of years[2]. I very much hope that this fruitful cooperation will continue. I am also very proud that Peter and I were asked to translate Ján Johanides's *But*

Crime Does Punish (Trestajúci zločin), published in 2022 as the first title in the Karolinum Press's Modern Slovak Classics series.

As the earthquake of the COVID-19 pandemic shook the literary market, the Slovak Literary Centre was one of the many institutions forced to refocus their promotional work from attendance at book fairs and live events to creating online resources. One of these was LitCast Slovakia, a series of podcasts on Slovak literature in German, English, and later also Hungarian. I was approached to take on the English-language podcast and host a series of interviews with translators, critics, and scholars of Slovak literature as well as writers and publishers, and after some initial reluctance I decided to give it a try. I ended up recording thirty interviews, broadcast between April 2020 and July 2021, and found the experience challenging (especially the technical side) and enjoyable in equal measure.

Another highlight that I mentioned in response to an earlier question was the 2019 UK tour with Ivana Dobrakovová, Uršuľa Kovalyk, and Balla, presenting their newly published books *Bellevue*, *Midnight Circus*, and *Big Love*. As part of *Raising the Velvet Curtain*, a project I organized to promote Slovak literature and culture in the UK to mark the thirtieth anniversary of the Velvet Revolution of 1989, the tour generated a lot of interest in these three writers and resulted in six or seven reviews of each of the books, a hitherto unprecedented number. This was certainly due to generous financial support from Arts Council England, the Slovak Arts Council, and the Embassy of the Slovak Republic in the UK, which enabled me to hire a professional PR and marketing specialist. A long-term legacy of this project is the website www.SlovakLiterature.com that I launched and continue to run jointly with Magdalena Mullek. And last but not least, you once told me that it was at the conference on contemporary Slovak literature, held at University College London in November 2019, also as part of the *Raising the Velvet Curtain* project, that your idea for the present publication was further developed and refined, and if that is really the case, I am very happy to have made a small contribution to this very valuable initiative.

NOTES

1 See https://ojs.latrobe.edu.au/ojs/index.php/AALITRA/article/view/1241.

2 The books published in the series so far are listed in the selected bibliography of Slovak literature in translation in the appendix of this book. Seagull Books is soon likely to become the most prolific publisher of Slovak literature in English as its Slovak list will extend into poetry – with collections by Eva Luka (translated by James Sutherland-Smith), Nóra Ružičková (translated by Ivana Hostová), and Katarína Kucbelová (translated by Julia Sherwood and Peter Sherwood) – and the prose collection will be expanded by Barbora Hrínová's *Unicorns*, translated by Isabel Stainsby.

APPENDIX

Selected Bibliography of Slovak Literature in English Translation

SLOVAK FICTION IN ENGLISH

Compiled by Charles Sabatos

As discussed in the introduction and mentioned in several of the chapters in this volume, the availability of Slovak literature in English has increased greatly in the past two decades. Some of the authors discussed above have appeared in recent anthologies, such as *The Dedalus Book of Slovak Literature* (edited by Peter Karpinský, 2015) and *Into the Spotlight: New Writing from Slovakia* (edited by Magdalena Mullek and Julia Sherwood, 2017). However, a large portion of translations (as Mullek describes in her chapter) appear only in excerpts in often short-lived journals, and most full-length works have appeared from smaller publishers that are not easy to find in bookshops. Nevertheless, most recent publications are available online for those willing to seek them out, and two new series are tied to established distribution networks: the "Slovak List" from the Calcutta-based Seagull Books, which began in 2021, and Modern Slovak Classics from Karolinum Press in Prague, which started in 2022. The bibliography below is intended as a starting point for readers interested in the novelists discussed or mentioned in this volume. However, it is not intended to be comprehensive and does not include children's literature, essays, and other nonfiction genres, nor does it include all translations of older works, or the stories or excerpts published in the collections mentioned above.

For more extensive details, one online resource is the "Slovak Literature in English translation," website: http://www.slovakliterature.com/index.

html. Slovak poetry in translation, which is usually published apart from fiction, is covered in the following separate bibliography compiled by Ivana Hostová.

Baláž, Anton. *The Camp of Fallen Women*. Translated by Jonathan Gresty. Ljubljana: International Foundation Forum of Slavic Cultures, 2016.

Balla. *Among the Ruins*. Translated by David Short. London: Jantar Publishing, 2024.

– *Big Love*. Translated by Julia Sherwood and Peter Sherwood. London: Jantar Publishing, 2019.

– *Dead*. Translated by David Short. London: Jantar Publishing, 2022.

– *In the Name of the Father*. Translated by Julia Sherwood and Peter Sherwood. London: Jantar Publishing, 2017.

Beňová, Jana. *Away! Away!* Translated by Janet Livingstone. Columbus: Two Dollar Radio, 2018.

– *Seeing People Off*. Translated by Janet Livingstone. Columbus: Two Dollar Radio, 2017.

Blažková, Jaroslava. "Forty Pink Flamingos" [from *Happyends*]. Translated by Lucia Otrísalová. In *Migrating Memories: Central Europe in Canada*, vol. 1, 339–44. Edited by Vesna Lopičić. Brno/Niš: Central European Association for Canadian Studies, 2010.

Bodnárová, Jana. *Necklace/Choker*. Translated by Jonathan Gresty. London, New York, Calcutta: Seagull Books, 2022.

Brežná, Irena. *The Thankless Foreigner*. Translated by Ruth Ahmedzai Kemp. London, New York, Calcutta: Seagull Books, 2022.

Cigánová, Zuzana. *Vanity Unfair*. Translated by Magdalena Mullek. London, New York, Calcutta: Seagull Books, 2023.

Dobrakovová, Ivana. *Bellevue*. Translated by Julia Sherwood and Peter Sherwood. London: Jantar, 2018.

– *Mothers and Truckers*. Translated by Julia Sherwood and Peter Sherwood. London: Jantar, 2022.

Johanides, Ján. *But Crime Does Punish*. Translated by Julia Sherwood and Peter Sherwood. Prague: Karolinum Press, 2022.

Juráňová, Jana. *Ilona: My Life with the Bard*. Translated by Julia Sherwood and Peter Sherwood. Philadelphia: Calypso Editions, 2014.

Kapitáňová, Daniela. *Samko Tále's Cemetery Book*. Translated by Julia Sherwood. London: Garnett Press, 2011.

Kepplová, Zuska. *The Moon in Foil.* Translated by Magdalena Mullek. London, New York, Calcutta: Seagull Books, 2023.

Klimáček, Viliam. *The Hot Summer of 1968.* Translated by Peter Petro. Simsbury: Mandel Vilar Press, 2021.

Kompaníková, Monika. *Boat Number Five.* Translated by Janet Livingstone. London, New York, Calcutta: Seagull Books, 2021.

Kovalyk, Uršuľa. *The Equestrienne.* Translated by Julia Sherwood and Peter Sherwood. Cardigan: Parthian Books, 2016.

– *The Night Circus and Other Stories.* Translated by Julia Sherwood and Peter Sherwood. Cardigan: Parthian Books, 2019.

Krištúfek, Peter. *The House of the Deaf Man.* Translated by Julia Sherwood and Peter Sherwood. Cardigan: Parthian Books, 2014.

Kucbelová, Katarína. *The Bonnet.* Translated by Julia Sherwood and Peter Sherwood. London, New York, Calcutta: Seagull Books, 2024.

Lacková, Elena. *A False Dawn: My Life as a Gypsy Woman in Slovakia.* Hatfield: University of Hertfordshire Press, 2000.

Macsovszky, Peter. *Making Skeletons Dance.* Translated by John Minahane. London, New York, Calcutta: Seagull Books, 2024.

Mitana, Dušan. *On the Threshold: Short Stories.* Translated by Magdalena Mullek. London, New York, Calcutta: Seagull Books, 2024.

Mňačko, Ladislav. *Death Is Called Engelchen.* Translated by George Theiner. Prague: Artia Pocket Books, 1961.

– *The Taste of Power.* Translated by Paul Stevenson. New York: Praeger, 1967.

Pišťanek, Peter. *Rivers of Babylon.* Translated by Peter Petro. London: Garnett Press, 2007.

– *Rivers of Babylon 2, or The Wooden Village.* Translated by Peter Petro. London: Garnett Press, 2008.

– *Rivers of Babylon 3, or The End of Freddy.* Translated by Peter Petro. London: Garnett Press, 2008.

Rankov, Pavol. *It Happened on the First of September (or Some Other Time).* Translated by Magdalena Mullek. Bloomington: Slavica Publishers, 2020.

– *On the Other Hand.* Translated by Magdalena Mullek. London: Terra Librorum, 2023.

Rozner, Ján. *Seven Days to the Funeral.* Translated by Julia Sherwood and Peter Sherwood. Prague: Karolinum, 2024.

Šimečka, Martin M. *The Year of the Frog.* Translated by Peter Petro. New York: Simon & Schuster, 1996.

Tatarka, Dominik. "The Demon of Conformism." Translated by Peter Petro. *Cross Currents* 6 (1987): 285–97.
Timrava [Božena Slančíková]. *That Alluring Land: Slovak Stories*. Translated by Norma Rudinsky. Pittsburgh, PA: University of Pittsburgh Press, 1992.
Vadas, Marek. *The Healer*. Translated by Julia Sherwood and Peter Sherwood. London, New York, Calcutta: Seagull Books, 2023.
Vilikovský, Pavel. *Ever Green Is …* Translated by Charles Sabatos. Evanston, IL: Northwestern University Press, 2002.
– *Fleeting Snow*. Translated by Julia Sherwood and Peter Sherwood. London: Istros, 2018.

SLOVAK POETRY IN ENGLISH

Compiled by Ivana Hostová

The following bibliography includes English translations of poets covered in this volume available in journals and a list of translated books by major, mostly older Slovak poets available in bookshops or libraries. The list of translations includes the anthology *One Hundred Years of Slovak Literature* (2000) edited by Stanislava Chrobáková, which provides the most representative and comprehensive picture of twentieth-century Slovak literature in translation. Unfortunately, there is no anthology in English covering the poetry of the last two decades. Single-author volumes of English translations of contemporary Slovak poets are also rare and often not available for purchase or in libraries. Most of the translations of poets discussed in this book remain scattered in magazines, anthologies, festival publications, and poetry websites such as Lyrikline.org or Versopolis.com. A notable exception is the selection from Mária Ferenčuhová's poetry translated by James Sutherland-Smith and Katarína Šoltis Smith under the title *Tidal Events* (2020).

Journals

Duero, Lucia, and Jesse Lee Kercheval, eds. "Fragments of the Vanishing Speech: Contemporary Slovak Poetry." Translated by Nina Varon, James Sutherland-Smith, and Viera Sutherland-Smith. *Tupelo Quarterly* 21

(2020). Accessed 2 April 2024. https://www.tupeloquarterly.com/editors-feature/fragments-of-the-vanishing-speech-contemporary-slovak-poetry-edited-by-lucia-duero-and-jesse-lee-kercheval/.

– "Fragments of the Vanishing Speech: Contemporary Slovak Poetry II." Translated by John Minahane, Jonathan Gresty, and Ivana Hostová. *Tupelo Quarterly* 26 (2022). Accessed 2 April 2024. https://www.tupeloquarterly.com/uncategorized/fragments-of-the-vanishing-speech-contemporary-slovak-poetry-ii-edited-by-lucia-duero-jesse-lee-kercheval/.

Ferenčuhová, Mária. "In the City of Dogs. Illuminated Cities. Tidal Events." Translated by James Sutherland-Smith. *Europe Now* (May 2017). Accessed 20 June 2022. https://www.europenowjournal.org/2017/05/02/three-poems-by-maria-ferencuhova/.

– "Poems." Translated by James Sutherland-Smith. *Verseville*. Accessed 20 June 2022. http://www.verseville.org/maacuteria-feren269uhovaacute.html.

– "Threatened Species." Translated by James Sutherland-Smith. *Asymptote*. Accessed 20 June 2022. https://www.asymptotejournal.com/poetry/maria-ferencuhova-threatened-species/.

– "Three Poems." Translated by James Sutherland-Smith. *PN Review* 239 (2018). Accessed 20 June 2022. https://www.pnreview.co.uk/cgi-bin/scribe?item_id=10094.

Habaj, Michal. "Caput Mortuum." Translated by John Minahane. *Slovak Literary Review* (2015): 84–9. Accessed 20 June 2022. https://www.litcentrum.sk/sites/default/files/catalogue_issue_files/slovak_literary_review_2015.pdf.

– "Seven Models. Trakl Track. In a Castle Park." Translated by Lyndon Davies. *Poetry Wales* 41, no. 2 (Autumn 2005): 57–8.

Kucbelová, Katarína. "All The Trees / She Can Scream and Fly / A Greenhouse Poem / The Forest Sucks Everything In / The Forest Is Advancing / They Lived Next To Each Other." Translated by Ivana Hostová. *Poem: International English Language Quarterly* 4, no. 2 (2016): 265–75. Accessed 20 June 2022. https://doi.org/10.1080/20519842.2016.1159037.

– "Little Big City." Translated by John Minahane. *Slovak Literary Review* 17, no. 1 (2012): 24–5. Accessed 20 June 2022. https://www.litcentrum.sk/sites/default/files/catalogue_issue_files/slovak_literary_review_2012_2.pdf.

Macsovszky, Peter. "Economy of Motion. Morporesonator. Lasting of the (L) one Lonely Text." Translated by Ian Davidson. *Poetry Wales* 41, no. 2 (Autumn 2005): 52–4.

– "From *Sarcangelium*." Translated by Ivana Hostová and James Alfred Sutherland-Smith. *Asymptote* (2019). Accessed 20 June 2022. https://www.asymptotejournal.com/poetry/peter-macsovsky-sarcangelium/.

– "Rhythm and Sun Forces Many / Treatment of Panic / Lose The Shell." Translated by Ivana Hostová. *Poem: International English Language Quarterly* 4, no. 2 (2016): 282–7. Accessed 20 June 2022. https://doi.org/10.1080/20519842.2016.1159040.

Ružičková, Nóra. "From Contemporaneities." *Asymptote* 12, no. 43 (2022). Accessed 11 August 2022. https://www.asymptotejournal.com/poetry/contemporaneities-nora-ruzickova.

– "Ornament. (untitled). Pins and Needles. Conception and Attack." Translated by Zoë Skoulding. *Poetry Wales* 41, no. 2 (Autumn 2005): 44–6.

– "Works and Intimacy." Translated by Ivana Hostová. *Poem: International English Language Quarterly* 4, no. 2 (2016): 276–81. Accessed 20 June 2022. https://doi.org/10.1080/20519842.2016.1159038.

Šulej, Peter. "nodes." Translated by John Minahane. *Slovak Literary Review* (2015): 50–7. Accessed 20 June 2022. https://www.litcentrum.sk/sites/default/files/catalogue_issue_files/slovak_literary_review_2015.pdf.

– "Poetry Untitled. May Be May Be. To See." *Poetry Wales* 41, no. 2 (Autumn 2005): 48–51.

Books

Buzássy, Ján. *Melancholy Hunter*. Translated by James Sutherland-Smith and Viera Sutherland-Smith. Mississauga, ON: Modry Peter Publishers Limited, 2002.

Chrobáková, Stanislava, ed. *One Hundred Years of Slovak Literature. An Anthology*. Bratislava: The Union of Slovenian Writers, the Association of Organisations of Slovak Writers, Literary Information Centre, and Institute of Slovak Literature of the SAS, 2000.

Ferenčuhová, Mária. *Tidal Events*. Translated by James Sutherland-Smith Bristol Shearsman Books, 2018.

Haugová, Mila. *Eternal Traffic*. Translated by James Sutherland-Smith and Katarina Šoltis Smith. Todmorden: Arc Publications, 2020.

– *Scent of the Unseen/Vôňu nevideného*. Translated by James Sutherland-Smith and Viera Sutherland-Smith Todmorden: Arc Publications, 2003.

Hochel, Igor, eds. *Six Slovak Poets*. Todmorden: Arc Publications, 2010.

Laučík, Ivan. *Cranberry in Ice*. Translated by James Sutherland-Smith and Viera Sutherland-Smith. Mississauga, ON: Modry Peter Publishers Limited, 2001.

– Poems. *Gedichte. Poesie. Dikter. Poemas*. Translated by James Sutherland-Smith, Štefánia Allen. Bratislava: Logos, 1994.

Milčák, Peter, and Braňo Hochel, eds. *Not Waiting for Miracles: Seventeen Contemporary Slovak Poets*. Levoča: Modrý Peter, 1993.

Novomeský, Laco. *Slovak Spring*. Translated by John Minahane. Belfast: Belfast Historical and Educational Society, 2004.

Ondruš, Ján. *Tightrope Walker*. Translated by Martin Solotruk and James Sutherland-Smith. Bratislava: GRAFIQ Studio, 1998.

Országh-Hviezdoslav, Pavol. *The Bloody Sonnets*. Translated by John Minahane. Bratislava: Literárne informačné centrum, 2018.

Podracká, Dana. *Forty Four*. Translated by Robert Welch. Cork: Southword Editions, 2005.

Rúfus, Milan. *And That's the Truth*. Translated by Ewald Osers, James Sutherland-Smith, Viera Sutherland-Smith. Wauconda, IL: Bolchazy-Carducci Publishers, Inc., 2006.

Strážay, Štefan. *Poems. Poesie. Gedichte. Poemas. Poemes*. Translated by David G. Murray. Bratislava: Logos, 1994.

Válek, Miroslav. *The Ground beneath Our Feet*. Translated by Ewald Osers. Levoča and Newcastle upon Tyne: Modrý Peter and Bloodaxe Books, 1996.

Contributors

RAJENDRA CHITNIS is associate professor in Czech and Ivana and Pavel Tykač Fellow at University College, Oxford University. His research has focused on Czech literature from the late nineteenth century to the present and Slovak and Russian fiction from the late socialist period to the present. In addition to two academic monographs, he has published numerous articles on Czech and Slovak literature. From 2014 to 2016, he was principal investigator of the AHRC Translating Cultures Research Innovations project "Translating the Literatures of Small European Nations."

PETER DAROVEC teaches contemporary Slovak and Czech literature as well as literary criticism at the Faculty of Arts of Comenius University in Bratislava. He is the author of several books, most recently the monograph on Peter Pišťanek, *On Pišťanek* (He, Pišťanek, 2020). Before that, he published *Pavel Vilikovský* (2007), *Mladá tvorba – časopis po čase* (Mladá tvorba: A magazine after time, co-authored with Vladimir Barborík, 1996), and *Násmešné rozmlúvanie o štyroch knihách* (A laughable conversation about four books, 1996). He was also the editor of the collections *K dielu Jána Števčeka* (On the work of Ján Števček, 2015) and *K dielu Pavla Vilikovského* (On the work of Pavel Vilikovský), as well as an anthology of modern Slovak short stories, *Miesto príbehu* (The place in the story, 1995). He was the editor-in-chief of the literary magazine RAK (*Revue aktuálnej kultúry*) and has been regularly publishing critical articles and studies on current literary production for several decades. He moderates a regular discussion show about new books called *Literary Quotient*.

KATARINA GEPHARDT is professor of English at Kennesaw State University. She has published a monograph entitled *The Idea of Europe in Nineteenth-Century British Travel Narratives, 1789–1914* (Ashgate/Routledge, 2014) and essays on nineteenth-century British literature, travel writing, Slovak literature, and pedagogy. She is currently working on a monograph on nineteenth-century British women's travel writing on Central and Eastern Europe.

IVANA HOSTOVÁ is a senior researcher at the Institute of Slovak Literature Slovak Academy of Sciences. She has published papers on the translation of poetry and on Slovak literature and edited and co-edited scholarly books and journals on poetry, translation, and world literatures (e.g., *World Literature Studies: Translation and Creativity*, 2022; *World Literature Studies: Communication, Compliance and Resistance in Inter-Contextual Encounters*, 2020; *Identity and Translation Trouble*, 2017). Her areas of interest include literary translation studies, poetry, gender studies, ecocriticism, posthumanism, identity, and Slovak studies. Her two academic books, both published in Slovak, *Haugovej Plathová, Plathovej Haugová* (Haugová's Plath, Plath's Haugová, 2013) and *Medzi entropiou a víziou* (Between entropy and vision, 2014), contribute to Plath studies and map contemporary Slovak poetry respectively. Her recent publications include a thorough investigation into the dissemination of Slovak poetry in the English translation "Slovak poetry in English translation after the collapse of state socialism" (*Meta* 68[1]: 159–79).

TAMARA JANECOVÁ studied Slovak and Russian at Comenius University in Bratislava. Her dissertation focused on the contexts and forms of the outsider condition in contemporary Slovak prose. She currently teaches in the Department of Slovak Language and Literature at Trnava University. She specializes in twentieth-century Slovak literature and has published several studies on inter-war period authors who wrote lyrical prose including František Švantner, Milo Urban, and Margita Figuli, as well as journal articles and reviews on contemporary prose. She is the author of *Proti wetrysku* (Against z great vind, 2022).

RAFAŁ MAJEREK is a Polish literary studies scholar at the Institute of Slavic Philology of the Jagiellonian University in Cracow. He is also a member of the Committee for Slavic Cultures at the Polish Academy of Arts and Sciences, the Polish-Slovak Committee for the Humanities, the Committee for Slavic Studies of the Cracow Branch of the Polish Academy of Sciences. His research focuses on questions of Slovak national and cultural identity as well as developments in contemporary Slovak literature, particularly the topic of women's writing and feminist prose. He has published a monograph entitled *Pamięć – mit – tożsamość: Słowackie procesy autoidentyfikacyjne w okresie odrodzenia narodowego* (Memory – myth – identity: Slovak self-identification in the period of the National Revival) (2011). He regularly publishes in academic journals and domestic and foreign collections of essays.

MAGDALENA MULLEK is an independent literary translator and scholar. She holds a PhD in Slavic languages and literatures from Indiana University. Her translations, reviews, and articles have appeared in *Asymptote*, *TWO LINES*, *Words Without Borders*, *Slovak Literary Review*, *BODY*, *Visegrad Insight*, and other journals. She has worked on two anthologies of Slovak literature: *Dedalus Book of Slovak Literature* (Dedalus Books, 2015) and *Into the Spotlight: New Writing from Slovakia* (Slavica Publishers/Parthian, 2017). Her translation of Pavol Rankov's *It Happened on the First of September (or Some Other Time)* was published in 2020 by Slavica Publishers. Her most recent translations include Zuzana Cigánová's *Vanity Unfair* (Seagull Books, 2023), Pavol Rankov's *On the Other Hand* (Terra Librorum, 2023), and Zuska Kepplová's *The Moon in Foil* (Seagull Books, 2023).

VILIAM NÁDASKAY studied English and Slovak at Comenius University in Bratislava. He is currently a postdoctoral researcher at the Institute of Slovak Literature of the Slovak Academy of Sciences. His research focuses on socialist realism, twentieth-century poetry, and contemporary literature. He contributed several chapters on the image of the Slovak capital city in Slovak twentieth and twenty-first-century poetry to the collectively authored monograph *Literárne krajiny Bratislavy: obraz mesta po roku 1918* (Bratislava's literary landscapes: portrayal of the city after 1918, 2023).

RADOSLAV PASSIA is senior research fellow at the Institute of Slovak Literature of the Slovak Academy of Sciences in Bratislava. He focuses on Slovak literature of the twentieth and twenty-first centuries in Central European contexts, area studies, and urban studies. He has published the monograph *Na hranici: Slovenská literatúra a východokarpatský hraničný areál* (At the border: Slovak literature and the East-Carpathian borderlands, 2014) and has co-authored and co-edited *Hľadanie súčasnosti: Slovenská literatúra začiatku 21. storočia* (Searching for the present: Slovak literature at the beginning of the twenty-first century, 2014) and *Literárne krajiny Bratislavy: obraz mesta po roku 1918* (Bratislava's literary landscapes: portrayal of the city after 1918, 2023).

DANIEL W. PRATT is assistant professor of Slavic culture at McGill University in the Department of Languages, Literatures, and Cultures. He works on Central European culture, narrative, philosophy and literature, and dissent. He has published on Witold Gombrowicz, Bohumil Hrabal, and the meaning of history in Central Europe. He is currently finishing his monograph *Against Narrative: Non-Narrative Temporalities in Central Europe*, and he is working on a second: *Bruno Jasieński, Internationalist.*

ZORA PRUŠKOVÁ is a literary theorist and a senior fellow emerita at the Institute of Slovak Literature of the Slovak Academy of Sciences. She focuses primarily on poetics and genre in prose texts of the second half of the twentieth century. She has written several monographs, including *Keď si tak spomeniem na šesťdesiate roky. Niekoľko pohľadov na súčasnú slovenskú prózu* (When I remember the sixties: Several perspectives on contemporary Slovak prose, 1993, 2008), *Rudolf Sloboda* (2001), and *Ako si porozumieť s literatúrou. Niekoľko poznámok o vzťahu medzi autorom, rozprávaním a žánrom v modernej próze* (How to come to terms with literature: Several notes on the relationship among author, narration, and genre in modern prose, 2016). She has co-authored several projects focused on pedagogy and literary editions.

CHARLES SABATOS is professor of comparative literature at Yeditepe University in Istanbul. His primary research interests are in Central and Eastern European literary histories, and he has held visiting fellowships in the Czech and Slovak Republics, the United States, the United Kingdom, Spain, and Portugal. He has translated contemporary Slovak fiction into English, including Pavel Vilikovský's *Ever Green Is ...*

(Northwestern, 2002), and published the monograph *Frontier Orientalism and the Turkish Image in Central European Literature* (Lexington, 2020).

JULIA SHERWOOD was born and grew up in Bratislava, Czechoslovakia, and lives in London. Since 2008 she has worked as a freelance translator, mostly of contemporary Slovak fiction, jointly with her husband Peter Sherwood. Her translations include Daniela Kapitáňová's *Samko Tále's Cemetery Book*, Ivana Dobrakovová's *Bellevue*, Balla's *In the Name of the Father*, Uršula Kovalyk's *Night Circus and Other Stories*, Peter Krištúfek's *The House of the Deaf Man*, Pavel Vilikovský's *Fleeting Snow*, Marek Vadas's *The Healer*, Ján Johanides's *But Crime Does Punish*, Katarína Kucbelová's *The Bonnet*, and Ján Rozner's *Seven Days to the Funeral*. She has organized events promoting Slovak literature in the United Kingdom and served as the editor-at-large for Slovakia for the online literary journal *Asymptote*.

IVANA TARANENKOVÁ is senior research fellow and director of the Institute of Slovak Literature of the Slovak Academy of Sciences in Bratislava. Her research focuses on the literary criticism and history of Slovak literature of the nineteenth century, problems of national and cultural identity, and contemporary fiction. She is the author of the monograph *Fenomén Vajanský* (A phenomenon named Vajanský, 2010) and many journal articles on literary history and contemporary literature. She also co-authored *Hľadanie súčasnosti: Slovenská literatúra začiatku 21. Storočia* (Searching for the present: Slovak literature at the beginning of the twenty-first century, 2014) and *Konfigurácie slovenského realizmu* (Configurations of Slovak realism, 2016). From 1999 to 2012, she was the editor in chief of the peer-reviewed journal *Slovenská literatúra* (*Slovak Literature*).

Index